THERAPEUTIC RIDING I
STRATEGIES
FOR INSTRUCTION
PART I

THERAPEUTIC RIDING I
STRATEGIES
FOR INSTRUCTION

EDITED BY
✳
BARBARA TEICHMANN ENGEL, M.ED, OTR

FOREWORD
✳
JOHN ANTHONY DAVIES, BA, BHSI

INTRODUCTION
✳
OCTAVIA BROWN, ED.M, CMTRI

ILLUSTRATORS
STEPHANIE C. WOODS, B.F..A
BARBARA T. ENGEL

PUBLISHED BY
BARBARA ENGEL THERAPY SERVICES

It is expected that the procedures described in this book will be carried out by trained and qualified practitioners according to recognized standards in the field of therapeutic riding. No warranty, expressed or implied, is made regarding the content of this book by the editor, authors, consultants, reviewers, or by its contributors. This book has been developed independently without the assistance of grants, sponsors or support of any organization. No endorsement has been requested or received from any foundation or organization.

✳✳✳✳✳✳✳✳✳✳✳✳✳

The opinions and/or experiences expressed in the articles of text are strictly those of each author and or contributor and do not necessarily represent the views of the editor, reviewer, Publisher or that of any organization. It is not an intention to give endorsement to author's ideas, methods, or techniques. It is the intent of this text to present the reader with many viewpoints from people who have extensive experience in the field, with the purpose of expanding and challenging each reader's base of knowledge. The dynamic field of therapeutic riding will prove its value **only** when those in the field *share their experiences, question, search, develop and continue to expand knowledge. The end result will be validation of the values of this unique discipline.*

Without question, there is no change;
Without change, there is no growth.

Published by   BARBARA ENGEL THERAPY SERVICES
10 Town Plaza, # 238, Durango, CO 81301 USA
Phone/FAX 970-563-9599; 970-563-6517; e-mail: engelbj@compuserve.com

Library of Congress Catalog Card Number: 92-71597

ISBN 0-9633065-5-3

Manufactured in the United States of America

Cover art work by **Judy Brey, OTR** of Durango, Colorado
Judy is both an artist and a practicing occupational therapist

We dedicated this book to **Carol Fuller**, a valued equestrian, a mentor to many riders with disabilities and staff. She was a contributor to this book. Carol died unexpectedly due to an accident, November 1996 .

❊❊❊❊

As a coach of the Great Falls Vaulting Club of Virginia, Carol Fuller recognized the many personal skills and values which could be learned through the sport of horse vaulting. She used the sport to teach young people about life, not just vaulting. Pride of achievement, self confidence, tenacious character, and caring for teammates were the Hallmarks of Great Falls Vaulters trained by Carol. With satisfaction and a sense of accomplishment she watched as her students moved across the United States, many of them starting new teams.

Carol also recognized the value of horse vaulting in opening opportunities for the youngsters with disabilities. Integrated into the Great Falls Trot Team when my daughter joined the club was a young man with Down Syndrome. John was a team member in every way, practicing and competing with the team and performing his share of the horse care and supports tasks.

When Carol retired as the coach of the Great Falls Vaulting Club, she continued her positive influence on young people by teaching therapeutic vaulting. Carol saw the good and positive opportunities in everyone and in every situation.

She saw every flower in any meadow and every ray of sunshine on the cloudiest of days. Her energy was infectious; her desire to see young people grow physically, mentally, emotionally, and socially was inspirational.

Carol's effort will continue on through those live's she influenced.

Charles Bittenbring
President,
American Vaulting Association
1997

CONTRIBUTORS

❀❀

TABLE OF CONTENTS

❀❀

CROSS REFERENCE
OF:
THERAPEUTIC RIDING I
STRATEGIES
FOR INSTRUCTION
and
THERAPEUTIC RIDING II
STRATEGIES
FOR REHABILITATION
❀❀

FOREWORD
❀❀
INTRODUCTION
❀❀
PREFACE

WHAT IS SUCCESS?

It's doing your work the best you can,

And being just to your fellow man;

It's making money, but holding friends

And staying true to your aims and ends;

It's figuring how and learning why,

And looking forward and thinking high,

And dreaming a little and doing much;

It's keeping always on close touch

With what is finest in work and deed;

It's being thorough, yet making speed,

It's daring blithely the field of chance

While making labor a brave romance.

It's going onward despite defeat,

And fighting staunchly, but keeping sweet;

It's being clean and it's playing fair;

It's laughing lightly at Dame Despair

It's looking up to the stars above,

It's struggling on with a cheerful grin;

It's sharing sorrow, and work, and mirth

And making better this good old earth;

It's serving, striving, through strain and stress

It's doing your noblest – that's success.

Anonymous

CONTRIBUTORS
✳✳✳ ✳✳✳

Barbara T. Engel, BS, M.Ed., OTR - EDITOR

Pediatric occupational therapist retired, private practice and consultant since 1976; administrator-18 years; university and clinical instructor-24 years; extensive work experience in pediatrics, rehabilitation medicine and psychiatry; 20 yrs training with Sensory Integration International, cerebral palsy treatment methods, NDT, CST and hippotherapy. Consultant and international lecturer in therapeutic riding and hippotherapy since 1981. Registered by the American Hippotherapy Association with advanced hippotherapy training in Germany. Hippotherapy Curriculum Development Committee. Edited eight therapeutic riding books and co-author of one. Active member of NARHA, of US Dressage Federation, US Combined Training Association, Rocky Mountain Dressage Society, and a member of AHSA; Board member local dressage & CT club; past Pony Club DC. Member of AVA, FRDI. President/owner of publishing company. Shows her Lipizzan stallion and mare in dressage, drives the Haflingers, and breeds her horses. She coaches a vaulting team with her Haflingers. She lives with her husband on their farm in Ignacio, Colorado with their two German Short Hairs, five cats and six horses.

Tebay, Jean M. BA, MS, CMTRI

A major contributor to Therapeutic Riding Programs: Instruction and Rehabilitation and Therapeutic Riding I Strategies for Instruction, supporter and advisor of these books.

Director Therapeutic Riding Services, Baltimore, MD; certified NARHA Master Therapeutic Riding Instructor; certified Therapeutic Recreation Technician; 26 years special riding population; NARHA Board of Directors; Delta Society Board of Directors; 1st NARHA recipient of the James Brady Professional Achievement Award; Delta Society Distinguished Service Award; coordinator of NARHA college curriculum project; Director of the Hippotherapy Curriculum Development Project to train occupational/ physical therapists as hippotherapy practitioners; member, special member task force for Riding for the Disabled International to develop an International character, initiated therapeutic riding programs in OH, Wash. DC, MD, and OR. Leader/teacher/ lecturer for the advancement of therapeutic riding. Board member, American Hippotherapy Association.

Galloway, Margaret (Meg), MS, BHSAI

A major contributor to Therapeutic Riding Programs: Instruction and Rehabilitation and Therapeutic Riding I Strategies for Instruction.

Special education K-6th, designs support curriculum for behavior modification & tutors, certified therapeutic riding instructor, Fran Joswick Center; Maryland Horse Center; California Dressage Society Qualified rider, instructor/trainer, NARHA member; Instructor-BOK Ranch, CA; therapeutic riding since 1986; NARHA member; life long equestrian; co-author, *The Horse, The Handicapped, The Riding Team.*, major contributor to this book and Therapeutic Riding Programs: Instruction & Rehabilitation.

A SPECIAL THANKS TO OUR INTERNATIONALLY KNOWN EQUESTRIAN SPECIALISTS FOR THEIR CONTRIBUTIONS

Peggy Cummings

An internationally-known equestrian clinician, instructor, trainer, and competitor; has develop her innovative technique of Connected Riding™ from years of classic training. Is certified as Master Riding Instructor in Centered Riding, and a TTEAM Practioner. She has authored many articles in national equestrian journals, contributor of books, producer of videos and a book, and presents workshops and clinics in the Americas and internationally and is part of the Women & Horses Workshops. She has ridden since childhood. See Chapter 34 for information.

Eleanor Kellon, VMD

Researcher & contributor to *Chronicle of the Horse*, authors many articles & scientific papers, *and books - The Older Horse*, and *First Aid For Horses;* equestrian, trainer, instructor, and judge.

John A. Davies, BA, BHSI

Internationally known. Assisted in the development of the field of therapeutic riding. Equine sciences; director/trainer St. James Farm Equestrian Facility; instructor/trainer/examiner; 33 years international experience; Dressage-combined training-steeple chasing through advanced level; 40 years experience in the field of therapeutic horseback riding in England and the USA; 4th president of NARHA; NARHA member; Author: *The Reins of Life, Riding in Rhyme*, and *I Saw A Child* in addition to many articles.

J. Ashton Moore, AVA "I", FEI "S"

Founder with Elizabeth Searle - the American Vaulting Assoc, international judge, technical delegate, instructor, lecturer, breeder, dressage trainer, United States Dressage Association committees, contributor-advisor to USPC.

Barbra Schulte, MS/CCC-SPL

Former national champion cutting horse trainer, became interested in sports psychology when she noticed that certain riders won again and again, regardless of which horse they were riding. Barbra considers mental training the third essential tool for anyone's success, after finding a compatible horse & learning the technical skills of your sport. She notes that people spend a lot of money on the horse, training, gear, & rig. They often neglect to train themselves. In 1987, she discovered the book, Mental Toughness Training for Sports, by Dr. James E. Loehr, Ed.D. She began applying the techniques, and became the first woman to win the National Cutting Horse Association Derby (1988), the NCHA Superstakes Classic (1992) and the Augusta Futurity (1992). Intrigued, she decided to find out more about Dr. Loehr and LGE Sport Science, Inc. in Orlando, Florida, a leading provider of performance training for athletes and business executives. (LGE stands for the three people who founded the corporation: Dr. Loehr, Dr. Jack Groppel and Pat Etcheberry). She opting to give up her successful horse training business to become certified as LGE's equestrian coach.

She offers a program called, "Mentally Tough Training for Riders" through the Center for Equestrian Performance in Brenham, Texas. Her work involves nationwide clinics, seminars and consultations. In 1996 year, she gave a presentation at the North American Riding for the Handicapped Association, Inc. annual conference. See chapter 34 for information.

Prof. Dr. med Carl Klüwer

Psychoanalyst, past President, The Federation of Riding for the Disabled International; member and consultant, German Kuratorium fur Hippotherapie; International lecturer, researcher, and writer on the subject of Hippotherapy.

Linda Tellington-Jones

Internationally known for *The Tellington Ttouch Techniques*, Life-long equestrian and accomplished rider, having competed in combined training, hunters, jumpers, dressage, Western and English pleasure, steeple chasing and endurance ride competitions. Held a world record for 7 years in 100-mile endurance racing; co-founder of Pacific Coast Equestrian Research Farm; Feldenkrais practioner; judge, teacher, trainer, researcher, and lecturer; developed the internationally known training technique of TT.E.A.M. lecturing and training all over the world; co-author of *Physical Therapy for the Athletic Horse, Endurance and Competitive Trail Riding, TT.E.A.M Approach to Problem Free Training,* and *The Tellington-Jones Equine Awareness Method, Riding with Awareness, The Tellington TTouch, Getting in Touch: Understand and Influence Your Horse's Personality, and* many new books, manuals and articles; produced more than 12 videos and holds regular clinics in North America and internationally; involved in riding with the disabled since 1958 and a strong supported of therapeutic riding, NARHA member. See chapter 34 for information.

Terri Barnes, PT

Director, Barnes Therapy Associates (PT & Hippotherapy,) Keller TX; advanced hippotherapy course in Germany; member, Hippotherapy Curriculum Development Committee; NARHA member; equine-assisted therapy practioner since 1984; national & international lecturer; equestrian since adolescence. Board member, American Hippotherapy Association, registered with AHA as a hippotherapy practioner.

Joann Benjamin, PT

NDT certified; Feldenkrais practioner in progress, NARHA & Delta Society member; involved in the field of therapeutic riding/hippotherapy as a physical therapy consultant since 1986 to several programs; charter member, American Hippotherapy Assoc. Board member &committees, NARHA Committees, registered with AHA as a hippotherapy practioner, equestrian

Christine Bennett, CRTRI

Cheff certified therapeutic riding instructor, NARHA registered therapeutic riding instructor, 4-H TR program, US Trot Assoc licensed driver, NARHA driving committee

Natalie P. Bieber, MS CAGA

Educational consultant, learning disabilities specialist, 6th yr diploma CAGS, therapeutic riding instructor 25 yrs, competition coach 20 yrs. national and international presentor and author of articles on learning disabilities and recreation therapy and competition, assisted in writing the original rules for national and international disabled competition, Honor award by Rehab Assoc of CT, awarded 2 time, outstanding educator by CT Community College System, an adjunct lecturer. At Southern Conn State Univ.

John H. Brough, OTR

Principal, Windward Preparatory School; founder with Nancy Winters of Wayne Dupage Ride & Hunt Club Program; past NARHA VP & chair of medical & research committee; therapeutic riding involvement since 1975- helped to develop early medical standards for NARHA; national lecturer in learning disabilities; member of many professional advisory committees.

Octavia J. Brown, EdM, CMTRI
Director of development of equine studies & assistant professor at Centenary College, Hackettsown NJ, founder & past executive Director, Somerset Hills Handicapped Riders Club; NARHA certified master instructor; Cheff Center certified instructor; Special Olympics Equestrian coach & event director, 25 years teaching therapeutic riding; 16 years NARHA Board member, 1st VP of NARHA and founding member, NARHA member, committees, board member of FRDI.

Elmer G. Butt, MD
Physician; Founding father and board member of NARHA.

Robin Hulsey Chickering, BS, MS
Teacher of hearing impaired, special school district of Saint Louis Country, MO; is hard of hearing herself, certified Cheff Center instructor; president & head instructor of Riding High Inc. since 1981; author: *Horseback Riding for the Hearing Impaired,*

Marylou Dickson
Marylou R Dickson received her Special Needs Riding Instructor Certification from the Cheff Center for the Handicapped in Augusta, Michigan in February of 1988. She has a Bachelor of Physical Education (1988) and a Bachelor of Education (1994) which were both received from the University of Alberta in Edmonton Alberta, Canada. She taught special needs horseback riding for the Friends of Whitemud Equine Centre Association in Edmonton. Marylou was the Program Coordinator of the Special Needs Riding Program in 1987-1988.

Barbara Di Stafano
Riding instructor and developer of Winslow riding program for persons with multiple sclerosis. Past Pony Club DC; 4-H leader; a founding member of Warwick Valley Polocrosse club. She has multiple sclerosis and is knowledgeable regarding program guidelines for those with multiple sclerosis. Community consultant.

Sandy Dota
American Judging Association Certified Judge; therapeutic riding instructor; Somerset Hills Handicapped Riders Club; NARHA Board of Directors; since 1985, faculty for NARHA Workshops; national lecturer; NARHA member; International riding competitor

Elizabeth Evans, OTR
Pediatric occupational therapist with MI school district, consultant therapist and board member of MI 4-H program -Midland county. NARHA driving committee.

Joy E. Ferguson, BA, Magr, CRTRI
NARHA certified instructor, certified Camp Horsemanship Assoc instructor, Executive Director of Therapeutic Horsemanship of El Paso, board member, two term past president Lone Star Therapeutic Equestrians Network, National Recreation Parks Assoc.

Jane C. Copeland Fitzpatrick, MA, RPT
Psychology; NDT certified; Executive Director, Pegasus Therapeutic Riding Inc., physical therapist for 15 years, private practice; Hippotherapy Curriculum Development Committee, NARHA medical committee, treasurer & board member Delta Society. NARHA member; executive committee, American Hippotherapy Association board member, registered with AHA as a hippotherapy practitioner, Who's Who of American Women, member of Am Soc of Assoc Executives, APTA, NARHA, FRDI.

Caroline Fuller, BA
Instructor, coach & administrator Great Falls Pony Club Vaulting Team since 1984, & Aft Us Up; Equestrian; board member, American Vaulting Association 1985-92; Vaulting Chair, USPC; member AHSA, published articles in Chronicle of the Horse, AVA Vaulting World, & USPC Newsletter; vaulting instructor for therapeutic & sports vaulting, 8 years. AVA and NARHA member. Died in 1996 of a horse related accident.

Anthony Z. Gonzales,
Master farrier for 21 years; developer of the PBM (proper balance movement) protector pads; lecturer; consultant; columnist & author, *PBM, a Diary of Lameness.*

Celine Green, BS, CMTRI
Majored in journalism; ex-director, Happy Horsemen Riding for the Handicapped; NAHRA certified master instructor; NAHRA instructor's committee, workshops faculty & program consultant; involved with therapeutic riding since 1979. 4H horse leader; Special Olympic certified instructor; member of NARHA, AHSA; therapeutic riding 1978.

Susan Greenall, BS
Animal science; teaching certificate in science (retired), free lance writer. Somerset Hills Handicapped Riding Club; competitor, judge & TD, American Driving Society; NARHA Driving Committee & member, equestrian competitor.

Edith Gross,
Born in Germany. Studied music and geography at Univ of Berlin. Dressage trainer and teacher in Mexico since 1981. She has worked in riding therapy since 1987 and published articles regarding dressage methodology and riding therapy.

Elizabeth Haartz, PT , CRTRI
NARHA life member, NARHA board member, NARHA committees, international presentor, registered hippotherapy practioner with AHA, member FRDI.

Kyle Hamilton, MS, PT
Physical therapist private practice; MS in sports science; experience with therapeutic riding since 1985. NDT certified, *Contributor to The Horse, The Handicapped, The Riding Team,* Competitive dressage rider.

Kathleen Harbaugh, BA, MEd, CRTRI
Exective director & founder, Triple H Equitherapy Center, 2 yrs driving for the disabled in England- qualified whip, 8 yrs therapeutic riding, NARHA registered instructor. Founder & exective director -Montgomery Area non-traditional Equestrian Center.

Kent Harbaugh, MA international affairs, MEd social studies
Teacher, vice president-Horses Helping the Handicapped inc, facility manager at Triple H Equitherapy Center.

Nancy Hendrickson
Volunteer

Philippa (Pippa) Hodge, BS, PT, BHSAI
Physiotherapist; head riding instructor, Valley Therapeutic Equestrian Association; examiner, Canadian Therapeutic Riding Association; board member, CanTRA; member Hippotherapy Curriculum Development Committee; advanced hippotherapy course, Germany; developed video, *Analysis of the Horse and Human Movement;* board member, American Hippotherapy Assoc., registered with AHA as a hippotherapy practioner.

Jean Hoffman, BS, DVM
Animal science; graduate pre-vet graduate program-Cal Poly Univ., CA; Vet degree - Colorado State Univ, instructor, therapeutic riding, since 1988; American Trakehner Assoc; CA Dressage Soc., Rocky Mountain Dressage Society, equestrian since high school.

Sandra L. Hubbard, BS, MS, OTR/L, CRTRI
Associate professor occupational therapy dept, U of TX, certified SIPT Sensory Integration & in Nursing-Child Assessment Satellite Training (NCAST), registered as hippotherapy practioner with AHA, NARHA registered instructor, NMU coordinator for rural outreach diagnostic evaluation program, 20 years clinical experience in pediatrics in developmental disabilities, early intervention, feeding intervention, and a hippotherapy practice.

Lita R. Hughes, BS
Pre-veterinarian science; teacher certificate; 5 years training with Sally Swift in Centered Riding; Caroll County Extension Service, therapeutic riding program; therapeutic riding with Baltimore Parks and Recreation; therapeutic riding since 1980; instructor in dressage; competitor in dressage and eventing; dog trainer; NARHA member.

Lorraine "Frosty" Kaiser, BA, MA
Teaching credential, learning disabilities; therapeutic riding program since 1976; Executive Director, American Riding Club; California Special Olympics Equestrian Director; established 1st all disabled equestrian drill team, NAHRA member, Special Olympics; Council for Exceptional Children; CA Jr. State parade champions, 8 times from 1983 to 1992. NARHA member.

Micheal Kaufmann
Director of education of the Humane Assoc., instructor, volunteer, camp director, Board member of NARHA, Equine Facilitated Mental Health Association board, NARHA

Robin R. Koehler, BS, MS
Assistant professor, riding instructor, equestrian studies program, Univ of Findley, Findley, OH; certified instructor, Fran Joswick Center; instructor of Equestrian Challenge Therapeutic Riding Program, Findlay OH; NARHA member.

Kerrill Knaus
Co-Founder, President, Executive Director, H.O.R.S.E.S for the physically challenged; 14 yrs animal behavior; 12 yrs, adaptive riding for disabled persons; disabled equestrian.

Marci Lawson
Riding instructor and consultant; disabled rider; board member, Therapeutic Riding Program; presenter 1990 at NAHRA; NARHA member.

Marty Leff, BA, MA, CRTRI
NCTR instructor certification; instructor for National Center for Therapeutic Riding; instructor since 1985 remedial/ psycho-educational riding, inner city public special education project (Washington D.C.); free-lance writer/editor in English and Spanish; NARHA member; co-author *Guide To Therapeutic Groundwork.*

Molly Lingue-Mundy, PT
Equestrian since grade school; advanced hippotherapy course in Germany; member, Hippotherapy Curriculum Development Committee; life-long equestrian. 1st Treasurer, American Hippotherapy Association., registered with AHA as a hippotherapy practioner.

Virginia H. Martin, BS, CMTRI
President and chief riding instructor: Borderland Farm Inc,; founder & executive director: Equus Outreach Inc; founder & consultant: Winslow Therapeutic Riding Inc; former NAHRA Board member; 4 years director: Metropolitan Therapeutic Equestrian Games, trainer of the 1984 U.S. Cerebral Palsy Team; trainer of New Jersey Special Olympics competitor at Indiana International Special Olympics. NAHRA certified master instructor.

Lisa Mayo, BS, PT
Physical therapist; NARHA Driving Committee member; founding member of National Association of Driving for the Disabled; active therapist associated with Saratoga Therapeutic Equestrian Program; teaches carriage driving for the disabled.

Joanne H. Moses, PhD
Founder in 1986, clinical & executive director Tucson Animal Assisted Psychotherapy Associates inc,- 1st out-patient equestrian psychotherapy program in AZ to qualify for Title XIX Behavioral health Licence, teaching since 1955 St Micheal's Indian Mission, Member International Transantional Analysis Assoc specialized in geriatric psychotherapy.

Mulhaupt, Patrick M.
Riding Instructor and author/originate of Barrel Ball.

Andrew Nanaa, Judge
Pleasure driving (A.D.S.); National Association of Driving for the Disabled; technical delegate, pleasure and combined driving/A.D.S.; secretary and certification instructor N.A.D.D.

Kay O'Daniel, MA, BS, CRTRI
Program coordinator and instructor - MI 4-H handicapped program, Michigan State Univ., Cheff center certified therapeutic riding instructor, NARHA registered therapeutic riding instructor, CHA certified instructor, Centered Riding certified instructor, author 4-H *Horseback Riding for Handicappers* notebook 4-H1392, member NARHA driving committee.

Ruth Debi Parker, MA, CMTRI
Special education (visually impaired) NAHRA certified master instructor; founded several therapeutic riding programs; involved in therapeutic riding as instructor since 1980.

Sunny Pfifferling, BS, CMTRI
Therapeutic recreation; NAHRA master instructor; Cheff Center head instructor certified; head equine trainer, International Special Olympics; director/head instructor of Loveway Inc; therapeutic horseback riding since 1982.

Kristy Pigeon, BA, CRTRI
Director Sagebrush Equine Training Center- 6 yrs, 3 yrs National Center for Equine Facilitation Therapy since 1991, NARHA registered instructor.

Rafferty, Sandra, MA, OTR, CATRI
Special education; certified instructor, John Davies course; occupational therapist and riding instructor with Therapeutic Horsemanship, St. Louis, MO; instructor/ head coach of the USA international disabled equestrian team; teacher of therapeutic riding since 1975, charter member, American Hippotherapy Assoc., registered hippotherapy practioner with AHA founder of NARHA competition organization.

Renker, Lorraine, BS, CMTRI
Cheff Center instructor certified; director & instructor of Special Friends-A Program for the Developmental Disabilities Inc; NAHRA accreditation committee member, NAHRA networking co-chair, 25 years experience with horses. St Andrews College Therapeutic Riding Program coordinator, NARHA James Brady Professional Achievement

Evelyn Refosco, AA, BA
NARHA board executive committee, NARHA standing committees, Founder, director & president of Horsepower & CO council for Handicapped Horseback Riding, workshop presentor, organizer for independent riders, advocate & spokesperson for disabled adult rides.

Max Read
College diploma in English, theater, psychology.
National examiner for Canadian Therapeutic Riding Association, certified CanTRA instructor, Canadian equestrian federation level 1 coach. Program director-Richmond Therapeutic Equestrian Society, Richmond, BC. Program director SARI-riding for the disabled 8 yrs.

Terri Richmond, BSc, Post graduate doctoral in process
Dip in progress, in equine science -biomechanics of jumping horses, horses movement and conformation & how this affects the rider. Research & Development & sales for Romurus Technology - Horse Power. Hon Research Fellow, Brunel Univ., Lecturer - colleges and RDA, author, Research & development of mechanical horse.

Wendy Shugol R. BS, MA
Special educator; USA International Equestrian Team for Disabled Riders, more than 8 years; volunteer; Board of Directors, Old Dominion School of Therapeutic Horsemanship.

Charla Shurtlef, CATRI
The Association for Horsemanship Safety and Education - Board member., NARHA member.

Dodi V. Stacey,
The Association for Horsemanship Safety and Education, Board member, CHA clinician, free lance riding instructor, horse trainer, free-lance writer for magazines. NARHA member. Was awarded the Girl Scout's Elizabeth Hayden Award and the North American Horseman's Association prestigious award '1999 Horsewoman of Distinction'.

Kitty Stalsbury, BS, CATRI
Program director High Hopes, past barn manager & instructor, NARHA advanced instructor, NARHA board, NARHA committees.

Jill A Standquist, OTR/L
Pediatric private practice, certified NDT, certified ski instructor for disabled skiers; advanced hippotherapy course- Germany; member Hippotherapy Curriculum Development Committee; 8 years occupational therapist with Pegasus Therapeutic Riding Program; NARHA member.

Eileen Szychowski
Founder/Director Camelot Therapeutic Horsemanship, Inc; former rehabilitation counselor & National Park Service Ranger; an equestrian with a disability; trained under Josef Rivers at the Dragon Slayers, CA.

Donn Taylor, CATRI
Barn manager for Heartland's School of Riding.

Philip Tedescdi, MSSW
Assistant Clinical Director, director-instructor of Therapeutic Riding; director of sex offender programs, Griffith Center, CO; certified NAHRA master instructor; WEMT; Cheff Center certified instructor; member of NAHRA instructor certification curriculum committee, medical committee, faculty of NAHRA workshops; co-chaired NAHRA research committee; experience in therapeutic riding since 1981, exploring equine-assisted psychotherapy.

Susan F. Tucker, BA, CMTRI
Certified instructor Cheff Center; certified NAHRA master therapeutic riding instructor; NAHRA program consultant; faculty NAHRA work-shop; NAHRA national accreditor, NAHRA accreditation & instructor certification committees, presenter, International Congress on Therapeutic Riding, Denmark 1991; instructor & vice president Pikes Peak Therapeutic Riding Center.

Lisa Walsh
Member U.S.A Equestrian Team for Disabled Riders in Sweden and Holland; presenter, International Congress for Therapeutic Riding; Rider.

Christine Wiegand, RN, MA
Clinical child development; family & child counselor, C.A.M.F.T.; therapist with Hillsides Families Together Program; early intervention instructor - Exceptional Children's Foundation, CA.

Nina Wiger, MA
Microbiology; independent instructor dressage-vaulting; horse trainer; remedial vaulting; Horsepower; California Carousel 4-H Vaulters; National AVA Training Clinics; member, NCEFT in remedial & therapeutic vaulting; gives clinics throughout USA in training vaulting horses; writer, lungeing for *Chronicle of the Horse*; AVA member.

Stephanie C. Woods, BFA
California special secondary/art teaching credential; consultant public relations; product/graphics designer; co-editor & illustrator- *Aspects and Answers; A Manual for Therapeutic Horseback Riding;* developed brochure for National Center for Equine Facilitated Therapy; riding instructor/trainer/exhibitor in trail/Western pleasure; owner, SpeCial Worlds Unlimited.

TABLE OF CONTENTS

PART II ~ THE HORSE

PART III ~ HUMAN DEVELOPMENT AND BEHAVIOR

PART IV ~ DISABILITIES

PART V ~ THE THERAPEUTIC RIDING TEAM

CHAPTER 14
COMPONENTS AND ORGANIZATION

CHAPTER 15
STAFF AND VOLUNTEERS

PART VI ~ THE EQUESTRIAN FACILITY FOR THERAPEUTIC RIDING

CHAPTER 16
FACILITIES

CHAPTER 17
TRAILS COURSES

PART VII ~ RIDING EQUIPMENT

CHAPTER 18
TACK

PART VIII ~ INSTRUCTION

CHAPTER 19
INSTRUCTIONAL METHODS

PART XI ~ RESOURCES

THERAPEUTIC RIDING I STRATEGIES FOR INSTRUCTION & THERAPEUTIC RIDING II STRATEGIES FOR REHABILITATION - - - A CROSS REFERENCE OF AUTHOR AND ARTICLES

Thou shall:

Practice "Safe First"

Do no harm to any rider

Present a professional appearance

Have a daily lesson plan appropriate to rider's disability

Be a task master: of your self and those around you

Simplify words and actions

Be creative, be resourceful

Bring each rider to his full potential, challenge each rider

Recognize your own areas of strength, and limitations

Inspire confidence

Enjoy yourself while teaching, enjoy your riders

Jean M. Tebay

FOREWORD

Over thirty-five years ago in Europe, horse and pony riding was first
introduced as a viable alternative form of rehabilitation therapy for persons
with physical disabilities. At that time, one of the most difficult tasks facing
the early equestrian pioneers was to try to convince a then skeptical medical
profession of the numerous therapeutic benefits that could be derived for
persons with a multitude of disabilities while they attempted to control or
"ride" a horse.

Provided the term "therapeutic" was not over-emphasized, medical advisors
went along with what was then considered the brainchild of a few eccentric
"horsey people." In spite of doubting the full extent of the benefits that were
claimed early on, therapists grudgingly admitted that in fact "no harm could be
done" given a certain safety requirements and medical guidelines were
followed. It took quite a few years of participation in operating programs
before doctors, surgeons, and therapists finally became convinced of its value,
and began to recommend this form of "treatment" for patients with a variety of
physical disabilities.

A group of German medical and equestrian experts, following a visit to the
Chigwell Center in England, finally recognized the multiple therapeutic benefits
of the horse's movement and subsequently coined the phrase "Hippotherapy."
This tern now applies to treatment of patients whose degree of disability or
involvement may contraindicate an actual progressive riding program, but who
may benefit from specific mounted exercises. These exercises are determined by
the therapist and the riding instructor and utilize the rhythm of the horse's
movement, the warmth of the horse, the rolling action of the horse's gait and
results in the adjustment necessary to maintain balance. These "patients" are
now mainly recommended by a medical professional and do not necessarily
ride by their own choice

For persons whose ability enables them, the emphasis was directed more toward recreation and rehabilitative effects of influencing or controlling the horse, albeit minimally. The enjoyment and social integration aspects of treatment outside of the "clinical atmosphere" was also a prime consideration. At the initial joint assessment or evaluation the individual desires of the student were taken into consideration, provided they were mentally aware and capable of making their own decision to ride. Hence, the adaption of the Chigwell motto, "It is Ability not Disability that Counts!"

During the last twenty-five years a great deal has been written by different authors, separately on both aspects. To my knowledge, however, the two approaches have never been described or compiled so logically together, to explain the natural progression from Hippotherapy to Rehabilitative riding, through all the natural transitions. This manual covers both in great detail. It is the result of close cooperation between experts from various fields, who have been involved in programs for many years and who obviously learnt a great deal from their person experiences. It also includes very comprehensively the opinions of riders with a variety of disabilities, who describe their own personal experiences. These I find particularly enlightening and informative.

For persons whose ability enables them, the emphasis was directed more toward recreation and rehabilitative effects of influencing or controlling the horse, albeit minimally. The enjoyment and social integration aspects of treatment outside of the "clinical atmosphere" was also a prime consideration. At the initial joint assessment or evaluation the individual desires of the student were taken into consideration, provided they were mentally aware and capable of making their own decision to ride. Hence, the adaption of the Chigwell motto, "It is Ability not Disability that Counts!"

During the last twenty-five years a great deal has been written by different authors, separately on both aspects. To my knowledge, however, the two approaches have never been described or compiled so logically together, to explain the natural progression from Hippotherapy to Rehabilitative riding, through all the natural transitions. This manual covers both in great detail. It is the result of close cooperation between experts from various fields, who have been involved in programs for many years and who obviously learned a great deal from their person experiences. It also includes very comprehensively the opinions of riders with a variety of disabilities, who describe their own personal experiences. These I find particularly enlightening and informative.

Anyone who has the opportunity to read this manual can learn and apply these unique principles to teaching their own students, and thereby enable many more, who choose, to take up and hold

"The Reins of Life"!

John A. Davies

May 1991
Former Chief Instructor, Riding For The Disabled Trust, England, 1964-1973;
President, North American Riding for the Handicapped Association, 1976-1982

INTRODUCTION

In ***Therapeutic Riding I & II Strategies for Instruction & Strategies for Rehabilitation,*** Barbara Teichmann Engel has tackled that most difficult task: being all things to all people. This two volume work represents the Second Edition of the popular Yellow Book otherwise known as Therapeutic Riding Programs: Instruction and Rehabilitation

Barbara T. Engel has put together a tremendous wealth of knowledge on every aspect of therapeutic activities conducted with the aid of the horse. Because of the depth and scope of the material she has wisely chosen to divide it into separate volumes, issues of primary interest to instructors, administrators, volunteers, and horse trainers appear in this book, Volume I. Topics relating to the use of the horse as a modality in therapy or education by therapists or special educators are grouped in Volume II which appeared earlier in 1997. The two are intended to be used together and a cross-referenced index appears in each.

The volume you have in your hands presents a significantly improved selection of in-depth information on how to establish and maintain a therapeutic riding program. ***Strategies for Instruction*** also represents a superb "refresher course" for experienced practitioners. Need to refresh your memory on suppling exercises or distances between cavalletti poles? Not quite sure of the placement of the dressage letters? You'll find it.

There is truly something for everyone here. There are chapters on the training and well-being of the horse. The instructor can find information on all manner of disabilities, as well as helpful hints on how to structure lessons, set goals and record progress. The importance of continuing education is emphasized and there are sections on stable management, facilities and equipment.

There are several articles that should be required reading for the therapist who has little or no equestrian knowledge to help him or her understand the needs of the horse. Other essays introduce the therapist's point of view for the instructor without strong background knowledge about disabilities.

It is becoming more important every year that instructors entering the therapeutic riding profession be well educated before they enter the ring to start teaching. The involvement of medical and educational professionals demands a matching level of expertise from the riding instructor. He or she needs to be well versed in human, as well as equine, physiology, anatomy, and physical, mental and emotional development. In the United States, we are fortunate that a number of colleges recognize the importance of "teaching the teachers" by including therapeutic riding in their curricula. This book, together with the companion volume, ***Strategies for Rehabilitation,*** is ideal as a college text book.

The great strength of this book is that it does not preach or insist on only one method or philosophy. Therapeutic riding programs come in all shapes and sizes. Some are concerned with the social-psychological benefits for their riders; others concentrate on providing hippotherapy; others again aim for success in competition, or emphasize equitation and horsemanship ideals. A number of programs incorporate all of the above. The reader will find essays dealing with these and still other approaches.

My personal favorite chapter contains the stories of riders who speak directly to the main point: riding driving and being around horses have enormous power to influence positively the lives and well-being of people with disabilities.

This book will assist instructors and therapists, volunteers and horse trainers to give each client the best possible setting to achieve his or her personal goals.

Congratulation, Barbara! You've done it again!!

Octavia J. Brown, Ed.M, CMTRI.
Gladstone, NJ

October, 1997

PREFACE

It is my privilege to bring to you the revised edition of *Therapeutic Riding Programs: Instruction and Rehabilitation*. Since it has grown in size, it has been divided into two volumes: *Therapeutic Riding I Strategies for Instruction* and *Therapeutic Riding II Strategies for Rehabilitation*. *Therapeutic Riding I Strategies for Instruction* was divided into two parts for easier handling. Both volumes include 40 to 50 percent new or revised material and are intended to be used together. All contributors must be commended for their time and expertise and their willingness to contribute to the reader's knowledge.

A special thanks must go the our busy national and international clinicians who were willing to give their time and contribute to this manuscript.

Therapeutic riding is not as simple as one might think. It involves much more then combining a horse with a rider who has a disability. Safety is of prime importance and to accomplish this, one must be knowledgeable in horsemanship, observation skills, teaching techniques, and in the various disabilities.

There are other needed skills such as people skills, team work, and paper skills. One must be able to reach out to others for knowledge that one does not have.

The size of these volumes give some indication of the vast knowledge needed to become proficient in the field. And much more material could be added, or, supplemented by, other sources. There are excellent reading materials and videos available, in addition to courses on the subject of therapeutic riding. A solid classic equestrian background is necessary to become proficient in the field in addition to a logical teaching approach based on the classical theory. These capabilities are acquired over time.

We look forward to the advancement of the field which is still young. Experimentation and exploration will help to further the field, but always remember that this must be done in such a way that the client's well being and advancement are not compromised. Hopefully this manuscript will both expand the reader's knowledge and provoke further development of the field.

Barbara T. Engel, M.Ed, OTR

Do nothing out of selfish ambition or vain conceit,
but in humility consider others better than yourself.
Each of you should look not only to your own interests, but also to
the interest of others.

Philippians 2:3-4

PART I
THERAPEUTIC RIDING

CHAPTER 1
WHAT IS THERAPEUTIC RIDING?

NARHA - THERAPEUTIC RIDING IN NORTH AMERICA ...
ITS FIRST DECADE 1970 TO 1980

Elmer G. Butt, MD

PROMPTING STEPS

Man through the ages has attributed to horseback riding extraordinary therapeutic benefits: Chiron, a centaur, a physical composite of man and horse, was a mentor to Aesculapius, the first physician and teacher of medicine. Medical writers of centuries past, Orebasius, Galen and many others, have alluded to riding as therapy. Lord Thomas Sydenham, an early English physician, after who is named Sydenham's Chorea, wrote in 1670, "There is no better treatment for the body and the soul than many tours each week in the saddle."

In contemporary times, riding as therapy assumed a new chapter in its history when Madame Liz Hartel of Denmark rehabilitated herself from a wheel chair to horseback, winning the silver medal for Grand Prix Dressage at the Helsinki Olympics in 1952. She had been stricken with polio. Soon thereafter, centers in therapeutic riding became known in Norway, Denmark and England.

In England in 1958, Mrs. Norah Jacques founded the Pony Riding for the Paralysis Trust, later named the Pony Riding for the Disabled Trust, and at Chigwell near London, it opened the first ever built indoor arena for riding for the disabled. Mr. John Davies was its first chief full-time instructor,

On the North American Continent in 1960, Mr. J. J. Bauer and Dr. R. E. Renaud of Toronto laid the beginnings of Community Association of Riding for the Disabled (C.A.R.D.), and in 1963, Dr. E.G. Butt of Windsor, Ontario, initiated a riding for the handicapped program. The Cheff Foundation of Augusta, Michigan in 1966 began its plans for the Cheff Center for the Handicapped as the first purposefully built riding for the handicapped center on the North American continent. Its chief instructor and executive director was Mrs. Lida L. McCowan. A professional horsewoman, Mrs. McCowan prepared for her role with the Cheff Center by visiting several riding for the disabled centers in England, and enrolled in a two-week course at the Disabled Trust Center at Chigwell under the direction of Mr. J. Davies. She received her certificate.

In England in 1964, the Advisory Council for Riding for the Disabled came into being and several national organizations for riding for the handicapped were formed in continental Europe.

THE FOUNDING

The Chronicle of the Horse and its editor, Mr. Alexander Mackay-Smith, played a very significant role in supporting the concept of NARHA. In the 1960's, the Chronicle of the Horse published articles submitted by some few in North America who had become engaged in riding for the handicapped on an occasional and small scale. It was thus natural and propitious that Mrs. McCowan might seek out that well respected gentleman, Mr. Mackay-Smith, as a sounding board and buttress. It seems that a letter written 28th July, 1969, by Mr. Mackay-Smith to Mrs. McCowan is the first record providing the opening bar for the overture to NARHA, for in it is penned "Furthermore, I like your idea of setting up an Advisory Council which could include

1

people all over the country." Following further discussion, the Red Fox Inn, Middleburg, Virginia, seemed an appropriate place for a founding meeting. It was well removed from the Cheff Center lest it be construed that the center might endeavor to assert unwanted influence; nor did it want to be labeled as a national center. Sunday afternoon, November 6, 1969, seemed an excellent time, falling as it were between two horse shows in the area. An appropriate notice of the meeting was placed in the Chronicle.

At the Red Fox Inn, Mr. Mackay-Smith presided; twenty were in attendance and eight delivered their regrets. Early in the meeting, Mr. John A. Davies of Chigwelt, England, Chief Instructor of Pony Riding for the Disabled Trust, gave a thumb nail sketch of the history of Riding for the Disabled. He presented its development in England and the founding of the Advisory Council for Riding for the Disabled in that country. He exhorted that all who were to be involved in riding for the disabled on this continent must learn early to work together and not each go his own direction. He reported on the assistance offered by the Pony Riding for the Disabled Trust and other related organizations and persons, should assistance be requested.

There was also total unanimity that an Advisory Councils be formed and that this should be accomplished through the suggested and readily accepted name of North America Riding for the Handicapped (NARHA). This name thus permitted direct participation by Canadians who wished to join. Thus, NARHA was founded. The time and place of the organization meeting were determined, and notice was given in the Chronicle of the Horse.

NARHA'S FIRST MEETING AND BOARD OF DIRECTORS
The meeting of NARHA that might be considered as the first was on January 28, 1970 at the Plaza Hotel in New York City with Mr. Mackay-Smith presiding. The following were in attendance:
Mr. and Mrs. Alexander Mackay-Smith, Mr. and Mrs. Dean Bedford, Mr., Robert Masson, Mr. and Mrs. David I.A. Pugh, Mr. J. J. Murphy, Dr. Elmer 0. Butt, Mr. Paul Klotz, Miss Octavia Chater, Mrs. W. H. Turner, Mrs. Lida McCowan, Mr. McLean, Mrs. Harry F. Black, Mr. Alan J. Zupko, Mrs. E. Haven Simmons, Dr. Jerry L. Adelson.

The proposed aims and by laws are read by the provisional Secretary and were accepted. The following were nominated and elected to the Board for one year:

Dr. Jerry Adelson	Mrs. F. Haven Simmons	Miss Octavia Chater
Mrs. Lida McCowan	Dr. Robert L. Banner	Dr. Janet Wassel
Mr. Harry B. Black	Mrs. Carl Spencer	Mr. Howard Haynes
Mr. J. Murphy	Dr. E.G. Butt	Mrs. L. P. Breithaupt
Mr. J. J. Bauer	Mr. Alex Mackay-Smith	Mr. Robert Masson

It became clear very early that the responsibility of each board member to the new organization was more than an honor; each at this first board meeting was assessed $10.00 for the purpose of creating the treasury. Little did each member realize that during his or her tenure on the board many would have spent hundreds to thousands of dollars attending the required number of board meetings held in widely separated cities across the country.

The attendance by some at board meetings during the decade was exemplary. Lida McCowan missed but one, followed closely by Octavia Chater Brown. Many others were very regular attendants and were so valued as to be re-nominated and elected. It was not an easy task each year to assemble nominations from across the country and Canada for a balanced board. This board required horsemen, administrators, teachers, medical and paramedical personnel, business persons and above all each with a concern for the handicapped. Since NARHA's inception, there were usually three board meetings per year. In 1971 however, only once was the board called to assemble. Many wondered if NARHA would survive.

In the first decade, NARHA elected four Presidents. Mr. Howard Haynes, the first president, was executive director of the Grafton School in Berryville, Virginia, and early he developed his own riding-for-the-handicapped program. His successor was Dr. Robert Banner, a surgeon, then of Nashville, Tennessee. Dr. Banner stressed the importance of the involvement of the medical and paramedical profession in NARHA and the importance of documentation with progress notes on each rider in the program. It was during Dr. Banner's term that overtures were made to medical organizations for support, but little of a direct nature resulted. This was not interpreted as a great discouraging factor.

Mrs. McCowan became President in 1974. As a professional horsewoman and executive director of the Cheff Foundation of Augusta, Michigan, she brought to the board firm direction and organization. In fulfilling NARHA's aims, standards for accreditation and examination of centers here began. Two years later, the certification of instructors to NARHA's standards was under study.

In March 1977, Mr. Davies was elected NARHA's fourth President. Mr. Davies, elected to the board in 1974, had left England and came to the United States as head instructor at Acorn Equestrian Centre, Naperville, Illinois. He early established NARHA standing committees of Finance and General Purposes, Standards and Education, and Medical and Research; within this organizational framework NARHA functioned to the close of its first decade.

NARHA has been served by three secretaries. Mrs. Harry Black (Chris), Mr. Leonard Warner and Miss Diana Seacord. Likewise in the first decade, NARHA had three treasurers; Mrs. Haven Simmons (Sally), Miss Seacord and Mr. Leonard Warner. Mr. Haven (Sally) Simmons, the husband of Sally, gave freely of his services as NARHA'S counsel. Mr. Mackay-Smith, NARHA'S Honorary Chairman since 1970, was elected Honorary Chairman, Emeritus in 1977. Mrs. McCowan was elected to the position of Honorary Chairman in 1977. Several retiring members of the board have been honored in a multiplicity of ways for their selfless service.

As in most successful charitable organizations, the challenges presented and the work to be accomplished outstrip the time available and the capabilities of the volunteers. In 1978, NARHA was indeed fortunate in having a board member, Mr. Warner, who had been secretary and treasurer, move into the new and very important position of executive director. NARHA started to move faster and farther.

The comradery at the board meetings was well sustained even when new members replaced the old. The meetings were always in good humor, and rarely did the super ego of a member rise above the surface of the *raison d'etre*, riding for the handicapped. Personal experiences of many of the board members outside the board room gave zest to the weekend business. The committee meetings of three, four or five persons were informal, convening on a Friday evening in a hotel room, at lunch or during recess of a board meeting.

The board meetings moved through cities of many states, Virginia, Massachusetts, Michigan, Washington, D.C., New York, New Jersey, Pennsylvania, Ohio, Illinois, Kentucky, Missouri, Colorado and Arizona. The areas selected were those where there seemed to be the greatest interest for riding for the handicapped. A program on a Saturday evening was arranged by a regional riding for the handicapped group wherein the public was invited to learn of some of the objectives and the many facets of NARHA. Attendance at these meetings at times was very gratifying and on other occasions disappointing.

THE MEMBERS AT LARGE
The membership classifications established by the bylaws in 1970 remained unchanged, sustaining individual members, contributing members, life members and operating centers, each with one vote. At the annual meeting in Washington, D.C. January 1971, there was reported a membership of 20 sustaining members, 36 contributing, 4 operating centers and 4 life members. In 1976 there was recorded a membership of 101 including all classifications. By 1980, the records reveal a 577 total membership with 150 operating center memberships.

The annual meeting held on a Saturday afternoon or evening, latterly in November, was in seven different states. These meetings, in some instances, were coupled with a clinic or demonstration sponsored by a local riding for the handicapped group.

Again, the annual meeting was endeavoring to reach to the location of the members and thus provide exposure of NARHA on a broad geographical basis. At all times, the members were encouraged to come to attend as observers at the Sunday morning board meeting and participate through the board members of their regions.

REGIONS

Regions in NARHA were geographical, nine in total, eight plus Canada. These divisions had appropriate board representation, but regional meetings and reporting therefrom had sporadic success in their intended function. Considerable distance within the regions was doubtless the greatest factor in the lack of appeal. Areas 1, 2 and 3 on the East Coast for some years were distinct exceptions having well-advertised meetings which featured slides, movies and discussions.

NARHA publications, its movie film service and other promotional printed efforts reflected a great deal of imagination and industry on the part of the members. The history of this organization is probably best preserved in the minutes of the board meetings and the annual membership meetings. The secretaries are to be commended for their diligence.

NARHA NEWS

In accordance with the early aims of NARHA, News Volume No.1 was published in October 1970. In the early days of the News, NARHA was most fortunate to have as editor, - Marilyn Massey, the wife of Mr. Mackay-Smith, editor of the Chronicle of the Horse. Furthermore, the publisher of the Chronicle of the Horse arranged for printing of the News. Marilyn Massey not only endeavored to present the activities of NARHA but also introduced its readers to many operating centers in the United States and Canada.

In 1974, owing to Marilyn Massey's resignation, the board found or "highjacked" a new editor, one of its original members and then vice-president, Mrs. Octavia Brown, with Mrs. Margaret Dunlap as co-editor. Three issues a year appeared. Philosophy of content changed slightly with biographical sketches of the members of the board, stories and photographs of handicapped riders, key note articles and editorials with quotes from writings of other publications. The circulation reached 500 copies per issue. In 1976, again owing to resignation, the board found its new senior editor in Mrs. L.B.P.(Sis) Gould, again a board member. Sis continued as her predecessors and encouraged some short papers worthy of a bibliographic record. In late 1978 and into early 1980, Laurie Kaplan Fox of Michigan was the editor in chief with Mr. Warner as publisher. The NARHA News as you know it today has now its editor and publisher in the name of Mr. Warner. His thesis was news of NARHA, one or two essays per issue, a letter to the editor and a later innovation, and classified advertisements.

NARHA-GUIDELINES AND HANDBOOK

NARHA first published its Guidelines booklet in 1974 wherein the suggested requirements for the operation of a program were briefly outlined. The experience gained at the Cheff Center for the Handicapped and the consultations with the British Pony Riding for the Disabled Trust provided the essence for this publication. The required medical supervision, the selection of mounts, the qualification of helpers and the desired equipment were among the items of major concern described. Miss Chater. Mrs. McCowan and Dr. Banner were the committee responsible for its preparation and publication; its cover was initially red and later green.

The Handbook bearing a blue cover supplanted the Guidelines in 1976. It was an elaborate expansion of its forerunner with additional chapters so, by following the instructions, one was well prepared to embark on a very creditable program. The Handbook, still available, indicates the committee as being Dr. Davies, Mrs. Kittredge and Dr. Butt. It should, however be recorded that Mrs. McCowan contributed greatly to this work. The original printing of the Handbook was made possible through a generous donation by Mr. and Mrs. L. B. P. Gould.

ANNUAL REPORT AND JOURNAL

The 1975 issue was the first of this periodical. There is little doubt from the outset that this was the creation of the newspaper-board member, Mr. Warner, as Chairman of Publications, with Mrs. Octavia Brown as editor and Mrs. Jean McCally co-editor of the first issue. Not only did it contain statistical data but also outlined some of NARHA's significant events of the past year and reports from many operating centers. The names of members of all classifications were recorded and readers could readily learn the benefits of membership in the organization. In summary, it was a rapid recapitulation of the happenings of NARHA of the past year and its current status.

BIBLIOGRAPHY

Miss Naomi Lorch can be given the greatest amount of credit for NARHA's first issue of "Bibliography of Therapeutic Horsemanship" published in 1975. In 1978, this publication was revised by a committee under the chairmanship of Dr. Michael McCally with Miss Lorch and Mrs. Octavia Chater Brown. This bibliography provided a list of books, professional journal articles, foreign language publications and audio visual aids. It was an extremely well prepared issue with a scientific format. It was the basis of a paper and seminar presented by Dr. McCally in 1979 at the Third International Conference of Riding for the Disabled in Coventry, England.

OTHERS

In addition NARHA has produced several other printings and promotional items. In late 1970 Mr. Mackay-Smith prepared and arranged for the printing of the very popular folded, a pocket size brochure which had been prepared by Mrs. Lida McCowan and Mrs. Harry Black. At a slightly later date, the bylaws including NARHA's purposes were printed on a similar sized folder and were available to members on request. Mrs. Brown arranged for the printing of a 16 by 13 inch NARHA colored poster and NARHA member buttons. Jacket patches, lapel pins and T-shirts have been produced bearing NARHA's emblem. On several occasions an NARHA display booth was assembled by an individual or a small committee for use at shows, meetings and dinners but the cost of transportation precluded a more permanent collection of articles.

NARHA'S EMBLEM

It was early apparent that such an organization as NARHA should have an emblem. At the second board meeting April 1970, which was presented by Mr. Mackay-Smith was discussed with his accompanying explanation "The symbolism of the side elements are the crutch, now broken into two pieces and discarded because the handicapped have achieved mobility through horseback riding as is illustrated in the centre." A modification of this was shortly in use with a full crutch replacing each broken half.

AUDIO-VISUAL (Film Rental Service)

This enterprise was among the most rewarding for NARHA in its support to local programs which are endeavoring to initiate or sustain interest in riding for the handicapped in a community. Probably the beginning of NARHA's involvement in this field was a slide collection prepared by the Cheff Center pertaining to its own program in 1970. Very quickly it was suggested that a larger collection be assembled to include the activities of many centers, but this was not fully accomplished. Its appeal was pre-empted by NARHA's purchase of two rental copies of the very excellent film "Exceptional Equestrians" produced in 1974 under the direction of Ms. Virginia Martin, Borderland Farm, Warwick N Y.

In 1977, a second film was added to NARHA's services, "Ability Not Disability," a production of the Latham Foundation, California. This film was a sensitive portrayal of activities at Cheff Center for the Handicapped, Augusta, Michigan. "Right to Choose" was made available in 1978. This was a beautiful film produced by Town and Country Productions Ltd. London, England. In 1980, the library added a fourth film "Yes I can Ride a Pony" a London B.B.C. production, featuring a riding center headed by a London Mounted Policeman.

The film service was a very big chore, initially fraught with frustration for Leonard Warner, the custodian of the film library. All too frequently the scheduled film delivery service broke down causing shattered nerves and abuse to many. One user kept the film in possession for almost two months. A film was often returned damaged and required repair before again being dispatched. Probably the most aggravating was the undependable Special Delivery Air Transport Postal Service, wherein excess of a week was required within the United States and more than one to two weeks for delivery in Canada. Delivery results became very satisfactory with the usage of United Parcel Service.

CENTER ACCREDITATION

In an early address as president, Mrs. McCowan, in February 1974, reminded the board of the aims of NARHA by stating "The time has come to get going on the accreditation program." Mr. Davies was appointed Chairman of the Accreditation Committee. Mrs. McCowan, Dr. Butt and Mrs. Kittredge as chairman were to establish the standards. This latter subcommittee had several heated meetings with all three members frequently differing in disciplinary opinions. Most of the contentious issues were resolved at the board meeting of January 1975, the NARHA accreditation questionnaire and examiner accreditation forms were approved; scores of 1 to 10 were given under the heading of condition and appropriateness of mounts, volunteers, equipment facilities, administration and, finally, the instructors' lessons. A satisfactory liability insurance policy had to be in force. Ever since 1973, the board had recognized that there must be a relationship between insurance and accreditation. A center was to be examined for provisional status and within a year permanent status or later know as full accreditation.

The Cheff Center was the first to be examined in the spring of 1975 by Mr. Davies and Mrs. Kittredge who recommended to the board that provisional accreditation be awarded. Many other centers were examined that year and several were successful. In 1980, the new streamlined mechanics of the accreditation process functioned well under the Standards and Education Committee. The examining team was enlarged and included non-board members. In 1980 also, full accreditation was awarded to a center obtaining 85 percent or more on the first examination and any center, at 3-to-4-year intervals, could be expected to receive a spot check to retain its accreditation.

Considerable credit must go to the persons who were selected in the early days for accreditation. Few were felt to be sufficiently knowledgeable and thus a few had to bear many demands; this, coupled with often great distances to travel, occasionally caused an embarrassing waiting period before the examination could be conducted. NARHA coffers being feebly low and the fee for accreditation covering scarcely more than the paper work, the expense allowance for the examiners travel accommodation and subsistence barely reached the poverty line. Indeed the examiners frequently adjusted their expenses downward or elected not to present an expense account.

Initially NARHA, at its own expense, was to provide examination for full accreditation but as the demand grew this was not permitted and, in 1980, the examination fee for a center, provisional or full, was fixed at $50.00. Despite this fee which to some seemed a deterrent, there apparently were 45 NARHA accredited programs in 1980.

INSTRUCTOR CERTIFICATION

Cheff Center for the Handicapped, Augusta, Michigan, probably even before its official opening in 1970, had embarked on an instructor education program. It realized there would be considerable demand for well-trained instructors across the continent and that the nature of its facility lent itself to this function. Through its graduates, other instructor training programs were initiated. In 1975, the NARHA board realized that it was time to seriously grapple with another of its early aims: to establish instructor standards. A training syllabus prepared by NARHA to which each instructor training center must adhere was seen to be unwieldily, uncontrollable, authoritarian and a completely unworkable approach. The board opted for the alternative wherein NARHA would prepare an examination for which any candidate could apply, regardless of the source or structure of training.

In 1976, the Standards and Education Committee was charged with the preparation and operation of the NARHA instruction for certification examination. Dr. Butt was chairman of the subcommittee to prepare the examination with Mrs. McCowan, Mrs. Kittredge and Mrs. Winter completing the committee. After a year of communication, mild dissidence, revisions and frequent progress reports to the board, the subcommittee felt its task completed and referred it back to the parent committee, Standards and Education, in 1978.

There were three instructors' certification examination classifications, one of which the candidate would select;
1. Non orthopedic handicapped.
2. Orthopedic handicapped.
3. Combined orthopedic and non-orthopedic handicapped.
The examinations were divided into sections: (a) the written, which were the open book concept to be completed at home in ten days. If successful the candidate proceeded to (b) the practical, at a specified center wherein the candidate was examined in horsemanship, horse-mastership and the teaching of a class or classes of handicapped riders.

There was much discussion as to who should be the examiners. Who should qualify the examiners? However, who better should know than NARHA what was required in this aspect of its aims. In March 1979, the board adopted the following resolution "to further implement the instructors' certification program, the board establishes a category of instructors under a grandfather clause so designated because of their long experience in the field. The following members were so designated: Dr. Elmer Butt, Mrs. M.V. Kittredge, Ms. Diana Seacord, Mrs. Octavia Brown, Ms. Virginia Martin, Mrs. Lida McCowan, Mr. John Davies, Mrs. John Davies, Mrs. Nancy Winter, Mrs. Frances Joswick, Mrs. Jean McCally, and Mrs. Bliss Brown. "The aforementioned may be called upon by the chairman to form a panel for each instructor examination." The first examination was at the Cheff Center on May 1979. Examinations were to be arranged at other centers having the required handicapped persons within their programs.

In April 1980, Mrs. Nancy Winter was appointed to the subcommittee of instructor certification as chairman and, in that year, new regulations appeared making the examination process easier and more effective. By the end of 1980, there were approximately twelve NARHA certified instructors. The individual fee for all or any part of the examination was $100.00.

In 1977, consideration was given to making application to the U.S. Department of Health, Education and Welfare for the purpose of attaining accrediting agency status. After correspondence, the effort for the time being seemed to outweigh the merit and application was deferred.

EDUCATION
NARHA efforts in education had, for the greater part, been directed through its influence on standards in Center Accreditation and Instructor Certification, through presentations at annual meetings and through the news. Particularly at the annual meetings, there was frequently a panel discussion of so-called experts on one or more subjects pertaining to riding for the handicapped. Mr. Brian Woodward, President of the New Zealand Riding for the Disabled Association, addressed the board in July 1980 in the administration of the program of that country. NARHA, also in a limited way, supported seminars or workshops sponsored by several centers.

In November 1980, NARHA had its first National Seminar, four days duration at the Cheff Center, Augusta, Michigan. One hundred and fifteen were in attendance from 50 states, Canada and West Germany. It was a definite success and comments received were most constructive. NARHA also endeavored to keep abreast with the international scene. In 1973, Mrs. Octavia Brown was NARHA's representative at the International Conference of Riding for the Handicapped, Warwickshire, England. In 1974, NARHA's representative was Mrs. Nancy Winter to the International Conference for Riding for the Handicapped in Paris, France. At the 1979 Third International Conference of Riding for the Handicapped in Coventry, England, NARHA had several delegates and Mrs. McCowan, Mr. Davies and Dr. Michael McCally were narrators.

MEDICAL AND RESEARCH COMMITTEE

It is true that, through the ages, it was a rare physician who realized the real therapeutic benefit of horseback riding. The dissidents were many, and they perceived the horse as an instrument of war, a beast of labor and animal of speed for wager, or a mode where man may have super ego exalted in sport. By most, the horse was not appreciated as a beautiful, docile, rhythmically moving animal whose latter characteristics when one is astride impart exhilaration, joint-muscular movements, coordination and many other effects.

The nonbelieiver, whether it is the physician, the paramedic or the lay person, asked what research data exist to warrant such an elaborate approach? It seems that NARHA's Medical and Research Committee, formed in 1977 under the chairmanship of Dr. Walter H. Warden, soon learned that its most productive role was not to pursue the difficult and expensive method of documentary proof, which at its best would be controversial. On the contrary it realized that it must work within the concept of "can't you see what has happened to Mary, to Jamie, to Sally and to John, since they began to ride?"

In 1979 under the chairmanship of Mr. John Brough, O.T.R. working with perceptual learning disabilities, the committee was enlarged and new horizons appeared. Information was gathered on research completed or in progress. Safety standards were considered. A standardized assessment form was developed and pamphlets on medical subject pertinent to the knowledge of the instructor of riding for the handicapped were planned. The first of these pamphlets, "Therapeutic Riding and Side Affects of Medication" published in 1980, was prepared by Miss Diana Seacord, R.N., a committee member.

SPORTS THERAPY

NARHA scarcely had been founded when the question of competition of handicapped riders within a center, or indeed inter center competition, was truly desirable. The handicapped were already struggling for identity and security, but it became appreciated that the aspirations of the handicapped frequently did not differ from the normal. It was acknowledged that the win-loss concept must be managed with great sensitivity for each rider.

Many centers had engaged in riding displays at different functions and had entered teams to games and competition. Some of these the NARHA board endorsed as requested and, on occasion, an official NARHA team was fielded. Mrs. McCowan, through her long interest with the mentally retarded and activities in riding, was appointed in 1975 as NARHA chairman of the Special Olympics Committee and with Mrs. Bliss Brown established standards. NARHA riders demonstrated at the State Special Olympics and at the International Special Olympics. In 1975-79 a demonstration was very well received and horseback riding became officially accepted as a demonstration sport by the Special Olympics Board.

INSURANCE

Insurance first appeared in NARHA's board minutes in 1972 when its members questioned the need of liability for themselves in the event of a suit against an NARHA member center. Very shortly the answer was rendered by Mr. Leybourne, of Leybourne, Olson and Anderson of Muskegon, Michigan, a firm knowledgeable in the Cheff Center operations. As long as the standards of NARHA are enforced upon centers, it is a remote possibility that any claim could be made against NARHA or its officers. However, it was recommended that NARHA take out a simple liability --policy for approximately $30.00 a year. By 1975, the operating centers of NARHA were learning of the advisability of liability insurance; Leybourne, Olson and Anderson again provided an NARHA master policy for each center on the provision of membership in NARHA and indeed such centers were required by NARHA to have filed an application for accreditation. Thus, this was the accreditation and insurance requirements for center membership.

Within an era of suits, generally in America, the rising cost of premiums so strained the budgets of some smaller centers that continued operation was threatened. The period from 1977 to 1979 was indeed a difficult period for the board in this regard. The executive director, charged by the board to come up with a solution, learned that the insurance companies did not like the mix of "horses and handicapped." The new agent and company engaged by the board proved to be somewhat less than honest.

8

After frantic and a rapid search in 1979, through information gained from the International Special Olympics, Mr. Harry Gustis, president of C.I.M.A. an agency in Washington, D.C., appreciated NARHA plight. After several weeks of work, Mr. Gustis and C.I.M.A. assembled a package which the board accepted, realizing the critical situation for many centers. NARHA became guarantors for a substantial amount of money wherein at the rate of $12.00 per person, there was coverage for riders, volunteers and instructors, operating centers and NARHA board members. It was not an attractive parcel for many centers and in the first year NARHA lost approximately $8,000.

The second year, the premium was reduced to $11.00 and a broader liability coverage was in the offing. This was overwhelmingly accepted, and in approximately 12 months, the number of insurance participating NARHA centers doubled. A new trend seemed certain. Fortunately, NARHA's treasury began to recuperate. NARHA's accident experience to the end of 1980 was almost nil. It was a great tribute to the association's total program and indeed a surprise to the insurance companies. The insurance program, after a six-year saga, made an outstanding contribution to the assurance of the growth of riding for the handicapped on this continent.

FINANCES AND FUND RAISING

The accomplishments of NARHA in that first decade were indeed considerable. One may well ask how was NARHA funded? It is understandable why NARHA might be an organization akin to poverty status. Persons and clubs would work and give for the handicapped in their own community - eager to build spires as it were. However, few would care to support an unwieldy national organization groping with its aims. In reality, it was the bricks and mortar for an emerging disciplined therapy.

The first record of concern of fund raising appears in the board minutes of 23 January, 1973 and probably correctly quoted as follows; "it is best we proceed slowly in fund raising, stress dues and membership, maintain a low profile; fund raising will come later," Indeed, the philosophy expressed at that date seems to have continued for the following three years, for at the annual meeting in the January 1976, the treasurer's report revealed an income of $3,424.23, expenses of $3,386.88, and a balance of $1,475.43. In addition to the dues, income from publications and film rental service was minuscule. Where it not for the donations that NARHA had received, NARHA probably would not have remained solvent.

It was at this time that the board realized NARHA was racing toward a crisis in that it could not sustain its accreditation program with its attendant costs. Centers were requesting to be examined, but examiners and monies for travel were in short supply. NARHA must now turn its efforts to fund raising coupled with promotion end publicity.

Octavia Brown sold hats for NARHA in 1973 that were donated by Banal Saddlery. Britches were donated by Mikes Saddle Shop of Geneva, Illinois and Mr. Davies donated a pony as an award In NARHA membership drive. In 1977, an NARHA Christmas card could be purchased bearing on its front a picture selected by a committee as the most appropriate in a contest submission by handicapped riders. At the close of the decade, a pony and carriage donation was announced as a possibility. Fund raising on a somewhat grander scale can owe its catalyst to the efforts of Mrs. Alys Cort of Pennsylvania. In Sept.1976, through the generosity of Mr. Jorie F. Butler, with Mrs. Cort assisting, NARHA was a substantial beneficiary from the polo match at the Oak Brook Polo Club, Illinois. The match was between Oak Brook Polo Team and the Guards Polo Teem Club of Windsor Great Perk, England. Although inclement weather curtailed the lull program, NARHA's demonstration proceeded well under the direction of a committee appointed by the board. The committee consisted of Mrs. McGowan, Mrs. Cort, Mrs. Winter and Mr. Davies as chairman. The 1976 Oak Brook day raised for NARHA more than $11,000.00 and provided excellent exposure of the association to the media.

In October 1976, Mrs. Alys Gort was made chairperson, with Mr. Davies as board representative, of a Special Charitable Funds Committee. This new subcommittee was under the Finance and General Purposes committee. The board also awarded life memberships in NARHA to several substantial contributors to the funds raised by the Oak Brook group.

If the September 1976 Polo day were dubbed as a "dress rehearsal", then the Sunday, July 10, 1977 NARHA benefit match and the attendant programing were "the grand performance," again through the generosity of Mr. Paul Butler and family. It was a glorious day! Preliminary to the exciting match, (Oak Brook versus Red Doors) was a luncheon under a decorated canvas followed by the Tempel Lipizzans in an NARHA benefit performance, courtesy Tempel Steel Company. This was succeeded by Mr. Davies presenting a group of handicapped students from Acorn Hill Riding for the Handicapped, Wayne Dupage program for exceptional children and St. James Farm Riding for the Handicapped.

This NARHA weekend was highly successful, both financially and through the publicity - not only by television but through reports and articles in publications with a national circulation. For the board it was memorable; a dinner in honor of the directors was hosted by Mrs. Cort at the Old Historic Chicago Golf Club. On Sunday morning, Mr. Davies arranged a tour of SI. James Farm Riding for the Handicapped facility, meeting with Mr. Brooks McCormick, its owner. Sunday evening, the board members were guests of Mr. and Mrs. Harry Lewis, honoring North American Riding for the Handicapped Association on the opening of their new restaurant, Hamburger Hamlet, Walton Street, Chicago.

Also, in Chicago in 1978, the Chicago Public Library sponsored a benefit dinner. A movie benefit in Chicago in 1978 netted NARHA $5,000.00. In the show world of 1979, NARHA broke into the big time at the National Horse Show, Madison Square Garden. Under the chairmanship of Mrs. Alys Cort, handicapped riders, students of Ms. Virginia Martin and Mrs. Octavia Brown, rode in a demonstration before the eyes of many thousand.

From 1975 to 1980, innumerable NARHA centers and horse organizations directed events to the benefit of NARHA in the nature of shows, ride-a-thons, game days, etc. These many efforts in the lesser cosmopolitan communities have been accomplished with dedication and to the enhancement of the image and financial return for NARHA. By the close of the decade, Mrs. Jean Baum was about to conclude arrangements with the American Horse Shows Association for an NARHA benefit class in selected recognized A.H.S.A. shows.

DONATIONS

NARHA had givers as well as workers. The donors not only provided much needed funds but gave the association the needed realization that thoughtful and important people and companies supported its aims and activities. The list of donors reached into dozens and dollars into the thousands. Some did not care to be named; others repeated their donations from year to year. The patrons among them were usually for a designated period of time.

CONCLUSION

The remarkable accomplishments of NARHA in its first decade are owed to dedicated people who share with one another in caring for the handicapped persons on the horse. But still so much remains to be done that we must consider the past as simply the beginning.

Elmer G. Butt, M.D
November 7, 1981
Canada

HORSEBACK RIDING FOR INDIVIDUALS WITH DISABILITIES
A PERSONAL HISTORICAL PERSPECTIVE

Natalie Bieber, MS, CAGS

The field of riding for the disabled, as it has progressed to the present, has not been without its conflicts, strong personalities and even stronger commitments to cautious innovations. Medical, educational and competition models developed, subdivided, and split into separate, but interconnected strands. Specialization, professionalism and accreditation are the focus today, but could not have been achieved without the efforts of many unsung hero(ine)s during the formative years. The earliest beginnings of the therapeutic riding movement and horseback riding for the disabled have been documented by various authors, as has the founding of NARHA. However, there were many developments through the years that were parallel to what has been publicized and the contributions of some individuals in the United States to the current state of the art may have been overlooked. The historical perspective presented here are based primarily on personal contacts, experience, and observations and covers the time from 1965 to 1985.

In North America, impetus to promote horseback riding as a credible activity for persons with disabilities was supplied by Joseph Bauer in Canada in 1965, Maudie Hunter-Warfel in 1967 with Happy Horsemanship for the Handicapped based in Pennsylvania and John Davies, Lida McCowan and the founders of NARHA. In 1967 in Colorado, Mary Woolverton, a medical social worker at Fitzsimmons Army Hospital (the 1997 president of NAHRA) for the Vietnam veterans, who shared her love of riding and horses, provided the opportunity for adults with amputations to experience the freedom of motion now denied many of them because of battlefield experiences. Hers was considered a very high risk activity because the men set many of their own limits of participation and devised unique methods of being stabilized in the saddle. This was treated with derision by some members of NARHA. Therapeutic programs were proliferating in the United States and Great Britain where there was a great deal of control over what the rider was or was not allowed to do--the decisions being made for the rider by a therapeutic riding instructor. With Woolverton, it was a shared decision. Adult riders assessed the risks they were willing to take and, with excellent horses and expert advice, rode for recreation and the pleasures of open competition. Dave Trexler (now a member of the NAHRA Board of Directors) was among those individuals. At the Third International Congress on Riding for the Disabled in England, Trexler gave a demonstration of western riding that was an eye-opener for all in attendance.

The role of lead organization, representing riding for the disabled, was contested for several years with NARHA and Happy Horsemanship vying for the honor. In a time of controversy and infighting, Mary (Sis) Gould, a woman with vision, dedication and deceptive strength, proved to be a moderating influence in many a volatile situation. Sis was the catalyst for the start of several programs in Connecticut and responsible for founding High Hopes in Lyme, CT. She was well aware, early on, that if there was to be credibility for the benefits of a therapeutic riding program, there had to be increased professionalism and less reliance on the inexperienced volunteers who were the mainstays of most early programs.

Pioneer programs were followed by independent programs conducted by dedicated, enthusiastic horse people and clinicians who volunteered their time, expertise and animals. The founding of the North American Riding for the Handicapped Association (NAHRA) in 1969 enabled therapeutic riding groups across the country to have a central body to coordinate efforts and serve as an information center. However, other non affiliated programs and groups also continued to grow according to the population served and the expertise of the professionals involved.

Continuing into the 1970's, programs for riders with disabilities were carefully controlled and the eligibility of riders accepted into established programs was generally based upon the ability of the rider to maintain his/her own stability in the saddle. A leader and one or two side walkers accompanied most of the riders. This excluded a large population, who could benefit immensely from the physical therapy that the movement of the horse imparted, as well as the recreational aspect. A program for the Little White Schoolhouse in New London, CT started using a physical or an occupational therapist as a backrider to position preschool children with physical disabilities to assist in their riding experience. This proved to be virtually a clinical therapy session and was enthusiastically endorsed by the participating therapists. Two years later, this strategy was adopted by the ACES Village School in North Haven, CT. Physical therapists in Connecticut and elsewhere began to view backriding as an auxiliary practice for patients they saw in a clinical setting. However, the thought of placing a rider who could not support him or herself independently on a horse remained a highly controversial subject. Barbara Glasow and Beth Stanford, both physical therapists, made major contributions through seminars and articles (unfortunately unpublished) by explaining what backriding and other techniques should and should not be. Through seminars sponsored by the Winslow Foundation (with strong support from Virginia Martin and Virginia Mazza) and by NARHA, they reached a wide audience of people in the field of therapeutic riding. Their expertise and ability to covey medical information, in an understandable format, had a definite impact on the direction that horseback riding as therapy was to take.

The use of horseback riding with at-risk students and/or persons with mental health problems has long been advocated and investigated. Students who qualify for adapted physical education programs have, and can be given, the option of being included, through an IEP, in a qualifying therapeutic riding program. Having a student as a captive audience while mounted provides options for all kinds of learning experiences, cognitive, physical and emotional. The possibilities are limited only by the creativity of the instructor and the safety factor. This is not something new, however. As early as 1975 Green Chimneys school, Brewster, NY, integrated a farm and riding program for the troubled inner-city children who were sent there. A curriculum was developed that included stable management and horsemanship skills. The special education class at Essex Elementary School had mounted and classroom activities provided by the Lower Connecticut Educational Riding Association (LCVERA), the precursor to High Hopes.

A therapeutic equestrian program was first introduced to the Village School, North Haven, CT, in 1976 by Cynthia Clarke, then a humane education specialist and coordinator of Self Improvement through Riding Education (SIRE) for the Humane Society of the United States. The initial program served the students from the ED/LD unit. It was expanded by Bieber to include students with physical disabilities and classroom activities complemented mounted time.

Another early (1975-82) and successful program for high risk students was administered through the Washington, D.C. school system with students riding under the direction of Robert Douglas. It was Douglas, who worked with James Brady, as part of his rehabilitation after he was shot during the assassination attempt on President Reagan. Brady's riding experience provided very favorable publicity for therapeutic riding programs around the country.

The interest generated by the programs mentioned above led in 1981 to Southern Connecticut State University offering an interdisciplinary, graduate level course, Applications and Implications of Animal-Facilitated Therapies, which was sponsored and taught through the Special Education Department. This course included an overview of the different ways animals are used as agents of therapy with special emphasis on riding as a therapeutic resource. The class was well attended by special education teachers, physical education specialists and horse people. It was intended to provide an awareness and appreciation of the possibilities of animal-facilitated therapies, not to train therapists.

Prior to 1979, there were few competitive opportunities for riders with disabilities. Stellar riders competed at open horse shows (see Woolverton above). On occasion, the Special Olympics had riding as a demonstration sport and individual programs or groups sometimes offered local competitions with games. However, there were few opportunities for formalized competitions with standardized rules that followed those of the American Horse Shows Association (AHSA) and the guidelines of the North American Riding for the Handicapped Association (NARHA). There was a need for riders who were physically challenged to have a venue where they could really compete against one another.

12

Through the efforts of Craig Huber of New Haven, CT, United Cerebral Palsy Association and, in conjunction with several adaptive physical education coaches and specialists, athletic competitions for persons with physical disabilities had become a reality in the U.S. in the 1970's. A classification system, based on the athlete's functional profile, was devised so that persons with similar physical abilities and limitations competed against one another. Though cerebral palsy and related disorders were the main focus of this organization, athletes with other disabilities, who were unable to find another sponsoring organization such as the wheelchair sports or blind groups, were invited to participate under the classification of Les Autres. Then in 1979, competitive options for riders with physical disabilities were incorporated into the events of a national sport organization for athletes with disabilities, the National Association of Sports for Cerebral Palsy (NASCP). Rules and guidelines, incorporating AHSA standards and those which had been used for Special Olympics riders, were developed. This opened the door to equestrian competition to riders with a physical disability who were able to meet the competitive standards for their functional profile.

Huber invited Bieber to coordinate the first such riding competition which was held at the Yale University Arena in conjunction with the 1979 NASCP Games in New Haven, CT. Most of the riders and coaches came from the New England area. Some brought their own horses, but most riders had horses provided for them. Among the group of riders, four would go on to be role models and make a definitive impact on the sport: Eileen Frischmann, Cynthia Good, Susan Rogowski, and Wendy Shugol. The opportunity for a competitive outlet motivated them to take their riding to a different dimension and higher levels in both the national and international events. These women also had an impact on the way adult riders were viewed and treated. They not only rode well, but were also able to articulate the point that they were highly intelligent, independent women who resented being patronized by service providers. Their legacy is the Adult Rider Committee now a part of NARHA. Good, an attorney, civil rights advocate and former Director of Consumer Affairs for United Cerebral Palsy Association, wrote several years ago of her experience:

> The historical pattern of rehabilitation has been to cut the client/patient into several pieces and send him/her into the world . . The "self" is disjointed; there is no "oneness." But, there is no reason why these different efforts cannot be coordinated. Through the physical and social impact of developing skills in riding comes all the ingredients of self-esteem: a sense of accomplishment, a sense of mobility, a sense of independence, a sense of participation in a recreational activity, and, above all, the ability to deal with people as equal and to be dealt with in a like manner. There is no other sport that not only tolerates, but indeed, and in fact, creates an environment that allows people to deal with people and not the paraphernalia that supports them in their daily life. In this lies horseback riding's therapy for all.

Support for that first competition in Connecticut came from Virginia Martin and Marge Kittredge, as coaches, and a group from CARD in Canada who came to observe. Martin, and the Winslow program with which she was associated, were instrumental in the encouragement and provision of opportunities for competition. It was in 1980 that the first international competition with teams from the United Sates and Canada participating in Toronto, Canada became a reality. NASCP, through its Connecticut affiliate, and Winslow sponsored the team. Bieber, Martin and Glasow went as coaches and facilitators. The Canadians at CARD fielded their team and provided horses for all the riders.

Riding competition became an established part of regional and national NASCP Games. In 1982, horseback riding was a demonstration sport at the International CP Games in Greve, Denmark and was accepted by the international governing body. Included in 1984 at the International Games for the Disabled, equestrian competition drew riders from Europe, Canada and the United States. Since that time, a multinational committee formalized the rules for equestrian competitions that are international in scope and are included by the United States Cerebral Palsy Athletic Association (USCPAA), the Paralympic Games and Special Olympics.

Therapeutic practices have come a long way from the time that backriding was regarded as suspect. There is a wide use of hippotherapy, "a form of treatment performed primarily by a physical or occupational therapist as a therapeutic intervention." (NAHRA). However, the early work of physical therapists Barbara Glasow and Beth Stanford dealing with positioning of riders, backriding and treatment appropriate for specific disabilities convinced many on the direction which therapeutic riding should take in the United States. In addition to the more traditional clients for riding therapy, Stanford did pioneer studies with traumatic head injury patients. Their material was always delivered in a manner that was relevant and understandable by both clinicians and lay people. In 1982 at the Fourth International Congress in Germany, Glasow with Jan Spink, and Stanford provided evidence that the United States had practitioners equal in caliber to those in Europe.

A special mention must be made of the work of two women whose diligence and determination are responsible for the documentation of so much valuable information. Both have to great extent worked outside of the system. From the 1970's on Jean Tebay persevered to raise the standards of professionalism expected in the field. She was also a catalyst who joined with the Delta Society for joint ventures involving therapeutic riding. In 1985 Barbara Engel started the daunting task of providing a bibliography of the growing literature about therapeutic riding. Though the need was widely recognized, she took on the responsibility for the job as an individual. She then went on to publish the two works widely used today by instructors and therapists.

It was this author's good fortune to be a part of the growth of therapeutic riding. With almost forty years of events in the United States to chronicle, this is an effort to fill in some of the blanks. It is good that there is an organization like NARHA to take a leadership role and coordinate the many facets of riding for persons with disabilities in the United States. However, for growth to continue, there must be a climate that encourages innovation rather than control, and openness rather than contention. Collaboration and credit, honestly given, are really what equestrian sport and therapeutic riding are all about.

SELECTED REFERENCES
Bieber, N. (1983). The Integration of a Therapeutic Equestrian Program in the Academic Environment of Children with Physical and Multiple Disabilities. New Perspectives on our Lives with Companion Animals. Philadelphia: University of Pennsylvania Press.
Glasow, B. (1980-4). Unpublished seminar materials.
Good, C. (1978). From Complete Paralysis to Riding Horses. Unpublished.
Stanford, Beth. (1981-4). Unpublished seminar materials.

Natalie Bieber
USA

THE FEDERATION OF RIDING FOR THE DISABLED INTERNATIONAL

Professor Dr. Carl Klüwer, med

In many nations in the last twenty years and, in some even before that, horseback riding as a therapeutic activity was developed. The sources of development varied from country to country. In some countries the development evolved from Dressage which is beneficial for the formation of personality. In most English speaking countries, the interest to bring riding within the reach of the disabled resulted mainly from an increased sense of life through leisure riding and cross-country riding. In Scandinavian countries, sport riding and competition were at the center of the development of therapeutic riding. In fact, Liz Hartel, a Scandinavian post-polio victim who won a silver metal in Dressage at the 1952 Helsinki Olympics, is credited with giving the concept of riding as therapy its modern day impetus.

In the German-speaking countries, the development was based more on medical experiences. For that reason the therapeutic aspect in its more scientific sense directed the early activities of therapeutic riding; including the use of the Swiss term "Hippotherapy" which came into common use to describe a specialized medical treatment (from Greek language = Therapy) with the horse (= hippos). Remedial-educational riding and vaulting, and riding as sport for the handicapped, described the non-medical specialties.

The International Congress on Therapeutic Riding was differently oriented depending on the interests of the host country. The first congress in Paris in 1974, and the second in Basel in 1976, had for their titles "Riding as Therapy" and "Therapy on Horseback." Since then, the title has changed in favor of the term Hippotherapy, in which scientific results were shown within the general scope of Riding for the Disabled, or therapeutic riding, which eventually became the generic, umbrella term.

The Third International Congress, held in Warwick, Great Britain, in 1979, highlighted the sportive and joyful enthusiasm of even the most severely disabled riders. At the fourth International Congress on Therapeutic Riding in Hamburg, 1982, an attempt was made to present an overview of a wide range of possibilities of the therapeutic use of the horse. Therefore, the program was subdivided under three headings:
  1) Hippotherapy
  2) Remedial-educational riding and vaulting
  3) Riding as sport for the disabled.
The results showed not only the very clear differences between these specialities, but also the common orientation regarding the possibilities of the horse in therapeutic settings.

These contacts made during these congresses led the participants to want a continuing exchange of information between congresses. As a result, it was planned for the fifth International Congress in Milian, in 1985, to create an administrative body to carry out such an exchange. During this congress, the delegates of the different national associations met and discussed this issue. Some pleaded for the immediate foundation of an international association, while others felt that they did not know each other well enough to form a legally binding commitment. All agreed, however, that two tasks should be worked on immediately:
  1) To set up a list of all national organizations who were concerned with therapeutic riding.
  2) To conduct a survey regarding national education and training programs for personnel in the field of therapeutic riding.

A loose cooperation was formed under the title *The Federation of Riding for the Disabled International* (Fed RDI) and an Interim Executive Board was elected as follows:
President, Dorothy Ames of Canada with the task: Congress in Toronto.
Secretary General, Jane Wykeham-Musgrave of Great Britain: task to develop a newsletter.
Jean Tebay of the United States: the task to develop a manual about national educational and training programs.

These tasks were all promptly carried out. But, it proved to be difficult to guarantee the financing of the newsletter because prospective sponsors asked for proof of a nonprofit organization in the form of a constitution with appropriate status. In response, Jane Wykeham-Musgrave asked each participating nation for proposals regarding the statutes. What she received however, was an enormous list of proposed wishes but no workable draft of statutes. Finally, however, as a result of international demand, in Germany a draft constitution was drawn up under the cooperative effort of several German therapeutic riding specialists including H. Reisser, H. Wolf, myself, and particularly Gerlinde Hoffmann. This draft included all of the proposed wishes. Jane Wykeham-Musgrave then forwarded this document to all national organizations for review and comment.

At the next meeting of all national delegates of the RDI during the sixth International Congress in Toronto, in 1988, this draft was discussed sentence by sentence and revised. As a Preliminary Constitution endorsed by an overwhelming majority of the 19 national representatives present at the meeting, it could then be legally examined and revised according to the requirements of international law.

The Congress in Canada was a big success; however, the energies of the Executive Board were largely directed to solving the problems concerning the drafting an international constitution. Because British law set such complicated conditions for the acknowledgment of a charity, there was finally no success in bringing all of the member organizations to a sufficient majority for agreement. In September of 1990, an extraordinary General Assembly was called in London, where a special committee was appointed to resolve the constitutional problems.

This special committee met in Cologne, Germany, in December of 1990. The goals of this committee were to finalize a working draft of the constitution to be presented at the seventh international congress in Aarhus, Denmark, in August 1991; and to locate a suitable country for the official organizational "seat" of the RDI.

Finally, at the General Assembly (International council, Fed. RDI) in Denmark, the result of the task force's work was passed nearly unanimously by 21 national delegates entitled to vote for their representative national organizations.

Some characteristics of the newly accepted constitution deserve specific review:
- The official name of the organization became *The Federation of Riding for the Disabled International* (Fed. RDI)
- The Federation would be registered as an international not-for-profit organization according to Belgian law with the official "seat" in Belgium,
- The Executive Board would be enlarged by a further member to be of Belgium nationality,
- In addition to the status of full membership for national representatives, there would be the status of Associate Membership. Associate membership does not carry the right to vote but entitles the member to receive all information and to obtain a hearing on any issue.
- An annual membership fee was approved by the International Council (1991).

NEW Executive Board was elected:

President:	Dr. med C. Klüwer, Germany
Vice-President:	Dr. D. Nicolas Citterio, Italy
Treasurer:	Dr. med Ad van Vliet
Secretary General:	J. Baillie, Great Britian
Members:	J.De Buck, Belgium
	J. Tebay, USA
	N. Pearce, Australia

It became necessary to strengthen Fed. RDI, as was shown at the congress in Denmark. At that congress, as a result of major efforts by a largely Scandinavian committee, a new group was founded on the initiative of the Disabled Sports Organization. This new group, International Para-Olympic Committee, (IPEC) was instrumental in organizing the splendid, world dressage championship for disabled riders at Wilhelmsborg, Denmark, just prior to the start of the International Congress. At this event, 11 coaches of national teams met to confirm the IPEC Constitution and elect its Board of Directors.

After intensive discussion between representatives of the IPEC and Fed. RDI, the 26 delegates of the International Counsel of the Fed. RDI came to the conclusion that the basic concerns of the specialty areas within therapeutic riding and the variety of approaches within the many countries practicing therapeutic riding, could not be adequately met by the IPEC with its strong sport and competition orientation. It was decided by the International Council of the Fed. RDI to develop good cooperation and communication with the IPEC, as with, for example, the Special Olympics Committee, and to support the mission of IPEC - riding as a sport for the disabled, especially regarding international competition. A. Van Vliet was appointed as the official liaison between RFDI and IPEC. Similarly, it was also decided that each national organization should promote contact with his national equestrian association and other national sport organizations for the disabled.

The Fed. RDI, as the international organization representing all aspects of the use of the horse to improve the quality of life for disabled individuals, began a new phase in its development. The Fed. RDI becomes the leading international service organization in the field of the therapeutic use of the horse. Individuals and organizations from all over the world contacted the Fed. RDI for information and assistance regarding the therapeutic use of the horse. The Fed. RDI provides consultation and assistance to all who asked for its services.

The VIII International Congress in Therapeutic Riding took place in 1994 in Hamilton, New Zealand. The Organizers tried to encourage the presentation of remedial-educational aspects and experience in Therapeutic Riding and, also, accepted new papers on Hippotherapy and Riding sport for the Handicapped. Advocate J. Buck (B), Dr. D. Citterio (I) and J. Tebay (USA) left the Executive Board and the International Council elected new members: R. Jaroscevics (B), Dr. G. Lawrence (CAN) and M. Longden (AUSTRALIA) as Vice-President.

The IX International Congress was held in Denver, Colorado, USA under the auspices of NARHA, the North American Riding for the Handicapped Association. The title "Riding the Winds of Progress" expressed the goals of this congress. The X International Congress will be held in Saumur, France, in the year 2000, where the first congress was held and it will be the 25th year celebration of the International Congress on Equestrian Therapy.

Professor med Dr. Carl Klüwer
Germany

17

THERAPEUTIC RIDING: ITS BENEFITS, PROFESSIONS AND DIVISIONS

Barbara T. Engel, M.Ed, OTR

> **KEY WORDS**
> BONDING, PHYSICAL
> RISK , HEALTH
> AWARENESS, TEAM

Therapeutic horseback riding is similar to all horseback riding. It is a *strenuous sport* involving all the muscles in the body with *risk factors*. It gives the rider the opportunity to *bond* with a large responsive animal. It provides a *team sport* --the horse--the rider that focuses on self improvement and, not necessarily, in competition with other humans. All riding provides the rider a *physical activity* which increases *general health* in the same manner as tennis, golf, running, biking, or swimming. (swimming and riding does not necessarily require strong legs). Riding can stimulate the cardiovascular system and strengthen muscles. It provides weight bearing and increases balance, coordination and body awareness. Because it is a leisure sport with the companionship of an animal, horseback riding has a soothing mental and social effect which may provide the rider with a feeling of well being.

It is important to remember that putting persons with disabilities on horses and teaching them to ride is therapeutic in the *same manner* as teaching able-bodied persons to ride. This is sports or recreational riding. This is an important factor to remember. Many adult and child riders with disabilities will express their desire to ride, ride in a safe setting with safe horses and with instructors who understand their difficulties. They may tell you that they are not there for "therapy" but for the pleasure and exercise of riding. *A horse + a rider with a disability does not = "therapy" but rather sports or recreational riding. However, because of riders' unique needs, they may continue to require a modified or therapeutic riding setting for safety and understanding for many years or indefinitely.*

SPECIFIC PROGRAMS CAN BE DETERMINED BY THE GOALS OF THE CLIENT AND THE TRAINING OF THOSE DIRECTING THE CLIENT.

Sports and recreational therapeutic riding has as its goal to **develop riding skills**. *Sports vaulting* and *developmental vaulting* have as their goals the **development of vaulting skills** according to the American Vaulting Association guidelines. These activities are carried out by trained riding and vaulting instructors. *Sports driving* has as its goals to develop driving skills.

Some clients need or want more than **sports or recreational riding**. They may come for *equine-assisted therapy*. There the word **therapy** is the objective with treatment by a certified health care professional in the fields of equine facilitated mental health, and hippotherapy. Hippotherapy, has as its goal the **rehabilitation (or habilitation) of persons with specific health care problems**. Equine facilitated mental health has as its goals the specific psychosocial rehabilitation of individuals with social and emotional disorders. The key terms here are addressing very specific problems under a treatment protocol that is billable to a third party - i.e., insurance. The developments of riding or vaulting skills are not a goal or a concern though maybe a result of the treatment. This therapy is carried out by health care professionals with specific training in the use of the horse in treatment who may use any aspect of the equestrian environment to accomplish their goals. The professionals are using the horse or equine setting to assist them in achieving specific client treatment goals. They are performing occupational therapy, physical therapy, or speech pathology while using the tools of hippotherapy. **These therapists are not hippotherapists** since there is no profession of hippotherapy. Remember that equine-assisted therapy is a **treatment process** carried out by a **medical or health care professional** who is using the horse as a treatment tool and intervention for **specific** health care problems.

A recreational therapist asked why she could not qualify to do hippotherapy. Recreational therapists are trained to re-socialize the total person into society or to work on social skills, not to work on specific movement, coordination or cognitive problems. We have in the medical field many specialities to deal with varying different problems and each is important to the total rehabilitation process. A recreational therapist certainly can use the horse in his or her rehabilitation process but only within the context of his or her profession.

Remedial riding and *remedial vaulting* can be used by special educators who use equestrian activities for **specific education gains.** Again, horsemanship skills are not a primary goal.

Clients have different goals and may work with riding instructors, equine science specialists, special educators, vocational specialists, activity directors, recreation or camp leaders or others with special skills that can be applied to the equine setting. The primary benefit may be educational, social, vocational or for special project-oriented activities, such as 4-H clubs. These activities are *animal-assisted activities* and should not be misrepresented as riding therapy or equine-assisted therapy. Those latter sessions require trained specialists in particular fields to carry out and direct each unique approach. The results of these sessions can be impressive and provide the clients with many gains.

When working with a specific population, especially with people who have disabilities, one takes on specific responsibilities. An instructor who takes on the responsibility of a "therapeutic riding instructor" is saying - I AM QUALIFIED TO DO THIS JOB. Would your qualifications hold up in the legal system during a law suit? If the program states that it is doing therapy, (could this be implied by the program title?) can the documentation be provided confirm the qualifications of the staff and the propriety of therapy procedures which are normally used in the health care "therapy session?" The more one **is** involved with this dynamic method of instruction or treatment intervention, the more one **becomes** aware of its complexity and its consequences.

The field of *therapeutic riding* is no longer in its infancy. It has a track record and has developed standards to ensure safety of the population it serves. Everyone involved in the field must abide by these standards and take the responsibility to up grade them as this becomes necessary. This is a professional responsibility which affects everyone in the field. One bad example can hurt other programs and possibly the national image of therapeutic riding. One can no longer put a child on a horse and call this therapeutic riding without putting **oneself at risk.** It is important to contact the agency that sets the standards for practice in your country for information and training. These agencies include RDA, NARHA, CanTRA, Kuratorium fur Therapeutisches Reiten, Associazion Nazionale Italiana Di Riabilitazione Equestre, Austrian Kuratorium fur Hippotherapie and those in other countries around the world.

The term THERAPEUTIC HORSEBACK RIDING is an *umbrella* term referring to riding in a setting which is specially equipped to handle people with special needs. The instructors and assistants are trained not only in horsemanship but also:
- To understand problems presented by each disability and are comfortable with them.
- To develop teaching techniques that accommodate special needs.
- To train horses specifically for disabled riders.
- To use special equipment to compensate for disabilities.
- To be concerned with safety factors unique to persons with disabilities.

The horse is unique, in that horsemanship and even the equine setting can be used effectively to treat or re-mediate many types of disabilities by many disciplines. The type of intervention used depends on the client's need and the professional training and skills of those directing the sessions.

It is important, as a therapeutic riding participant, to take pride in one's own knowledge and skills and in one's accomplishments. Being placed in the "therapeutic riding setting," however, does not turn us all into therapists, trainers or instructors since each of these functions requires specific knowledge and skill. We remain what we have been trained to be: special education or adaptive physical education teachers, psychologists, recreational therapists, occupational therapists, physical therapists, riding instructors, vaulting coaches and so on. But, by working with a special population, we do need to acquire specific knowledge about that population and then apply our skills differently. The equine setting also requires special knowledge and additional training to manage the horse and his environment correctly. When a special population is combined with the equine setting, a team is needed to provide the technical medical expertise and the specialized equine training needed to relate to the client's needs. For example, teaching adults requires a different base of knowledge than teaching small children. Teaching an individual who cannot move in the normal way requires particular knowledge, but your professional skills as a teacher or instructor do not change.

A WORD OF CAUTION: DO NOT SAY THAT WHAT YOU OR YOUR PROGRAM IS DOING IS PHYSICAL THERAPY UNLESS, OF COURSE, YOU ARE A PHYSICAL THERAPIST. IN MOST STATES IN THE U.S., IT IS ILLEGAL TO PERFORM PHYSICAL THERAPY UNLESS YOU ARE A LICENSED PHYSICAL THERAPIST. NOR ARE YOU DOING SENSORY INTEGRATION UNLESS YOU ARE A QUALIFIED OCCUPATIONAL THERAPIST. IF YOUR BACKGROUND DOES NOT QUALIFIED YOU FOR THESE SKILLS, YOU COULD PUT YOURSELF AND THE PROGRAM IN A POSITION TO BE FINED OR SUED. The term is used in an understandable way. Riding is physical; riding is therapeutic. Therefore, it must be physical + therapy = physical therapy. **WRONG!**

There are many aspects of riding that have brought people to the stable, but it is the horse who is the major focus. The horse has a unique nature and provides a rich assortment of movements which can do wonders for the human mind and body.

Therapeutic effects from riding may include:

EXERCISE. Children and adults with disabilities ordinarily have little access to the quality of exercise that riding provides. Riding involves all of the muscles in the body and, in addition, stimulates all body systems. A strong cardiovascular system and a strong set of lungs are required to make a person function. Many children and adults with severe physical problems have poorly developed lungs due to their limited ability to challenge their cardiovascular systems. Exercise can be like giving the system a whole new set of batteries. This author has been impressed with the great changes she sees in clients in her practice even after a month of therapy or riding. This change is due to increased exercise which is imposed on the client as part of the treatment as well as the "therapeutic" intervention.

THE THREE DIMENSIONAL SWINGING GAIT of the horse causes the rider's pelvis, trunk and shoulder girdle to react in ways very similar to those produced by the normal human adult walk. On a horse, a non-walking person can actually *feel* what walking is like without the need for weight bearing through the legs. A little eight-year-old client of mine stated, *"the horse is giving me long legs and walking for me."* as he sat on the shoulders of the horse. One frequently hears therapeutic riding instructors mention riders who began to walk more easily after riding. The horse has provided the rider with the upper and lower body sensation and mental images of walking.

BALANCE. The side to side, back and forth, and up and down movements of the horse have the effect of gently shifting the rider off balance to the right, on balance to the center, off balance to the left and back to the center. This constant shifting helps develop balance in the rider. Many people with physical disabilities have difficulty with balance which causes major problems in normal function.

STIMULATION. The undulating movements from the gait of the horse are transferred to the rider providing neuromuscular stimulation while increasing cardiovascular output and respiratory excitation. This offers the rider a rich source of sensation. Rhythmic movement on the horse has been found to be relaxing and soothing to the human mind and body.

BONDING. The horse is a social creature who will readily bond with humans. The horse will accept a rider with no prejudgement. He will tolerate behavior from a rider that humans find difficult to accept. He immediately returns kindness and affection and will respond to the rider's commands. Bonding has been found to be basic to the development of human communication.

RESPIRATION. Exercise increases respiration which in turn increases the ability to vocalize. Speech requires strong lungs. The lungs pass air over the vocal cords to produce sound. Further, the increase in respiration also increases alertness (Oetter, 1989). As a result of both the bonding (an early form of non-verbal communication) and the effects of movement on speech, one may see increases in social language and speech.

HAPPINESS AND PLEASURE. Norman Cousins (Cousins, 1989), with his physician, has documented the healing effect of positive emotions and laughter upon the human body. Certainly, the horse brings us pleasure and the environment gives us determination, hope, faith and purpose: all the elements which Cousins feels will heal the mind and body. Most of the clients in a therapeutic riding program are not "sick," but may be recovering from illness or injuries due to accidents. Even the child with cerebral palsy is attempting to gain motor control. Every therapist, and anyone working with children, has observed that when the client is happy and motivated, progress comes more easily. A good attitude does seem to help when one is working to regain the body's functional abilities.

The concept of riding for the person with disabilities has grown rapidly since the 1970's. For therapeutic riding to gain the full respect of the community, medical and health care professionals, educators and the equine society must be managed in a professional manner. This requires all those involved to take responsibility for their own roles and to represent themselves appropriately. If one takes on the task of head instructor of disabled riders, clients will expect this person to have the knowledge, skills and education to carry out the job. Many countries require each person in this field to pass qualifying tests. Where tests are not required, each person must take on the responsibility to make sure he or she is qualified for the job. One must always remember that when one takes on the responsibility of caring for others, he or she also takes on legal obligations. Your education and licensing credentials--be it an educator, a psychologist, a health professional, a physician, or a qualified riding instructor will determine your ability to carry out a specified skill. All those involved may one day move their training to a higher level. This was strongly supported at a forum at the 9th International Congress on Therapeutic Riding. The professional in the field should have college level training. In many countries, college level courses in therapeutic riding already exist and are increasing.

RESPECT WHO YOU ARE, THE SKILLS YOU POSSESS, THE PROFESSION YOU REPRESENT AND GIVE YOUR CLIENTS THE MOST YOU CAN WITHIN THE LIMITS OF YOUR PROFESSION AND TRAINING.

References
Cousins, N. (1989). *Head First*. New York: Penguin Books. 126-27.
Oetter, P. (1987). Course notes. University of New Mexico.

Barbara T. Engel
USA

PROFESSIONS INVOLVED IN EQUINE-ASSISTED THERAPIES

Barbara T. Engel, M.Ed, OTR

Therapeutic riding programs may seek the services of physical or occupational therapists as the programs' major consultants. As a consultant, the therapist provides information to the program staff regarding the needs and disabilities of the clients. Specialization has become necessary in order for one to develop a complete understanding of groups of disabilities and methods of dealing with them. Specialized training is necessary, for example, if one is to work with children and adults with cerebral palsy or other neurological and developmental disorders.

An *Occupational Therapist* (OTR™) is presently a master's degree with past OTs at a bachelor's degree level college graduate with a major in occupational therapy. In addition to the academic training, the therapist will have completed internships in such areas as pediatrics, psychiatry and physical disabilities. The therapist must pass an examination at the end of his or her training before he or she is certified to practice as a registered occupational therapist. Post graduate education may be in such areas as hand therapy, sensory integration treatment, geriatric care, neonatal care, arthritis, rehabilitation, developmental disabilities, community mental health, work hardening and other highly specialized areas. Most states require therapists to be licensed as well as certified. The occupational therapist treats clients with the use of activities with the aim of returning them to their useful "occupation." "Occupational" can mean activities of daily living, work, or play/leisure.

A *Physical Therapist* (PT) is a graduate of a four-year college with a major in physical therapy with a master's degree. In addition to the academic courses, a physical therapist also completed internships in various specialty areas. The physical therapist must pass a state examination to be licensed by the state in which he or she practices. He or she may seek additional postgraduate training in neurodevelopmental treatment, various sub-specialties in orthopedics, pediatrics, sports science and medicine, and other areas of acute or chronic care. The physical therapist treats clients with the use of modalities such as light, heat, water, electricity and with movement activities such as exercises and neurological stimulation. The aim is of gaining maximum mobility in the client.

A *Speech and Language Pathologist* is a graduate with a Master's degree. He or she is certified by a national association (ASHA) and is licensed by some states to practice. He or she may specialize in specific areas as do physical and occupational therapists. The speech and language pathologist facilitates the development of the oral-motor area and provides language focused treatment with persons of all ages who have communication problems.

A *Clinical Psychologist* is a graduate of doctoral level university programs. He or she usually specializes in distinct areas of human behavior, normal or aberrant, and offers counseling and support to individuals with problems of adjustment to their social environment.

Counselors have a Master's degree in counseling. He or she may specialize in working with children, marriage problems, at risk teens or any other field of social behavioral dysfunctions.

Recreational Therapist (RTR) is a person who has graduated from a four-year college with a major in recreational therapy. The academic requirements include internships with various special population groups such as developmentally delayed, emotionally and physically disabled persons. A national competency exam, and state certification in some states, are required. The recreational therapist uses participation in leisure activities to improve functional behavior in clients while giving them the opportunity to acquire skills, knowledge and develop effective use of leisure time that assists them in social integration.

Barbara T Engel, USA

GLOSSARY OF TERMS USED IN THERAPEUTIC RIDING

ADAPTIVE EQUIPMENT
1) Riding equipment which has been changed in structure or form to allow a person with a disability to ride.
2) Equipment which has been specially developed to allow a physically disabled person to ride a horse.
3) Equipment which is used to elicit specific responses.

ADAPTIVE PHYSICAL EDUCATION
Physical education which has been modified for special populations who cannot take part in regular physical education activities.

ADAPTIVE RIDING
Horseback riding adapted for a special population.

ANIMAL-ASSISTED ACTIVITIES (AAA)--A person who provides AAA possesses specialized knowledge of animals and the populations with which they interact in delivering motivational, educational, recreational and/or therapeutic animal-oriented activities. Volunteers are often involved in AAA. Individuals may work independently when they have specialized training.

ANIMAL-ASSISTED THERAPY (AAT)--is a goal-directed intervention in which an animal that meets specific criteria is an integral part of the treatment process. AAT is directed and/or delivered by health/human service professionals with specialized expertise, and is within the scope of practice of their profession. AAT is designed to promote improvement in human physical, social, emotional, and/or cognitive functioning. AAT is provided in a variety of settings, and may be group or individual in nature. This process is documented and evaluated. An alternate term to identify such action is "pet-facilitated therapy." A less acceptable term is "pet therapy."

BACKRIDING
When two people ride on a horse together. In therapeutic horseback riding, specifically hippotherapy, backriding is used as a therapeutic tool to develop posture in the front rider (the client) by the backrider (a therapist). On a limited basis, an instructor may backride a child until that child feels secure.

BONDING
The establishment of an attachment/union between two persons or a person and an animal.

CERTIFIED OCCUPATIONAL THERAPIST ASSISTANT
A person with credentials as an occupational therapy assistant who works under the supervision of a registered occupational therapist and treats disease and injury by the use of activities with emphasis on adaptation.

DELTA SOCIETY
An organization, headquartered in Renton, WA, that supports research studies and educates people on how companion animals benefit human physical and emotional well-being; establishes community programs to build a partnership between animals and people; operates the national information center and library for the field of human-animal interactions.

DEVELOPMENTAL EQUINE-ASSISTED THERAPY
A specific treatment method, using NDT (neuro-developmental treatment techniques), which are carried out by a specially trained physical or occupational therapist during a treatment session with a client with a neuromuscular dysfunction.

DEVELOPMENTAL VAULTING
Vaulting (gymnastic activities on the back of a horse) for persons with special needs, supervised by a vaulting instructor.

DISABILITY
Restriction or lack (resulting from impairment) of ability to perform an activity in the manner or within the range considered normal for a human being (World Health Organization, 1980).

EQUINE-ASSISTIVE THERAPY
Treatment with the use of the horse and the equine setting by a qualified health care professional.

HANDICAP
Disadvantage for a given individual, resulting from an impairment or a disability, that limits or prevents the fulfillment of a role which is normal (depending on age, sex, and social and cultural factors) for that individual (World Health Organization, 1980).

HIPPOTHERAPY
"Hippos" means horse in Greek. "Treatment with the help of the horse." A treatment for clients with movement dysfunctions and/or neurological disorders used by physical and occupational therapists trained in the use of the horse as a treatment tool. In classic hippotherapy, the horse influences the client rather than the client controlling the horse (Hippotherapy Curriculum Development Project, 1991). The therapist may use modalities within his/her profession such as exercises or activities to achieve specific treatment goals.

23

HORSE HANDLER

A person trained in horsemanship skills who knows the psychological and physical needs of a horse.

HORSE LEADER

A person who has had training in horsemanship skills and who is knowledgeable in the emotional and physical needs of a horse. In addition, he or she knows how to handle a horse with specific needs for the disabled rider.

HUMAN-ANIMAL BONDING

The attachment that develops between humans and animals involving strong feelings and psychological ties. Studies have supported that the love and attentiveness given by people to animals is reciprocal and both animals and people benefit (Anderson, 1983).

IMPAIRMENT

Loss or abnormality of psychological, physiological or anatomical structure or function.

LEADER

Same as horse leader. One who leads the horse.

LONG REINING

A technique used in hippotherapy and training. The horse is "driven" from the ground by the use of reins that reach from the bit to one stride or more behind the horse. The client sits on the horse while the handler controls and reins the horse from behind.

METER

A unit of measurement in the metric system. A riding ring, such as a dressage arena, is measured by the metric system. One meter = 39.37 inches.

MOUNTING BLOCK

A device used for mounting a rider onto the horse.

MOUNTING RAMP

A ramp designed for mounting a person onto the horse from a wheelchair. It may be also used by ambulatory riders to mount the horse.

NORTH AMERICAN RIDING FOR THE HANDICAPPED ASSOCIATION (NARHA)

NARHA is a service organization created to promote the well-being of individuals with disabilities through equine activities.

OCCUPATIONAL THERAPIST REGISTERED /and licensed OTR-OTR/L

A person with a credential in occupational therapy who treats disease and injury by the use of activities with emphasis on adaptation (Clark & Allen, 1985).

PHYSICAL THERAPIST--PT

A person with a degree in physical therapy who treats disease and injury by physical means, such as light, heat, cold, water, ultrasound, massage and exercise and with emphasis on mobility (Clark & Allen 1985).

PROBLEM SOLVING

The mental process by which one sequentially identifies a problem, interprets aspects of the situation and selects a method to alleviate the problem (Fleming, 1991).

RECREATIONAL THERAPIST--RTR

A person with a degree in recreational therapy who treats disease and injury using usual or adaptive leisure activities.

REMEDIAL RIDING

Riding activities, which are adapted to help the client gain educational and psychological goals under the direction of a specially trained educator or therapist.

REMEDIAL VAULTING

Vaulting which is adapted to help the client to gain educational and psychological goals under the direction of a specially trained educator or therapist.

RIDING THERAPY

The integration by therapists of neurophysical or psychosocial treatment procedures with exercises and horsemanship to gain specific medical goals. Riding therapy is a part of equine-assisted therapy.

SCHOOLING FIGURES.

Circles, figure eights, straight lines, curves and other patterns used in riding training to develop precise control of a horse through one's aids or actions.

SENSORY INTEGRATION (SI)(Term coined by A. Jean Ayres, Ph.D, OTR.)

An occupational therapy treatment technique to facilitate the brain to organize and coordinate sensation and behavior, which leads to adaptive responses that permit a higher level of function. Sensory Integration procedures are initiated by the client with the occupational therapist manipulating the environment to gain specific therapeutic results. The Sensory Integration procedure is based on occupational therapy practice theory. Sensory Integration is a specific treatment technique developed by A. Jean Ayres and her associates for children who have been identified by specific measures to have deficits in Sensory Integration.

SENSORIMOTOR INTEGRATION

This term refers to a group of techniques used by therapists to treat neurological disorders. It may incorporate Sensory Integration methods along with other techniques to increase a person's function.

SHEEPSKIN

A pad made out of sheepskin secured with a surcingle. The pad is used with clients during exercises with a therapist or with riders who are more comfortable with the softness of sheepskin. It can be used with a standard surcingle or with a **vaulting** surcingle.

SIDE-AIDE or AIDE, SIDEWALKER.

A person who has been trained to assist a rider. This person walks next to the horse, at the rider's side (so he or she can place his or her arm across the rider's thigh when necessary), may assist the rider with balance, provides necessary security, and/or help the rider carry through with a lesson. Side-aide is more often use by therapists since the term is more descriptive to the task.

SPECIAL EDUCATION

Educational programs which are adapted to meet learning needs for a population with special needs (and problems).

SPECIAL NEEDS POPULATION

Persons with special needs--these can be physical, psychological, psychosocial or a combination of these.

SPEECH AND LANGUAGE PATHOLOGIST

A person with a degree in speech and language pathology who treats persons with deficits in speech and language, both visual and audible.

SPORTS VAULTING

Same as vaulting. Gymnastics on horseback. Vaulting is carried out according to the primary six vaulting exercises and additional creative exercises called a "kur." Vaulting is an equine sport.

SUPPLING THE HORSE

Riding exercises to increase the flexibility and balance of the horse.

THERAPEUTIC RIDING

Therapeutic Riding is an umbrella term. It encompasses Recreational and Leisure riding. Sports riding, Educational activities and Hippotherapy (NARHA Guide 1999).

THERAPEUTIC VAULTING

Standard vaulting exercises performed at the level of a special vaulter. Sports vaulting for special needs vaulters.

THERAPY

The meaning employed in effecting the cure or management of disease. Implies diagnosis using special criteria (or diagnostic and procedural coding systems used in medicine for billing purposes); involves prescribed treatment by a health care professional who is liable for his or her actions according to the standards of his or her specialty, and is billable to a third-party payer (i.e., insurance carriers). Hippotherapy and equine assisted therapy are recognized treatment procedures when used by especially trained physical and occupational therapist in a treatment situation by the American Physical Therapy Association and by the American Occupational Therapy Association.

TT.E.A.M.

The Tellington-Jones Equine Awareness Method, a unique training protocol developed by Linda Tellington-Jones, for the horse to make him safer, more attentive to the handler, less distracted by the environment, more pleasurable, less stressful to ride and a better performer. The training method involves a detailed step by step procedure (taught during a series of courses) which produces a friendly horse who is eager to learn (Tellington-Jones, Bruns 1988).

VAULTING

The gymnastics on the back of a moving horse. Vaulting is carried out according to the primary vaulting exercises and additional creative exercises called "kur" and free styles. Vaulting is an equine sport acceptance within the Olympics.

25

VAULTING SURCINGLE

A surcingle with handles. A vaulting surcingle used with a bareback pad or sheepskin, mainly for holding on, can be constructed of leather or webbing with two handles (internally secured to a metal plate) and can flex at the center. A vaulting girth used in gymnastic vaulting, must be constructed with a solid plate (internally) from well below the handle on one side, across the top to well below the handle on the other side. The construction of this vaulting girth is much stronger than the one required for "therapeutic riding."

VAULTING THERAPY

The integration by therapists of neurophysical or psychosocial treatment procedures with exercises and vaulting to gain specific medical goals. Vaulting therapy is a part of equine-assisted therapy.

References:

Anderson, R.K. (1984). *The Pet Connection.* Center to Study Human-Animal Relationship and Environments, Univ of Minn. Minn., MN

Clark & Allen. (1985). *Occupational Therapy for Children.* St. Louis: C. V. Mosby Co.

Dorland's Medical Dictionary, 28th Ed. (1994), Philadelphia, WB Saunders.

Fleming, H.M. (1991). *American Journal of Occupational Therapy.* Nov. 45, 11, 989.

Gould Medical Dictionary. (1979).New York: McGraw-Hill Book Co.

Hippotherapy Section, *NARHA Conference.* Los Angeles. 1991

Hippotherapy Curriculum Development Project (1987-1991). Therapeutic Riding Services, Inc. Riderwood, MD. 21139

World Health Organization. (1980). *International Classification of Impairments, Disabilities, and Handicaps: A Manual of Classification Relating to the Consequence of Disease.* Geneva: World Health Organization.

CHAPTER 2
PROFESSIONAL DEVELOPMENT OF THERAPEUTIC RIDING

ESTABLISHING THERAPEUTIC RIDING AS A PROFESSION: DEVELOPING STANDARDS

Jean M. Tebay, MS, MCTRI

WHY ARE PROFESSIONAL STANDARDS IMPORTANT?

This is a time in the history of the United States when the concern for excellence is at a high level of public consciousness. It appears that excellence in many areas of endeavor is in the minds not only of state and federal officials, but also educators and the public. One stimulus for such a phenomenon comes, perhaps, from product advertising--the biggest, the best, the most that money can buy.

The primary distinguishing characteristic of any profession is its willingness to commit itself to quality as well as to excellence, and to govern itself and its practitioners in the promotion of both, in order to protect the clients it serves. The development of standards of educational preparation and performance by a national organization is the enactment in, reality, of such a philosophical commitment. Without such policies, many disciplines--in our case therapeutic riding as conducted at the more than 525 operating centers registered by North American Riding for the Handicapped Association (NARHA)--may be viewed as a non-vocational or an avocational activities. In addition, without such policies, the activities these operating centers offer are more likely to be regarded as para-professional in the eyes of professional practitioners, of the disabled communities served and of the public in general.

Those active in therapeutic riding in the U.S., though a comparatively small entity, have answered a national call to join in this pursuit of excellence. Many individuals who engage in therapeutic riding have been influenced by the growing momentum and rising popularity of the activity and seek to serve as leaders in the field. They have acted together to professionalize both the field's activities and its personnel in their quest for excellence and quality.

Let us contrast with therapeutic riding for a moment, the venerable profession of nursing which, through nationally accepted policies, seeks to assure consistently trained personnel, who work in uniformly recognizable settings, governed by constantly updated sets of practice standards. Therapeutic riding, on the other hand, has within its ranks a variety of individuals who differ greatly in the strength and focus of their educational preparation and vocational qualifications. There is no unique type of setting in which they work, no nationally recognized goals for their work, and until recently, no established standards to govern their service activities.

Therapeutic riding has reached a time in its growth and popularity when it has become more than a pleasant recreation for disabled individuals. It has established itself as a feasible rehabilitation tool used to make significant changes, both physically and psychologically, in the lives of disabled individuals. In the United States, many therapeutic riding practitioners have worked to make the field a viable profession. A vital step in this development process has been the establishment of standards, an accreditation process and instructor certification levels for operating centers and their personnel which comprise the NARHA membership.

WHAT EXACTLY ARE STANDARDS?

Standards are a written set of mutually agreed-upon criteria providing a guideline or measure by which to evaluate an activity. For therapeutic riding programs, NARHA's comprehensive list of standards is helpful for assuring quality services to clients and in helping to define the scope and purpose of service. In addition, such standards assure personnel a safe, suitable work environment and satisfy prospective clients as well as outside agencies, of consistent operational quality.

The NARHA standards were developed by a committee within the organization, and subsequently submitted to a larger sample from the organization's total membership for review, verification of content and comment. Following revision, the final standards were published as a manual and circulated to NARHA operating centers. Subsequently, the standards are being reviewed and updated every three years or sooner when such a need is indicated. It is important to understand that compliance with such standards is now purely voluntary. Such standards are not enforceable until and unless adopted into state or federal law or incorporated into health care regulations.

The *NARHA Operating Center Standards & Accreditation Manual* for therapeutic riding updated by NARHA in 1996 (with yearly revisions), was prepared in order to meet several objectives:

- To provide guidelines for the planning and organization of therapeutic riding programs
- To provide an educational resource for orientation and training of staff and other personnel
- To provide organization and definition of activities on a level consistent with current knowledge and practice
- To provide an authoritative source of information for use in program promotion
- To provide a set of requirements which would be met in order to be eligible for and subsequently retain accreditation
- To provide a means for ongoing assessment and improvement
- To provide a resource for risk management and safety administration
- To provide for the health and welfare of animals involved in therapeutic riding programs

WHAT ARE THE AREAS IN WHICH STANDARDS WERE DEVELOPED?

The current standards in therapeutic riding focus on administration, facilities and programs. Standards for hippotherapy and backriding have been field tested in 1996-97. Areas for future development include those for specific groups of professional personnel (for example, therapists) as well as for adjunct activities such as vaulting, competition and driving.

SUMMARY

With its set of standards firmly in place, along with a well-established process for accrediting operating centers, the field of therapeutic riding, operating under the umbrella of NARHA, has joined the ranks of a full-fledged professional discipline in the realms of therapeutic recreation and rehabilitation. The field has reached a recognized level of ongoing professional development in its determination to provide consistent quality service to its clients.

Sources:

American Society of Association Executives. (1988). *Self Regulation: Accreditation, Certification and Standardization.* American Society of Association Executives: Washington, D.C.

Commission on Accreditation of Rehabilitation Facilities. (1988). *Standards Manual for Organizations Serving People with Disabilities.* Tucson, Az.

Joint Commission on Accreditation of Hospitals. (1985). Consolidated Standards Manual. Chicago, IL.

North American Riding for the Handicapped Association. (1996). NARHA Operating Center Standards and Accreditation Manual. NARHA: P.O. Box 33150, Denver, CO 80233

Professional Standards in Special Education. (1987). ERIC Clearinghouse on Handicapped and Gifted Children. Reston, Virginia.

Riles, B. ed., (1989). *Evaluation of Therapeutic Recreation Through Quality Assurance.*

Voelkl, J.E. (1988). *Risk Management in Therapeutic Recreation.* American Therapeutic Recreation Association. State College: Venture Publishing, Inc.

Jean M. Tebay
USA

HOW NARHA's ACCREDITATION SYSTEM HAS DEVELOPED AND ITS EFFECT ON "THE INDUSTRY" OF THERAPEUTIC RIDING

Octavia J. Brown, Ed.M, NARHA, Master Instructor
Jean M. Tebay, MS, CMTRI

INTRODUCTION: THE NEED FOR STANDARDIZATION

In most fields of human endeavor, there is a process of development that begins with a **good idea.** The pioneering work on that idea is usually done by energetic, visionary people who may not accurately document their progress and results. These are the revolutionaries that are the makers of change and the inspires of others. This generation is followed usually by a less visionary, more practical-minded set of people who take the pioneering work and further the process of starting the new discipline. The **good idea** is no longer free to follow any path that appeals to its creators; it must be studied, its effects documented, the practitioners trained, a body of literature established, scientific research undertaken and the results published and applied in increasingly specialized ways.

Soon there are so many different people in the field that rules and regulations about how to use the **good idea** begin to be developed. Different schools of thought arise, each proposed by well-meaning, well-educated individuals. These people may or may not communicate with each other productively because their egos get involved with their **good idea**. The issue of "turf" becomes important: in the language of equines: "Get away from that pile of hay: it's MINE!" Those wishing to enter the field, as well as the consumers of its products, begin to wish that there were a set of criteria by which the quality of the **good idea** could be judged.

Our **good idea**, of course, is Therapeutic Activities with the Horse. For the sake of clarity, we will use the term "Therapeutic Riding" in this presentation to cover any and all equine activities that can be done to improve the quality of life of a person with a disability.

STANDARDS AND ACCREDITATION SYSTEMS

In their development, almost all institutions and services-providing organizations arrive at a point where they need standards. A set of standards is a series of specific rules of performance and quality against which a product or performance can be measured. In our case, the product is **therapeutic riding.** To ensure that standards are adhered to, a system of accreditation becomes necessary. This paper will trace NARHA's experience as it has dealt with the creation of standards and an accreditation system over the past 25 years.

THE UNITED STATES EXPERIENCE

In the United States, the North American Riding for the Handicapped Association was founded in 1969. In the mid-1970's, the Board of Directors decided that a system of accreditation should be created to verify the quality of its member centers' work. Several knowledgeable individuals from the membership were invited to become peer reviewers. One or more members of this group would visit every program once every three or four years to assure that it was being well run and safe for riders and volunteers. A checklist and a system of scoring were then developed. The peer reviewers reported to the Board of Directors whose job is was to issue certificates of accreditation to approved centers.

There were several problems with this program:
- The subjectivity of the system: no list of *objective standards* existed against which the individual center could judge itself;
- The peer reviewers were not given *in-depth training* to perform the visits.
- As a result, the *quality* of accredited centers varied widely.
- It was the *personal opinion* of the individual peer reviewer that determined which centers were accredited and which were not.

The positive side of this early accreditation system was that the people who went on these visits were generally extremely knowledgeable and spent more time teaching and informing their hosts than they did accredit. The centers were generally very happy to receive this supportive, friendly person and felt that they benefitted greatly. Because of the lack of objective scoring, almost all centers passed - even some that had unsafe conditions and practices.

As the number of centers grew, a large backlog developed. The peer reviewers were volunteers, received only their travel expenses, and had to be based within driving distance of the center. They simply could not cover all the centers in a timely manner. It was clear that something new had to be instituted. In 1985, thanks to a financial grant, NARHA was able to hire one person whose full-time job it was to visit centers all over the country. Her title was "National Accreditor." This solved the problem of difference in outlook resulting from the peer review team approach. Those who were visited by the National Accreditor were happy. She spent as much time on educating and encouraging as she did on objective measurement of the center's way of doing business. This system was in place from 1985 to 1987.

However, it became clear that the backlog was still accumulating and a new approach had to be found. At this point, the need for a more objective standardized system of accreditation was keenly felt. With about 400 centers waiting for accreditation, a completely new system was developed. This relied not on a personal visit, but on videotapes and self-reporting. The system was also made mandatory; all centers' membership fees included the cost of accreditation In order to maintain NARHA insurance coverage, centers had to apply within a year of starting to operate. This system was put into place in 1988.

THE IMPORTANCE OF A STANDARDIZED APPROACH
In the two systems of accreditation which preceded the 1988 version, inconsistencies between peer reviewers and reviewer subjectivity were the two major weaknesses. An answer also had to be found that would reduce the large numbers of operating centers waiting to be reviewed. Creating an efficient, standardized approach was seen as the major concern of the eight member Accreditation Committee.

A set of 160 standards was created, to be used in three major ways:
- As a guide for the creation of a therapeutic riding center.
- As a *self study guide* for established centers.
- As a guide to prepare for official accreditation.

The Standards were divided into eight major areas:
- Administration
- Equipment
- Facilities
- Horses
- Instructor/instruction
- Mounting /dismounting
- Therapist/therapy
- Volunteers

An evaluation tool was developed based on these eight areas and a team of eight to ten people was sought to serve on the Accreditation Committee that was charged with evaluating video tapes, photographs and paperwork submitted by each of the NARHA centers. All the member operating centers were to be reviewed in the space of three years. Accreditation was granted for two to five years based on the quality of performance of each applicant.

Selection criteria were drawn up for Accreditation Committee members. Applicants had to submit an application and be approved by the Board of Directors. They had to be fully conversant with NARHA policies and procedures, the day-to-day running of operating center and the evaluation of teaching methods for a wide range of disabilities. Physical and occupational therapists were included in the group to evaluate hippotherapy tapes.

This system did what it was designed to do: it ensured that each of NARHA's operating centers was in some way evaluated and measured against a set of standards. What was missing was the opportunity to see the facility in person. Reports came back to NARHA about a few centers that had major safety problems that could not be detected under this system of reviewing video tapes and photographs.

The standards that were created for this system of accreditation were of enormous help to centers. If center personnel took each of them into account, and used them as guidelines, the center would certainly benefit. However, they were only a partial step since many of the standards were still subjective and not measurable.

It became clear that it was time for NARHA to take the next logical step toward quality assurance for its member centers: a return to accreditation visits by qualified peer reviewers. But this time, existing models would be used to create a peer review system that would solve the problems of inconsistency and subjectivity.

To develop the new accreditation system, a task force was created in 1994 to completely revise the existing standards and recommend a new approach. The basic approach of the task force was to create a peer review system that would be **voluntary.** The fees would no longer be included in membership and NARHA insurance would be available to all member centers, accredited or not. The philosophy behind this change was that in the United States, any system of accreditation has historically always been voluntary. In almost all instances where accreditation is offered, most members of national organizations *choose* to apply for it. The public looks for assurances of quality when seeking everything from hospitals to colleges to summer camps. NARHA's clients would do the same when it became clear that accredited centers had been measured against a high standard of excellence.

PROCEDURE

Each existing standard was scrutinized for objectivity and measurability. In other words, a peer reviewer going to a center must be able to give a direct Yes or No response to each standard. Either the center is in compliance or it is not. There could be no room for an individual's personal judgment.

Examples of old and new standards:
H 10 - The horse shall be of suitable temperament and correct size for the rider's height, weight and disability
H11 - The horse shall possess the type and quality of movement appropriate for the rider's disability.

Who determines any of these parameters? There are legitimate differences of opinion on how much weight a given horse can carry. Temperament? Without working around a horse for a period of time, how can you measure that? Quality of movement? Horse people have trouble agreeing on the definition of "a working trot," how could two people agree on what is or is not in compliance with this? Both of these standards were deemed to be subjective.

NEW: *P1 - Does the operating center have guidelines to determine selection of prospective horses' for the riding program?*

Interpretation: Guidelines for horse selection are determined by the individual needs of the operating center. Considerations include soundness, activities offered (i.e., vaulting, driving, hippotherapy), size of participants accepted, disability of participants and type/quality of movement needed.

Compliance Demonstration: Personnel explanation of horse selection process.

The peer reviewer interviews a center representative about their process of selection. If the person hems and haws and indicates that the center takes any and all horses offered to **it** and there really is no systematic approach to this problem, the answer is NO. If the person reels off a list of what the center does, when and by whom - the answer is YES. The peer reviewer is not asked to assess the quality of movement of a horse or try to ascertain if it has bad stable manners. If the peer reviewer sees examples of lameness or dangerous behavior, he or she can write a note for the Accreditation Committee to review. A procedure for dealing with this is in place.

There are now 80 standards, divided between Administration, Program and Facility. From these, a list of ten Mandatory standards was compiled. These are as follows;

The operating center must provide written evidence of the following;
● Insurance coverage for liability and accident/medical expense.
● Signed release of liability.
● Signed permission or signed non consent, to seek emergency medical treatment.
● NARHA certification for all instructors.
● Nationally recognized license or credential for all health professionals conducting therapy sessions or consulting to the center.

Assurance must be given that:
●Health professionals providing direct service must be NARHA certified or assisted at all times by an NARHA certified instructor.

The following mandatory standards relate to equipment and facilities:
● All participants must wear protective equestrian headgear that is ASTM-SEI approved.
● All English-style saddles must have safety stirrups at all times.
● All Western-style saddles must have safety stirrups - OR - a written policy must be in place requiring participants to wear riding boots or hard-soled shoes with heels.
● A working telephone or similar communication device must be available and emergency information must be posted beside it.

HOW THE NEW ACCREDITATION SYSTEM WORKS:
The Accreditation Committee and NARHA Board of Directors adopted the following statement of purpose for Accreditation Program: *The purpose of NARHA Accreditation is to provide a process of evaluation that recognizes an operating center's program as meeting basic standards for health and safety to promote the well-being of all participants and horses.*

As mentioned before, a major change of policy accompanied the proposal for the new Accreditation system: **it had to be voluntary.** In addition, two **training programs** have been created: one for the **center personnel**; one for **new peer reviewers.** Representatives from operating centers take a three-hour seminar to become familiar with the standards and the procedures involved in becoming accredited. The peer reviewer applicants take an in depth course and have to pass a rigorous examination to be considered for the position.

The operating center receives a **self study form** listing all the standards to ensure that all paperwork and training are in place and correct. Accreditation visits are scheduled at the convenience of the center - but all aspects of its work must be shown to the peer reviewers. For example: if hippotherapy, backriding, therapeutic riding and driving are all offered, an example of each must be shown.

All visits are conducted by two trained peer reviewers and all peer reviewers agree to go on at least two visits per year if asked. The entire accreditation visit takes place on one day, if at all possible, and, before the peer reviewers leave the center, everyone knows whether the center passed or failed. Each standard receives a "yes," "no," or "not applicable" response. The center must score at least 75% on anyone section, and must achieve an overall score of 80%. All mandatory standards must earn a "yes": even a single "no" response to a mandatory standard causes the center to fail.

The granting of accreditation is then subject to approval by the Accreditation Committee and Board of Directors and is valid for five years. Should a major safety problem be reported to the Accreditation Committee, a center may be revisited at random. Checks and balances are built into the system to ensure the right of all concerned and a code of ethics must be signed by both operating center personnel and peer reviewers.

CONCLUSION
The issue of standards and accreditation are crucial to the reputation of each individual NARHA member operating center. As the public becomes more knowledgeable about therapeutic riding in all its aspects, parents and riders will want to know that the center they attend meets a high level of professionalism and safety for themselves and their loved ones. No less than the credibility of the entire industry rests on how well each individual center conducts itself. Accreditation plays a very large role in ensuring a continuing trend to raise standards of excellence.

Jean M. Tebay
USA

CERTIFICATION OF THERAPEUTIC RIDING INSTRUCTORS

Lorraine Renker, BA, NARHA Master Instructor

There is often confusion regarding the terms certification and accreditation. Accreditation refers to a program NOT an individual. A program must meet predetermined standards in order to achieve accreditation. Certification is obtained by individuals. To achieve certification, an individual is tested and evaluated to determine mastery of specific bodies of knowledge. Certification determines competency of an individual. In a nutshell, therapeutic riding centers can become accredited and riding instructors can become certified. It is important to be clear about the differences between accreditation and certification.

This article is concerned with the certification of therapeutic riding instructors. The American Society of Association Executives (1988) defines the objectives of a certification program as follows:

❑ To raise the standards of a profession.
❑ To encourage self-assessment by offering guidelines for achievement.
❑ To identify persons with acceptable knowledge of principles and practices of the profession and related disciplines.
❑ To award recognition to those who have demonstrated a high level of competence and ethical fitness for a profession.
● To improve the performance in the profession by encouraging participation in a continuing program of professional development.

As the field of therapeutic riding continues to grow, certification is an important component of professional growth. Other American equine organizations have recognized the importance of instructor certification as demonstrated by the programs offered by the United States Dressage Federation (USDF), the American Riding Instructors Certification Program (ARICP), The Association for Horsemanship, Safety, and Education (CHA), and Horsemanship Safety Association (HSA). In the United States, the North American Riding for the Handicapped Association (NARHA) is the organization looked to for the certification of therapeutic riding instructors. NARHA currently offers three levels of instructor certification: Registered, Advanced, and Master.

HISTORY OF THE NARHA INSTRUCTOR CERTIFICATION PROGRAM

NARHA has been interested in the education and certification of therapeutic riding instructors since its inception in 1969. Initially, therapeutic riding centers, such as the Cheff Center in Michigan and the Fran Joswick Center in California offered training courses to prospective therapeutic riding instructors. At the successful completion of the course, instructors received therapeutic instructor ratings. In 1975, the NARHA board of directors was ready to tackle an early aim of establishing instructor standards.

In 1976, the Standards and Education Committee of NARHA undertook the development of an instructor certification program. A committee was established and, in 1978, a completed program was presented to the NARHA board of directors. The program offered three certification classifications: non-orthopedic, orthopedic and combined non-orthopedic and orthopedic. Potential examinees first successfully completed an open-book exam before moving onto the on-site practical examination. The practical exam was divided into three sections: written tests, teaching and horsemanship and horse-mastership.

To start off the program, the NARHA board of directors designated the first certified instructors who would become the first examiners. The first therapeutic riding instructor's certification examination was held in 1979 at the Cheff Center in Michigan. By the end of 1980 there were approximately twelve NARHA Certified Instructors in addition to the initial eleven examiners. This process continued through 1987 when there were 28 certified instructors listed in the NARHA Annual Report and Journal. NARHA went through a lot of changes in the period between 1987 and 1989 and the on-site instructor's certification examinations were put on hold.

In 1989, an instructor certification committee was established. This ten-member committee was charged with the task of reviewing the instructor's certification program and making recommendations to the NARHA board of directors. It was decided that the previously certified instructors would be given the opportunity to be renamed NARHA Certified Master Therapeutic Riding Instructors. A new level of instructor certification would then be developed and tested through a video tape process. Instructors could become certified in physical and cognitive, cognitive only, or physical only levels. The applicants would be required to go to a predetermined site to take a closed-book, written examination and to turn in a video tape demonstrating teaching, riding and evaluation skills. The first instructors were certified under the new videotape process in 1992.

A need was recognized for an entry level instructor certification, so in 1994 a registered level was developed. This level was evaluated through an open book exam and a video tape demonstrating teaching and riding skills. The first registered instructors were certified in 1994. Starting in January of 1995, it became a requirement that all instructors at NARHA operating centers must achieve at least a registered level instructor certification. Operating centers would comply with this requirement as their accreditation expired. This requirement supported the trend toward professionalism of therapeutic riding. Riders with disabilities could be assured that their riding instructors had demonstrated at least an entry level competence.

By 1994, three levels of instructor certification were available to therapeutic riding instructors: registered, certified, and master. In 1996, the certified level was renamed the advanced level because of the confusion in terminology, thus the current terminology: registered, advanced and master NARHA certified riding instructors.

Specific criteria are available for all three levels of instructor certification. The criteria are divided into five areas: Equine Management, Horsemanship, Instruction, Teaching Methodology and Disabilities. Each section is further divided into areas of knowledge or skill required at each level of certification. The criteria provide instructors with specific information to help them prepare for each examination.

By 1995, there were several options available for obtaining instructor certification at the registered and advanced levels. NARHA continued to offer the video tape option for obtaining certification. In addition, in 1995, NARHA developed an Approved Training Course Program which enabled approved training centers to administer the registration and advanced certification examinations at the end of a successful completed training course. NARHA also entered into a joint venture with CHA in 1994 to offer CHA/NARHA certification clinics for therapeutic riding instructors. More information about any of these programs or new programs that might be developed can be obtained from NARHA.

Riding instructors that pursued NARHA certification at the registered and advanced levels in 1997 indicated that 558 became registered instructors and 150 completed the advanced, physical and cognitive certification, 25 advanced completed the cognitive certification only and three advanced persons completed the physical certification only. Several master instructor examinations had been offered, but did not fill until the fall of 1997. In 1997, there were 27 NARHA master instructors.

The instructor's certification program is designed to promote continuing education and professional development. Annual renewal requires certified instructors to show proof of current first aid and CPR as well as a predetermined number of continuing education hours. Instructors are encouraged to upgrade their certification level as they develop the required skills and knowledge.

OTHER INTERNATIONAL THERAPEUTIC RIDING INSTRUCTOR CERTIFICATION PROGRAMS
NARHA is not alone in the recognition of the need for the certification of therapeutic riding instructors. Many other countries offer some form of therapeutic riding instructor certification. Many countries tie into a strong national equestrian federation that has long-standing programs for training and recognizing equestrian instructors, coaches, and/or trainers.

The Canadian Therapeutic Riding Association (CanTRA) offers certification as an assistant instructor and an instructor with a third certification level in development. Australia offers two levels of certification. England offers a three level certification program. Germany offers three instructor certifications to three different fields: hippotherapy, remedial education vaulting/ riding, and sports riding certificates. These are only a few examples of the instructor's certification programs offered in other countries.

CONCLUSION:

In order for therapeutic riding instructors to be viewed as professionals, it is necessary to embrace instructor certification programs. Certification provides increased professional credibility. In the United States, certification of riding instructors in general and therapeutic riding instructors specifically is in its infancy. Certification is an important key in the development and acceptance of the "professional therapeutic riding instructor."

References

American Society of Association Executives. (1988). Accreditation, certification, and standardization Background Kit-Self Regulation: Accreditation, Certification and Standardization) Washington, DC.

Butt, E. (1981), NARHA- its first decade 1970 to 1980 . NARHA, Denver, CO.

NARHA. (1987). North American Riding for the Handicapped Association inc. annual report and journal 1986-1987. NARHA, Denver, CO.

NARHA (1997), NARHA guide, 1997 update pages. NARHA, Denver, CO.

Lorraine Renker
USA

CHA A CERTIFICATION PROGRAM FOR INSTRUCTORS OF RIDERS WITH DISABILITIES

Dodi Stacey & Charla Shurtlef

In today's world of competitive equine professionals, certification is becoming more of a necessity than a choice. There are many good reasons for seeking certification, but there are four basically essential reasons:
- Safety and Standards provided by the certifying body.
- Liability, responsibility, accountability and Liability Insurance.
- Education.
- Validation of professionalism and skills.

HISTORY OF THE CHA INSTRUCTORS OF RIDERS WITH DISABILITIES CERTIFICATION PROGRAM

Certified Horsemanship Association (CHA) has been certifying instructors for people without disabilities for thirty-two years. CHA was founded as a private organization in 1967 by Dan Hemphill, who owned and operated Camp Summer Life in Vadito, New Mexico. The organization rose from his frustrations on hiring riding Instructors who not only were not qualified, but also could not live up to the information that he gleaned from the resumes sent to him. In 1976, the organization was turned over to a board of directors. The Board then applied for and was granted, non-profit status. During the ensuing years, CHA's unique certification process has been highly lauded. The process is continually monitored and reviewed in an effort to stay competitive and current in the industry. There are CHA Certified Instructors on five continents and in twelve countries. CHA also provides standards of the industry, instructional manuals for students, instructional manuals for instructors and many other support materials and products for the riding instructor.

In 1991, the first steps were taken toward a CHA certification process for Instructors of Riders with Disabilities, utilizing NARHA and CHA Standards, and NARHA's expertise on riding for people with disabilities and the CHA's certification techniques. The CHA Instructors of Riders with Disabilities Committee was formed with members from both organizations. Over the course of the last five years, this committee developed a strong and well-defined process that certifies Instructors of Riders with Disabilities.

The first responsibility of the Committee was to develop a criterion to govern the development of a strong process. The first decision, based on the premise that to successfully teach riders with disabilities one must be able to teach riders without disabilities, dictated the prerequisite of certification in the Standard CHA program for riders without disabilities. This criteria also allows the inclusion of riders with disabilities in classes of riders without disabilities, *and* the instructor will be certified in both programs! Classes for riders without disabilities can also be given to supplement the income for the program for riders with disabilities. The second decision was that there would be no "Grandfathering" of instructors or clinic instructors, into the program. This decision would make a stronger process from the start. The final decision was based on the needs of the program horse, the prospective CHA Instructors of Riders with Disabilities must have the ability to care for and school all the horses involved in the program for riders with disabilities. The prerequisite of prior certification in CHA's Standard program allows the CHA Instructors of Riders with Disabilities certification clinic material to concentrate on the needs of the client riding in programs for riders with disabilities. The entire clinic is devoted to safety, teaching techniques, mounting and dismounting, required documentation and specific information for the instructor of riders with disabilities.

Many people have been asking the questions, "Who? How? Why?" The "Who" is any instructor that teaches equine activities to persons with disabilities. The "How" is discussed throughout this chapter! The "Why"? CHA has provided this certification process to give instructors an alternate method of certification with a different philosophy. Then one might ask, "Which?" If the person is a solid, experienced instructor and only looking for certification, NARHA Certification is probably the best choice. The newer instructor or the instructor trying to improve their skills might want to look at the CHA Instructors of Riders with

Disabilities Certification process. Following is an in-depth discussion of the clinic process, but in a nutshell, a CHA Instructors of Riders with Disabilities Certification Clinic provides an instructor with five days of hands-on experience, sharing of information, and collection of new ideas and new information through lectures by the qualified staff. The instructor candidate receives instant feedback on successes and problems. Instructors are given the opportunity to practice their teaching skills during role-playing lesson before being tested with students with disabilities. During the clinic there are daily lectures to gather new knowledge or to validate old knowledge.

THE CHA INSTRUCTORS OF RIDERS WITH DISABILITIES CLINIC

The Benefits and Requirements. It must be stressed here that CHA Instructors of Riders with Disabilities Clinics are *certification* clinics, not teaching clinics. However, it is virtually impossible to come to a clinic without learning a great deal of information. There are five full days of each clinic that will be spent in practice teaching, evaluation, sharing of information and interaction with fellow candidates. All of the currently certified Clinic Instructors are talented and knowledgeable instructors in their own right.

All CHA Instructors of Riders with Disabilities clinics must be held at facilities that fulfill the needs of riders with disabilities and who has on site specific adaptive riding equipment and tools for use with riders with disabilities! This requirement guarantees the Clinic Instructors that all necessary equipment for the successful completion of a clinic will be at the site when they arrive. It also assures the instructor candidate that they will have the necessary equipment they need to teach their assigned lessons.

Since the Standard CHA Instructor Certification is a prerequisite for participation in the CHA Instructors of Riders with Disabilities certification program, some sites will host a Standard CHA Instructor Certification Clinic prior to the CHA Instructors of Riders with Disabilities clinic. Other sites will do the CHA Instructors of Riders with Disabilities format only, expecting *the prospective instructor candidate* to find a clinic for Standard CHA Instructor Certification before arriving. The instructor desiring certification can receive a listing of Standard CHA Instructor Certification Clinics by calling the CHA office at 1-800-399-0138.

The CHA Instructors of Riders with Disabilities clinics are designed to provide instructor certification for people who work with riders with disabilities. The qualified candidate, with properly documented required hours and all completed required forms, who successfully completes this clinic, will receive CHA Instructors of Riders with Disabilities certification to teach riders with disabilities. Current First Aid and CPR certification are a prerequisite.

The following clinic forms are required, and must be completed and brought to the clinic when the candidate comes to the site. These will be sent to prospective candidates on registration for the clinic.
- Instructor Candidate Registration Form.
- Instructor Candidate Resume Form.
- Documentation of Hours Form.
- CHA Standard Instructor Certification Certificate (May be earned immediately prior to this clinic.)
- First Aid/CPR Certification Certificate or Card with the expiration date clearly visible.

The entire focus of the CHA Instructors of Riders with Disabilities Certification Clinic is on certifying qualified instructors, at their individual levels of competency, to teach riding to people with disabilities safely and knowledgeably. The materials and curriculum are specific to the various considerations, adaptations, applications, contra-indications, adaptive equipment and horses used in riding programs that serve people with physical and/or cognitive disabilities.

THE CLINIC SYLLABUS:

Clinic must be scheduled for a full five (5) days and include a minimum of forty (40) hours.

I. Welcome and introductions (Clinic staff and candidates get acquainted).
   A. Host Site - Introduction.
      1. Introduce site staff.
      2. Site Rules and information on site. (Facilities, grounds, meal schedules, rules, barn orientation, etc.)
   B. CHA
      1. Brief history, mission and goals, programs.
      2. CHA Certification Standards.
      3. NARHA Certification Standands.
   C. Clinic syllabus, clinic schedule, daily schedule, explained.

II. Lecture and Discussions
   A. Taught by clinic staff.
      1. Safety in teaching riding for people with disabilities.
      2. Working with disabilities and how to adapt your teaching skills to people with disabilities.
      3. Confidentiality (riders rights).
      4. Preparing students for a trail ride.
   B. Three (3) to four (4) hours lectures concerning:
      1. Disabilities.
      2. Contraindications to riding for people with disabilities.

III. Familiarization with CHA and NARHA Standards
   A. Recommended Reference reading materials for testing: CHA Standards, NARHA Operating Center Standards and Accreditation Manual; CHA Instructor's Manual; NARHA Precautions and Contraindications; CHA Composite Manual, NARHA Instructor Educational Guide; Therapeutic Riding I Strategies for Instruction, edited by Engel.
   B. Discussion and Practice.

IV. Practice Teaching and Evaluations of Teaching Skills.
   A. Assistant for Instructors of Riders with Disabilities and Level One - Minimum of participation as sidewalker, horse handler, or assistant instructor for two lessons with role playing students and two lessons with riders with disabilities having cognitive disabilities, physical disabilities, or both.
   B. Level One - Minimum of two lessons with role-playing students and two lessons of riders with disabilities.
   C. Theory lessons and any additional teaching sessions assigned.

V. Practical Experience
   A. Horse knowledge.
      1. Choosing the correct horse for riders with disabilities.
      2. Matching the horse to the rider with disabilities.
   B. Correct mounting and dismounting procedures and techniques.
   C. Special Equipment - Purpose of each, how to select, and how to use.
   D. Volunteer training.

VI. Testing and Evaluation.
   A. Feedback from group after teaching lab session, plus clinic instructors comments.
   B. Written test on disabilities and theory on arrival.
   C. Clinic Instructors' evaluations of candidates teaching skills, safety practices, horsemanship for riders with disabilities. knowledge, knowledge of all aspects of disabilities, and standards.
   D. Clinic Participants' evaluation of clinic and clinic instructors.
   E. Issue CHA certificates for CHA Instructors of Riders with Disabilities Certification.

Days are long and filled with activity. Each candidate will teach a minimum of four lessons, two with role-playing students and two with riders with disabilities. Candidates for higher levels may be asked to teach additional lessons. At the conclusion of each lesson the candidate will be asked to self evaluate the lesson, as an instructor cannot improve their lessons at their home facility if they have not developed this skill. The rest of the candidates will then be given the opportunity to make comments and suggestions, either as a role-playing student or as an observer. Finally the Clinic Instructors will tell the candidate those things that they did well and will mention areas that might benefit from change or should be added to the lesson. The Clinic Instructors will then give suggestions on how to achieve the changes for best results. Lecture and/or discussion will be held each evening. Candidates must come prepared forboth riding and teaching. One can bring his/her favorite teaching aids, ideas to share and an open mind. The professional clinicians place primary importance on the candidates' knowledge that is in their possession on arrival at the clinic site, prior experience attained and the performance during the practice teaching sessions.

Many of the clinic facilities will be able to house and feed the clinic participants, while others can not. The clinic fees charged for the course will always include the use of the site, the equipment, and the certification fees. Candidates should contact the clinic site directly to determine what accommodations are available and what one needs to bring for ones comfort.

Clinicians base the levels of certification awarded on the candidate's individual performance, scores on written examination, documentation of hours and other prerequisites as listed on the application form and the active Standard CHA Riding Instructor certification level.

During the last day of the clinic, candidates will attend a private interview with their clinic instructors. At this time the clinic instructors will inform the candidate of the level of certification awarded. The CHA Instructors of Riders with Disabilities Certification is effective immediately, there is no waiting period, as the clinic instructors in this program have the final authority. They will fairly and accurately certify the candidate at the level they feel is appropriate and where they feel they can accept legal responsibility for the certification.

Examination and certification results can be appealed to the CHA Instructors of Riders with Disabilities Certification Committee within thirty (30) days of the close of the clinic. A Candidate submitting an appeal will be notified of the committee's decision within (30) days of receipt of the appeal. If the candidate cannot accept the ruling of the CHA Instructors of Riders with Disabilities Committee, he/she may submit a request in writing to appear, at his/her own expense, at the next CHA Board meeting for a final judgement. This request must be submitted to the Instructors of Riders with Disabilities Committee within thirty (30) days of receiving the Committee's decision regarding the original appeal.

LEVELS OF CERTIFICATION AVAILABLE

All levels of certification have prerequisites. These prerequisites are listed below. Actual level of certification achieved will be based on these prerequisites and the candidate's performance during the certification clinic.

CHA ASSISTANT TO INSTRUCTORS FOR RIDERS WITH DISABILITIES.
CERTIFICATION IS FOR COGNITIVE AND/OR PHYSICAL DISABILITIES.
CANDIDATE MAY BE CERTIFIED AS A SIDEWALKER, HORSE HANDLER, OR ASSISTANT RIDING
INSTRUCTOR.

- Sixteen (16) years of age.
- Current CHA Standard Level 1 Instructor Certification for Certification as an Assistant Instructor for Riders with Disabilities.
- Current First Aid/CPR Certification.
- Documented 5 hours of field experience in disabilities.
- Demonstrate participation safe, effective, and enjoyable lessons for Riders with Disabilities.

CHA INSTRUCTORS OF RIDERS WITH DISABILITIES LEVEL ONE.
CERTIFICATION MAY BE IN COGNITIVE DISABILITIES, PHYSICAL DISABILITIES OR BOTH.
- Eighteen (18) years of age.
- Current CHA Standard Level 2 Instructor Certification.
- Current First Aid/CPR Certification.
- Document 25 hours of instructing Riders with Disabilities. Fifteen hours must be teaching riders with or without disabilities. Ten hours must be working with persons with disabilities inside or outside of the equine industry.
- Pass the CHA written examination with a score of 70% or more.
- Successfully pass this clinic for certification and an award of an additional 40 hours of experience teaching riders with disabilities.

CHA INSTRUCTORS OF RIDERS WITH DISABILITIES LEVEL TWO.
CERTIFICATION MAY BE IN COGNITIVE DISABILITIES, PHYSICAL DISABILITIES OR BOTH.
- Twenty-one (21) years of age.
- Current CHA Standard Level 3 Instructor Certification.
- Current First Aid/CPR Certification.
- Document 120 hours of instructing Riders with Disabilities (May include any hours of teaching Riders with Disabilities used in total hours for Level One).
- Pass the CHA written examination with a score of 80% or more.
- Successfully complete this clinic for certification and an award of an additional 40 hours of experience teaching riders with disabilities.

CHA Instructors of Riders with Disabilities Level Three. Certification may be in Cognitive, Physical or Both.
- Twenty-one (21) years of age.
- Current CHA Standard Level 4 Instructor Certification.
- Current First Aid/CPR Certification.
- Document 160 hours of instructing Riders with Disabilities. (May include any hours of teaching Riders with Disabilities used in total hours for Levels One and Two).
- Demonstrate knowledge of competitive equestrian activities for Riders with Disabilities.
- Pass CHA Instructors of Riders with Disabilities written examination with a score of 90% or higher.

All CHA Instructors of Riders with Disabilities Clinic candidates will be chosen from those who have successfully achieved CHA Instructors of Riders with Disabilities Level Three, passed the Assistant Clinic Instructor Examination, and documented prerequisites.

RECERTIFICATION REQUIREMENTS FOR ALL LEVELS ARE:

CHA Instructors of Riders with Disabilities Instructor Recertification Process requires instructors who are applying for recertification to submit documents of the following requirements annually. Please submit the required information with payment for your annual membership fees, before January 1 of each New Year.

CHA INSTRUCTORS OF RIDERS WITH DISABILITIES LEVEL ONE
- Instructor Membership with CHA must be submitted with Recertification requirements.
- Documentation of currant First Aid and CPR Certification.
- Documentation of ten (10) hours of continuing education.

CHA INSTRUCTORS OF RIDERS WITH DISABILITIES ADVANCED INSTRUCTORS, LEVELS TWO AND THREE

- Instructor Membership with CHA must be submitted with Recertification requirements.
- Documentation of currant First Aid and CPR Certification.
- Documentation of twenty (20) hours of continuing education.

CHA INSTRUCTORS OF RIDERS WITH DISABILITIES CLINIC INSTRUCTORS AND ASSISTANT CLINIC INSTRUCTORS.

- Instructor Membership with CHA must be submitted with Recertification requirements.
- Documentation of current First Aid and CPR Certification.
- Documentation of Thirty (30) hours of continuing education.

HOSTING A CHA CLINIC

Any sites can host a clinic if they are accredited by NARHA and a member in good standing with both organizations. Membership in CHA can be submitted with the application. The current location of the NARHA operating center must be the same location where the most recent NARHA accreditation status was granted. The site should call the CHA office and request a clinic application form. After the prospective clinic site completes the form, it must be mailed to the CHA office with a check for purchase of CHA clinic insurance. CHA will then process the form and forward it to NARHA. Once the approval process has been completed, the new clinic host site will receive detailed information regarding how to host the clinic. There is a maximum limit of eight participants and a minimum limit of four participants per clinic.

HOSTING A CHA INSTRUCTORS OF RIDERS WITH DISABILITIES CLINIC

Any sites can host a clinic if they have or purchase a current membership with CHA. NARHA membership and accreditation are a plus! Membership in CHA can be submitted with the application. The site should call the CHA office and request a clinic application form. After the prospective clinic site completes the form, it must be mailed to the CHA office with a check to purchase CHA Clinic insurance. CHA will then process the form. Once the approval process has been completed, the new Clinic Host Site will receive detailed information regarding how to host the clinic. There is a maximum limit of eight participants and a minimum limit of four participants for group situations per clinic.

The Host Site must order and pay for all required clinic and reference materials. Required forms are included in the administration fees but the site must mail required instructor candidate forms and materials to each participant on receipt of his/her application with a deposit or payment. One set of recommended reference material must be available at the site for candidate to use. The reference materials may be purchased by the site or borrowed from the library. A list of these materials is provided to both the candidate and the host site.

The required information must include: Candidate Registration Form, Instructor Candidate Resume Form, Documentation of Teaching Hours Form and a copy of first aid/CPR certification with expiration date clearly visible. Each registrant accepted into the clinic must supply a copy of his/her CHA Instructor Certification Certificate unless the candidate is also registering for a CHA Standard Clinic in conjunction with the CHA Instructors of Riders with Disabilities Clinic. The Host Site must then mail copies of all required information to the Clinic Faculty a minimum of two weeks before the start of the clinic. This gives the Clinic Instructors the time necessary to verify that all persons have properly completed their paperwork before the start of the clinic. It is a real "bummer" to arrive at the clinic site and find out that you cannot participate because your forms are not complete. The Host Site will be notified of any missing information by the clinic instructors, so that the prospective candidate can be made aware of the problems before he/she arrives.

Auditors may come and observe to learn from the activities at the clinic. Aiditors can create extra income for the host site but auditors must be informed that they will not receive certification. Auditors are not included in the maximum of eight participants. Last minute applications can be accepted but these candidates must be warned that they will only be allowed to audit if the required forms are not complete and/or do not meet clinic entrance standards after being reviewed by the Clinic Staff. The Host Site must provide a Liability Release Form to be signed by each candidate and by spectators at the time of arrival on the site. The release must include CHA and the Clinic Staff. The Host Site must have reference materials available during the clinic as resource material for instructor candidates. The Host Site is responsible for paying all CHA Instructors of Riders with Disabilities clinic fees but not the fees of the participant. The Host Site must include these fees in the cost of the clinic to the candidates. The Host Site must provide a Site Liaison Person. This may or may not be the same person as the designated Contact Person for the clinic. The site liaison person must be available to assist with clinic needs during scheduled hours.

Each Host Site must arrange accommodations for housing and feeding the instructor candidates. It is preferred that accommodations are on the site, however, housing and eating facilities within twenty minutes drive of the site that conform to ADA Standards are acceptable. On-site accommodations should arrange for all meals and snacks. All lunches must be on-site, but can be catered. Evening snacks and drinks should be made available on site during the evening hours. Meals, at discounts, can be arranged at one restaurant for off-site accommodations. Host Site must provide transportation, if needed by candidates without cars, to and from off-site accommodations.

The *minimum* clinic cost the Host Site may charge to participants is $400.00 if they provide housing, and the minimum salary for Clinic Staff is $600.00. The average cost per participant for candidates is currently an approximate $500.00 with housing included.

The CHA Instructors of Riders with Disabilities Clinic is an activity program of the host site. There is a set administration fee to CHA for the processing of the clinic and the successful candidates. The site, however, gets to keep any profits made after these fees are paid. Hosting a clinic can be a smaller fundraiser if only outside participants are accepted. It is also an excellent way to certify all the instructors at a facility at no or low cost, depending on the number of site instructors that will attend. It is commonly accepted that four or five outside participants should pay the expenses incurred in conducting a clinic. Any additional participants are then profit. This means that with appropriate cost analysis, a site could conceivable have a nice profit to use for the benefit of the program.

The Host Site is responsible for hiring and paying the salaries and expenses of Clinic Staff, from the list provided by the CHA office. The CHA office will assist in the event of difficulties, but does not guarantee staff availability.

The Host Site must provide:
- Exclusive use of all facility and equipment requirements for each clinic.
- A covered or indoor arena is nice for inclement weather. If one is not available on site, arrangements can be made to borrow or rent the arena of a nearby facility or clear out a building suitable for indoor riding at a walk (High implement shed, hay shed, etc). The building must be large enough to provide 32 linear feet of space on the rail per horse. Thirty-two (32) feet per horse allows space for one horse, one horse handler, and two sidewalkers for each student in a group lesson. Ceilings or rafters must be a minimum of 12 feet high, 14 feet high recommended. The emergency indoor arena does not have to meet CHA standards other than those listed above but provisions must be made to transport and supply necessary adaptive equipment to the emergency facility.
- Sufficient tack and adaptive equipment to accommodate needs of the clinic, candidates, and riders with disabilities.

Equipment to include the following:
- A minimum of one mounting ramp and one mounting block.
- Mobility aids, with a minimum of one wheelchair and one pair of crutches.
- Safety stirrups. Devonshire boots to meet needs of riders with disabilities.
- ASTM-SEI Approved Helmets or other helmets as described in NARHA Standards for use by specifically indicated disabilities.

- Seat savers, sheepskins, fleece pads as needed.
- A minimum of one surcingle.
- Lunging equipment.
- Bareback pad with NO stirrups.
- English and Western tack.
- Miscellaneous adaptive equipment, as required by riders with disabilities.
- Miscellaneous games for riders with disabilities. (Cones, rings, nerf balls, bean bags, etc.)
- A minimum of two classes of riders with disabilities per instructor candidate. (The classes to include riders with cognitive disabilities and physical disabilities. It is recommended that lessons progress from cognitive disabilities to physical disabilities. Daily clinic schedules will be determined prior to the clinic by the clinic staff, with considerations for the host site needs.) A rider may be assigned to more than one class, provided allowances are made for that rider's stamina and attention span.

- A sufficient number of horses to accommodate needs of the clinic candidates and riders with disabilities. The horses must include various types of conformation, movement, and level of responsiveness to aids; and be sufficiently trained to allow practicum instruction and evaluation for suitability as therapeutic riding mounts by instructor candidates.

- An appropriate number of trained volunteers to meet the demands of the riders with disabilities and instructor candidates during the course of the clinic.

The CHA Office is now accepting applications for CHA Instructors of Riders with Disabilities Clinic Sites and they are keeping a list of instructors who would like to attend a CHA Instructors of Riders with Disabilities Certification clinic. CHA can be reached at 1 800 399-0138!

*THE NARHA ON-SITE CERTIFICATION PROCESS

Kitty Stalsburg, BS, NACI

North American Riding for the Handicapped (NARHA) accreditation is a voluntary membership-driven program. Accreditation focuses on education and evaluation of an operating center's program(s) using standards that are developed and approved by the membership that are considered basic to therapeutic riding. Standards are written in an objective manner to assure consistent interpretation by operating centers and to be easily evaluated by trained site visitors. The standards are reviewed regularly and updated by the Accreditation Committee. Accreditation involves education, preparation and communication. The process should help to strengthen the center's therapeutic riding program.

WHAT ARE SITE VISITORS?

There are three classes of NARHA site visitors.

- **Associate visitors**: an NARHA member who has completed the Operating Center Training Course. He or she relates well to therapeutic riding professionals, has knowledge of and administrative experience in therapeutic riding, has had three years experience of the day-to-day operation of an NARHA accredited center, is willing to volunteer time to conduct site visits and to participate in training and updates and is recommended by the course instructor, Accreditation and Standards Committee, and NARHA Board.

- **Visitor**: a current NARHA member who has successfully completed the associate visitor training course. He or she has successfully completed three visits as an associate visitor under supervision and evaluation of a minimum of two different visitors, has met all associate visitor requirements and is capable and ready to assume ultimate authority during the visit for compliance decisions and applicability of specific standards and section of standards.

- **Mentor:** A mentor visitor must remain an NARHA member, be available to participate in two visits per year and attend a visitor update training every two years to maintain site visitor status.

THE ACCREDITATION PROGRAM OBJECTIVES:

- Establish national standards for the therapeutic riding industry.
- Provide a means for accreditation, continued self-evaluation and a constant striving for improvement.
- Provide standards for use by operating centers for planning and implementing services.
- Provide resources to help center's ability to assure quality service.
- Assist the public in selecting centers that meet established standards.

NARHA standards identify practices considered basic to quality therapeutic riding. These standards do not require that all programs "look alike" but allow each center to address its own criteria by the NARHA standards while maintaining common professional goals.

THE BENEFITS OF ACCREDITATION:

- Quality Assurance - prospective donors, volunteers and riders are more willing to establish relationships with organizations that have attained this respected benchmark. The center staff can take pride that it meets national standards.
- Accreditation provides an advantage when raising funds, grant writing, especially approaching state and organizations that require proof that the center meets industry standards.

ALL MATERIAL INCLUDED IN THIS ARTICLE HAS BEEN TAKEN FROM NARHA STANDARDS & ACCREDITATION MANUAL, NARHA PAMPHLET ON ON-SITE ACCREDITATION, AND THE JULY 1997 STRIDES ARTICLE BY KITTY STALSBURG - REPRINTED BY PERMISSION FROM NARHA.

- When key staff members change, the rider can be assured that they will continue to receive therapeutically valid services that meet safety standards. Accredited centers are listed or designated in all NARHA publications and public recognitions of these centers are made at meetings.
- Only accredited centers may use the NARHA logo and "Accredited Center" on their printed material.
- Accreditation is an opportunity to involve staff, volunteers and board members in the safety, operation and administration of each operating center.
- A center may need to recruit the advice of experts in various fields from their community and in turn, to meet compliance standards. The contact with community agencies will help a center gain recognition.
- Accreditation allows all members of the organization to participate in written policies and procedures and in turn train and educate of staff and volunteers.
- Guidelines help to increase the longevity and consistency of the operating center.

The on-site accreditation of centers is accomplished by <u>peer review.</u> The peer review system is the strongest role model for successful accreditation of programs. It strengthens professional respect and encourages networking. The dissemination of information occurs faster through the peer review process.

THE ACCREDITATION PROCESS

Only NARHA member centers are eligible for accreditation. The process is set-up on a yearly schedule where established deadlines must be met. Failure to meet the scheduled deadlines will automatically refer the process to the next calendar year.

Step One:
- The center receives the *Operating Center Standards & Accreditation Manual*.
- A self-study evaluation form must be completed to allow a center to determine its readiness to become accredited.
- A member from the center must attend an operating center Training course to insure that all operating centers applying for accreditation understand the NARHA standards and process.
- A member must attend this course within twelve months prior to the peer review site visit.

Step Two:
- The operating center will send to NARHA by March 1st, a completed accreditation application, the self-study form and $500.
- The application covers a five-year period for centers that pass the accreditation.
- By submitting the application, a center acknowledges that it has assessed itself according to the NARHA standards and is prepared for a site visit.

Step Three:
- By April 1st, the operating center will be notified of its assigned site visitor.
- The site visitor (consisting of two visitors - one lead visitor) coordinate a mutual agreeable visit date.
- The operating center will host the visit prior to September 15th.
- NARHA Accreditation Committee reviews the site visit scores.
- Operating centers that fail the accreditation are notified by September 30th.
- The operating centers that pass the accreditation are announced at NARHA's annual conference.
- Accredited operating centers must submit an annual statement of compliance for each year during the five-year period.

After the site visit is completed and all questions have been answered, the form is signed by the visitor and the operating center representative. One copy is given to the operating center representative and the other copy is sealed and sent to NARHA the same day. There is a review - appeal process through NARHA.

MAINTAINING ACCREDITATION STATUS
- Operating centers will receive a membership invoice and a statement of compliance each December.
- Operating center must renew its membership annually.
- Accredited operating centers must submit a signed annual statement of compliance no later than January 1st.

COLLEGE-BASED TRAINING FOR
THERAPEUTIC RIDING INSTRUCTORS

Octavia J. Brown, Ed.M, NARHA Master Instructor

INTRODUCTION

Therapeutic riding has an intrinsic appeal for most horse people. They think of their own joy in their partnership with horses and immediately understand the emotional significance such a partnership could have for someone with a disability. This innate comprehension of the horse-human bond causes dozens of riding instructors to decide to add clients with disabilities to their schedules.

Beyond this gut reaction and willingness to be of help, there are some serious issues that must be considered. People with disabilities, who want to learn how to ride, have a right to expect safe, medically-appropriate lessons that not only challenge their minds but also attempt to improve their bodies in ways consistent with any other forms of treatment they are receiving.

The instructors, who teach such riders, have the obligations to be as well trained as possible for the task. There is a large responsibility to "do no harm." More than that, there is the need to interface with the medical and educational establishments for the best possible combination of approaches for each rider in every lesson. As we learn more about the effects the horse can have on the rider's body and mind, we are constantly obliged to reexamine the methods by which instructors are trained.

Concurrent with the growing acknowledgment of therapeutic riding as a legitimate form of therapeutic recreation and treatment has been a rise in demand for qualified therapeutic riding instructors.

This article will address the following question: What role can/should colleges and universities play in providing appropriate, thorough training for the next generation of therapeutic riding instructors?

OVERVIEW AND HISTORY OF THERAPEUTIC RIDING INSTRUCTOR TRAINING IN THE UNITED STATES

A college setting is a far cry from the early days of therapeutic riding instructor training efforts.

The North American Riding for the Handicapped Association (NARHA)[1] was founded in 1969. At about the same time, the Cheff Center in Augusta, MI, opened its doors. Cheff offered its first therapeutic riding instructor training course in 1971. Following Cheff's lead, a number of such courses started to appear. In New York, Winslow Therapeutic Riding Unlimited was among the pioneers to offer hippotherapy and sensory integration workshops; in New Jersey, the Somerset Hills Handicapped Riding Center offered its first instructor training course in 1977. However, the vast majority of instructors did not have the opportunity to enroll in these courses and they learned how to instruct clients with disabilities by enrolling in the 'School of Hard Knocks' - more commonly known as OJT (on the job training). Riding instructors with experience used a common sense approach, observing their clients with disabilities closely and adapting their teaching techniques accordingly.

The lessons taught were safe, for the most part, but the lesson plans were based on the teaching of riding skills, and not usually on the specific, individual, physical, emotional or cognitive needs of each client. Few instructors already had the educational background that could give them in-depth understanding of many different disabling conditions. For experienced instructors of able-bodied students, it was hard to find the training and education which would prepare them to work closely with a physical or occupational therapist to incorporate into the riding lesson exercises or movements designed to complement what the therapist

---

[1]NARHA may be reached at 1-800-369-RIDE for more information on any of its programs.

was doing in therapy sessions. In some cases, a physical or occupational therapist was invited to be present at lessons, but usually in an advisory capacity. It was generally understood that the goal was recreational riding rather than medically therapeutic adapted riding.a grant from the Kellogg Foundation.

In 1985, NARHA's annual conferences began to offer scholarly and practical information, through papers and round tables, prompting research and in-depth study of a wide variety of topics in therapeutic riding. In 1990, NARHA instituted Instructor Workshops through
a grant from the Kellogg Foundation.

The paradigm was as follows:
An experienced instructor of able-bodied riders decides to open a therapeutic riding program.
Learns by doing about various disabling conditions.
Goes to workshops and conferences to gain more in-depth knowledge or attends a formal training course.
Returns to program to put new knowledge into practice and pass it onto new instructors.

Most people, now active in the profession, had no choice but to acquire their knowledge in this somewhat piecemeal fashion.

There are few other professions where this would be tolerated. Does a surgeon start operating and then learn the details of anatomy? Of course not. Does a sailor take the wheel and learn how to steer without studying winds, tides, the mechanics of ships, the physics of steering? Not if he wants to stay afloat long! A lawyer, who did not go to law school, would have a difficult time in court!

Now that therapeutic riding is widely recognized as a viable profession, it is time to make the next logical step: incorporation of rigorous training and education in therapeutic riding at the college level. Students will then have the academic and practical training necessary to become certified according to NARHA's guidelines.[2]

This is consistent with the surgeon's training. You get all the book learning, then you learn how to cut and stitch. The new paradigm would be:
Get a college degree that includes therapeutic riding and a solid liberal arts background.
Take an internship or teaching practicum for hands-on experience to learn how to be an effective instructor.
Join an accredited program to gain the experience necessary to be certified.
Only then, consider starting a program

Many people believe that this approach will be the wave of the future. This is, in part, because our society is highly litigious and you'd better be credentialed and approved if you are to defend yourself in a law suit. There is also growing pressure within the therapeutic riding industry to standardize the educational background of the next wave of therapeutic riding professionals. This will give clients and their families the security of knowing that the quality of one therapeutic riding program will be comparable to others throughout the country[3].

---

[2]NARHA offers three levels of certified therapeutic riding instructors: Registered, Advanced and Master. Each level requires examination of instructional skills, equestrian skills and stable management, and knowledge of disabilities.
[3]NARHA is in the forefront of this emphasis on standardization through its Accreditation program for member operating centers as well as the Instructor Certification program. The American Hippotherapy Association (a NARHA-affiliated organization) is at work on certification for therapists practicing hippotherapy.

COLLEGES[4] AND THERAPEUTIC RIDING

"College becomes a must for a career with horses" trumpets a headline in a 1997 publication with an entire section devoted to equestrian education. **"To succeed in today's competitive market, horse people need the same types of skills that lead to effective careers in any industry."[5]** These words are as true of therapeutic riding instruction as for any other equine-related profession.

Let's take a look at a profile of the education needed for a person setting out to be a therapeutic riding instructor. He or she needs a strong equestrian background which includes the following:
- Ability to design a training and schooling program for therapeutic riding horses and to assess new horses for suitability.
- Ability to recognize unsoundness and make intelligent decisions on when to call the vet.
- A firm understanding of equine nutrition, conditioning, physiology, lameness, illness, the problem horse and daily maintenance requirements.
- Sufficient riding skill and knowledge of riding theory to deliver a well-planned lesson to a group or individual from beginner through (at least) intermediate; a good communicator.

Specific subjects that need to be studied to fully comprehend the challenges facing each individual client with a disability include:
- Human anatomy.
- Theories of learning.
- Theories of normal and abnormal physical, cognitive and emotional human development.
- The nature of acquired and congenital disabilities.

Finally, in order to run a successful therapeutic riding program, the student needs education in:
- Business management, including nonprofit issues.
- Computer skills.
- Basic bookkeeping/accounting.
- Public relations, marketing and fund raising.

The obvious place to look for such an education is a college or university that offers a strong degree program in the field of equine studies.

IDENTIFYING AN APPROPRIATE EQUINE STUDIES PROGRAM

A strong equine studies department is built on several factors:
- A broad-based equine curriculum that can cater to a variety of career goals. This might include:
  Science-based courses in equine anatomy, physiology, nutrition and performance.
  Stable management, including care of sick and injured horses and management of lameness.
  Theory of instruction.
  Theory of training, including dealing with problem horses and conditioning for various needs.
  Equine business management.
  Equine-related legal and insurance issues.
- A liberal arts curriculum which gives students and their parents the feeling that the equine degree is underpinned by a strong all-around education.

---

[4]From this point on, "college" will refer equally to "university."
[5]Martha Barbone in The Horse of Delaware Valley, p. 7, May 1997

- A barn full of reasonably sound, sensible "schoolmaster" horses at a variety of levels to match the range of riding skills represented by the students.
- A faculty consisting of people with a variety of backgrounds and skills to match the curricular needs. For example:

   Ability to instruct all levels of riders in the disciplines offered in the catalog (hunt seat, dressage, combined training, western riding, etc.)

   Academic qualifications to teach the necessary science, business, equine management, liberal arts and theory classes called for by the curriculum.

   Experience managing a barn and ability to maintain the level of school horses' training.

   Experience coaching riders for competition if that is a goal of the program.
- Access to internships which can expose the student to the "real world" of equestrian job opportunities.
- A list of elective courses that allows students to study specific areas of interest. For example: breeding and reproduction, judging, therapeutic riding instruction, facility design, etc.
- A comprehensive instructor-training program that exposes would-be instructors to various methods of teaching, and educates them in how to make lesson plans, assess progress and set appropriate goals for each pupil.

COMPONENTS OF A THERAPEUTIC RIDING CURRICULUM

Faculty Credentials

Any person, who teaches therapeutic riding courses, should have attained NARHA certification at the Advanced or Master level.

Curriculum Design

A comprehensive therapeutic riding curriculum will emphasize the following:

- Understanding of disabling conditions
- Adapting the teaching of riding skills for various populations
- Assessing horses' gaits, temperaments, way of going for individual riders
- The basics of how to be part of a hippotherapy team and the handling techniques required
- Selection and training of the horse used for hippotherapy
- Creating and maintaining a viable therapeutic riding program

Prerequisites

As discussed earlier, a number of related courses in other academic disciplines are necessary to lay the groundwork for studying therapeutic riding; for example: human development, psychology, education and business. These courses should be readily available to the student wishing to specialize in therapeutic riding.

PRACTICUM REQUIREMENTS AND CERTIFICATION BY NARHA

Students, who are serious about earning NARHA certification, will have to take a teaching practicum or internship at an accredited NARHA member center. Some colleges have their own therapeutic riding center; others rely on centers in the vicinity. Each college has its own requirements/agreements for practicums or internships in terms of supervision, course requirements, grades awarded, etc. Ideally, this experience will be rewarded with a certain number of credit hours toward the bachelor's degree.

For NARHA certification at the Registered Instructor level, applicants must complete 25 hours of teaching. This usually translates into a two-semester teaching commitment, since the student needs to develop his or her individual teaching style and learn how to integrate his or her academic learning with the hands-on situation of instructing riders with disabilities. If hippotherapy is being performed, the student instructor should also work with the therapist at least one hour per week.

As with all college choices, you should plan a visit, preferably when classes are in session. Try to schedule your visit to coincide with activities at the local therapeutic riding program so that you can visit there as well, or at least talk to someone on the phone about their involvement with the college.

Look carefully at the course catalog to understand the various core requirements and how they interact with the therapeutic riding course requirements. Consider whether you are looking for a four-year degree in therapeutic riding or an equine study degree with a concentration in therapeutic riding. Or, are you interested in a degree in the education, psychology or business departments with a minor in equine studies and therapeutic riding? If your goal is to achieve NARHA instructor certification, seek a program that will prepare you for it.

CONCLUSION

Acquiring a degree has been shown to have a profound influence on a person's future income level. Given the realities that young people have to face nowadays, there is an imperative to prepare for more than one career path through a diversified college degree program. In response to the uncertainties of their future careers, **students** are increasingly becoming aware of the need to acquire a variety of skills that will give them increased flexibility to find rewarding work. To train people to go into "the horse business," **colleges** are offering a smorgasbord of courses from accounting to equine nutrition, from marketing to breeding.

The graduate from an equine study program with therapeutic riding instruction as a concentration will be firmly grounded in the skills necessary to teach both able-bodied students and those with disabilities. He or she can join any NARHA program as a Certified Instructor. He or she will be ready to continue the lifelong learning that all of us in the profession joyfully undertook when we decided to add therapeutic riding to our lives. And, should the student decide to make therapeutic riding an adjunct to another career, he or she will have the necessary general educational background to make a success of both.

Building on the work of the pioneers in the field, today's college-educated therapeutic riding instructors will be well prepared as they develop their instructing skills. The ultimate beneficiaries, of course, will be the riders with disabilities who learn from the new generation of instructors.

Last but not least, another new career path is being created: that of "Professor of Therapeutic Riding Instruction." This will involve the development of master's degree options, which are already being considered seriously in a few institutions. This trend, in its turn, will lead to more reliable research being undertaken to assess the physical, cognitive, psychological and social benefits of therapeutic riding as the profession takes its place in the academic spectrum as a legitimate field of study.

"The degree that includes training and education as a therapeutic riding instructor opens the door to one of the most fulfilling careers that exists in the equestrian world."

Octavia J. Brown
USA

COMPETITION ASSOCIATION OF NARHA - CAN

Sandra L. Rafferty, MA, OTR

The Competition Association of NARHA - CAN was founded in 1996 as a section of NARHA. CAN has its own board of directors and bylaws. It operates within NARHA guidelines and standards.

CAN's MISSION STATEMENT:
To promote standards, education, training, competition, representation among riders, instructors, judges, coaches and other interested in competition for those with disabilities.

CAN's OBJECTIVES:

❑ To promote standards and guidelines for riders with disabilities in accordance with the standards set by the American Horse Show Association.

❑ To promote communication, education and training for judges, riding instructors, trainers, coaches, riders and those interested in competition for riders with disabilities.

❑ To advocate access to competition for equestrians with disabilities.

❑ To actively encourage competition and help establish competitions in the eleven NARHA regions.

❑ To establish NARHA as a leading authority in competition for those with disabilities by working with other appropriate organization - United States Cerebral Palsy Athletic Association and The Special Olympics to:
     a. help set qualifying standards for competitions,
     b. help select riders for international competition,
     c. represent the United States at international competition.

Sandra L. Rafferty
USA

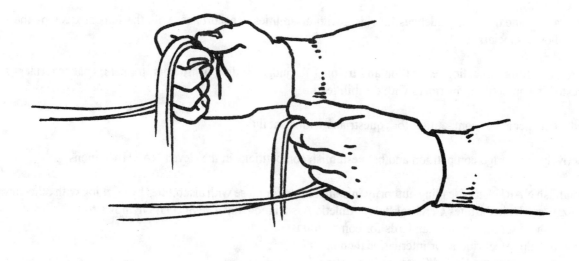

CHAPTER 3
PHILOSOPHICAL CONSIDERATIONS

Webster gives a definition of the word philosophical as "a particular system of principles for the conduct of life, a study of human morals, character, behavior and the original love of wisdom or knowledge. Chapter 3 contains a collection of articles by the authors who are presenting original insights that are of particular interest to those in the field of therapeutic riding. All are unique in their focus. They certainly present original wisdom and knowledge that will be of value to the field.

Editor

INDIVIDUALS WITH DISABILITIES AS A DISTINCT CULTURAL GROUP: A CALL FOR CULTURAL COMPETENCE IN THERAPEUTIC RIDING.

Michael E. Kaufmann and Evelyn Refosco

Authors Introductory Note: We would like to formally recognize the tremendous growth in leadership and competency of the work being done in therapeutic horseback riding by individuals and organizations throughout the world. The intent of the following article is not to place blame or overlook major accomplishments. By identifying and highlighting significant areas of weakness, we seek to challenge and animate the industry toward continued development, education and excellence.

It has been estimated that there are 54 million individuals with disabilities in the United States. While there is great diversity within this number, Americans with disabilities have emerged with cultural, political and social agendas that define their shared experience. Similar to African Americans, Asian Americans, American Senior Citizens and Gay and Lesbian Americans, the disabled population is defining itself as a distinct cultural group within the greater patchwork of the American experience.

Cultural values are fluid and constantly evolve and change. Therefore, no cultural group can be rigidly stereotyped as to behaviors, attitudes or customs. Although there can be commonalities of beliefs or customs in certain groups, individual members will always represent considerable variation. Cultural competence cannot rely on a simplistic and static set of rules that dictate policy or behavior toward a cultural group. For example: It would be deplorable if an organization, in an attempt to become culturally competent, fell into a pattern of treating all sight impaired individuals in a certain way based on one or two stereotypes (i.e., All sight impaired individuals read braille and use guide dogs). This prejudicial approach does not allow for individual traits to be appreciated. Inclusion of viewpoints from various cultural perspectives, sensitivity and education are key to the development of cultural competence. It is an approach that acknowledges diversity and is inclusive of diverse views and interests.

While there is great diversity among those with disabilities in terms of ethnicity, gender, age, socioeconomic background and type and extent of ability, there are specific issues that impact all members of this diverse group. Traditional patterns of relating to people with disabilities in a negative fashion are deeply ingrained. Discriminatory practices in the work place, unfair treatment of individuals with disabilities, fear of the disabled and intentional or casual insensitivity toward this group is well known to those who experience this type of treatment. Pity is an emotion frequently directed toward that group as is the relatively new stereotype of the over achieving individual with a disability who performs on the "superhuman" level. It can be frustrating to live in a world that subtly or blatantly judges one's character by the presence of a wheelchair, a prosthesis or a cognitive impairment. The reality of coping and living with these stressful outside pressures, in addition to the actual disability, is largely unknown to outsiders.

A new relationship needs to emerge in how the currently able bodied relate to Americans with disabilities. In the work place, at home, in the political arena and in every aspect of society, Americans with disabilities are emerging as a vibrant, active and vocal presence. Where individuals with disabilities once were shunned, hidden and ignored, political activism is creating a new climate where a person is acknowledged for his or her uniqueness and abilities and not for physical or psychological limitations.

The Americans with Disabilities Act has been, perhaps, the greatest leap forward in an effort to acknowledge and ensure the rights and expectations of the disabled population. The basic concept is simple: Americans with disabilities merit admission to all environments accessible to the currently able bodied. Individuals should be judged on ability and skill in the work place, and every other walk of life, and be afforded the same basic rights as any other citizen. When accommodations such as ramps or specialized equipment can facilitate participation of the disabled population, then such accommodations must be provided by law.

While the United States is now a leader in the legislative implementation and application of the ADA, there still is a great need for improvement in how individuals with disabilities are treated in the work place and in every day, social situations. A greater level of cultural competence on part of the currently able bodied is evolving. Although individuals with disabilities are leading the battle to redefine their role in society, too often their experience is still defined by the able bodied.

The field of therapeutic riding has a unique role in that it provides services to individuals with disability of all ages in various environments. While equine sport therapy and recreation are the goals of therapeutic horseback riding, a concurrent obligation of such agencies should be to approach individuals with disabilities with the highest level of cultural competence. In order to accomplish this, therapeutic riding organizations, their administrations, staff and volunteers must be aware and trained in the concept of cultural competence as it relates to Americans with disabilities. This proficiency extends far beyond a cognitive familiarity with the terminology and symptoms of disabilities and requires more subtle understanding of the psychosocial reality of living with a disability. Once developed, such awareness must be translated into actions to further integrate Americans with disabilities into the general fabric of society. Above all, the perspective of Americans with disabilities must be solicited by the field of therapeutic riding so that the targeted population has vocal participation in creating programs, services and treatment plans. A culturally competent response is indispensable in all facets of therapeutic riding.

WHAT IS CULTURAL COMPETENCE?
Cultural competence is a set of congruent behaviors, attitudes and policies that come together in a system, agency, or between professionals and enables that system, agency or those professionals to work effectively in cross-cultural situations. The word "culture" is used because it implies the integrated pattern of human behavior that includes thoughts, communications, actions, customs, beliefs, values and institutions of a racial, ethnic, religious or a social group. The word competence is used because it implies having the capacity to function effectively. A culturally competent system of care acknowledges and incorporates - at all levels - the importance of culture, the assessment of cross-cultural relations, vigilance toward the dynamics that result from cultural differences, the expansion of cultural knowledge and the adaptation of services to meet culturally-unique needs. (Cross, Bazron, Dennis, Isaacs, 1989)

CULTURAL COMPETENCY IN THE THERAPEUTIC RIDING CENTER:
While therapeutic riding personnel may focus their energy on teaching riding, providing hippotherapy or equine facilitated mental health, the clients of their agencies are people with disabilities in all their diversity. Every aspect of therapeutic riding begins with an effective and holistic approach to that diverse public. Many therapists, riding instructors and therapeutic riding center operators are compassionate and caring individuals who enter this field for altruistic reasons. The large majority of the "practitioners" are currently able bodied, while most of the "recipients" of therapeutic riding intervention are individuals with disabilities. No studies have been conducted and published to assess the cultural competence among therapeutic riding providers. Based on anecdotal evidence, it can be asserted that most therapeutic riding center personnel have an incomplete awareness of the profound cultural issues that have a direct impact on the clients/riders with whom they work with. Organizationally too, many procedures and policies may not fully meet the needs and expectations of the clients/riders with disabilities who are the target

group of therapeutic riding. For example: How knowledgeable are therapeutic riding instructors about the issues of aging for people with various disabilities? Or how cognizant are most physical therapists with the psychological development of adolescents with Down Syndrome? Yet, these issues can be very relevant when designing treatment plans for individuals or deciding on the composition of a class. Topics like these have been explored by various professionals and information has been published. For example: Courses in issues of aging are offered in many areas for people with disabilities (and their families.) A therapeutic riding center merely needs to tap the community resources that address these concerns and infuse this information into its work and staff training.

Based on the experience of several adult riders with disabilities, it could be asserted that most therapeutic riding centers in the United States fall between cultural blindness and cultural pre competence. The culturally blind center fosters the belief that color or culture makes no difference and that all people are the same and share a common mission when it comes to experience, customs and outlook on life. This leads to a belief that the world-view of a dominant able-bodied culture is universal. It denies the unique perspective and experience of people whose lives are different. Internally, such a center often has low level or no participation by people with disabilities in its policy making or among its staff. Even though there may be a heightened sensitivity to the needs of individuals with disabilities that group (as a culture) often is not included in basic decision making and policy setting. In this situation, the rider or staff member with a disability is simply treated as "being just like everyone else." This denies the person with a disability his or her own unique experience, the positive and negative attributes that make daily life with a disability different. Glossing over this difference, and even denying it, cheats the individual with a disability out of a significant aspect of his or her life.

Culturally pre competent therapeutic riding centers maintain that issues of culture are relevant both internally and also, in terms of community outreach. These agencies realize that there are significant differences between various cultural groups and also between individuals with disabilities in their approaches to every aspect of life. At this stage, agencies seek staff diversity, attempt to comply with the ADA and address the needs of a diverse clientele. Having a board member with multiple sclerosis, a therapeutic riding instructor who, is recovering from a traumatic injury or maintaining a committee of riders with disabilities to serve as program advisors are positive steps toward including relevant perspectives in program design and delivery.

Deplorably, some therapeutic riding centers have settled into cultural incapacity. These agencies lack diversity in their staff and express the condescending and paternalistic belief that "we" are here to help "those people." Policies and programs within this type of agency may be well intentioned but rarely serves the needs of the riders fully and have been developed based on the opinions of the organization leadership. In many riding centers, it is common for riding instructors to plan lessons for adult riders mostly based on what is recommended for a specific disability rather than working with individual riders to develop a distinctive program that is specifically tailored to that individual. Often individuals with disabilities, especially adults, feel excluded, uncomfortable and even insulted by this kind of treatment. The driving forces behind programs like this often are "charity, compassion and sympathy for the disabled." Such sentiments create an "us" helping "them" climate, and can be extremely upsetting and repulsive to individuals with disabilities.

APPLYING THE CONCEPTS:
Compelling reasons for a call for cultural competence in the field of therapeutic riding.

1. a) Therapeutic riding centers, their staff and programs, must reflect and meet the needs of the community they serve. Negative messages are sent when no individuals with disabilities are present among the staff, volunteers, on the board, and no effort is made to include riders with disabilities to help create the program. The capacity to be inclusive and reach out to a wider clientele dramatically rises when a staff and board reflect the diversity of a community at every level. Riding centers that seek to include individuals with disabilities in program development and operation create vibrant programs that reflect the diversity of its riders. It can be challenging to be inclusive in a riding center that primarily serve

children with disabilities or adults with Down Syndrome, yet one, nevertheless, can be as inclusive as possible to best serve this group. Outside expertise from medical experts, psychologists and also from family members of those with various conditions, can increase responsiveness and sensitivity to these groups.

1.b) Although staff and rider diversity is important, care must be taken to actually incorporate the views and suggestions in of both staff and rider into practice. Some therapeutic riding centers that have staff diversity and that try to include the viewpoints of colleagues/riders with disabilities, but receive staff/rider complaints of discontent due to the perception (or reality) that their views are not treated in an equitable fashion as those of other staff. Especially those independent adult riders that have stated they "have no place" in the rigid structure of a therapeutic riding center. For example, in an attempt to have a safe program, many therapeutic riding centers do not allow the use of any creative adaptive equipment (such as velcro in saddles or special restraints to assist riders with limited balance in staying in place on the horse.) While safety and liability are a significant concern for a riding center, adult independent riders want to decide for themselves if a piece of equipment works for them. A working compromise would be to form a task force consisting of adult riders, therapists and center operators to create a flexible policy and process that make room for the need for special adaptive equipment. It is very important for a riding center to be responsive to these adult riders who have very specific and individual goals and objectives for their riding regimen. Responsiveness and flexibility by centers to input from populations served will facilitate consumer satisfaction and program delivery.

2. Training in cultural competence can make a therapeutic riding center more effective in its work. Cultural competence helps raise the standards of work performance and service delivery. A culturally competent therapeutic riding center is ready to meet the demands a diverse public during the riding lesson, in fund-rasing, community relations or in the creation of policy. Simultaneously, such an organization can advocate for the activity of therapeutic riding while also modeling inclusiveness. Because, too often, others try to define people with disabilities in language, law and custom, it is vital that a therapeutic riding center stays updated and attuned to that population. Language itself can be a starting point. What terms are considered proper and which are not? The words "handicapped" and "retarded" have been eliminated from currently acceptable terminology. Even the difference between "a disabled woman" and "a woman with a disability" have significant meaning and trigger various responses among people with disabilities. Similarly, not all will have the same responses to language. Anyone designing brochures for a program or selecting a name for a riding center must be sensitive to these trends and seek the proper assistance when creating such materials. "Happy Hollow Handicapped Riders," while a descriptive name for a therapeutic riding center, should not be an acceptable choice today. Even organizations that are burdened by a name that includes outdated terminology must be willing to change. Such considerations go beyond mere political correctness and try to reflect the actual experience of individuals with disabilities.

SPECIFIC AREAS OF FOCUS:

1. The field of therapeutic riding currently is not culturally competent on various levels, largely because the majority of administrators and staff members are white and able bodied. There is a notable lack of ethnic diversity of people with disabilities within the ranks of staff, volunteers and clients/riders. Since Americans with disabilities are a significant minority with members from all ethnic groups, therapeutic riding ought to be made available to an ethnically diverse cross section of Americans with disabilities. An exploration of why ethnic diversity is lacking within therapeutic riding is needed. Further investigation is warranted to discover why so few individuals with disabilities are in leadership positions within the therapeutic riding field? Since such under representation often is systemic and unintentional, old procedures and patterns may need to be shattered. An example of an ingrained system that results in exclusionary practices, is the nominating committee of a therapeutic riding center board of directors, who consistently creates a board slate of people, who replicate the ethnic/social make-up of the current group. A common, and inadequate, defense is the claim that the group "tried" to find diverse representatives, but couldn't "find" any.

2. a)   Many therapeutic riding centers in the United States provide services primarily to children. Typically, the average age ranges between seven and fifteen. There is significant attrition among riders as they mature, and adults are a small proportion of riders in many centers. According to an informal survey, some therapeutic riding centers even have an age limit after which riders no longer are accepted. Why do many children who participate in therapeutic riding discontinue this activity as they mature even if the possibility to continue exists? And, why are there not more adult riders in many therapeutic riding centers that provide services to this age group? One could speculate that many therapeutic riding centers focus on providing services for children with disabilities because it is easier. These clients/riders are still under the care of their (usually) able bodied parents or care givers and have not yet developed a full sense of the cultural realities of living with a disability. Children, generally, do not question policies and procedures and are modest in their demands. Further research and exploration is needed to substantiate such a claim.

2.b)   However, even a therapeutic riding center that intentionally limits its services to children, can provide a valuable service by fostering a climate of cultural awareness that supports and strengthens the personality development of children with disabilities. An intentional policy to support the personality development of children with disabilities may be as valuable as equine sport, therapy or recreation. Mentoring programs that bring together adults and children with disabilities must be developed, input from adults with disabilities in program improvement sought and training of staff and volunteers in cultural competence must become the norm. Depending on ability, the children themselves can participate in creating lessons, therapeutic exercises or other activities. By valuing group decision making, independent thinking and encouraging feedback from children with disabilities (when appropriate), lifelong values and living skills can be casually modeled at an early age.

3.   How effectively do the staff and volunteers relate to individuals with disabilities as a distinct cultural group? While most therapeutic riding centers intend to provide safe and pleasurable recreational or therapeutic activities to riders with disabilities, there are fluctuating levels in proficiency among their administrators, staffs and volunteers. The relationship between riding center representatives and riders often is very authoritarian. Adult riders with disabilities, in particular, report they are treated like children and denied even basic autonomy, even though they are often older and more accomplished than the staff. Since teens and adults with disabilities might already be sensitized to intolerance and bigotry, it may not take many negative experiences at a riding center for them to withdraw from therapeutic riding. One adult rider with a visual impairment withdrew from his lessons because his instructor refused to let him take even the most basic risk. He felt that his instructor was so afraid of him getting hurt that she denied him the challenges he desired in his riding. The attrition and absence of large numbers of adults in therapeutic riding in itself are a major justification for the necessity of cultural competence.

4.   How effectively are the needs and aspirations of individuals with disabilities acknowledged and integrated into policy setting and program development? Often ignorance and organizational inflexibility fail to include the views and experiences of the population that is served by a therapeutic riding center. For example: One adult rider wanted to learn more about horse care and barn management, yet there never was enough time available for her to have time in the stable after her lesson. The instructors barely let her pet her horse upon dismounting and the rider soon realized that the center staff had no time or interest in accommodating her. Other adult riders have experienced the same hesitancy on part of center operators to let them get more involved in horse care. Few centers currently have adults with disabilities on their boards or hold focus groups among their riders to gauge responses regarding policies. If a few adult riders want to learn about horse care, then why can't such activities be conducted in a safe and structured fashion? More input from adults with disabilities would provide timely feedback to a riding center and allow for refined services based on the recommendations of the riders.

5.   In order to appraise the current state of cultural competence within a therapeutic riding center, regional, state, national and international organizations might conduct a cultural self-assessment. This process would examine all policies, services, written materials and procedures for inclusiveness according to the Americans with Disabilities Act. This Federal law outlines the legal obligations for inclusive policies and practices. However, as a model, a therapeutic riding center should exceed the minimum requirements set by the ADA. Since this is a relatively new goal for many therapeutic riding organizations, assistance may have to be solicited from related fields that have undergone such a process. Services, procedures and approaches can be revised as necessary. Thorough consideration of culturally and ethnically diverse individuals with disabilities will yield new answers and prompt a heightened level of professionalism.

CONCLUSION:

It has been projected by demographers that the American society of the next millennium will be shaped by an increase in cultural diversity through immigration and population shifts of existing minorities. The aging of America and a current rise in births will undoubtedly increase the ranks of Americans with disabilities. This shift of an up to now, able-bodied mainstream population will impact all areas of daily life. It will significantly influence language, culture, commerce, education, law enforcement, and politics. Culturally competent service delivery to people with disabilities will become ever more relevant to educators, architects, engineers, law makers, commerce and society as a whole.

The field of therapeutic riding can provide leadership in recognizing and supporting individuals with disabilities as a unique cultural group within the fabric of a diverse society. By becoming more attuned to people with disabilities as individuals within a larger cultural group, tremendous growth, expansion and adaptation of current services can be anticipated in therapeutic riding.

T. Cross, B. Baron, K. Dennis, M. Isaac (1989) "Towards A Culturally Competent System of Care: A Monograph on Effective Services for Minority Children Who Are Severely Emotionally Disturbed."
Can be ordered from: Georgetown University Child Development Center, 3800 Reservoir Road N.W., Washington, DC 2007 (202) 687- 8635

Michael E. Kaufmann and Evelyn Refosco
USA

The Cultural Competency Continuum:

Several stages of "cultural competence" have been identified. These levels of awareness hold true for organizations, such as a therapeutic riding center, yet also have relevance to gage the level of cultural competence of an individual.

Cultural Destructiveness: The negative end of the continuum. The dehumanization and intentional destruction of a culture. For example: Nazi genocide of individuals with disabilities.

Cultural Incapacity: A biased approach to cultural communities, based on fear and ignorance. This approach fosters discrimination in hiring practices and devalues other, non-mainstream cultures. For example: Denying employment to individuals with disabilities based on prejudice.

Cultural Blindness: The belief that culture and ethnicity do not matter, that everyone is the same. This well intentioned approach leads to the belief that everyone thinks, acts, and believes the same. Example: An agency that claims to be welcoming of the disabled, but does not have any individuals with disabilities on their staff or board.

Cultural Pre-Competence: This term implies movement toward integrating cultural issues. Questions are asked on how better to serve a multi-cultural clientele. Although this level can lead to a false sense of accomplishment and "tokenism", it is the start of cultural competence. Example: Having one or more individuals with disabilities on the staff or board.

Cultural Competence: The stage of viewing minority groups as distinctly different yet equal. Agencies seek staff diversity to meet the needs of a multi-cultural world. Cross-cultural situations are comfortable both philosophically and in practice. Example: A therapeutic riding center that has a founder with a disability, maintains a diverse board, as well as committees of riders to help develop policies.

Cultural Proficiency: The most positive end of the scale. Culture is held in high esteem. Agencies hire a multi-cultural staff proficient in culturally competent practices. Cultural competence is valued in every aspect of policy and practice. All levels of an agency, individual, administration, board, policy makers and clients participate in the process. Example: The Americans with Disability Act Adapted from Cross, Baron, Dennis and Isaac (1989) Toward a Culturally Competent System of Care

FIGURE 1.

TREATING PEOPLE "G1NGER"LY

Joanne Henry Moses, PhD

While horses have been assisting physically challenged people in therapeutic riding programs in the United States and in Europe for about thirty years, they have only recently begun to help those suffering from often hidden, but very real, temporary and permanent psychiatric problems. Tucson Animal Assisted Psychotherapy Association has worked exclusively in mental health and personal growth since 1990. The horse acts as an integral member of the treatment team. Perhaps the easiest way to explain the process is to let one of the horses tell her story.

Although my real name is DSK Bakira, you will probably call me Ginger. That's what Lobmanns called me during my brief stay with them. Their two little girls couldn't handle my registered name, so they called me Ginger. Thus, I was Ginger to Joanne until, after three years of research, she cleared my papers through the Arabian Horse Registry and discovered the beautiful name I'd been given at birth.

I had a good start in life with the Gurrs when I was born on February 27, 1982. They bred me and raised me until I was a little more then three. But they couldn't afford to keep me. With the best of intentions, they donated me to the Arizona Boy's Ranch. But I was barely green broke and they didn't know what to do with me. When Mr. Lohmann bought a reliable old gelding from them for his two daughters, officials at the ranch offered me as part of the deal.

Since I'm a registered Arabian (#0248590), Mr. Lohmann thought I'd bring a good price and agreed to take me. However he was much too large to ride me himself and his daughters were far too young and inexperienced. So he asked a friend, Gay, to keep me exercised for him. It was hard for me going from a home where I was very much loved, to being an anonymous horse in a herd, to being an investment.

One morning after Gay had worked me on the ground, I was standing beside Joanne as she was untacking Peach. I liked her energy. I blew in her ear and sent her the wish, "I want to be your horse." I could see how much she loved Peach, and I felt sure she would love me, too. I knew I could win her heart. She blew back and went on brushing Peach. I had to make my point. I put my head on her shoulder, pressed, and blew harder. She blew back, this time putting her arm around my nose and talking tenderly to me.

Gay sized up the situation. "Joanne, this is your kind of horse. She's what you need for the program you're planning. You really ought to buy her." Joanne asked it I were for sale and for how much. Gay strategized wisely. "Well, the owner is asking $5,000, but I think he'd let her go for a lot less. Offer $500 about the time he has to pay her board again."

Joanne tried me out right then and there. I knew she was scared but she got on anyway. I did my best to remember all I knew and responded instantaneously to her slightest cue. She was satisfied and I was hopeful. She made an offer to Mr. Lohmann the next day, but he promptly refused. She was hesitant, anyway, and made her offer contingently on being able to lease space at the Jewish Community Center. She left Mr. Lohmann with the thought that should he reconsider and should she get the JCC stable, her offer was still good.

When it came time to pay board again, Mr. Lohmann called her and accepted the offer. However, he transferred title under the terms, "For due consideration and $1.00" because he felt I was too valuable to have anything on record that I was sold for such a low price. He did have some sense of my real worth. But for Joanne, even that price was a sacrifice.

When we moved to JCC, I joined Peach and Wacin in a large pasture. I guess I just was not prepared for Wacin. Joanne's first love among the horses, she held the position in the herd that I wanted. But Joanne and Wacin had already been together for two years and had been through experiences that had bonded them like glue. I was hurt. I was angry. So, I challenged Wacin at every turn. Although we both bore the scars, I got the worst of it by far.

Joanne quickly realized that I wanted to be her only special horse. "I can't give you that," she lamented. "Wacin holds that place in my heart. But I'll look for someone who will appreciate you and love you the way you deserved to be loved." She kept me confined to a stall most of the time to keep me safe, although it broke her heart to do so.

Then Jack came into my life. All along, Joanne was thinking about her therapeutic riding program and experimenting with how it would work. Often, she would invite people to ride with her to get an idea of how they would react to the horse and how the horse might help them. One day, Yolanda, a former day patient at the psychiatric hospital, phoned her. "Remember how you used to take us on field trips out to your horses? Well, I got so much strength from that! And now I am facing a crisis, and I need to recapture that strength --- Jack (her husband who had been sentenced to eighteen months in prison for abusing her and the children) is being paroled. I just want to go out and stand by the horses and be with them."

Several times, Joanne ran into Yolanda at the pasture. "As long as you are here, would you like to ride with me?" she invited. Yolanda and Joanne became Saturday morning riding companions. One day, Yolanda confided, I'm really anxious. Jack is coming home on Wednesday." Without even thinking it through, Joanne suggested, " Do you think he'd like to ride with us next Saturday?"

I was still quite green and full of myself. But Jack had plenty of self-confidence when it came to riding. He sheepishly came along that next Saturday morning in 1988. We got along great! He wasn't at all afraid and he liked my energy. When Joanne realized how much unstructured time was a problem for him, she suggested that he ride me whenever he wanted. That proved to be a great outlet for both of us. We both let off stream loping through the hills. He could experience his deep sensitivity and put it to positive use in reading my needs. I allowed him to be tender and soft without compromising his need to control.

"Besides riding Ginger, work with the babies!" she said. TaWacin was a little over a year old and Waida was eight months. Jack began training them with ground work in addition to riding me daily. Meanwhile, Joanne wanted me be that one special horse in someone's life, and kept reassuring me that she would somehow find just the right person who would love me the way I deserved to be loved and would appreciate my potential. I knew Jack wanted me but he couldn't afford me.

Just before Christmas, Yolanda called Joanne. "I can't thank you enough for what's happened to our family over these past months. Before he went to prison, Jack never touched the children except to hit them. But since he has been working with your babies, he's learned to handle authority and play at the same time. Now, he gets down on the floor and tussles with the boys. They are spontaneously hugging and kissing him goodnight. And, he's responding. He could never do that before! ... I know you want to sell Ginger. But, if she's still there when Jack's through school and has a job, he'd like to buy her."

"If he wants her, I'll give her to him as soon as he can afford to support her!" Joanne was elated! She saw the warmth between Jack and me, and it was just the kind of relationship she wanted for me to enjoy. So she talked to me often about my future when I would be someone's only, special and cherished horse. While I was fond of Jack, she was still the owner I'd chosen.

By the time Jack was well enough established to support his family, he was really too busy to have much time for me. When Joanne suggested transferring my papers to him, he observed, "Ginger seems really happy now and works so well with the clients. You need her in your program. Let's leave it the way it is. I know I can ride her any time."

By mid-1990, Joanna had incorporated TAAPA (Tucson Animal Assisted Psychotherapy Association) and immediately started working on its nonprofit status. As she planned for taking clients once her insurance was in place, she began bringing out more people to study the equestrian psychotherapy process more fully. By the time patients began coming in 1991, I grasped the special role she had envisioned for me. Just as Jack needed me in order to heal through a process that respected his dignity and independence and minimized talking, many other people came with similar needs. Then, I suddenly realized just how much Joanne needed me. I could be protective, reliable and extremely psychic. While I couldn't play athletic process as often as I might like, I could give these people my heart and soul in an intensely therapeutic encounter.

Once I had grasped the vision and my job description within it, my attitude changes completely. I no longer needed to challenge Wacin. While Wacin has a special gift for this program, what I bring to it is unique. Wacin takes care of patients because Joanne wants her to. Those long, quiet hours with Jack taught me to feel my riders, sense their needs and act accordingly. Sometimes, I take care of them, but often I challenge, encourage or invite them to play.

Let me tell you about some of my riders. I had Sam the longest. He suffered from PTSD (post-traumatic stress disorder). Most of the time he dissociated. Joanne tried to get him to stay in the here and now by experiencing his body. I tried with all my might to help him. I responded clearly to his most obscure signal. (Believe me, I won't do that for many riders! But, Sam was special to me.) Once a week she took him out on a trail and tried to get him to feel his five senses.

On a trail, Joanne discovered that even when he was on my back and out in the beauty of nature, Sam could not perceive his surroundings. "What do you see on your right?" she inquired, as we passed a stand of brilliantly colored blooming cholla."A gray wall," he responded flatly. She then began directing his attention to flowers, animals, mountain vistas. He never responded to the overwhelming beauty around him so trapped was he in his sealed world of despair. And, that world was hopelessly gray. Working in the arena one day, Joanna directed him to turn left at the green jumps. When he could not do so, he finally admitted that he could no longer distinguish color. Yet, he had no history of color blindness.

In arena work, Joanne fought the dissociation with body work to help him become aware of sensation. He barely breathed enough to stay alive. With vaulting exercise, she and the riding instructor were able to bring his breath as deep as mid-chest. He never achieved full, diaphragmatic breathing. With these exercises going on while I was moving, I stepped ever so cautiously. When he went the least bit off balance, I carefully adjusted myself to right him in the saddle.

I was still working with Sam when my son, Chonteh, was born. While the birth was not difficult, I retained the placenta and was very ill when he came for his appointment early the next morning. The veterinarian had already been called and was on his way. I needed to be walked. That morning, Sam was more aware of my need then he had ever been before. He volunteered to walk me around the arena until the vet came. I can still see him leading me with Chonteh frolicking at my side.

Joanne was so touched by his gentleness and concern that she invited him to choose my baby's name from a list that she was considering. She always names the foals in Sioux to remind herself and her riders of the Native Americans' profound reverence for life and for the place of every species in nature's scheme of things. The strange sounding names lead people to ask if they mean something special. Chonteh, the name chosen for my son, means heart, valor, faithfulness.

Much as I would like to report that Sam got better that did not happen. But, for a time at least he bonded with me and seemed to take comfort in our relationship.

Milissa was another story. A troubled thirteen year old, she learned many lessons with my help. In the first session, I worked exceptionally hard with her. Joanne noticed that all though she kept purporting how much she loved horses, she showed me neither affection nor praise. After her first ride, Joanne reminded her to get some carrots from the tack room and give me a reward. "OK," she acknowledged, then got herself a snack from her backpack but forgot about rewarding me.

Praising me, giving me treats, and taking care of me became key components in Milissa's treatment plan. She was able to carry over her new behaviors to dealing with her family. As she lived through a turbulent period in her life, I became her consoler and confidante. She gained self-confidence, poise and the ability to cope as she learned to be in control of herself and me at the same time.

Sometimes she wanted to get ahead of herself and take on more of a risk than she could handle. Keeping her stimulated but safe challenged both the riding instructor and therapist. Insightful as she was, Milissa readily grasped the metaphor. She struggled with wanting to grow up too quickly, to take on experiences she wasn't yet mature enough to handle. She advanced step by step with me helping her to accept limits and guidance in other areas of her life.

Clare suffers from multiple personality disorder. When she was Clare, her core personality, she rode me. As Mary, a fearful and fragile little girl needing nurturing, she rod Wacin. And when she was George, a feisty nine year old boy, she chose Echo's Fire. Clare experienced the natural high induced by the motion of the horse and always felt better after she rode. But her depressions were frightful. Just being with me, stroking me, and brushing my name and tail comforted her.

As a rider, she reveled in the lightness of touch it takes to get me to respond. And when I love someone the way I love Clare, I react almost before the signal is given. Joanne always says I'm the most psychic of her horses. When I'm in tune with the rider, it's true I can almost read his or her thoughts and work hard to do so. Clare and I were almost magical together when we were "on." Of course, not every ride was like that. But, she almost always felt better after she rode. Most of the herd helped with her therapy, but I knew that I played a special role.

Cynthia represented the other end of the spectrum. Subtlety and gentleness were not her forte. She came to Joanne for grief counseling. A bright, articulate and highly educated professional, she engaged readily in talking therapy. Recognizing that this gift could delay the therapeutic process, Joanne suggested trying equestrian psychotherapy. Cynthia readily agreed. She had ridden for many years but had been injured thirty years previously in a jumping accident and had not ridden since. Getting back to riding in a safe and controlled environment appealed to her.

A harsh disciplinarian especially with herself, Cynthia allowed little room for pleasure. The way she groomed me reflected the intensity she thrust into every aspect of her life. Was I grateful when Joanne described what she observed and invited Cynthia to "work easily!" By surrendering her drive to groom me perfectly, quickly and with all her strength, she has to examine her belief pattern that demanded such severity. That examination took her far beyond her grief – back to an emotional abusive childhood and the feeling that she had to earn her right to exist. Her overwhelming sense of shame led her to feel personally responsible for the mistake and misfortunes of those she loved. So, undeserved guilt complicated her grief over her husband's death.

In tutoring Cynthia to being gentle with me, I taught her to be considerate with herself as well. She quickly learned to soothe both me and herself in the way she groomed. At first, her signals were sharp and harsh. By jumping into gaits and wresting the reins out of her hands, I quickly let her know that I would not tolerate sharp signals. Joanne and the riding instructor insisted that she find the lightest possible signals to get my response. She learned quickly, amazed at how light a touch could gain my enthusiastic cooperation. As far as I know, she now owns a horse again. And she continues to "lighten up."

No two people respond to me the same way, nor I to them. Yet I play an integral role in their therapy. Being a therapy horse makes unique demands on the equine psyche. I feel proud that not every horse can deal with this kind of work. I know how special I am, even without being told. I got so exhilarated when I can lift a patient out of depression just by my rhythmic movement. We horses absorb so much information through our bodies! Subtle changes in pressure, temperature, and energy radiate into my nerve endings. And, deep within my being, I mystically perceive the physical, mental, emotional, and spiritual integration my riders are achieving.

I participate in the therapeutic process at a profound level–so much so that I choose my riders carefully. We horses size up new clients instantaneously. When I like someone, I'm at the fence inviting them to pet me. When I don't, I quietly walk away and make myself scarce. I've even been known to flatten my ears and obviously turn my back on a few people. The rider and I need to "click" because we will share intimate moments and deep emotions. Being an animal, I can get by with being so blatant about my likes and dislikes.

But once I engage with a client, I'm with that person every moment we're together. If it's someone very needy, I'll take care of him or her. But if it's someone capable, I won't tolerate sloppiness. I demand his or her best. And in doing so, I help them feel proud of themselves and what they have accomplished. Being a therapy horse is a sacred trust. Somewhere deep within my being, I sense my role in somehow making the universe more whole by an interspecies process of restoring that wholeness.

THE "INTUITION" FACTOR IN THE EQUINE THERAPY.

Edith Gross

**"Only with the heart
is it possible to see with certainty;
that which is essential
is invisible to the eye".**
Antoine de Saint-Exupery

A LITTLE STORY...
SOME PERSONAL FEELINGS AND SENSITIVE INSIGHT ON THE THERAPY RIDING EXPERIENCE

Victor has arrived - he's six years old and suffers from cerebral palsy. Half walking, half dragging his legs, he's supported by the arms by his parents. His head and trunk arrive first than the rest of his body, because he wants to run, to move on, to play, he wants to ride...

Oh, my how can. I show him what riding is?! - to become one with the horse, dancing without moving yourself, harmony of both in one in rhythm and speed? His body - arms, trunk, legs - is stiff because he wants to do, to act

Up we go, Victor - I get on the horse with him, behind him, his pelvis fitting well between mine and the girth, his head and trunk slightly resting against me. Fine Victor - now we go, relax - let it go, let the horse lead you... I talk to him, I sing to him, I do the exercises for him - head to the left, to the right, forward, backwards...I bend his arms, his elbows, his wrists... Victor still has his hands in fists. Oh, how can he pet the horse with hands like that?!

We are walking along - one, two, three, four...I constantly correct his pelvis, his trunk and his head - straight, Victor, so that the rhythmic impulses can go up and reach your brain. I close my eyes and wait....there is an absolute calmness. What can I do? Oh, I really wish Victor can run, play, ride..... Suddenly I begin massaging him in the inside of his forearm. I take his fist and tighten strongly on the outside of the back of his hand; the fist is relaxing slowly and the hand begins to open. Well, finally...he will be able to pet the horse. I put his hand on the horse's neck, - feel, Victor, feel the softness of the hair, feel the warmth, feel the life vibrating under you!

Meanwhile, I massage his back, specially the lower back. I softly squeeze the sides of the spinal column - Victor feels very comfortable, his arms relaxed and hanging to the sides, then he turns around toward me, laughing - he's happy! He begins to feel that there is nothing to do, only sitting straight, allowing the horse to lead him... Shall we try a trot, Victor? - you and me together, slowly, with rhythm, very smoothly? I rest his head and trunk against my body - there's a little bit of fear - but it goes away, because there I am, behind him, protecting him - and Victor relaxes, and lets himself be led by the horse, adapting his pelvis to the movement...one, two...one, two. I start to vocalize the syllable "tchu" in a loud voice, following the rhythm of the horse - and Victor relaxes more and more, enjoying riding! At the end, now walking, I put his leg up; Victor pets the horse with his bare foot. I massage his toes and when they are docile, I can rotate the whole foot from his ankle. That's wonderful - Victor relaxed his spastic muscles - at the moment, there is no contraction, there is no defense....Victor gets off - now he can set his whole foot on the ground. He stands beside the horse, petting it and thanking it - rather straight, because he's learned - there is nothing to do, only sitting straight, allowing the horse to lead him..... **Victor started to ride!**

ANOTHER LITTLE STORY...

Arriving home, I am still thinking: how is it that he suddenly relaxed? What did I do? And how did I do it? My intellect is tormenting me and I begin to search in the books - Do-in, Acupuncture, Music Therapy..... I cannot find a satisfactory explanation. Many weeks later, a friend of mine lends me a book on Acupuncture, a very thorough account, and there it is: what I did was to massage the heart's meridian "Shaoyin of the hand" [6] - the indications for the majority of these points say: "Pain in elbows and arms, contraction of elbow and arm, contraction of the wrist." Almost euphoric, I keep on searching - what points are there in the back of the hand? - I find it: "point I.D.3 Houxi: indication - contraction of elbow, arms and fingers." My mind is clearing, my doubts disappear. Can it be possible that my intuition led me to apply what the Chinese already did 2,000 years ago?

The massages certainly helped to liberate the energetic channels (meridians), in which the energy gets stuck due to the high spasticity. What a relief for my intellect, to find a logical explanation! But I wonder: does the healing process always have to be logical, rationally grounded? What is more important in a therapy, including Equine Therapy - the method or the results?

Isn't it positive result that creates the method?

The two little stories demonstrate that the therapist's intuition can play a very important role in the therapeutic process. Undoubtedly, as a therapist, I need a system, a methodology as a framework to support my work and which yields parameters for the evaluation of the therapeutic process and its advances. But let's not forget that in every one of us there is an inherent intelligence, an internal healer full of wisdom, who indicates to us what to do and how, in just the right moment. We should not forget, either, that each patient is an individual being, with different physical and psychic needs, changing day by day.

Each therapeutic session is always a unique and very personal experience for both therapist and patient, and it is often the case that a fixed methodology cannot satisfy the needs of the latter. The internal receptivity to the physical and psychic need of the moment is a key factor to therapeutic success. Because of this, it is of utmost importance to develop the sensitive-intuitive capacities of the equine therapist, along with the practical and cognitive abilities.

In order to be able to transmit the enchantment of the act of riding to the patient and stimulate the patient's motivation for the therapy, the equine therapist must experience equitation sensorial, as something enjoyable, relaxing and harmonious. Or he or she must also be aware that this harmony is only attainable if the horse is well trained, moving with rhythm, suppleness, impulsion, straightness and submission.

The equine therapist must be able to feel his or her own muscle tensions and those of the horse in order to be able to correct them. The three physical and psychic bodies of the therapist-patient-horse establish and intimate connection during the therapy and experrence a mutual interdependence. Muscle tensions and body asymmetries of each one effect those of the others, affecting the whole therapeutic process. For this reason, the equine therapist needs enough experience in equitation (especially Dressage), and must know him/herself in depth. The therapist's body consciousness, must be highly developed, in order to detect his or her own tense and conflictive body parts and know how to correct them, so that he or she can correct those of the horse and the patient.

Developing body consciousness while riding, the therapist can reach an enormous amplification of his or her sensorial perception and of his or her intuitive faculties. The therapist's psychic sensibility will grow, and he or she will spontaneously begin to feel the conflictive body parts in him/herself, the horse and the patient. The therapist will also develop mental concentration and self-knowledge of his/ her personal physical and psychic expression. This sensori-perceptive capacity, will increase, which will in turn increase his or her riding ability and therapeutic sensibility.

---

[6] Fundamentos de Acupuntura y Moxibustion de China. Beijing, Republica China.

Thus, the therapist knows that the most significant thing for riding and for riding therapy is to be in a constant dynamic balance on the central point, legs in soft contact with the horse's ribs, knowing that the balance, body symmetry and state of relaxation of the patient and horse depend on his/her own! The therapist experiences the benefits of riding him/herself and these are valid also for every rider, being disabled or not:

1. The propagation of the rhythmic impulses of the horse upward to the top of the head, relaxing body segments that are tense and stimulating the respiratory and circulatory systems.
2. The three-dimensional pattern of the movement stimulating and relaxing the pelvic area, thus developing a better psycho-motor coordination.
3. The physical and psychic relaxation as a consequence of a centered seat in dynamic balance, harmonizing with the rhythm of the horse.

With time, the therapist realizes that:
1. The pelvic relaxation and stimulation are key factors during the therapy, with physical and psychic consequences for the patient.
2. The straightness of trunk and head are essential for a harmonious ride and for a correct motricity.
3. The horse reacts with submission and suppleness when the rider keeps his or her centered seat, in a dynamic relaxation, thus increasing the therapeutic effects.
4. Guiding the patient to a state of physical and psychic relaxation so he or she can experiment the same joy of riding and receive the physiological and psychological benefits of riding.

So, the equine therapist knows that what he or she has to teach the patient - is simply to relax and ride!

The sensitivity and body consciousness are not static factors in human beings, but are instead in constant development and expansion throughout life. It is for this reason that it is possible to stimulate their growth by means of different techniques and exercises.

The following sensori-motor exercises will help the rider to observe and feel him or herself, increasing his or her sensitive potential and expanding his consciousness. These exercises are carried out riding, first walking and then, after having developed more body consciousness and body control, can be experienced in trot and canter:
1. Riding without stirrups and longeing girth.
2. Riding while being longed with eyes closed.
3. Paying mental attention to different parts of the body, imagining a liquid that runs from the top of the head downward, concentrating itself in the lower abdomen.
4. Touching different parts of ones own body with the hand (top of the head, nape of the neck, shoulders, chest, shoulder blades, buttocks, etc.) and experience the body sensation that is caused by this and the consequences for the posture.
5. Imagining that the lower extremities and the trunk are growing like a plant, from the waist upward toward the sky and from the waist down rooting in the ground.
6. Performing the following neuromuscular exercises in slow motion, with closed eyes:
   a) lateral movements of the head
   b) shoulder movements, alternative, and simultaneously (going up and down close and open)
   c) bending and straightening the trunk and diaphragm
   d) rotating the trunk very slowly
   e) putting one hand on top of the head and let the arm fall *heavily*, first on the shoulder and then onward,
   f) open and close the hands very slowly

g) opening the legs to the maximum toward the sides (alternatively and simultaneously opening each leg)

h) moving the legs up slowly, alternatively and simultaneously each leg

i) letting the feet's tips fall downward

j) rotating each foot slowly toward the inside and the outside

7. Performing the gymnastic exercises that the therapist will demand from the patient, during the therapeutic session,
   experiencing them physically, psychically and sensorially.

8. Riding consciously with asymmetric postures.

9. Experiencing different types of breathing (abdominal, diaphragmal and intercostal).

10. Breathing rhythmically, adapting to the pace of the horse's movements.

11. Slowly exhaling, imagining the air coming out through different body parts (top of the head, nape of the neck, higher and lower back, neck, ribs, elbows, vagina, knees, heel, tip of the feet).

12. Exhaling strongly through the mouth, following the horse's rhythm, imagining that the air comes out of the body part that feels tense and contracted.

13. Vocalizing rhythmically, in loud voice, the vowels and different syllables (especially tchu, tcha, ha, hu), trying to perceive the effects of these on oneself and the horse.

By means of these exercises, the therapist becomes increasingly aware of the physical and energetic workings of his or her body and the relationship of these to the horse's own. It becomes more imperative to him or her to keep the rhythm and the relaxations of his or her joints and muscles and those of the horse in order to achieve a harmonious ride, experiencing its benefits in full. The increase of the physical and psychic sensibility induces the therapist to expand his or her perception of the realities and needs of the patients, and motivates him or her to respond in a sensitive and intuitive manner.

We must be aware that in every therapy there applies the "law of resonance," which means that any psychic or physical tension of the therapist will be transmitted to the patient and the horse in little time. A stressed and tense equine therapist, because of assisting many patients at the same time or having to work with badly prepared horses and without help, will be incapable of inducing a physical-psychic relaxation in his patient. The therapist's capacity of keeping an internal receptivity, admitting and integrating his own body and psychic sensations and his self-confidence combined with his will to help, open the channels for the flow of his internal wisdom - the intuition! This is how every therapeutic session becomes an act of unique creation, very personal for both patient and therapist!

Equine therapy, in the end, is riding as therapy, where therapist, patient and horse form an interdependent trinity, at the physical, psychic and spiritual levels!

"What is inside of you is also outside.
What is not inside of you is nowhere".

Edith Gross
Mexico

COACHING RIDERS TO DEVELOP CONFIDENCE

Barbra Schulte, MS/CCC-SLP

The information in this article contains valuable insights to be a more effective coach within the therapeutic riding program. The information can be applied to all support person roles including trainers, leaders and side-walkers. In the first part of the paper you will learn about yourself as a coach. You will also discover what a great support person or coach's job really is. You will learn how to stay positive and control your own emotions. And, you will learn how to increase your ability to handle stress. The second half of the article will show you eight proven ways to support and coach a rider.

THE ORIGINS OF MENTALLY TOUGH TRAINING

This information is dramatically effective. It is based in sport science. For the past 20 years, a team of professionals at LGE Sport Science in Orlando, Florida has studied human performance and the research continues today. They understand what makes people perform at maximum levels under pressure. It is state of the art technology based on research with Olympic and professional athletes. It applies to you as a coach of a handicapped rider as much as it does to a coach of a world class Olympian. It's training for the entire person, mind, body and emotion. It is for performance on demand and for living. The information is unique and has been developed by a team of professionals, not just one specialization. The research is pioneered by Dr. James Loehr, a world renowned sports psychologist. Other professionals include an exercise physiologist, a biomechanist, a nutritionist, a sports medicine professional and a psychoneuroimmunologist. This program approaches coaching from many professional disciplines.

SIMPLIFY YOUR JOB AS A COACH

A coach's job is to help the rider develop confidence and have fun. Fun is what makes learning new skills possible. Without confidence and fun, the rider's performance is below her ability every time. Whether you are the coach or the rider, making mistakes is a necessary part of learning. When situations become very difficult, the perspective needs to stay on gaining confidence and having fun. Technique improvement may be involved, but that is only one of the ways to gain a sense of control and good feelings. It takes strong, positive emotional, mental and physical skills. If a coach doesn't have a way to maintain confidence, no matter what happens before or during a client's ride, the rider will ride below technical skill level. In therapeutic riding, a sense of calm may be necessary to maintain safety. This training program is about helping you, the coach understand how to develop emotional toughness for yourself and for the rider.

TRAIN THE IDEAL PERFORMANCE STATE

There is a condition within called the Ideal Performance State (IPS). It is a skill, not a talent. It is the core of the Mentally Tough program. All great performers have something happening deep within themselves when they are achieving peak levels. They can summon a combination of positive emotions in an instant, no matter what is happening around them. They feel confident. They know they can do it. They feel calm or a very profound sense of inner stillness. There is a feeling of boundless physical energy. They feel relaxed, free of fear, as if pressure didn't exist. They are focused, intently tuned in. They feel in control, no matter how crazy things are around them. And most of all, they're having fun. There is a sense of total enjoyment even though they know they could lose it all if it didn't happen.

IPS is all of these emotions happening at the same time. You don't just feel energized . . . or just calm or just focused. You feel them all and that is what makes IPS exhilarating. I'm sure you've felt this way before. You probably didn't realize it was even happening. Take a moment and remember a time when you felt nothing could go wrong. You were in control, feeling relaxed and free and loving the moment. You knew you could handle it. It was as if everything was going your way and nothing could stop you now. The only problem might have been when it was all over. You didn't know how to repeat it or if it would ever come back.

Here's the really great news for you personally and for your coaching. Calling up IPS is a skill. You learn it and you teach it the same as any other skill. You understand what it is, why it is important and how to do it. The more you practice, the better you get. The more you can do it yourself as a coach, the more you'll be able to help a rider find her sense of confidence.

Here is why it is important to achieve IPS. There is no separation of mind, body and emotion. Every emotion you feel has a specific body chemistry. Biochemistry affects your ability to perform technical physical skills. Thinking and emotions are not invisible. Thinking is an electrochemical event in the brain and, therefore, physical. Emotions are neurochemical and therefore physical. When you're feeling positive, your brain waves have a specific wave pattern. Your muscles are more relaxed. Your vision is soft and broad. When you're in IPS, you have the potential to coach at your highest level. If a rider is in IPS she has her best chance to ride her best. When anyone feels negative, their body chemistry actually blocks high level performance, physically. Coaching or riding happens at some level, but not at its best. IPS control is the goal. Your ability and your rider's ability to call up positive emotions on demand determines if talent and skill come to life when you want it most. If you haven't been able to do that before now yourself, or if you haven't known how to coach for it, it's only because you haven't learned how to do it. This training is about being able to create the conditions for and coaching for confidence.

UNDERSTAND THE PERFORMER SELF AND THE REAL SELF
You arrive at the equestrian center late. You are very upset. Nothing has gone right this morning. You feel tired. Your friends greet you and you feel like not responding. You have a session in 15 minutes. Instinctively, you know something has to change or this is going to be a very difficult day.

You have a better chance of helping yourself if you are aware of the distinction between your "Performer Self" and your "Real Self." It is important to understand what each is and how the two interact. The way you really feel is your Real Self. It has everything to do with your everyday life. For example, being physically prepared and well rested from adequate sleep. You have great energy from good nutrition and exercise. You feel emotional harmony in your home life, just to name a few considerations. Real Self needs must be met or you can't do your best work. Sometimes though, the Real Self feels less than ideal. Now, enter the Performer Self. It is the way you need to feel to perform at your peak via IPS anytime. The Performer Self's job is to move from the actual feelings of the Real Self to IPS on demand before and during the ride. When you arrived at the equestrian center, your Real Self was tired, hungry, grumpy and unfocused. For your riding session you need to kick in your Performer Self skills to coach calmly, yet be alert and focused. If you don't engage your Performer Self and, if you coach the way you really feel, your student's ride will be affected. For your client and for your highest potentials to emerge, IPS must be happening prior to and during your client's entire ride. And, if disaster strikes in the middle of the ride, just by maintaining emotional control, you can respond in the best possible way to the situation at hand. It's a skill that's developed with practice. Tough times provide the best chances to see how solid IPS skills really are and to practice them.

Let's be clear that the rider has her own positive or negative feelings before and during a ride. You do not have direct control of them. But, as a coach you can do so much to help her learn how to stay positive and you can create an environment that aids her control of positive emotions. That is your job. You will only do your best as a coach of technical or emotional skills if you can bring up your own positive emotions no matter how you really feel. During coaching time you, too, are a performer. You are performing your coaching and support skills.

ACQUIRE HIGH POSITIVE EMOTIONS THROUGH ACTING, MENTAL CONDITIONING AND RITUAL SKILLS
You can help yourself and your client's acquire the positive energy of IPS in three ways, through - acting skills, mental conditioning skills and rituals. The most dramatic results happen when the skills are combined.

The first way is through acting skills. It is called "outside in training." You use your body to call up positive emotions. You become an actress or actor in the arena and the script is always the same - "confidence, calm, focus, energy and fun" - no matter how out of control things seem. If you are a bad actress, you can't bring positive feelings to life when you are having a bad morning. If you feel badly, you will act that way. Your shoulders are slumped, eyes are down, head shaking.

If you are skilled in IPS control, you will never show any negative emotion on the outside. That is the cardinal rule of tough acting. Signal loud and clear, with your body, that you love being right where you are. Show only strength on the outside. It works and here is why.

God wired our mind, body and emotions all together. Different body positions connect to different emotional states. For example, the physiology of sadness is shoulders slumped, eyes down, a turned down mouth, drawn facial muscles and shallow breathing. The physiology of confidence and joy is shoulders back, chin up, eyes up, determined facial expressions and deep breathing. If you are skilled in IPS control, you control your emotions by controlling your body. By conditioning your body to "act" like a calm, confident and successful coach, you become that coach.

There are three main acting skills: breath control, eye control and posture control. Breathing immediately improves your emotional state because it accomplishes three things at once. It slows brain wave activity, which allows you to think clearly. It increases oxygen flow to muscles which relaxes them and it provides an internal focus which is calming and helps concentration.

When you become aware that you are feeling negative emotions, start breathing all the way into your abdomen. Inhale slowly and deeply. Make sure the exhalation is longer than the inhalation. Then, get into a comfortable breathing rhythm. The more rhythmic repetitions you do, the calmer and more focused you'll become.

Eye control is the next acting skill. It is critical because your mind follows your eyes. When you're anxious or nervous, your eyes go down and your vision narrows. The effect is like a vice closing in on your head with huge side blinders. But when you keep your eyes up and your focus wide and scanning, no matter how you really feel, your mind stays focused on what you want to accomplish. You feel calmer and see all the options.

Posture control is the third acting skill and simply means you look confident no matter what. You can feel more positive just by maintaining a "look" of confidence. Shoulders stay back, proud and erect. Your chin remains level or slightly raised, all the time. As a coach, make sure you have the look of confidence. Walk and move with your shoulders open, your chin level, and eyes up. Breathe, relax and be an example of the very emotions you're coaching. Never show any weakness on the outside and feel only strength on the inside.

The second way to control IPS is through strategic thinking with words and pictures called scripting and imaging. They help maintain concentration and help handle errors in a positive way. Chances are you may be grumbling to yourself about your bad morning and complaining that things are awful. When you have that thought, you are probably seeing mental pictures of yourself at your absolute worst. If you keep those thoughts, IPS is out of the question. So, here are some suggestions:

The first skill is imaging. Create in your mind a picture of being a great coach and all the joy that job brings to you. When you do this exercise, it forces you to decide exactly how you want to be instead of having some vague idea and hoping it all works out. Once the images are created, they automatically program your subconscious. Your subconscious then goes to work on its own to make that picture real. You become what you imagine.

Visualization is developed through practice. Start at home in your favorite easy chair or lie on your bed and completely relax. Imagine your coaching in as much detail as possible. Add vibrant color, sound and smells. Smell the hair coat conditioner, see the smiling face of a child or her parents, feel the coarse hair of a horse's mane. Know you are making a difference! Charge your mental image with emotion. Get excited. Believe deeply in yourself. Go for it.

The second tough thinking tool is scripting. Program yourself for positive emotions and actions with strategic words. It is like having a personal coach or guardian angel on your shoulder saying the right words to keep you on track. Program yourself for positive results and encourage yourself when times get tough. You plan what to say to yourself at very specific times. Talk to yourself about things to do with your client or the horse or about staying cool and feeling good and confident.

The third tool to condition IPS is the use of rituals. Design a personal routine right before training sessions for you and your client. Decide on a specific script and way of acting that makes you feel strong. Get yourself into IPS. Rituals are habitual ways of thinking and acting that call up positive feelings in an instant. They can be mental, physical or both. You could lift your chin, pull your shoulders back, breathe deeply several times and say to yourself, "I'm really in tune with this client. I feel good. Now, stay relaxed. I'm ready." Rituals are powerful, they work and here's why. The association of what you do mentally and physically with strong positive emotions becomes conditioned deep within the body.

INCREASE YOUR CAPACITY TO HANDLE STRESS THROUGH RECOVERY STRATEGIES
Do you think it is stress that usually gets the best of you? I have a new definition of stress for you. I think of it only as putting energy out. Now, think of the term "recovery" as getting energy back. You can put lots of energy out as long as you get energy back and maintain balance. The problem we have in our culture is not the stress, but instead, our lack of recovery. Stress is actually good for us. It stimulates our growth. But, we must have recovery too, because that is when we grow. Stress without recovery is deadly. We can all handle massive doses of stress as long as we recover. Mentally Tough training focuses on training recovery as a huge priority...not on reducing stress. Much of the research at LGE has been on training recovery for performance events as well as in our lives.

The first is the most important recovery activity of life, sleeping. You need 7 - 8 hours of sleep every night. A well-rested body has reserves of energy at really critical times. When the energy is gone, the fight is over.

The next recovery strategy is strategic eating. Eat often, eat light and eat with variety. Every 90 - 120 minutes our blood sugar drops. When blood sugar drops, energy drops along with emotional strength. Without the right body chemistry, we just can't perform. Eat every 90 - 120 minutes and make sure it is healthy food low in fat and sugar. It's called grazing.

The third recovery strategy is to make sure you relax periodically throughout the day. That is absolutely necessary for you to maintain your ability to coach well. If you find yourself putting out extra energy for a day or several days for reasons out of your control, take a longer recovery time when you can. Balance is the key. Training recovery is as important as anything else you do. It's equally important to train in your rider as well. Make sleeping, eating and relaxation times a priority in your scheduling.

EIGHT SPECIFIC COACHING SUGGESTIONS:

1. UTILIZE A BASIC STRENGTH BUILDING PHILOSOPHY
   One of the biggest coaching challenges is to know how much to push. If you push too hard, a rider will deteriorate. That's called overtraining. If you don't push hard enough, she'll never reach her potential. That is called under training. One of the main premises of the Mentally Tough program gives you guidelines to know exactly how much information you can present.

First, understand that to get stronger mentally, emotionally or physically, a rider must go beyond their normal limits. They must do what is uncomfortable for a part of the training in every practice. If they always do what is comfortable, they will either get weaker or maintain their current skill level. The key is to know the difference between comfort, discomfort and pain. Never go the route of pain. The "No pain, no gain" philosophy is damaging. The language of pain is individual. That is where your coaching awareness comes in. If a rider feels mental, emotional or physical in pain, stop, period. You are in overtraining. A great marker for pain is lack of fun. When the fun is gone, stop.

During a confidence building session, the rider starts out doing something that feels comfortable. Then, she does some skill that stretches her to being slightly uncomfortable. She then experiences success, even if only partially. It should feel stimulated, highly challenged, a bit pushed and some pressure, but the level of discomfort is manageable. If a rider doesn't feel pushed or extended at all, she will probably not get tougher. Then, after some success at the level of discomfort, go back to a comfortable skill. Then, over the course of the ride, go back to uncomfortable, back to comfortable. Create a wave by moving back and forth between the two. Always end with success. The key is to know the difference between pain, discomfort and comfort levels for your rider. Be sure to structure the lesson or riding experience accordingly.

There are eight specific ways to coach, support and help a rider grow to her full potential. These suggestions are guidelines. Use them to brainstorm even more ways to build confidence. I'll give you an idea, explain why it works and then show you how to do it.

2. SHARE MUTUAL EXPECTATIONS

The second coaching suggestion is to share mutual expectations and keep the channels of communication open. Many difficulties between a rider and a helper come from not understanding what the other is expecting. When possible, I suggest you become the initiator and monitor of an ongoing channel of communication. You will establish trust. Trust is a powerful emotion which connects to confidence and calmness. Creating a positive environment begins by establishing mutual expectations. It remains when you share changing desires as time goes on.

At the beginning of a relationship, or anytime with ongoing clients or their parents, ask them how you can best help them. Ask them what they want from their riding and how they see you fitting into that scheme. Every person sees things from his or her own perception. Understand what that is. You are in a sense "selling" ideas to your riders. I'm not talking about money. I'm talking about the riders fully accepting your help. You open those doors when see it from their standpoint. And it's equally important for you to share your expectations. Explain to them what works for you. What makes helping them efficient and fun? Mutually decide, what are the roles? Who is responsible for what? Then, once you've shared that, set up a way to keep those communication channels open. As the coach, you take responsibility to establish a type of review weekly, monthly or whatever works for both of you. Don't leave it up to the rider. You will discover changes in each of your needs. Always ask, "How can I best help you?", and then really listen. Give honest feedback if you can or can't meet those needs. Keep working on the plan until it feels good to both of you. That may entail some compromise.

3. COACH THE PERFORMER SELF AND THE REAL SELF

You can condition Performer Self skills over time when you remember to coach for positive emotions with the technical skills. It's so easy to view the rider as a technician and forget about how she is feeling. Positive emotions run the show. When the rider is feeling good, she has the best chance of a positive outcome. When she does not have them, you don't. So, help the rider stay on track with emotional control. For example, monitor if the rider looks relaxed or not.

If she does not look relaxed before giving technical instruction say, "Relax. Everything is okay. Breathe. Good, now use your right leg." Or, coach eye control in a technical way and remind her of the connection to confidence, like "Look past the jump and feel the confidence." Coaching the connection of the mind, body and spirit is the most powerful teaching you can do.

Use the power of rituals to engage the Performer Self. Before hand, talk about what ritual the rider intends to use. Reemphasize how important it is. Then, if for some reason when it gets close to time for the session and the rider feels upset or distracted, that's when you can help her stay calm and focused. Just remind her to take the time to do a ritual, no matter how hectic things may seem. Perhaps do one together. It will anchor her in IPS and mentally slow things down. For only for a few seconds of invested time, rituals have such powerful results.

4. SET PERFORMANCE GOALS

The fourth suggestion I have for you in your coaching is to set performance goals instead of outcome goals. Focus is on setting things up for success by achieving things over which the rider has control. Performing a ritual, maintaining eye control for the entire ride, using cues properly or keeping her cool if something goes wrong would all be performance goals.

Identify progressive technical, mental and emotional mini steps along the way of your long term goals. Identify which of these steps will be the focus during a particular session. When the ride is over, resist the tendency to negatively judge it in terms of bad, awful, etc. Instead, identify and acknowledge what worked and celebrate it. See the ride as multidimensional with many parts to train for and execute. Feeling confident about the good stuff should be positive and separate from dealing with the parts to improve. Technical or emotional improvements need to be viewed in terms of finding replacements. No negative judgments about a person's eventual ability to do the job. Only specific information of how to do the desirable thing the next time. What specifically needs to happen? It's important for you to understand that a rider can never improve his skills by trying not to do something. Identify what needs to be replaced and focus totally on the new. When you focus on replacements instead of on the person's inability to do it. It takes tremendous pressure off of the rider. She needs to be reminded that learning is a process and finding replacements and mastering them is fun. We never arrive. We just keep getting better and better and stronger and stronger.

5. COACH IN POSITIVE STATEMENTS

Have you ever said, "Now, don't pull too hard?"...or...."Don't lean?".....That is the way most people instruct. Some only express suggestions in the negative, and there's no alternative given. Others point out the negative prior to the idea they want communicated. It's a natural thing to do unless you're trained otherwise. Of all the coaching errors, this one is very prevalent and very destructive.

The fifth suggestion is about coaching in the positive. This idea is very powerful and here is why. When we give ourselves or someone else a suggestion, our minds don't process the negatives very well. A void exists. Our brain seems to take the negative idea and put it in the spotlight without its replacement. When I say to you " Don't lean.", Don't you immediately have the idea of someone leaning? Coaching in the positive bypasses all that. Get right to the point of what you want.

To do this you must be clear in your mind about the specific behavior you desire first before you ever state it. Then, tell the rider what you want, all stated positively. Instead of "Now, don't pull too hard," you might say, "Be soft with your hands. Feel the horse's response as you pull on the reins." If you're in a situation where you can discuss why and how using the reins that way is most effective, a rider will respond even more. People are more apt to internalize and follow through with an instruction if they understand why they're doing something. But obviously, we're not always just sitting around talking or that may not be appropriate for your client. You can also help a rider internalize ideas by mutually deciding on some words, they can say to themselves at a certain place. The riders then rely on themselves to say it instead of relying on you. This fosters self confidence and responsibility. Coach positively and train your rider to think and talk to themselves about what needs to happen.

6. KEEP IDEAS SIMPLE

The sixth coaching suggestion is to keep ideas simple. This works because the entire experience feels controlled. Feeling in control is a major part of feeling calm and confident. Keep things simple and help the rider stay focused.

When I teach, one of the biggest things, I remind myself, is that learning is a process. It's my job to get in touch with the flow of that process. I need to present and teach my students foundation skills. I let them master them solidly, and then move them onto the next skill level. It's so easy to want to jump ahead in the interest of progress. My suggestion is to get the teaching sequence clear in your mind. Keep it simple, then move back and forth between comfortable and uncomfortable skills.

There are two questions I want to introduce to you to help keep things simple. Both will help your rider tune out distractions and the questions help a rider to stay focused on the job. Consider this powerful fact. All the rider has is herself, her horse and the task at hand. Everything else is out of her control and concerning herself with them is not her job. Her job is to get herself and her horse ready mentally, emotionally and physically. If she asks herself "What is my job?" and "What do I have control of?" she will do her job at her highest level. All the other people and things over which she has no control will never affect her. When you coach, help her to keep things simple by reminding herself of those powerful questions, especially at times when she feels threatened and distracted.

The last way to keep things simple and focused are two powerful phrases: "No problem" and "Next time." Saying "No problem" the instant an error occurs keeps the rider from replaying the error in her mind. She stays on target and in the moment. The phrase "Next time" lets her replace what didn't work with the idea she can do it the next time that opportunity comes up. It also affirms her belief in herself. "No problem" and "Next time" are absolutely necessary when Performer Self skills are engaged.

7. TRAIN RECOVERY

This seventh coaching strategy helps a rider stay cool. I'm going to take the concepts of stress and recovery we discussed on side one and apply them to the actual ride.

When you're coaching, strategize a plan with the rider, for her eyes, her breathing and her thinking during planned recovery times. Riding recovery times are opportunities to stop and relax, if only for a few seconds. A recovery plan allows a client to stay focused without feeling a sense of ever losing control. It's the ability to recover, even if only for a few seconds, that determines if a rider maintains a focus and keeps a sense of control and confidence. Coaching for recovery in and out of the arena is one of the most effective strategies you can do. Everyone, including you, will enjoy experiencing periodic feelings of relief and gaining control.

8. SHIFT GEARS FOR INDIVIDUALS

My eighth suggestion is simple. Take the time to shift gears for individuals. It's so easy in a hectic situation, to get into a groove and become unaware of each person's individual needs. If you have a number of kids or students in a fast-paced situation, script yourself to change gears for each person. Take a moment, breathe and remind yourself, "This is Bill. I need to encourage him, but basically leave him alone and not be too technical." When it is time to help Sara, you remind yourself, for example, that the two of you both decided you will help her remember to use her right leg. Just make sure you keep yourself calm and centered in the moment with whomever you're helping. When you feel that way, chances are you'll be a great example for your rider.

SUMMARY

Coaching, helping and supporting riders is one of those jobs that's rarely recognized. When things go well, the credit is given to the rider, as it should be. When things go wrong, we're there to help. Life in general is not about gaining recognition, it's about giving to others. Your job as a coach is important. You can truly make a difference in a rider's life. Know for yourself and for your client that it's not about the achievement, but about the journey to get there. It's about building feelings of belief in oneself, about helping someone to let go and go for it. It's about creating a place where it's safe to make errors. Create an atmosphere of fun, humor and passion for riding and growing. In this context, your fears and your rider's fears will go away.

Good luck on your journey to becoming a great confidence builder behind the scenes.

Barbra Schulte
USA

CHAPTER 4
THE VALUE OF RIDING - FROM THE RIDER'S POINT OF VIEW

RIDING AS ABLE, THEN DISABLED

Marci Lawson

I have been riding horses ever since I can remember. First they were farm horses that my cousins and I jumped onto bareback and rode with a halter and lead rope. Next it was working at a stable and leading trail rides, always riding a rent string horse. Then came mucking stalls for the privilege of a "real" lesson from a trainer. And finally on down the line, came my own business which kept me on the show circuits with pleasure horses, hunters, jumpers, and a handful of junior riders to promote as well. Then came life in a wheelchair.

Like most people that go through a devastating change in their life, I wasn't quite sure what to do with myself. I spent the first year quite depressed. It seemed I had to give up everything I liked to do most: sports, riding, camping, and worst of all, my business. I could find absolutely nothing to do from a wheelchair. That is until I found a small article in the newspaper about a local program that offered horseback riding to--what--yes--disabled individuals. It took a few weeks to muster the courage to call the program as I wasn't sure what I could possibly do. Finally I did call to get more information and to see how I could be of any help. Little did I know then the possibilities that lay ahead of me.

After visiting the program and observing the first lesson, I knew that I was hooked. The program's founder and director and I became friends as she put me to work in various capacities based on my previous background in horsemanship. I immediately became a board member, primarily as a spokesperson for the disabled students, and represented them, as well as their families and friends. I still had many contacts in the horse world and had new ones throughout the general disabled community which helped to attract more riders into the program. My favorite capacity, though, was as a "disabled rider consultant." Many times I was asked to consult with a riding instructor and help problem solve a rider's particular problem. I often explained to the teacher what a handicapped rider's body was feeling, as I could relate the experience to how my own body would react in a particular circumstance. Often I could formulate ideas to make some process easier, or possibly more independent for the student in either grooming, mounting, riding, or dismounting procedures because of methods I had myself experimented with. It became quite a challenge to identify my limitations, as well as abilities, and to try to match them with other students to help improve their own skills.

It is truly amazing to me as a wheelchair user to realize exactly what a good ride, meaning the combination of the right exercises and activities, plus the right horse, can do to a disabled body. I have seen drastic changes in other riders, which, of course is always impressive, but when I can feel it happening to my own body it's unforgettable! I have a neuromuscular disease called familial spastic quadraparesis which can be similar in symptoms to many other types of neurological diseases including multiple sclerosis and Lou Gehrig's disease. As the name of my disease implies, there is a strong spastic component to my disorder which tends to keep my limbs rather stiff and makes moving in a coordinated fashion difficult. Some muscles are constantly tight and contracted. After a while the muscles begin to tire and although they tend to stay tight, they begin to ache as though I had a bad case of the flu. I take medicine for the spasticity and do some range of motion exercises to keep the muscles as loose as possible, but spasticity does not just disappear. You learn to live with it.

As the time finally neared for me to actually mount and ride a horse for the first time as a disabled person, I had a lot of mixed feelings and thoughts racing through my mind. As a person who craved independence, I realized that this would not be an independent feat in the least. I was still picturing myself on a 17-hand thoroughbred, galloping around the arena heading toward a five-foot solid wall, ready to feel the adrenaline rush as my horse lifted his front feet and coiled like a tight spring in the rear, to leap over the obstacle looming in front of us. But as I was wheeled over to the wheelchair mounting ramp, I was suddenly snapped back to reality. I saw a large, broad horse standing patiently at the ramp with a leader at his head, a side walker at his offside, and my second side walker and the instructor on the ramp ready to assist me onto the horse. As I have minimal trunk control, I also required a fifth person to stabilize me on the horse. Imagine, five people just so that I could ride for ten minutes at the walk! I was feeling pretty humiliated by then.

My first conscious thought after I mounted was how wonderful it was to look down at my sidewalkers. Since I have been using a wheelchair, all I have done was look up at people, which can easily make you feel childlike again. To actually look down on all those around me was a most pleasant surprise! That first ride went very smoothly and was indeed quite pleasant, mainly riding on the rail at an even, long, and swinging stride. The horse was great. I remember how peaceful I felt and how comfortable and relaxing the long rocking rhythmic walk felt to my stiff body. It was at this point that I started to learn about, or maybe just be aware of, new aspects of riding.

As I worked mentally to get my body relaxed, I suddenly became aware of the cadence of the horse's foot falls. Not just the cadence, but also the actual sequence. We all know that the horse's walk is a four-beat gait, but I had never been aware how much stronger the first and third beats are. I guess it makes sense, as those beats are from the rear legs which automatically imply some thrust and drive. But I had never noticed the difference until I rode as a disabled rider and my body reacted more to those first and third beats.

Another thing that I discovered was *that if a horse was at all lame, even just slightly off, it could ruin my whole ride in that my body would stiffen even more each time the horse would step down onto the affected leg.* It therefore became of utmost importance to pick the horse that I would ride on the soundness and purity of his gait. A nice long even swinging stride proved to be the best for me, and for that the horse needs to be fairly tall. What seems to work for me is to match the size of the horse relative and proportionate to the size of the rider. If I ride a horse under 15 to 15 ½ hands, the stride tends to be too short and the positive effect is not nearly as pronounced as if I ride a larger horse with a longer, flowing stride.

I think that the greatest thing for me about riding a horse now, is what it can do for my body. I can mount the horse being stiff and rigid, but when I dismount after a good ride I come off the horse similar to a wet, soggy noodle. To date I have found no other exercise or activity that can even approximate the extreme relaxation I get from riding. My body got so relaxed that for a few minutes after my ride it is difficult to coordinate any voluntary movement and I must in fact be strapped into my wheelchair just to keep me from slipping right out onto the floor. It may sound terrible, but in reality it feels absolutely wonderful.

I have one suggestion to make to instructors of the disabled. My favorite lesson plan as a physically disabled rider is to have a three-part lesson. The first part contains some mild stretching and exercising routines to limber and loosen up enough to perform the second part of the lesson, which can be anything from serious equitation to just fun and games. Whatever the second part consists of make it challenging mentally as well as physically. Frequently, physically disabled riders have few chances to be stimulated mentally, especially if they are unable to attend school or work. So, challenge their brains and make them think and plan and concentrate within their lesson. The third and best segment of the lesson is the relaxation part.

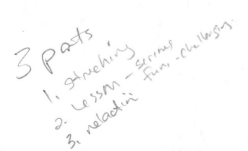

I like to end the lesson and get off the horse feeling better both mentally and physically than when I got on. I believe to achieve complete physical relaxation, one must give up the reins and control of the horse to a leader, so that the arms can be free to relax as well. Depending on the rider and the disability, the technique used can vary from simple exercises to full hippotherapy. Find what works best with your student, then make it part of your lesson plan.

In summary, I guess that I would have to affirm that horseback riding is a great sport whether you do it from a wheelchair or as an able-bodied person. The parameters are different, but the challenges are always there. The challenge comes from what a person can feasiblely do, not from what is realistically unattainable.

"My own challenge now comes not from facing a tough round of five foot jumps, but rather possibly doing an independent transfer from wheelchair to the horse. I will always continue to keep meeting the challenge!"

Marci Lawson
USA

EDGING TOWARD FULFILLMENT

Eileen Szychowski

"Come to the edge," he said,
    They said "We are afraid".
"Come to the edge" he said.
    They came... he pushed them
And they flew!

Author Unknown

Standing on the narrow, swaying bridge, I savored the wind in my hair and watched it lift my horse's mane. This wonderful horse and the sublime world of the Inner Canyon made me forget I had just ridden seven hours on slim, winding trails that edged thousand foot cliffs. Instead, I felt that I had been carried into an unearthly world on the mist of the river--the great Colorado--which churned and roared sixty feet below.

It was hard to believe that a year previously I was denied, on the basis of handicap, the opportunity and the right to ride the Grand Canyon. I owed this historical ride and the confidence to do it to a wonderful teacher named Josef Rivers who operates a therapeutic riding program in California called the DRAGON SLAYERS. Josef was my first disabled role model and continues to inspire me today. Among the many special gifts he has given me was the knowledge that, despite crutches, leg braces and paralyzed hands, I could be or do anything! He also gave me several years of training and several magnificent horses to begin my own program, CAMELOT, here in ARIZONA.

What makes CAMELOT and DRAGON SLAYERS unique among handicapped riding programs is that they are among a handful of programs which are run by persons with disabilities. I have always felt that my handicap is my greatest asset in teaching. My disability experience increases my sensitivity to my students and also increases my expectations of them. Living with my own disability helps me in creatively overcoming obstacles while the heightened expectations enable students to discover their potential. Research shows that students will perform according to expectation. Disabled persons can and want to work hard. Indeed, there is therapeutic value in hard work and, if the truth be known, hard work is part of daily living with a disability. Don't be afraid to send us home tired. It will be a "tired" we can feel good about.

Growing up with a physical disability, I grew frustrated at programs which failed to challenge me, which treated me "special" when what I wanted and needed was to be treated equal. Those of us in the helping professions--including disabled riding programs--continue to make this mistake today which results in limiting the potential of the people we serve.

Those of us who go into the field of disabled riding are by nature caring people who want to make life better for others. But let us begin by honestly examining our perceptions. Do we see the people we serve as our equals, having a unique combination of strengths and needs with the potential to become independent persons integrated into our community? Or do we see them as "kids" regardless of their age, who will always need us, who will never leave the lead line or show in anything but "special" shows. Do we see them in terms of possibility or disability? It is true that some disabled persons will go farther than others but all of us with disabilities will go farther in a teaching environment which supports our right to explore risk and does not, however well intended, attempt to keep us separate or protect us from disappointment. We are failing a vast contingent of physically disabled persons who are not being appropriately served by our therapeutic recreation programs simply because of our own attitudes about risk and failure. And so, places like the Grand Canyon, the forests, shorelines, mountains and deserts which belong to all of us are accessible to only a few. When I began my lessons under Josef Rivers I wanted more than a pony ride. I wanted to someday own a horse so that I could have complete access to nature, perhaps even to show, breed and train horses. I wanted things to be made accessible to me--not made easy for me. And that is what I got: a tough but empowering teacher who did not give me ribbons just for being disabled but gave me the incentive to win or lose like anyone else. In this way horses became the greatest equalizers in my life.

This experience of empowerment is what I seek to pass on to my own students at CAMELOT. Like the DRAGON SLAYERS, CAMELOT operates on a few basic truths. The first basic truth is that dreams are essential to quality of life. Dreams involve risk. Risk is a basic human right. We must honor the need to dream and the right to risk by building challenge into our programs. Out of my frustration with programs and activities which failed to meet my needs for challenge and integration grew the commitment to design a curriculum with more emphasis on personal development than physical therapy. Frankly speaking, most of us have had therapy up the kazoo! Our parents, teachers and therapists have lovingly done their best to enhance our lives, but all too often the development of muscle has been stressed while overlooking our human need for fun and the kinds of social interactions which lead to a healthy adult life.

CAMELOT is offered as a salute to disabled persons who want to pilot their own ship rather than be a passenger. Our students come with the desire to feel the wind in their faces, to ride the trail and experience the outdoors. We encourage them to set their own goals, reminding them not to think small. Most of our work is done outside the arena, moving always toward independence and goal fulfillment. All of this means of course, increased risk which requires horses and staff that are absolutely exemplary, jewels which can only be found through rigorous screening and training. Accordingly, CAMELOT requires of staff a minimum age of 21 and some basic knowledge of horses. This means not everybody will be suitable as a rider assistant. We utilize them in other ways. Safety and challenge can happily co-exist but only when the strictest standards are adhered to.

Yes, this is especially difficult when we are all in need of more volunteers. At CAMELOT we make our commitment to do a small job well through a well-structured, individualized program rather than trying to serve everybody. (After all, the world is changed one life at a time). We have found that serious trail riding and horse trekking for the disabled can only be approached in this way, an approach which has led to several CAMELOT students acquiring their own horses or landing jobs in the horse industry. All of this comes back to our personal attitudes about dreams, risk and possibility. Another basic truth we believe at CAMELOT is that disabled persons should be in control of their own lives. CAMELOT, therefore, is a program where disabled persons provide their own leadership. Our teaching model is based on mentorship. This is not to say that able bodied instructors should not be operating programs or teaching disabled students. What I am saying is that the role model is a most powerful way of teaching. Cultivate this precious resource! Use your advanced riders as assistant instructors, advisors and board members to insure that you are hitting your mark. Solicit the input of the people you serve in all aspects of your program!

I am excited to see that programs are improving as the field of adaptive riding matures. We are all seeing more riders, and they are asking more of us as their teachers. Let's continue to allow our disabled students to define their own horizons, and when they have arrived, encourage them to go a step further. We will all grow in the process, after all we are all both teacher and student. At CAMELOT we call this the Round Table philosophy.

HOW DOES IT WORK? They come..I push them...and WE FLY!

Eileen Szychowski
USA

FROM THE RIDER'S PERSPECTIVE

Wendy R. Shugol, MA

How do I begin to unfold the myriad of feelings and opinions which I have come to formulate over the years when it comes to the topic of therapeutic riding? So much has occurred, and horses have come to play such a very significant role in my life, since I first became involved with a therapeutic riding program in 1976. As a result of this partnership with horses, I have become an owner and a contender in both disabled and able-bodied competition on many different levels.

When I began riding, I had no idea what an impact it would have on me. I had always loved horses, from the time I was a small child, and suffered from a terminal case of "Black Beauty Syndrome" (something many young people experience). I never outgrew it, and, as an adult, finally received my chance to be involved with a program where I could begin to see just whether or not I really wanted to ride. I became thoroughly engrossed in horses and the therapeutic riding program right from the beginning. I was able to ride independently almost by the end of the first lesson. This experience motivated me to the point where I wanted to get as much as I could possibly get as soon as I could get it. It was the biggest "pick-me-up" I had in a long time. Here was something that **I** could do that was unique to my able-bodied peers! Finally, there was something physical that put me on equal footing with them!

From the beginning, the sky became the limit. I spent every weekend with the program, learning all I could about horse management, grooming and tacking, equipment management, and how I needed to manipulate my environment to accomplish the tasks around the farm. I figured out how to muck out stalls from my wheelchair, bring horses in from the field, clean feet and fully groom horses of all sizes.

Then, my family donated a horse to the program I was involved in. Now, I had a mount whom I could ride any time the program was in session. I continued to spend just about all my free time working with, and for, the program. However, as time wore on, my enthusiasm was waning. I continued to care for the horse donated by my family but something just was not the same. I could not put my finger on it right away, but it finally occurred to me what the problem could possibly be. The problem was that I was reaching the end of what the therapeutic riding program could offer me. I was ready to move onto a higher level of riding which the program could not provide. It was becoming time for me to move on.

By this time, I was now the proud owner of the horse which my family had donated. Not knowing how I would support him, I managed to get him involved with another therapeutic riding program so I could keep my expenses to a minimum and, also, to give the program the benefit of a very suitable mount for all the aspects of its curriculum (hippotherapy, vaulting and recreational riding). I had also sought out this group because of the dressage background which the instructor possessed. I had become involved with dressage and competition, and wanted to further my knowledge and ability level. Another situation arose at about this time in my riding career: the aspect of competition. This was truly the shot-in-the-arm that I was looking for. In 1979, the National Cerebral Palsy Games was hosting the first competition ever to be held in the United States for riders with disabilities. I suddenly had a goal to work for again as I began to set my sights on this new opportunity. This was to be my first show experience.

Being a rather competitive person by nature, riding competition appealed to me immediately. The instructor I was now working with helped me in every way possible. She provided me with extra riding opportunities in preparation for this, as well as letting me know when there was a horse show competition in the area that I might benefit from watching. All these experiences were beneficial in fostering my new interest. I "repaid" the program with additional volunteering and fund-raising hours. It was a very amicable (and successful) working agreement. I was, and continue to be, very motivated in this endeavor of competitive riding.

It is an avenue which continually gives me a new goal to work for. With dressage, I will never run out of new things to learn. It is always a feeling of great accomplishment when I finally achieve a new skill. Each competition is a new challenge which I look forward to very much.

In the past several years, I have graduated from the therapeutic riding programs. I have received all the benefits I can derive from their expertise. It was unfair for me to continue to take up a space on their roster when I now had two horses (I had received a second horse as a gift), both of whom were being used extensively in the program, and I was fully "mainstreamed" most of the time. I was fortunate because the program borrowed space and horses from a private facility which provided lessons on a large scale to the non disabled public. It was quite easy for me to make the transition into mainstream riding.

My current instructor (whom I have been with for the past several years) accepted me as a student as soon as I presented my case to her. Her philosophy was much the same as mine, so we decided to give it a trial. Needless to say, it has worked out. She has extracted performance levels from me that I never thought possible. Although she pushes me to my limit and beyond, I let her know when my abnormal neurological reflexes are going to impede my performance. Then I adapt my positioning to accommodate my disability in order to achieve the desired end result. We have established an extremely successful team.

However, despite my now more advanced level of riding, competition among those in my disability group (individuals with cerebral palsy) is limited. I am currently the top-seeded rider with my level of disability in this country. This is an honor I have held since the inception of the competitive movement in 1979. It is very difficult for me to attend the regional and national qualifiers when I am fairly sure that there really will not be much, if any, competition for me in my disability classification. My experience has been, in the many programs throughout the country which I have visited, that instructors are afraid to push their students with disabilities for fear that they might be hurt if something should happen. Riding is a controlled, high risk sport, and riders who undertake this endeavor knows that they are taking a chance. More than anything else, we want the right to choose the route of competition just like any other rider. We know we are taking a risk to do this, but we deserve the same opportunity as anyone else. Too often I have visited programs where there were students, still dependent upon leaders and sidewalkers, who were more than able to be riding independently. When questioned, instructors admitted that they were afraid to let the students go for fear they may have problems. But yet, they talk about wanting their students to have the experience of competition. Riders need the tools at the program level in order to be successful in the competition arena.

Then there is the subject of space availability within a program. What happens to the riders with disabilities once they have reached as high a level of achievement as they can in their therapeutic riding programs? I was one of the lucky ones who had developed a network of people who could help me find an instructor that was willing to accept a rider; one needed different techniques of teaching in order to accomplish her goals. I was also extremely fortunate in that I was given a horse so I always had access to a mount. But, this is rare.

I have met so many people with disabilities who have said to me, *"Oh, I used to ride but once I graduated from the program, there was nowhere else for me go. Now I am no longer riding."* It is a shame that there are so many riders out there who are singing the same song. *It should be a cooperative effort on the parts of both rider and instructors to help the rider to continue riding* (if this is what the rider desires).

Competition and mainstreaming are there for those who wish to pursue it. There are many would-be talented riders with disabilities who just need to be provided with the tools and opportunities to make it happen.

Wendy R. Shugol
USA

THE VALUE OF HORSEBACK RIDING

Lisa Walsh

Horseback riding has played a large role in my life. I have been riding for the past 16 years and I couldn't imagine not having it be such a large part of my life. It is now not just an activity but it is part of my work week. I do not take it for granted; it is missed greatly if I cannot ride.

The value of horseback riding is priceless. When I began riding, I thought it would be great therapy for me. Little did I know how much else in my life riding could affect. I do depend on my horse's body warmth to stretch my muscles and allow them to lengthen. The horse's movement during his walk, trot, halt and other transitions have taught me how to "think ahead" and prepare my body for different actions. My balance has become keen both on horseback and on the ground, whether I am in my wheelchair, on a bench, or on the ground.

My eye-hand coordination has strengthened as I am now an independent rider and have gained positive thought process through the use of horseback riding. My spasticity can be overwhelming at times along with my athetoid movements. Through the use of horseback riding, I have been taught a great philosophy--"MIND OVER BODY." My instructor and her many leaders have allowed me to accept my cerebral palsy and its many difficulties and utilize my strengths. It is not easy but this theory does work. If we put our minds before our actions, great things do happen! That's exciting and possible.

Horseback riding has increased my self-concept 110%. In the beginning, it gave me pride, pride that I could do an activity that nobody else in my family would even think of doing. Sixteen years later, I would never have thought I'd be where I have been today:

❏	I have traveled to the West Coast to demonstrate that horseback riding is a positive thing in a very therapeutic way.
❏	I have competed locally, regionally and nationally against persons with my disability, with different disabilities, and with no disability at all.
❏	I have traveled abroad - once as an alternate member to the U.S. Equestrian Team to compete in the First World Championship held in Orust, Sweden. And once as a member on the U.S. Equestrian team to the Games for the Cerebral Palsied in Assen, Holland.
❏	I was chosen to present a paper on horseback riding and its many positive attributes, with responses from other disabled riders, to the International Conference on Animal-Human Relationships held in Monaco in November 1989.

The above four activities focused greatly on how I felt about myself. Through horseback riding, I am able to leave my disability behind and stress my abilities. It may have started with confidence that my horse will remain still as I mount, allowing my body to respond with awkward movements. I think as my body moves, everything will be fine, and I complete my movement while I am thinking about it. "MIND OVER BODY" can be powerful, and simply, it can work. As I try to keep in mind that very powerful theory and practice, I need to remember that nothing is perfect. Spasms do happen. Differences can be present. Above all, nothing is perfect.

Horseback riding has also taught me a great deal about relationships both between human and human and/or animal and human. With any relationship, one must continue to give and take. I trust my family, and I trust my horse. I acknowledge the presence of goodness in my friends and family. I see the gold upon my mount. As my horse moves, I need to allow him to feel as free as I do, yet acknowledge that I do have control with trust. With my friends and family, it takes more than just one person to get something good finished. Even better, to be independent, I have to acknowledge my needs and how they should be met.

As an adult rider, I believe that I have received topnotch instruction. Dressage is understood, but I always can better my ride. My instructor has taught me how to use my abilities and deal with my disabilities. Upon a horse, I have no limitations. I expect my instructor to accept me as I am, and teach me to ride as she teaches many others, disability or no disability.

In summary, horseback riding is priceless. It has given me dignity. I know that it is okay to be me no matter what. I am proud of my past, my family, my friends and myself. It has allowed me to say "yes, I use a wheelchair and **I have** many **abilities.**" I am a teacher. I am disabled. I have a great number of friends and family who believe in me and my abilities as I do. I am a human being with dignity like everyone else.

Lisa Walsh
USA

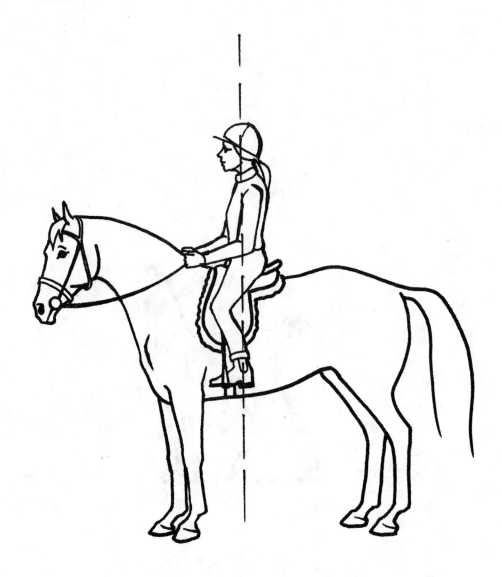

CHAPTER 5
HOW DOES THERAPEUTIC RIDING WORK?

HOW RIDING AIDS THE CHILD WITH DISABILITIES

John H. Brough, OTR

Why is horseback riding a valuable tool in helping the child with a disability? It is recognized that horseback riding aids the child with a disability in neuromuscular and psychological development (Bertoti, 1988; McCowan, 1972; Davis, 1968). A need exists to demonstrate the reasons why and how therapeutic riding techniques benefit the child. This article attempts to present one person's point of view regarding the body's response, especially the response of the autonomic nervous system, to the activities of riding.

The autonomic nervous system is the portion of the central nervous system that controls the automatic functions of the body. It is divided into two parts which work in opposition to each other. The *parasympathetic system* maintains body function in a normal state. The *sympathetic system*, commonly called the "fight or flight" system, prepares the body to deal with emergencies. This sympathetic division of the autonomic nervous system takes charge in an emergency. It causes the eyes to dilate, the hair to stand up, goose bumps to appear, and the heart and lungs to work faster. Blood is directed away from the skin and organs of digestion, and is directed to the skeletal muscles. There is an increased urge to empty the bladder. The whole body is in a state of readiness. Functions which are of no particular assistance to defense are slowed down. The bladder wall is relaxed, digestion is slowed, and the activities of the sex organs are inhibited.

In the riding milieu children with disabilities **MAY** be ruled by the sympathetic portion of the autonomic nervous system. Think of the probable stress of a child entering the stable for the first time. The instructor may see signs that tell him or her that this child is being ruled by the sympathetic division. These signs include different degrees of some or all of the following:

SYMPATHETIC NERVOUS SYSTEM STRESS SIGNS THAT THE CHILD MAY SHOW:
- ❏ Wide, dark appearing eyes
- ❏ Irregular, rapid, shallow breathing
- ❏ Light, jerky, restless movements
- ❏ Escalation in strength of movement
- ❏ Being easily irritated or distracted by sights, sounds, or smells
- ❏ Sensitivity to touching things or being touched
- ❏ Increased frequency of swallowing
- ❏ Complaint of thirstiness
- ❏ Cold, clammy skin
- ❏ Voice loud and higher pitched and/or quavering
- ❏ Frequent requests to go to the bathroom, or "accidents" occur
- ❏ Trembling of the hands, legs, or jaw
- ❏ Inability to attend to a task--"spaced out"
- ❏ Inability to remember what was done
- ❏ Reduced efficiency of learning

After prolonged stimulation by the sympathetic division of the autonomic nervous system, the person may complain of being *weak, faint* or *tired*.

If control of the sympathetic division decreases, the control by the parasympathetic division increases. The person will demonstrate subsidence in the sympathetic system's behavior and show improved function.

In general, there are three principles for helping a person to change from dominance of the sympathetic system to the parasympathetic system. The person needs:

- ❑ WARMTH applied to the muscles
- ❑ RHYTHMICAL MASSAGE
- ❑ MODULATED SENSORY INPUT

In riding, **warmth** to the muscles comes from the result of the physical activity. However, increasing the temperature of an area can also enhance the application of the principle. Garments which retain constant body heat are preferable to achieve the desired results.

Rhythmical massage, the second principle for producing faster change to control by the parasympathetic nervous system, is accomplished by the horse. After mounting, the rider's body is stimulated by the horse's rhythmic gait. Sufficient time should be allowed for the child to acclimate to the rhythmic pattern of walking before changing to another gait. The gaits enhance rhythmic vestibular and joint receptor stimulation. Muscle spindle and Golgi tendon organs are also stimulated. All of these receptors enhance neuro-integration. The rhythmic movements of the horse further acts on many other sensory receptors thus creating an integrated sensory experience. This experience's affect the balance mechanism, position sense, sense of motion, as well as muscle activity, and relaxation.

Modulated sensory input is a necessary concomitant in helping the parasympathetic system to become more dominant. Reducing sensory stimulation to the ears and eyes will enable the rider to cope more successfully with the task at hand. Quick movements or loud yelling should be avoided at all times but especially once the child is mounted. The smaller the arena, the better, since it takes less visual stimulation for a person to organize in a confined area. Bright colors and clutter in the arena should also be avoided. Soft, quiet classical music may be added to the arena to aid in relaxation and help concentration. Achieving parasympathetic control of the body will aid the child. He or she will be more successful as he or she can attend to the riding lesson. He or she will then be ready to learn and progress in his or her riding abilities.

Emotional changes can also be aided by parasympathetic control. When the fragile, explosive child becomes stable, he or she can tolerate frustration more easily. He or she will now be easier to handle astride the horse for a longer period of time. The control of the fight or flight mechanism is overridden. The child is better able emotionally to handle the task.

CONCLUSION:

The *elements* found in horseback riding are very effective for sensorimotor integration in the child with a disability. These elements augment the transfer of control of the child's responses by the sympathetic to the parasympathetic nervous system. These elements also aid relaxation and learning. One needs to be aware of the effects and power of the autonomic nervous system since it can work for or against the child with a disability.

John H. Brough, OTR
USA

References

Basmajian, J.V. (1964). *Primary Anatomy*. Baltimore: The Williams and Wilkins Co.

Bertoti, D.B.(1988). Effects of therapeutic horseback riding on posture in children with cerebral palsy. *Physical Therapy*. 68.10. Oct. 1505-1512.

Davies, J.A. (1968). *Reins of Life*. London: J A Allen.

Gray, H. (1959). *Anatomy of the Human Body*. Philadelphia: Lea & Feiberger.

Guyton, A. (1964). *Function of the Human Body*. Philadelphia: W.B. Sanders Co.

McCowan, L. (1972). *It is Ability That Counts*. Augusta MI: Cheff Center.

AN ANALYSIS OF THE EFFECTS OF THERAPEUTIC RIDING ON A STUDENT WITH DISABILITIES: A CASE STUDY

Jean Hoffman, BS, DVM

The author, as a volunteer, was an instructor in a therapeutic riding program while completing her bachelor's degree in Animal Science. In fulfillment for a senior project, a case study was developed about one of her students. The use of the case study is described here to demonstrate both the steps required to develop a study and how easily one can be accomplished. The method can serve an important place in further validation of therapeutic riding. More of those involved are encouraged to gather information on the results of their riding activities using the case study technique. Ultimately, the purpose of most case studies is to show change in a subject over time. The case study process, described as a model here, is no different. It was designed and is presented in this instance to show that horseback riding is therapeutic in many ways and can help people having many different kinds of problems.

PREPARING TO DO A CASE STUDY

This study involved a student relatively new to a therapeutic riding program. Brad had only been riding with the group for a few months when the instructors and parents began to notice many positive changes in him. Immediately, as one of his instructors, I made the decision to document these changes in Brad in case study form. By so doing, it was hoped to illustrate that riding was, for him and others, therapeutic.

Since course requirements limited the time in which to complete the project, Brad's riding lessons were documented for three months with **written logs** of lesson plans and results of each lesson, in addition to **photographs** taken during the lessons. **Evaluation forms**, routinely used for all the therapeutic riding students in the group, were also completed to record Brad's progress in several mental and physical areas, such as comprehension, balance and coordination.

A **literature search** was carried out to see what kinds of studies had already been done in this activity with what results. It is best to do the research first, before the case study starts, as this can help one decide what a study needs to examine and how to shape the process. However, one should not be influenced by another person's findings. Those are used later in evaluating one's own findings. The results of a case study must stand alone, based on facts presented. This is more difficult than it sounds since so many "facts" are the subjective observations of instructors, relatives, volunteers and physical or occupational therapists. But, observation is a critical research skill in any qualitative study. A student's lack of improvement or even decline during a study can be caused by many factors, including, in this example, the rider's health and the type of riding being done. All results, positive or negative, when evaluated will help others shape their instructional programs to better benefit their students.

LOCATING REPORTS OF RELEVANT STUDIES

Finding publications on therapeutic riding may be difficult, but in general, public libraries have little to no information on this subject. University libraries may be more helpful, but the best hope in therapeutic riding at present usually lies in private sources. Some people involved in therapeutic riding have started their own collections of related books and journal articles. In addition, riding groups/organizations in various countries publish collections of articles from their annual conferences. Thus, networking with those in riding groups to locate materials related to your subject is a good alternative to libraries. In this project, when articles were found relating to Brad's condition and his current program, they were read and highlighted and saved for later citation. Various important points relating to the study and its results were then easy to find later to be used to reinforce the case study findings.

PRESENTING THE CASE

When the study period was over, that is, the approximately three-month period of documenting Brad's progress, the **handwritten reports** of riding plans as well as comments written after each lesson were organized chronologically and typed up. Next, the **photographs** were developed, duplicated and identified as to activity. A **questionnaire** was written to give to Brad's mother to complete. It asked for information about his schooling, his disability, his previous riding experience, and other sports in which he was involved. There were also questions concerning his mother's observation of his progress; had his parents, physician, teachers or others noted any physical, mental or emotional changes in him since he had started riding? The completed questionnaire was included in the finished study along with the uncut written log of lessons. Only clear, representative photos were chosen to be included, four each from five sessions, to illustrate Brad's form and progress.

The photos were presented with captions describing the intent and results of the activity shown and were in chronological order. With more time and forethought, a short video of several sessions could have been made. This would have better illustrated points such as coordination, flexibility and response time to instructions.

Finally, after the photo section, in a **summary** section, the instructor's overall evaluation of Brad's progress was detailed in the areas of performance mentioned previously and in areas such as attentiveness, endurance, attitude and confidence. In a section called **conclusion**, Brad's experiences were compared to the findings of other studies found in the literature searched.

The **appendix** included samples of the evaluation forms used, a **bibliography** of sources (49 in this case), forms for admission to the riding program: consent and release, medical information, physician referral and occupational/physical therapy assessment. The last form(s) is particularly useful to include in a study, with both pre- and post study data recorded.

CONCLUSIONS

This case study went very smoothly from start to finish; only two make-up sessions were required. The student, instructors, therapist, parent and volunteers were completely cooperative and showed up for each weekly session as scheduled. In addition, the results were uniformly positive, showing mild to major improvement in all areas of performance measured. Thankfully the pictures supported the results. Subsequent studies by this researcher are not expected to always go as well as this first one did, but they will in any case cover a longer period, using more in-depth observations and include better documentation techniques, such as video.

Following the simple steps described can help a person learn not only how to produce a case study, but also to appreciate what is valuable to students in a riding program, and how to observe the changes in students over time. Even with this kind of single case research one can help improve therapeutic riding programs everywhere and thereby ultimately increase the riders' learning and enjoyment.

Jean Hoffman
USA

SPECIAL NEEDS HORSEBACK RIDING: CASE STUDY OF A CLIENT WITH AN ACQUIRED TRAUMATIC BRAIN INJURY

Marylou R. Dickson
Brenda L. Belec

The following article describes the work Brenda Belec has achieved and the progress she has made while riding as a student at the Friends of Whitemud Equine Centre Special Needs Riding Program under the instruction of Marylou Dickson. The purpose of this article is to give a description of the goals set by the student and the instructor and the procedure used to reach these goals.

HISTORY:

On March 30, 1991, Brenda Belec received a serious brain injury which left her in a coma for three months. As a result of the injuries, there were impairments of short term memory, speech and language skills, muscle spasticity and weakness, poor sense of balance and reduced self-esteem. She was unable to lift her right arm but did have some use of the right hand and fingers.

Before the accident, Brenda was an accomplished rider. Being able to continue riding, an activity that she loved, gave her a connection with her past. Goals were set by Brenda and her instructor. Goals included using horseback riding to improve memory skills, using techniques she was using in her therapy sessions. Memory was improved by memorizing the names and uses for different tack, horses' names and a dressage pattern. Other goals included strengthening the legs and back, improving posture and regaining self-confidence. Brenda stated "I hope that this therapy can help others as much as it has helped me. Horseback riding has given me, my family and my therapist a way of evaluating my on going progress."

EVALUATION

Brenda was first evaluated at the Friends of Whitemud Equine Centre Special Needs Riding Program in May of 1993 by riding instructor Marylou Dickson. The client was accompanied by her family who needed to be assured that riding would be safe and something the client could manage physically, mentally and emotionally.

The client was observed and asked applicable questions. Balance, strength and cognition were observed and evaluated. Her reaction to the horses and other animals at the barn was noted. Because a stable is a place with a large number of allergens, her reactions to the barn environment were observed during this evaluation. One of the concerns that her father had was the use of an English saddle rather than a Western one. He was assured that by using an English saddle, Brenda would have a closer contact with the horse as well as increasing her balance.

Brenda showed no sign of fear or uneasiness. She appeared relaxed in the stable environment. Her balance was weak. She needed to hold on to someone while walking. She appeared to have potential for increasing her strength while riding. Brenda understood everything that was asked of her and answered questions in a well thought-out manner.

GOALS: Physical, Mental, Emotional:
1. Increase balance, physical strength, and memory skills
2. Relaxation during independence in mounting
3. Increase cognition while riding
4. Strengthen application skills
5. Increase self-esteem and self-confidence

HORSE TYPE AND EQUIPMENT

The horses used were quiet, reliable, patient and of varying heights (14.2 to 16 hands). Quarter horse or Quarter horse-cross horses seem to be the most appropriate for Brenda. We found that the Arabian cross-horses were a little too nervous for her. The horses that Brenda rode had gaits that were fairly regular and smooth. This allowed Brenda to not have to worry about her balance. As Brenda's balance, strength and confidence increased, we changed from shorter mounts (14.2 h) to taller mounts (16.h).

Tack used included: a helmet, and all-purpose English saddle, saddle aids, bridle, loop reins and a standing martingale. Brenda had one of the tack shops make her reins with loops in them. Without the loops, the reins tended to slide through her hands. Loops helped her keep consistent contact on the horse's mouth.

VOLUNTEERS

Brenda had an aide who came with her and was able to act as a leader as was needed. The aides for Brenda had been around horses and were quite capable volunteers. Also, they were very responsive to any volunteer training given.

PROCEDURES

The procedures were split into the following sections: evaluation, orientation, first few lessons, first year, second year and conclusion.

THE FIRST GROUP OF LESSONS:

Brenda rode either once a week or every other week. The lessons lasted one hour with riding and general horse care, ie: grooming, tacking-up. Horses used were 14.2 - 15 h, quiet, patient and average in width. During the first few lessons, the client was evaluated for riding ability. I also was able to determine the horses that would best suit Brenda's needs. The first lessons took place in an indoor riding arena with the goals to improve balance, coordination and memory.

Lessons consisted of basic position, steering, natural aids, both spoken and physical and a variety of exercises. These exercises included reaching toes, touching the horse's hip with opposite hand and reaching for the horse's ears. These were done at a halt and walk. As Brenda began her lesson she showed a great determination to excel in her progress as a rider. Not only did Brenda retain her horse sense but her basic seat was strong as well.

FIRST YEAR:

As the first year progressed, Brenda's confidence increased as well as balance and ability to remember instructions. We went from a basic seat at walk and halt, at the sitting trot and posting at a walk. We even got a canter one day and Brenda managed beautifully, sitting well. Brenda would go through obstacle courses where she would have to steer her steed between jump standards and stop and turn in various directions.

The steering was a bit of a problem because the reins would constantly slide through Brenda's right hand. Loop reins were obtained which insured that Brenda could hold onto the reins without them sliding through her fingers. The loops are just the right size so that it is very difficult for her whole hand to slip through them. With the rein problem solved, Brenda's ability to maneuver the horse increased drastically.

As the warm weather approached in the spring, Brenda's lessons consisted of grooming, tacking and a trail ride. Brenda rode along the trails dealing calmly and skillfully with any obstacles encountered. Independence was one important aspect that Brenda had desired in every area of her life so, of course, this included her riding. Brenda was given the opportunity to groom as independently as possible. She managed the brushing and currying well. Because of Brenda's difficulty with balance, it was difficult for her to bend over and hold the hoof while picking out the foot. To assist her, the hooves would be held up for her as she picked them. Sometimes, Brenda would hold up the hooves, and then they would be picked out for her. Grooming was a small area where Brenda found some independence. Remembering the names of the tack and grooming tools helped Brenda work on her memory. Brenda's balance improved enough so that she could step up onto the mounting block with little assistance and mount without me stepping up with her. I stood to the back of the block so I could be there if Brenda required any assistance with balance or assistance to get her right leg over the horse's hindquarters. This assistance would consist of me gently helping her abduct her leg.

SECOND YEAR

At the beginning of Brenda's second year, she mounted without a mounting block. I still assisted her by gently holding her side as she put her foot in the stirrup, and then giving her a slight boost as she pulled up into the saddle to ensure she did not lose her balance. While mounting, one of the problems Brenda had had been abducting her right leg enough as she swung it over the horse's hindquarters so she would not rub the horse with it. The client was given stretching and abduction strengthening exercises to assist in mounting. Within a few weeks, Brenda was able to mount without touching the horse's hindquarters with her right leg. She was given assistance lifting her leg depending on how she was on a particular day. Usually, there was very little assistance required.

Dressage patterns were used (see Appendix A) to develop Brenda's riding and memory skills. In the second year she began to walk without a leader while in the arena. The horse's martingale was lengthened a number of holes so that it could be used as a handhold when Brenda was doing exercises. Brenda's muscular control of her head and neck and partial paralysis of her hand, caused her hand to bob quite a bit so we no longer trotted. Brenda did, however, do the posting motion at a walk to improve her balance and strength.

RESULTS AND CONCLUSIONS

The goals that were set at the beginning are being met and will continue to be met. Brenda's physical strength, flexibility, balance, and skill have improved as described in her mounting ability. Her mental abilities, such as memory and cognition, have improved. She increased her ability to apply what she has learned. She knows the names of all the tack and grooming tools. She can perform the dressage course without help. She has become more independent at something she loves to do. The increase in independence has increased her emotional strength, self-esteem, self-confidence and self-concept.

Brenda has bought her own horse and will continue to enjoy, learn and develop her abilities as she rides and carries on with her rehabilitation.

Marylou R. Dickson
Brenda L. Belec
USA

APPENDIX A

DRESSAGE PATTERN

Halt at X facing B.

Walk on to B and turn right.

Walk around the whole arena to B and halt at B.

Walk around arena again, this time halting at each letter F, A, K, E, H, C, M, B.

Walk around the arena to K and walk across the diagonal to M . Turn left to C.

At C begin a serpentine by going from C to H, from H to M, M to B, B to E, E to K, K to F, F to A.

At A walk on around the arena to C.

At C walk straight but at an angle towards B.

At B walk straight but at an angle towards A.

At A walk to B and turn right and halt at X.

At X change reins into your best steering hand and grab onto the martingale with the other and ride in the two-point position to B.
Turn left.

Continue in the two-point position all around the arena till A.

At A post at the walk until C. Sit.

At C turn left towards X and halt.

Main Door

PART II
THE HORSE

CHAPTER 6
THE CONFORMATION OF THE HORSE - ITS SIGNIFICANCE TO THERAPEUTIC RIDING

The Horse

Oh horse you are a wondrous thing,
No buttons to push, no engine that pings.
You start yourself, no clutch to slip,
No dead battery, no gears to strip.
No license buying every year,
With plates to screw on front and rear.
No gas fumes polluting each day,
Taking the joys of nature away.
No speed cops dashing into view,
Writing a ticket out to you.

Your super-treads all seem OK,
And hoof-pick in hand, they should stay that way.
Your spark plugs never miss and fuss,
Your motor never makes us cuss,
Your frame is good for many a mile,
Your body never outdates its style.
Your needs are few, and happily met,
We honor you, we're in your debt!
You serve us well, as our riders you carry,
Making instructors, volunteers - the whole team merry.

Yes, Horse, you are a wondrous thing,
Teacher--Therapist--Friend,
your praises we sing!

Jean M. Tebay

CONFORMATION FACTORS AND THEIR RELATION TO THERAPEUTIC RIDING

Barbara T. Engel, MEd, OTR

The horse is the *focus* of any equine-assisted activity such as therapeutic riding, equine-assisted psychotherapy, equine-assisted speech pathology and hippotherapy. The characteristics and the quality of the horse determine, to a great degree, the quality of services which are provided to the consumer, the persons with disabilities. Instructors and therapists **MUST** understand the horse in terms of its anatomy and kinesiology, its nature and trainability, and its effects upon the rider under specific conditions. This chapter directs the reader's attention to areas that are of major concern to all those who are involved in the field of therapeutic riding.

Conformation, according to Webster (1966, *Webster's New World Dictionary of the American Language.* 1966, Cleveland: The World Publishing Co.), is the complete and symmetrical formation and arrangement of parts. The conformation of a horse is a major factor in determining the quality of movement, structural soundness and usefulness with specific riders and appropriateness for individual tasks. Conformation alone will not produce a good balanced and forward-moving horse. The horse must also be trained to develop its athletic abilities through cultivating the muscular, cardiovascular and nervous systems.

Therapeutic riding programs have developed on the concept that the horse influences the rider. Over the years many specialists have studied how the horse influences the rider and what qualities are desirable for specific tasks. Tasks may include dressage training, driving, vaulting, gymkhana, jumping, trail riding, equine-assisted therapy or developing physical and recreational skills in the rider with a disability. Each of these tasks requires the selection of an appropriate horse. The instructor must have knowledge of conformation and how the horse moves in order to effectively train and direct the horse's influence upon the rider.

The selection and training of a horse to meet a program's needs will be discussed. The appropriateness of the horse will lead to the achievement of both the goals of riders and the program's aims. The horse that is well trained in basic dressage techniques (either through English or Western training), is responsive, supple and *balanced.* It can be used for therapy and for riders who wish to develop riding skills. The vaulting horse is used for the gymnastics on horseback. The carriage horse is used in driving programs. Some horses will have characteristics which will meet several needs while other horses may be used specifically, just for one task. The knowledge of these characteristics is important in developing a program and in the selection of horses appropriate to the task.

It is important to understand conformation components in relation to training and to maintaining the horse in a healthy state. Some defects can be compensated for by other good points or by training the horse to overcome negative factors. One must always keep in mind what it is that the horse is to do.

- ❑   What form must the horse take to accomplish the requested task?
- ❑   How can the horse be helped to accomplish the task?
- ❑   Has the horse been trained to the level essential for a given task?
- ❑   Is he presently in condition for the task or has there been a year or so of lapse in training?

This section is not intended to be a text on conformation but rather it highlights major factors and thereby underscores to the reader the importance of the subject. A full understanding of conformation can be acquired by reading text books on the subject.

THE HORSE'S SKELETON

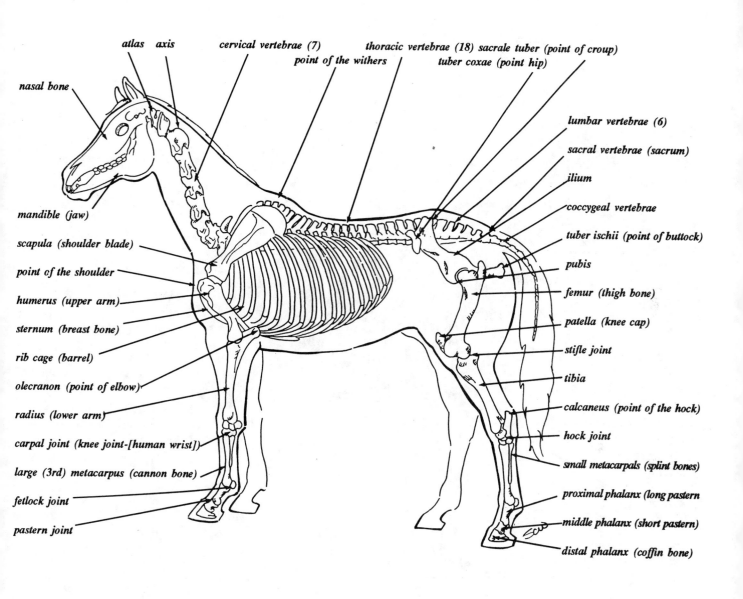

atlas *axis*   *cervical vertebrae (7)*   *thoracic vertebrae (18) sacrale tuber (point of croup)*
point of the withers   *tuber coxae (point hip)*

nasal bone

lumbar vertebrae (6)

sacral vertebrae (sacrum)

ilium

coccygeal vertebrae

mandible (jaw)

scapula (shoulder blade)   *tuber ischii (point of buttock)*

point of the shoulder   *pubis*

humerus (upper arm)   *femur (thigh bone)*

sternum (breast bone)   *patella (knee cap)*

rib cage (barrel)   *stifle joint*

olecranon (point of elbow)   *tibia*

radius (lower arm)   *calcaneus (point of the hock)*

carpal joint (knee joint-[human wrist])   *hock joint*

large (3rd) metacarpus (cannon bone)   *small metacarpals (splint bones)*

fetlock joint   *proximal phalanx (long pastern*

pastern joint   *middle phalanx (short pastern)*

distal phalanx (coffin bone)

FIGURE 1.
THE SKELETON OF THE HORSE

101

POINTS OF THE HORSE

Points of a horse define distinct "parts" of a horse and each horse has these same parts regardless of breed. Collectively the **points** define conformation. Variations in conformation can be found from breed to breed and horse to horse. For example, the conformation of a Hanoverian is different than that of a Thoroughbred or Iceland horse - for example in the shape and set of their necks.

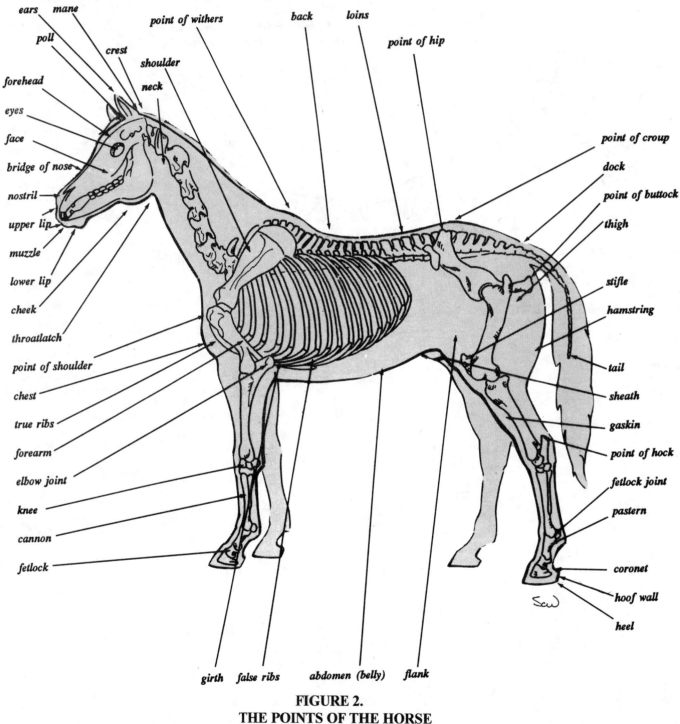

FIGURE 2.
THE POINTS OF THE HORSE

CONFORMATION TERMS AND FAULTS--ILLUSTRATED

Barbara T. Engel, MEd, OTR

> **Conformation influences balance, smoothness, quality of movement, soundness, strength and endurance**

This section on conformation terms and faults is an overview of some current literature on conformation. It is the intent of this section to emphasize the importance of conformation as it can influence the rider in a therapeutic riding program, and it should encourage instructors and therapists to expand their knowledge in this field by reading standard texts on the subject and attending clinics. "A horse's conformation holds the clues to his soundness and performance potential (Practical Horseman, 1992)." **In the field of therapeutic riding, performance potential relates to the effect the horse has on a rider in addition to the skills the horse must perform. Conformation faults may have a negative impact upon a rider and as a result the *therapeutic* riding value may diminish or may actually be detrimental to him or her**. If a horse has difficulty finding his own balance with a rider astride due to conformation faults or poor muscular development, he will not stimulate balance in the rider. Balance is the basis of human function and of primary importance in rehabilitation. Balance is the basis of developing riding skills. It is, therefore, clear that the knowledge of the anatomical structure and movement of the horse is of primary importance to both instructors and therapists involved in therapeutic riding programs.

Throughout this section, it is important to refer to the illustrations of the skeleton and points of the horse on the proceeding pages. Become familiar with the terminology of the parts of the horse and the names and location of the major supporting bones. For therapists, this is an easy task since the skeleton of the horse is not so different from the skeleton of the human. The muscle system is of major importance to conformation. It should be studied in order to understand leverage, strength and endurance and to assist maintaining health and performance of the horse. Some faults are more serious than others; while some can be counterbalanced with training and conditioning. Remember that a horse who carries a rider with imbalances that is stiff or has poor muscle tone, carries a load that is 20 to 30% heavier than the normal athletic horseman. This requires the horse to maintain his athletic ability. Coming to a therapeutic riding program has not placed the horse on semi-retirement. It has placed him in a job of constant changes and requiring him to carry difficult and imbalanced riders whether they be small or large.

Since therapists are more familiar with the structure of bones, muscles and connecting tissue, and instructors have the knowledge of horsemanship, it would be beneficial for the instructors and their assistants to join with the therapists to study the subject of conformation. This subject is of prime importance to both the therapist and the instructor.

OVERALL GENERAL APPEARANCE OF THE HORSE

At a distance, the horse should look well proportioned, balanced and have well-developed muscles. All parts should flow smoothly well into each other[16]. The following descriptions are in anatomical terms, not necessarily in terms used in judging. A general guide to overall **body proportions** is fitting the body and legs of a horse into a square box [5,20,6,16]*; there will be some variation from breed to breed. The top of the square is equally divided between the shoulders, the back, and the hip.

* In this article numbers will indicate the references listed at the end of this chapter, due to limitations of space.

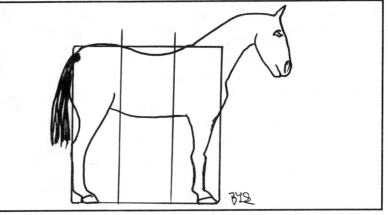

The size of the **head** (from the poll to the muzzle, **1 to 2**) is generally equal to[4,20,6,16]:

1. The point of withers to point of shoulders **(6 to 7)**
2. Point of shoulders to throat latch **(7 to 3)**
3. Cervical base of the neck **(4 to 5)**
4. Waist (point of hips to flank) **(14 to 11)**
5. Point of stifle joint to point of hock **(15 to 13)**
6. Point of the fetlock to point of elbow **(9 to 8)**
7. Point of hip to point of buttocks **(14 to 12)**
8. Point of buttocks to point of the stifle **(12 to 15)**
9. Point of hocks to the ground **(13 to ground)**

Other **body proportions** are[20,5,16]

10. The withers to abdomen equal abdomen to ground **(6 to 8 to ground)**
11. Withers to ground equal point of shoulders to point of buttocks **(6 to ground = 7 to 12)**
12. Top of the croup to the ground equals the top withers to the ground (equals ½ times the size of the head.) **(10 to ground = 6 to ground)**

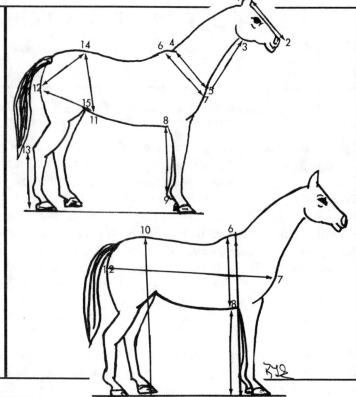

FIGURE 4.

The horse's **head** is composed of the skull and houses the brain, eyes, teeth, jaw and nasal cavity. It is used as an oscillating pendulum to vary distribution of body weight and to effect the center of gravity during movement[7,15,21,22]. The average horse's head weighs forty pounds which he uses to effectively mobilize his body[7].

1. The skull should be well structured and proportioned to size of horse[15,21,22]

The **head** should:

2. Be well set on, with smooth connection to neck[5,16]
3. Have a forehead wide enough to comfortably and efficiently house the brain, sinus, eyes and upper jaw[16,15]
4. Have good width between eyes, good length between the eyes and nostrils to allow free breathing and air intake to be heated or cooled before entering the lungs[16,15,21,22]
5. Have a jaw proportional to the head[16,15,21,22]
6. Have space between lower jaw and neck to allow for bending at the poll and space for windpipe[5,6,9,10]
7. Have a good expression--expression portrays the horse's emotions, moods and temperament[5,6,9,10]

FIGURE 5.

Possible problems with the **head** include:

1. A head too large for the body puts added weight to the forehand
2. A large head on a long neck puts too much weight on the forelegs[9]
3. A large head on a short neck displaces balance less than a large head on a average size neck[11]
4. A small head is better balanced on a long neck[11] but may not provide a balance leverage for a large horse.
5. When head is set on too close upon the neck, breathing maybe restricted[22]
6. When angle of the head to neck is too acute, it compresses the larynx[10]
7. Horses with excessively long heads may have larger blind spots in front of them on the ground[12]

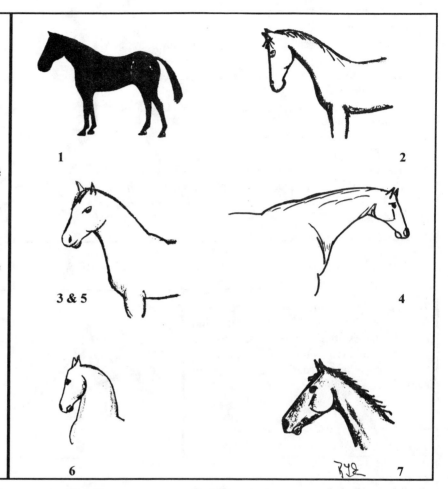

FIGURE 6.

1. Shape of the horse's **face** is triangular from the front and generally straight from a side view.
2. Roman nose/Ram-headed (convex) may impair vision[5]. A roman nose is found in some draft horses.
3. Dish-faced (concave) enhances vision[5,20].
   Dish-face is characteristic of Welsh and Arabian breeds.

FIGURE 7.

105

Eyes should be:

1. Large, round and bright. Increases vision up/down, front/back[22]
2. Wide set to increase the vision field. May indicate good intelligence[15]
3. Warm, friendly, alert and expressive depicting a good temperament[11]

Negative factors are:

4. **Bovine eyes** (popeyed)(bug-eyed) may impair vision[4]
5. **Pig eyes** are small and set far back into head limiting vision and may make the horse nervous because it cannot see the source of sounds[4,5,15]

FIGURE 8.

To enhance hearing the **ears** should be a good size but not too big. They should be relaxed and mobile to hear well in all directions. Alert ears means the horse is attentive to its surroundings. "Back" ears indicate a sour temperament, mad, pain and possibly dangerous horse[4,5,15].

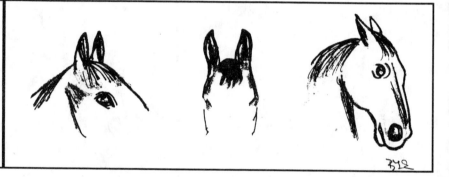

FIGURE 9.

The **muzzle** includes the nostrils, lips and covers the front teeth.

The **nostrils** should be large, sensitive, well-formed and mobile to allow for adequate flow of air into the respiratory system. **Lips** should be firm, muscular and oppose each other evenly. They should have good prehension[5] ability since the horse uses his lips, (especially the upper lip) as a `hand' to feed. The **jaws** influence the lips and must meet evenly. If they do not meet evenly they will interfere with grazing and chewing[11,15]. The size of the jaws determine the size of the bit.

Negative factors include:

1. **Parrot-mouth**--the lower jaw recedes and upper jaw appears buck-toothed[5,8]
2. **Monkey-mouth**--the lower jaw protrudes and the upper jaw recedes[5,8]

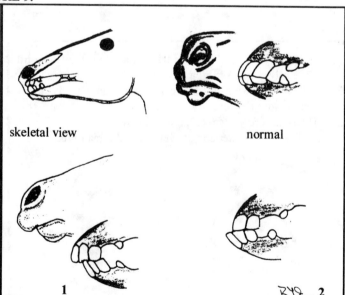

skeletal view

normal

FIGURE 10.

The **neck,** along with the head, plays an essential role in balance and movement of the horse[18]. It acts as a counterbalance and lever to support changes in the horse's center of gravity as he bends, shifts speed or directions[16]. It is composed of 7 cervical vertebrae. The 1st cervical bone, the atlas, enables the head to move up and down upon the neck. The 2nd cervical bone, axis, allows minimal rotation upon the neck. The last five joints allow lateral movement of the neck with some degree of arching[2a,9,20]. The neck must be as long as the horse's forelegs to facilitate grazing[7]. When the head is brought closer to the body, the horse can shift its center of gravity backward. The neck muscles must tie into the body smoothly and hold the neck at such an angle that it can effectively balance the body and help move the shoulders[7,18].

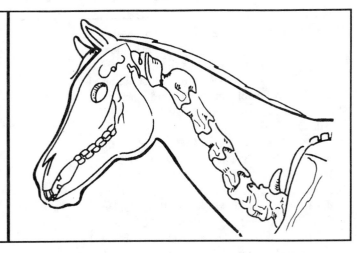

FIGURE 11.

In order for the **neck** to function effectively it should have the following characteristics:

1. Well proportioned length to the rest of the body to assist in balance and movement[6,11,15]
2. Set well into the shoulders (equal on both sides) without hollowing at the shoulder line, to aid over all balance[21,9,5]
3. Be convex with a slight arch between the poll and withers[5]
4. Be more muscular on the top than the underline[11,13]
5. Underline should appears as though it slips into the shoulders with smooth muscles[11,21]
6. The neck should be thicker at the base than at the poll[5]
7. Attached at the head with wide and open throat latch so the head can flex to accept the bit and air can pass through the trachea[4,5,12,20]
8. Long, smooth neck muscles that forms an "S" curve between the poll and point of the withers allowing for flexion at the poll and good head carriage[4,5]
9. Two fingers or more space behind the cheek bones allow for better flexion[11]
10. In motion, the horse's neck should move in tandem, gracefully with the body. It should not jerk, wobble or bob[15].

FIGURE 12.

Negative characteristics affecting the **neck** are:

1. A thick **throat latch**, and/or a severe angle of the neck to the head prevents flexion at the poll[11]. Therefore, the horse may resist the bit and be less flexible for balance and mobility.

2. **Set on to high** and straight causes poor balancing ability[21,9].

3. A **big neck** and large cheek bones decrease the ability to flex at the poll and respond to the bit[15].

4. A **short necked** horse will have shorter strides due to the neck as it will restrict the shoulder' forward[17]. A short neck decreases the horse 's ability to assist in balance and aid in mobility.

5. A **ewe neck** is curved like a sheep's neck with no crest and a bulky muscular lower line. The sagging topline makes flexing at the poll difficult. The head tends to go upward, and control of the bit becomes difficult by the rider[11,3]. The horse may also be under muscled which limits its stride[17]. The angle of the head decreases vision[7].

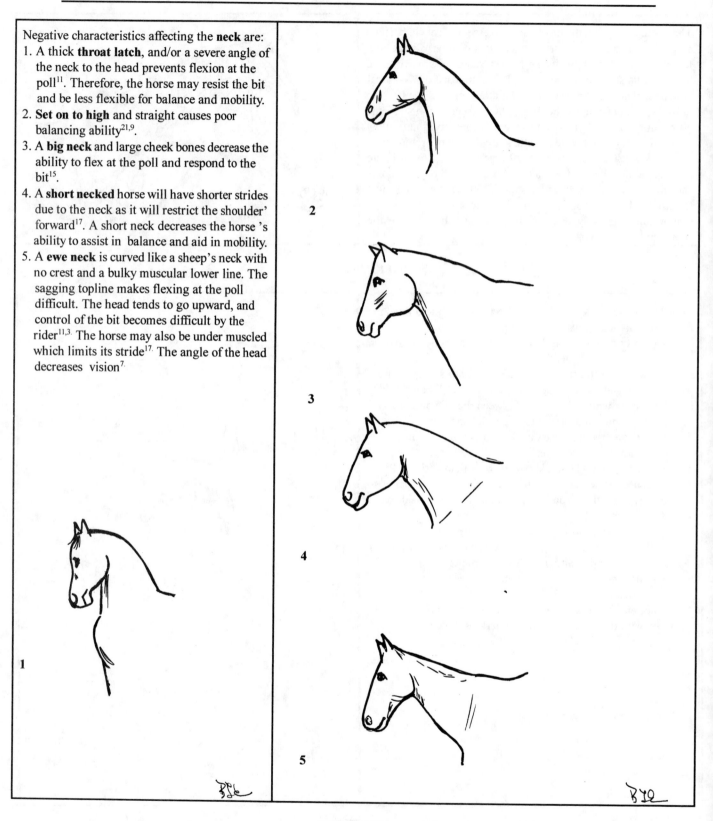

FIGURE 13

Swan neck is a long slender neck held high[11]. It is a long **S**-shaped neck which allows the horse to flex at the poll. The swan neck is not necessarily a negative factor and alone does not influence balance.

Close-coupled or upside-down neck has a heavy muscled underside causing:
1. Discomfort when the horse attempts to flex at the poll or he may not be able to flex at all.
2. Center of gravity shifting forward which may predispose to foreleg unsoundness.
3. Difficulty in reining with light reins because of the head set and rigidity of the neck.

Low-set on neck causes the horse to go on the forehand. Balance and schooling are hindered[9]. The neck shifts the weight forward and may drag down causing weight on the forehand[8,11,10]. Muscles on the lower neck will lose some of their mechanical effectiveness[18,8,10,11].

FIGURE 14

The **shoulder blade** (scapula) rests next to the rib cage and should be flat, long[11], and slope forward 45° to 60°[5]. The length of the scapula determines the degree of slope. A short scapula is more upright than a long scapula[22]. The shoulders are attached to the body by muscles that allow the shoulder-arm joints to absorb the concussion of the forelegs (sling effect)[5,22]. It is the only joint (not a true joint) that is not held together by ligaments - instead muscles and tendons move the limb and hold it together[19]. The deeply defined slope of the shoulders determines the forward angle of movement of the forelimbs. A long shoulder blade causes a longer springy stride on a longer lever, giving more flow of movement and power[19,13,9,5,2c]. An upright shoulder makes the legs susceptible to greater knee action[2b]. But, it shortens the forward stride and dispenses jarring movements to the rider[19].

Positive **shoulder** characteristics include:

1. Shoulder blades close together at the top. Wide apart blades makes the shoulder lumpy, difficult to fit a saddle to, provides poor movement, and is uncomfortable for the rider[21].
2. A distance of one fist between the ribs and the shoulders and at the point of the elbow. This allows freedom of movement of the forelimb[11].
3. Long, broad, sloping shoulders, forming a right angle with the humerus which give a springy stride with a longer forward reach and more ground covering[9].
4. Long shoulder bones which provide for better muscle attachment (the longer the bone, the more acute the angle, the less downward stress is placed on the horse's limbs[16])
5. Withers that are set well back allow the limbs the capability of straightening, increasing the length of stride[19].
6. The shoulders (point of the withers to the point of the shoulders) should not be shorter than the length of the head, to gain the greatest freedom of stride[16].

The angel of the shoulder blade (point of the withers to the point of the shoulder.)*

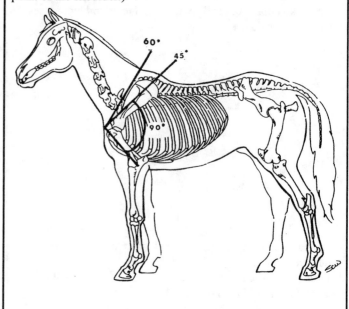

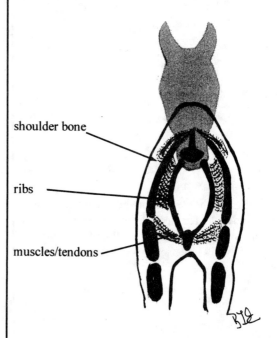

The "sling" construction of the shoulders and forelegs.

FIGURE 15.

Negative shoulder characteristics:
1. Too steep a shoulder: causes stress on the front legs and a hard ride since the concussion is not absorbed by the joints and passes on to the rider[3].
2. Upright shoulder: restricts movement of the humerus, restricts endurance[4,19], and allows the saddle to slip forward[21].
3. Upright shoulder: is more suitable for a harness horse, (providing good pulling power[21]) than for a gaited horse[2b].
4. A short shoulder: is poor for a driving horse - it needs to be well set on the neck with a short back for strength[3].

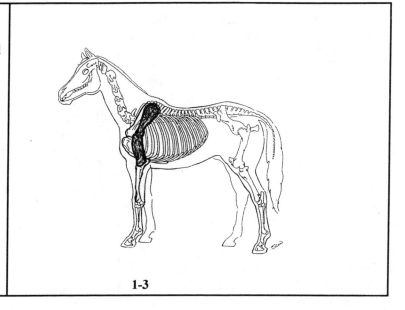

1-3

FIGURE 16.

The **withers** on the top line are made up of the long spinal processes of the 3rd through the 9th or 10th thoracic vertebrae with the scapula laying over the first 7 vertebrae[22]. The spines of the vertebrae taper upward to the 4th vertebrae and then decrease in height to the 15-16th[19,23]. The vertebrae processes should be long, high and broad in conjunction with sloping shoulders to provide effective slant for the attachment for muscles and ligaments of the neck, shoulders, and back. Good withers provide for correct muscles to develop behind the shoulders[6,8].

Good withers characteristics include:
1. Clear definition with sufficient height[14].
2. Similar height as that of the croup[13,11,17].
3. Point of the withers to the point of the elbow generally equals from the point of the elbow to the ground (see figure 4.)

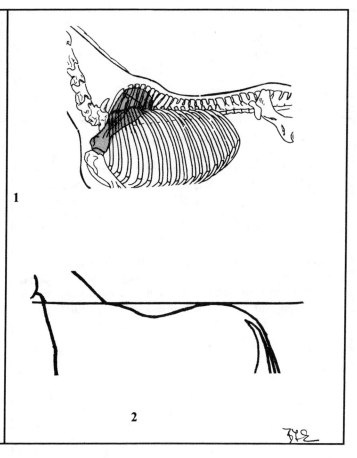

1

2

FIGURE 17.

Negative characteristics of the **withers** include:
1. Withers that are too high; cannot accomodate a saddle fit[21]
1a. Short steep withers
1b. Long steep withers

2. Mutton withers that are low and predispose the horse to clumsiness, forging, and restrict rotation at the shoulder causing him to move in a rolling motion[5].

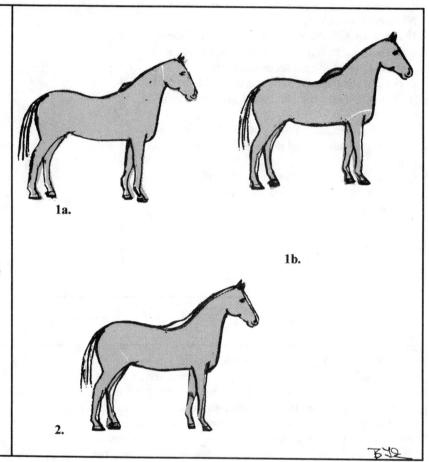

FIGURE 18.

The **topline** of the horse runs from the poll to the dock - in line with the spine[2d,7,11] and is supported by the neck, shoulders, back, loins and croup. It is influenced by the skeletal structure, the spine and muscular development[22,11].

It should not have protrusion, dips or hollows, but have a smooth flowing curves as viewed from the side - slightly concave behind the withers and convex over the loins[15]. Viewed from behind (from a high platform), the topline should form a straight line[2d].

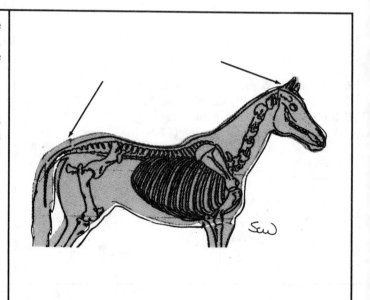

FIGURE 19.

The **trunk** is composed of the chest, abdomen, back, loins and croup. It is slung between the forelimbs (figure 17) in a muscular cradle and attached by a bony union with the hind limbs at the pelvis. It holds the vital organs of the horse in place[22,9,14]. The spine lies in the upper portion of the trunk and allows for limited movement.

The major areas of movement occur in the head-neck region, the cervical-thoracic area, between the last thoracic and 1st limber vertebrae, the lumbar-sacral junction and in the tail - see pointers.

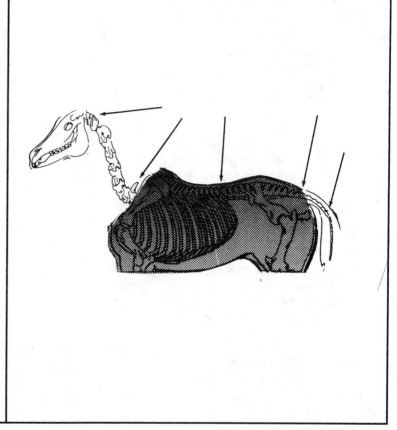

FIGURE 20.

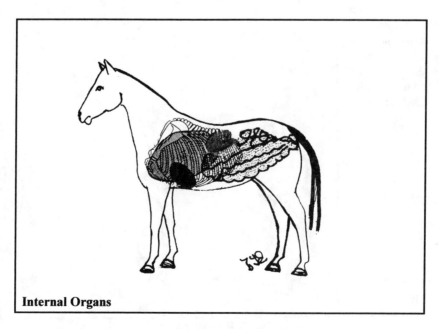

Internal Organs

FIGURE 21.

The **internal organs** of the horse are housed in the **chest** formed by the rib cage and the muscles and the **abdomen** (flank or belly.) The chest protects the lungs and heart, and should be of generous depth to provide space for these organs and be in proportion to the rest of the body. Ribs should be curved outward (well sprung) not flat, set apart, carried well back along the body and not cramped together, to provide good points for attachment of the forelegs and the shoulder muscles and tendons[14,10,4,9.]

The **abdomen** lies below the loins and is formed by many layers of muscle which hold up the belly, intestinal organs and help to support the back[2d,2 3.]

1. The chest should be oval, not oblong or round, placing the legs straight, providing a good seat **(1a)** and straight way of going **(1b)**[6,22].
2. Too narrow a chest (slab-sided) places the front legs close together causing a narrow stance and brushing **(2a)**.
3. Too wide a chest (rounded) may cause a rolling, paddling way of going **(3a)** or criss-cross of the front legs. The rider cannot sit correctly to use the leg and seat aids **(3b)**.
4. A pendulous belly goes with a hollow back - shows lack of fitness and poor strength - see figure **23 (1)**[2d]
5. A belly line that goes downhill will cause the saddle to slide backward[11].

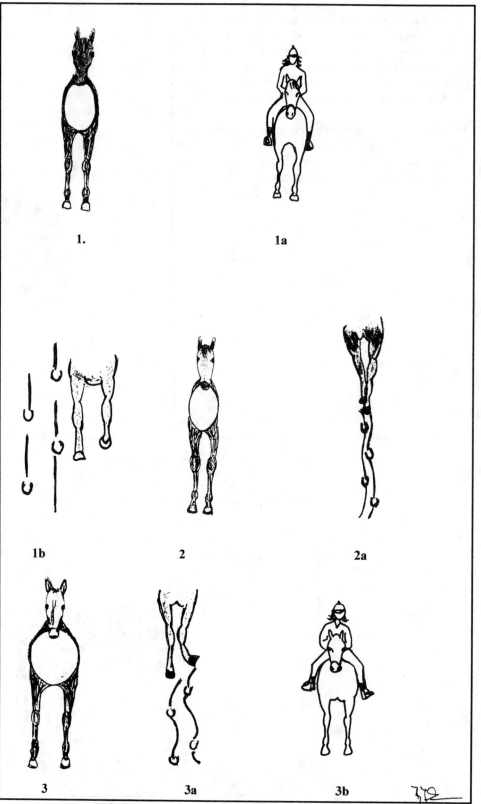

1.   1a

1b   2   2a

3   3a   3b

FIGURE 22.

The **back** is composed of 18 thoracic vertebrae. It should be in proportion to the rest of the body and be well muscled[5,9]. It should be of medium length and almost level. Long backs are comfortable but weak[6,21]. A strong well proportioned, supple back aids good movement of the rider[11].

1. A **hollow back** indicates weakness, poor conditioning, causes damage to the spine, and is difficult to collect[10,21].

2. A **roach back** is arched upward, strong but uncomfortable to sit to, and the stride is short.

3. A **long back** in proportion to the body but with a weak loin, makes it difficult for the hind legs to come underneath the body (collection)[8,11].

4. A **very long back** may be weak and makes it difficult to find an effective center of gravity. This horse may have a swing motion in his stride. These backs must be kept conditioned to avoid weakness[8,11,15].

5. A back that is too **short**, viewed from the side, is difficult to supple and uncomfortable to sit on[8,9,10,11].

6. A **straight back** (top line) restricts the horse's movement and power.

7. A **narrow back**, especially when long, maybe weak and provide a poor base of support for the rider.

8. A back that is **too wide** is difficult to sit on causing the rider's femur (upper leg bone) to hyper-abduct, preventing the use of the seat bones, "seat aids" leg aids, causing the pelvis to tilt and the back to lose its balance and suppleness.

9. The spine must be straight from the poll to the dock as viewed from above 9b. A crooked spine (9a) will cause the horse to be off balance, and the rider cannot sit straight and in-balance.

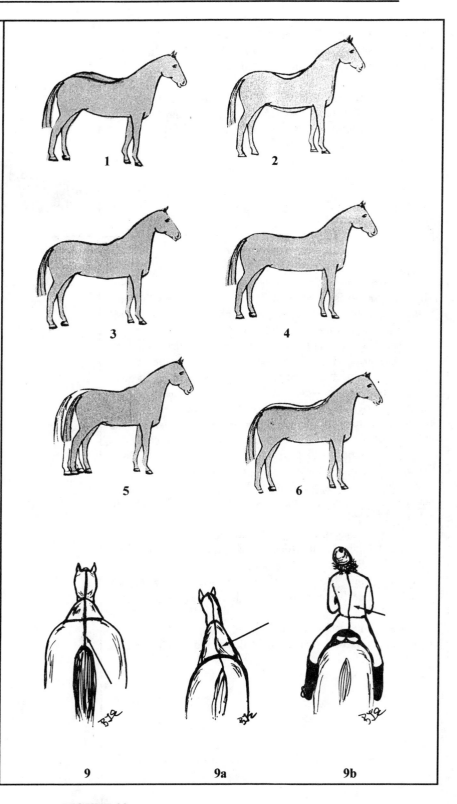

FIGURE 23.

The **loins** are formed by the lumbar vertebrae and have no support other than muscling. They are the weakest part of the back and should be short and well muscled.

1. Lack of muscling usually leads to a sagging back[6,11].
2. A long-coupled horse [2a](one with long loins) may have more difficulty carrying weight than a short-coupled [2b] horse[5,6,7,11].

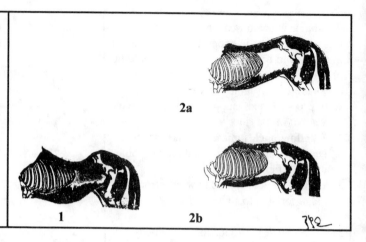

2a

1   2b

FIGURE 24.

The **hindquarter** is the posterior part of the trunk, from the loins to the dock of the tail. It is composed of the (5) fused vertebrae (sacrum), the coccygeal vertebrae (18), the pelvic girdle and the hind legs. The croup is formed by the sacral vertebrae and the first three coccygeal vertebrae. The tail is formed by the remaining coccygeal vertebrae. The pelvic girdle is composed of three bones fused together which are fused to the sacrum at the top. The hindquarters provide the lever, or driving power, of the horse and should be long and slightly sloped and well muscled. A good distance between the point of the buttock to the point of the hip increases movement. The angle of the croup affects the angle of the legs. The angle of the haunches (hindquarters) and the point of the hips should be level and equal. A well set, relaxed tail is not too high on the topline or too low, and aids the horse in balance[5,6,14,15,21,22].

1. A **flat croup** has little flexibility, can cause the stride to be long and flat, makes it difficult for rounding the hindquarters and with collection, and poor power for jumping[11].
2. A **steep croup** (goose-rump) tends to be weak and produces a limited stride due to the lack of angle between the ilium and the femur[13].
3. A **short croup** lacks flexibility, speed, and power[7,9].
4. A **clamped tail** hinders over-all balance and may indicate nervousness[9].

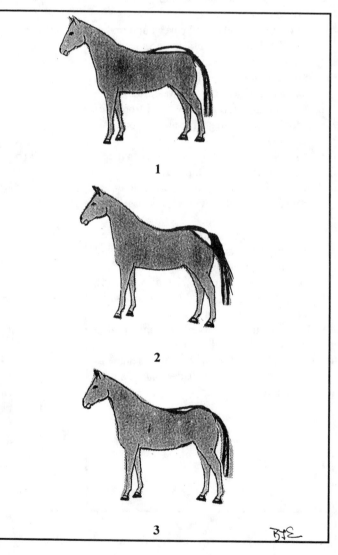

1

2

3

FIGURE 25.

116

The **hind legs** are attached to the pelvic girdle at the hip joint and therefore have a direct influence on the spine. The rear leg is designed to push the horse forward (the engine). The stifle should be in line with the body. The part of the leg below the knee or hock has no muscles, and movement is influenced by the muscles above the knee and carried through by tendons with ligaments holding the structures together. The hocks and stifle joints coordinate their movements[21,19,22].

1. The leg should be **straight** as viewed from the rear.
2. Viewed from the side, the point of **hock** should be directly below the point of buttock.
3. The hocks (7 bones) should be prominent, wide, and deep for attachment of tendons. The hock is a major joint.

Negative characteristics of the hind legs are:
4. **Bowlegged or bowed hocks:** as viewed from the rear, the hocks turn out with the toes turning in. This tends to cause an uneven load, twisting the hocks outward and causing strains[10,21,9,16].
5. **Cow-hocked:** as viewed from the rear, the hocks turn inward and close together with toes turned out. They cause the limbs to move outward or rotate instead of forward motion. This tends to strain the hocks, and can cause brushing[21,9,12,16].
6. **Cramped out legs:** legs set out behind the line with the buttocks and prevent the horse from stepping under himself or prevents being "strung out." The legs tend to dig into the ground and cannot lift the body - are poor power producers[5,15].
7. **Cramped in - legs:** legs under the horse decreasing the base of support and decreasing power[5,15].
8. **Post-legged** (upright leg); legs are too straight, lacking spring and length to the stride, causing a short hard ride.
9. **Sickle-hocked:** an increased angulation of the hock toward the front of the horse which over-stresses the ligaments predisposing them to injury[10,12,16].
10. **Straight hocks** - cause more concussion and are prone to strains. A horse with straight hocks also has straight stifles; Therefore it is difficult for him to sit back on his haunches[21,9].

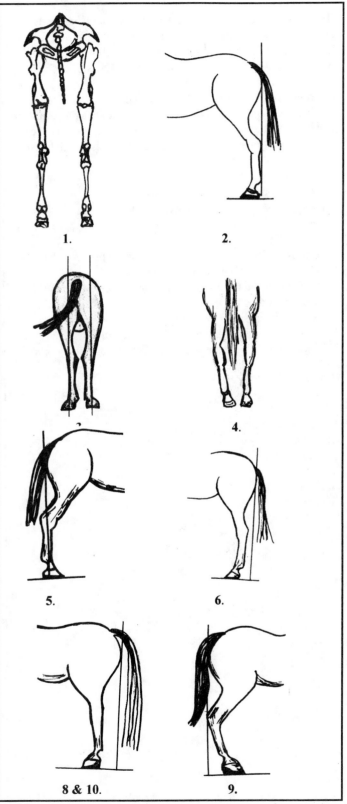

1.   2.

3.   4.

5.   6.

8 & 10.   9.

FIGURE 26.

The **forelegs** are joined by a system of muscles, ligaments and fascia to the body. This system decreases the concussion force to the body when the limb hits the ground and allows the shoulders to drop providing additional "bend" during turns[22].

The **forelimbs** support 2/3rds of the body weight. The foreleg position is dependent on the position and length of the humerus[10,5]. The elbow should be clear of the body so not to interfere with the motion of the leg - about one fist width between the body and the upper limb[3,4,9,11,12,21,22].

The **forelegs** should:

1. Have a knee large, flat and deep to allow attachments of tendons and ligaments to the seven knee bones (there are no muscles below the knee)[21].
2. Be straight from the front, from the point of the shoulder to the ground, to provide a forward gait [21,5].
3. Be straight from the elbow to the fetlock from the side view.[21,5].
4. Have cannon bones short and straight to increase stability[21,3].
5. Have flat[21] fetlocks.
6. Have pasterns of medium length for strength[21].
7. Travel straight in balance causing less stress to the joints[11,10].

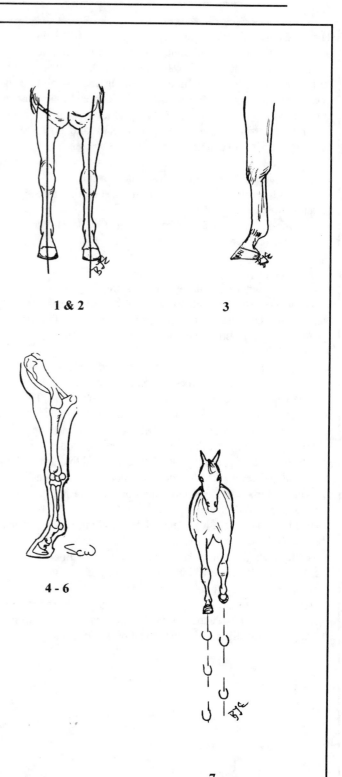

1 & 2

3

4 - 6

7

FIGURE 27.

118

Negative characteristics of the foreleg:

1. Lack of straightness of the legs from the front will affect motion and put strains on the tendons, ligaments and joints[21,5].
2. **Long cannon bone**s - increase weakness and breakdown[22,3,11].
3. Narrow base with **toes out** makes the horse stand on the back of the knees causes winging or dishing[16,5].
4. **Buck-kneed** (over at the knee) are bent forward and become unstable, dangerous for the rider if the leg buckles[12,16].
5. **Calf-knee** (back of the knee) - hyperextension of the knee joint (concave) in front, lacks strength and tends to strain ligaments[12,16,5].
6. **Pigeon-toed** causes the horse to stand with his toes pointing in toward each other and causes paddling[16].
7. **Cramped in legs** are under the horse decreasing the base of support and decreasing the power[5,15].
8. **Splay footed** (toed out) that cause "winging" to the inside and may hit the opposite limb and prone to injury[16,5].
9. **Knock-kneed** the knees are closer together than at the chest or feet, restricts movement and strains the knees[16,5].
10. **Bench kneed** (offset) is caused by the cannon bone being offset set the knee joint - not lined up at the center of the joint[12,1].
11. **Tied in below the knee** when the cannon bone is narrower below the knee than at the fetlock.

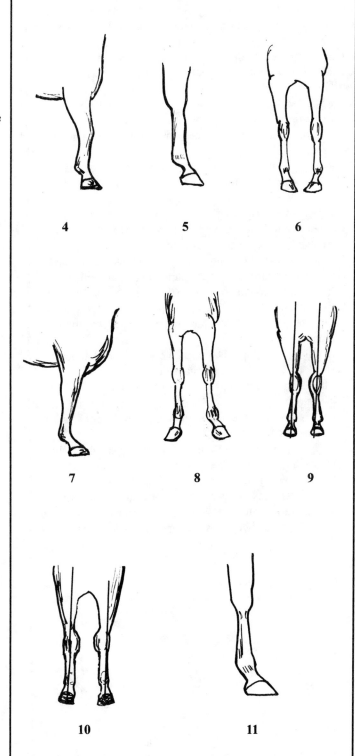

FIGURE 28.

Hoof and pastern should be in proportion to the size of the horse: ie; large horses with large and broad hooves; ponies, with smaller and more upright hooves. Healthy frogs act as shock absorbers, provide a foothold and aid in the pumping action and circulation of the blood to the leg. The horn should be hard, the frog well developed and healthy and open at the heel[5,6,9,18,14].

1. Pasterns:
   a. Short-upright--increased shock on the pastern and fetlock joints with increased risk of injury and a harsh ride[9,11,12].
   b. Long-sloping pasterns provide a springy ride but are predisposed to strains, bowed tendons, and navicular unsoundness[21,3,15,11,12].
   c. Pasterns that are very flexible cause a slow pace[9]
2. Front and hind feet should be the same size, matched in frog size and angle to the ground[19].
3. The heel of the hoof should be wide (3a). A closed-contracted heel (3b) hinders the pumping action needed in the circulation of blood flow to the leg[12].
4. The sole should be concave; aids gripping power.
5. Flat-feet are less shock-absorbing, prone to corns, weakness and bruising[12].
6. Small feet develop foot unsoundness because of major shock to the absorbing mechanism.
7. Slope of hoof wall should be 45 to 55 degrees.
8. The slope of the hoof wall should be the same as the angle of the pastern. The normal angle of the hoof forms an even arc in foot flight[5].
9. Boxy feet, (mule-footed) that have a high heel and a short toe have little weight bearing surface and are prone to breaking down and incorrect foot flight[5].
10. Long toe with low heels may cause bruising to the heel or navicular area, interferes with balance and balanced foot flight. A low heel deprives the leg of the necessary spring [5,10,11].

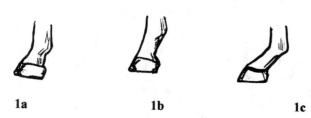

1a   1b   1c

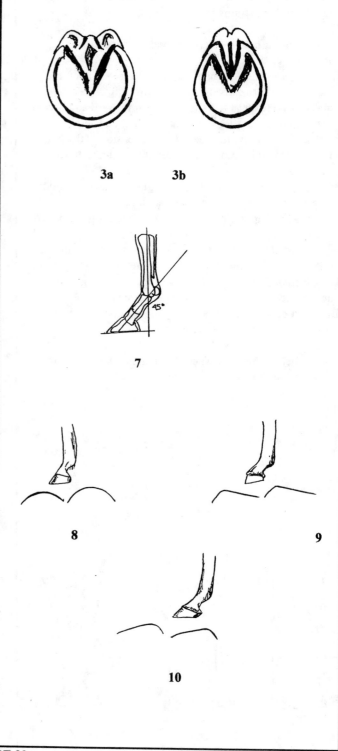

3a   3b

7

8   9

10

FIGURE 29.

BIOMECHANICS:

"Biomechanics applies mechanical principles to the study of living systems"[24] Equine biomechanics involve the study of the moving system of the horse. "This process, which is known as gait analysis, measures a horse's performance objectively and allows us to quantify some aspects of performance that are not visible to the human eye."[24]

Areas such as:

a) Measurements of the horse's performance and/or level of training can be compared to other horses of equal abilities.

b) Detecting subtle lameness or asymmetries.

c) Measuring strains in different parts of the body.

d) Measuring8 the effect of footing and shoeing on the performance and soundness[24]

We shall watch closely the research that Dr. Clayton is involved with at Michigan State University regarding the movement of the horse as a equine athlete with the emphasis in the area of dressage.

Barbara T. Engel
USA

References cited in Figures

1   Adams, O.R. (1987). *Lameness in Horses*. Philadelphia: Lea and Febiger.

2a   Bennett, D. (1990). Clinic, Los Angles.

2b   Bennett, D. (1988). *Principles of Conformation Analysis, Vol I*, Gaithersburg: Fleet Street Publishing Corp.

2c   Bennett, D. (1988). The right angle on shoulders. 130, 100-105. *Equus*. Gaithersburg: Fleet Street Publishing Corp.

2d   Bennett, D. (1989). *Principles of Conformation Analysis, Vol II*, Gaithersburg: Fleet Street Publishing Corp.

3   Bromily, M. (1987). *Equine Injury and Therapy*. New York: Howell Book House Inc.

4   Borton, A. (1990). Selection of the horse. In Evans, Borton, Hintz, & L.D. Van Vleck. *The Horse*. New York: W.H. Freeman and Co.

5   Evans, J.W. (1989). *Horses*. New York: W.H. Freeman and Co.

6   Froissard, J. (1967). *Equitation*. Cranbury: A.S. Barnes and Co.

7   Green, Ben K. (1991 revised). *Horse Conformation*. Northland Publishing.

8   German National Equestrian Federation. (1985). *The Principles of Riding*. New York: Arco Publishing Inc.

9   German National Equestrian Federation. (1987). *Horse Management*. Gaithersburg: Half Halt Press

10   Hadfield, M. (1982). *The Manual of Horsemanship*. New York: Barron's Educational Series Inc.

11   Henriques, P. (1991) *Conformation*. Buckingham, GB:Threshold Books

12   Hill, C. (1988). *From the Center of the Ring*. Pownal: Garden Way Publishing Book

13   Kidd. J. (1984). *The Better Horse*. New York: Arco Publishing Inc.

14   Oliver, R.,Langrish, B. (1991). *A Photographic Guide To Conformation*. London: J.A. Allen & Co. Ltd.

15   Pascoe, E. (1986). *The Horse Owner's Preventive Maintenance Handbook*. New York: Charles Scribner's Sons

16   Practical Horseman, Editors. (March, April, May 1992). *Conformation*. Coatesville: Practical Horseman

17   Practical Horseman, Editors. (1988). *In the Design of a Head, What Really Matters*. Coatesville: Practical Horseman

18   Practical Horseman, Editors. (1988). *What do You Like About a Neck*. Coatesville: Practical Horseman

19   Roomey, J. (1974). *The Lame Horse*. Cranbury: A.S. Barnes

20   Savitt, S. (1981). *Draw Horses*. New York: Bonanza

21   Smallwood, P. (1988). *The Manual of Stable Management: The Horse. British Horse Society. Gaithersburg: Half Halt Press*

22   Smythe, R.H.(1975*). The Horse Structure and Movement. 2nd Ed. Revised by P.C. Goody. London: J.A. Allen & Co Ltd*

23   Way, R.F. (1983). *The Anatomy of the Horse. Millwood: Breakthrough Publications*

24   Clayton, HM. (1997). Biomechanics of the Horse. USDF Conference, LA.

THE VITAL PARTS OF THE HORSE

Barbara T. Engel, MEd, OTR

1   PULSE

2   RESPIRATION

3   ABDOMINAL SOUNDS

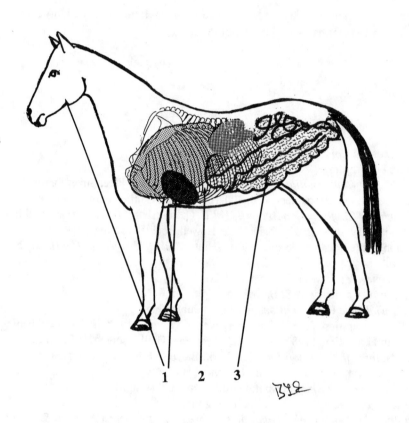

HORSE VITAL PARTS

MEASUREMENTS OF THE HORSE

SIZE OF THE HORSE IN <u>HANDS</u>: 4 INCHES = ONE HAND
A 15 hand horse is 60 inches high at the point of the withers to the ground

MEASUREMENT FOR A HORSE BLANKET

The Age of a Horse

To tell the age of every horse
I inspect the lower jaw, of course;
The six front teeth the tale will tell,
And every doubt and fear dispel.

Two middle nippers you behold
Before the colt is two weeks old;
Before eight weeks two more will come;
Eight months the corner cut the gum.

The outside grooves will disappear
From middle two in just one year,
In two years from the second pair;
In three, the corners, too, are bare.

At two the middle nippers drop;
At three, the second pair can't stop;
At four years old the third pair goes;
At five a full new set he shows.

The deep black spots will pass from view
At six years from the middle two;
The second pair at seven years;
At eight the spot each corner clears.

From middle nippers upper jaw
At nine the black spots will withdraw;
The second pair at ten are white
Eleven finds the corners light.

As time goes on the horsemen know
The oval teeth, three-sided grow;
They longer get, project before
Till twenty, when we know no more.

Anonymous

INTRODUCTION

The horse in movement can be appreciated at many levels. A passe
seemingly fragile limbs in play at pasture, their attempts to emulate
and alarming. The potential buyer will watch with a critical and pract
potential, suitability and soundness for the task in mind. The veter
move with confidence and grace both with and without a rider, as it
its soundness of movement. As scientists study the movement of hoi
of them, the ability of horses to move four legs, in various sequences,
more amazing, not less.

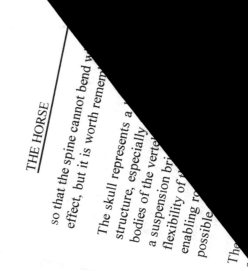

In order to better understand the horse's movements, the skeleton, joints and muscles are viewed from a functional
The appearance of the horse will tell one not only what is possible for it to do, but much of what it already has done. By looking
at the functional anatomy of the horse and appreciating the consequences of the anatomy, one optimizes the use of the horse and
avoids the battle of trying to get the horse to do something that, in terms of functional anatomy, it is not designed to do.

THE SKELETON

The skeleton acts as a series of levers, articulated by joints, stabilized by ligaments, moved by muscles and tendons and coordinated by nerve impulses. The limits of these systems will dictate the workings of the whole. The skeleton has three major
functions, support, protection and movement. The architecture of the component bones of the skeleton is a compromise between
these three and as such will always have some areas of weakness for a given function.

It is worth remembering that about 90% of bone growth occurs in the first 18-24 months of the horse's life, dependant upon
the breed. During this time bones are easily deformed, but need to be allowed to respond to the range of movement that will
expose the developing bones to loading patterns to be met in later life. This means that keeping excess weight down and
maximizing natural exercise patterns, in other words, being a horse. Bone is a living tissue that responds positively to loading
by becoming more dense. Response time is delayed, commencing after about three months of exposure to loading. Overload
the bones will result in degenerative changes. Ligaments and tendons also respond to exercise, but research suggests that this
response may be slower than bone. During this crucial development time, diet is crucial, as sufficient nutrients must be supplied
to lay down quality bone, without encouraging over development of muscle or, even more unforgivable, fat.

The axial skeleton comprises the skull and the specialized bones of the spine, the vertebrae. These bones provide a protective
covering for the brain and the spinal cord. Comprising the bony box of the skull and in excess of 36 different vertebrae, each
vertebra is cushioned from the next by an inter-vertebral disc. The spine is stabilized in its range of movement by bone to bone
connections called ligaments. These are important as they limit the range of movement of a joint. No amount of muscle
development will allow movement out of this range without damage to the ligaments and a joint. Thus the spine has some
movement, in discrete areas, elicited by active muscle contraction, passive muscle relaxation, triggered by nerve impulse but
constrained by the position of ligaments around joints. Limiting the lateral movement and flexion and extension of the spine
minimizes the likelihood of injury to the spinal cord and maximizes the ability to make use of the power produced by the hind
limbs.

The sequence of the types of vertebrae of the spine allows maximum stability when weighted from below. As a nomadic
herbivore, the horse is designed to carry a load of digesting grass in its guts. These hang below the spine, suspended by
mesenteries, in the abdomen. This weight has the effect of locking the spinous processes (which point caudally then cranially)

ith the direction of the load. Putting a load on top of the spine (i.e., a rider) has much the same
bering that a horse did not evolve for this specific purpose!

heavy weight placed at the end of a relatively long and flexible neck. This is a potentially unstable
when moving. Again, the neck is stabilized by ligaments, running between the vertebrae and from the
rae to the spines of the first half dozen or so thoracic vertebrae, rather like the steel hawsers that hold up
dge. These ligaments then blend into those stabilizing the thoracic spine. Thus the cervical spine has the most
he axial skeleton, the sacral spine the least. The lumbo-sacral junction has some movement in the saggital plane,
tation of the hindquarters under the horse but little lateral movement. Some lateral movement is thought to be
through the thoracic vertebrae, but only in the most cranial and most caudal areas.

appendicular skeleton includes the limbs that are associated with the axial skeleton. The primary functions of the limbs
e support and movement. Only the hind limbs are attached by bone to the axial skeleton, via the pelvis at the lumbo-sacral
junction. The fore limbs are attached by muscle and connective tissue, the horse having no clavicle.

The limbs themselves are not simply columns of bone, but many individual bones and they are stacked at unstable angles.
Again, ligaments hold these bones together around the joints as well as limiting the movement of the individual joints. Such is
the unstable nature of the component parts of the limbs, a sophisticated interplay of all the ligaments and tendons in the limb
are required to prevent muscle fatigue whilst standing still (the stay apparatus of the front and hind limbs).

The limbs and the neck of the horse are linked in their proportions, as the limbs cannot be too long for the neck or the horse
could not graze in comfort, indeed foals can be seen to splay their front legs in order to get their relatively short neck low enough
to graze. Not being a fighting animal, the horse depends on fright and flight as the basic responses for survival. Speeds have
been the evolutionary pressure requiring light distal limb bones, with long tendons attaching these structures to muscles located
above the "knee" and hock. These same tendons are paradoxically seen as the weak link when asking a horse to perform at the
limits of speed.

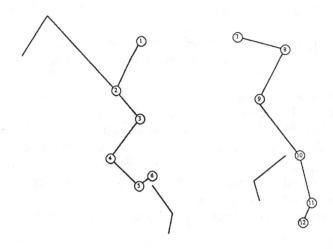

2D Marker Placement
FIGURE 1.

Elegance of design is displayed in the strength of the radius, the curve of the shaft and the off set position of olecranon complementing the lines of force shown in the loaded bone. The bones of the hock joint are precisely designed to cause the rotation outward of the stifle when the hock is flexed, so that the horse neatly avoids jabbing itself in the belly each time the hock and stifle are flexed. The synchrony of the flexions is ensured by the linking of the tendino-ligamentous structures of the hind limb in the reciprocal apparatus.

Number	Skeletal Reference Points
1	tuberosity of scapular spine
2	caudal edge of the greater tubercle of the humerus
3	instantaneous centre of rotation (ICR) of the lateral epicondyle of the humerus,
4	lateral styloid process of the lateral malleolus of the radius
5	lateral collateral ligament as it crosses the joint space of the metacarpophalange al joint
6	continuation of the palmar pastern axis on the caudal, lateral quarter of the hoof capsule
7	ventral, caudal aspect of the palpable tuber coxae
8	cranial aspect of the greater trochanter of the femur
9	proximal extremity of the cranial aspect of the tibial crest
10	lateral malleolus of the fibula
11	lateral collateral ligament (as 5)
12	lateral quarter of the hoof capsule (as 6)

Diagram and table to illustrate the position of the Skeletal Reference Points (SRP's) used to assess left-right symmetry in the horse.

FIGURE 2.

Horses are asymmetric left to right. Have a close look at the pasterns and joints on the fore and hind limbs with the horse standing square. Are the left and right pasterns the same slope? Does the angle of the hock on the left match that on the right? Are the hips level? Do not assume a back problem yet! The hind limbs may be of a different length, rendered functionally similarly by compensation at the hip or stifle and hock. An inspection of the component bone lengths in the fore and hind limbs of the horse suggests that 85-95% symmetry is usual, with 95% being associated with the more elite performers.

The nature of the limbs as levers is well documented. The interplay of these levers will produce the movement of the horses' back that is so desirable at all level of riding therapy. An appreciation of the proportions of these levers by those using the horse is more difficult to impart, as the picture becomes clouded by the accepted tenants of conformation.

Most of us do not have much of an option with the conformation of the therapy horse. We have to work with what we are given. Using markers located on SRP's (see the diagram) palpable landmarks can be visualized. This aids the evaluation of the static and dynamic form of the horse. Simple photographic and video techniques are then applicable to individual horse over time or different horses with each other. Much is happening when a horse moves. If nothing else, these markers serve to concentrate the eye and make sure everyone is looking at the same thing!

MALLEABLE MUSCLES

Clothing the skeletal framework are layers of muscle giving the form that fills the eye when we look at a horse. Comprising contractile proteins assembled together in a hierarchy from component fibrils to individual muscle, muscles are attached to bones by tendons. They can perform work by contraction resulting in stabilizing a joint, by contraction resulting in moving a joint and by contraction preventing movement in a joint. All contractions require energy.

Muscle works on a "use it or loose it" principle. A horse is designed as a lawnmower, and not a very efficient one at that! It must move to eat. Thus head down and weight over the forehand is the natural balance point for the horse, except when fleeing. During flight, the head and neck are extended in order to maximize airflow into the lungs, as in the racehorse. Only in play and display do we see the collected paces so admired by riders and trainers.

The musculature of the horse will tell the observer what muscles it uses during daily activities. The development of these muscles demonstrates what level of activity is being performed. Tension and inequality of tone or even pain will tell one a tale of compensation and discomfort. One of the joys of thorough body brushing during the grooming process is the familiarity gained with the muscles of your horse and the gentle massage that this grooming gives. When a muscle contracts it gets shorter, rounder and more tense. Repeated contractions during a movement sequence result, by muscle fibre cells getting either bigger or more in number, in the muscle concerned getting more developed. Strapping works by taking advantage of this process. Correct muscle development requires that the movement be appropriate and performed correctly. Incorrect muscle development requires that we first establish why the muscle is being used incorrectly before attempts are made to "retrain" or "rebalance" the horse.

The influence of the performance discipline cannot be over emphasized. The racing thoroughbred will, during the gallop, utilize components of the long strap muscles of the neck (sternocephalic and braciocephalic) to maximize the reach and pull of the forelimb. This can result in the appearance of an upside down neck, with pronounced muscle on the underside. Similarly, a dressage horse that has well-established lateral paces, will exhibit a pronounced roundness in the region of the tensor facia latae, due to the development of the muscles associated with adduction and abduction of the hind limbs.

Just as sporting discipline can influence muscle development, acquired movement patterns designed to minimize pain associated with lameness can result in major muscle asymmetry. Swinging front leg lameness can result in a delay in the hoof leaving the ground. This has a knock-on effect on the timing and footfall of the hind foot on the same side, as it can only contact the ground when the front foot is out of the way, if self injury is to be avoided. The compensation in the movement pattern shown by the horse is the movement of that hind limb to the inside track (with consequent risk to the inside of the opposite hind limb) or shortening of the forward swing phase of that hind limb by altering the flexion and extension of the component joints. In an effort to avoid further injury, the horse may push the hindquarters away from the affected front leg, compounding the error of the movement pattern. The muscles of the hind quarters will respond to the different movement pattern, developing unequally. Interestingly, this acquired movement pattern of the limbs can also be elicited by a rider with too much inside rein contact or a leader trying to control a pace, especially the slow walk.

Optimizing the performance of a horse in any sphere means that the horse person must take on accommodating all these factors, monitor the horse's movement patterns, question the importance of changes in that movement pattern, and locate the cause of those changes so that appropriate steps can be taken to increase the quality if life and use for the horse. Looking through the muscular clothes of the horse to the common structure of the skeleton will ensure that the training and development of musculature will be made with the constraints of the framework in mind.

THE GROUND CONTACT POINT - THE HOOF

The single most important thing that we can do for the horses that we use in any way is to ensure that their feet are correctly balanced throughout their life from the first week to the last. Irrespective of whether shoes are ever attached to the feet, the correct medio-lateral and cranio-caudal balance of the hoof with respect to the limb above it, is crucial to maintain the efficient action of the component joints of the limb. If the limb rotates medially, then the foot and hoof must be allowed to follow that rotation; no cosmetic shoeing allowed! There is nothing wrong with remedial farrieries as this supplies an aid to the support surface in the case of a foot that is not supporting the weight bearing structures above it. This is to be applauded as long as the remedy is not so radical as to render the horse seriously uncomfortable.

The sole of the foot is not designed to bear weight. The hoof wall, supported by the bars of the foot, is the main supporting structure. This is further enhanced by well-formed heels and correctly trimmed toes. Except in mid-stance, when the limb is maximally loaded from above, the frog is not designed to be in touch with the ground. Heel expansion occurs at mid-stance and inspection of a cast shoe will readily testify to this movement, showing marked rubbing at the heels of the shoe, on the surface that was applied to the hoof. The same shoe will show the point of break-over, where the toe rolls over prior to the swing phase. This should be in line with the point of the frog.

Break over and toe-off are rapid movements, 0.02 sec. at the trot, and yet this short time can be crucial to avoid striking by the hind foot. Should a horse continually pull off a front shoe with the hind, the owner may ask for the heels of the front shoe to be reduced in length. Yet, this length is often required to give essential support for the heel, especially in the flat-footed horse. Close inspection will often show that the offending shoe may not have been pulled off from the heel, but from the toe, (especially at speed) indicating that the hind is approaching contact when the fore has barely achieved break-over. The answer to either heel or toe strike, is to speed up toe off by shortening the length of the toe, getting the required effect and keeping heel support.

There are few horses that can be said to have an ideal limb conformation. A correct farriery will ensure that whatever the limb conformation, it will be optimized by a correctly balanced foot. Much is made of concussion when the foot is in contact with the ground. Concussion occurs when the hoof first impacts the ground, which occurs prior to full weight bearing. The high impact forces measured at impact are of short duration. In human athletes, the correlation between highest impact forces and degenerative changes on the joint are well established. Some elite athletes put their feet down in such a way as to have significantly lower impact spikes. This group showed a markedly lower incidence of joint changes. These two groups were termed "macroclumpers" and "microclumpers" respectively. It would be interesting to see if the same correlation could be said of horses, and if so, would optimising hoof balance in "macroclumpers" have the effect of minimizing these changes. Work at Bristol University's Equine Sports Medicine Centre, has already established that poor foot balance and symptoms associated with navicular syndrome are linked.

Compression, acting down the limb from above, is the dominant action at mid-stance. The duration of a mid stance varies with the gait and speed. During mid-stance it is essential that the limb's joint surfaces are loaded evenly. The cartilage covering the articular surfaces of the joints is susceptible to point pressure, forcing contained water away from that point, resulting in degeneration of the cartilage, forming pits, cysts and loci for a degenerative breakdown. So, at impact, it is the foot balance that is crucial, at a mid stance, it is the loading of the joints which will be optimized by correctly balanced feet.

GAIT ANALYSIS - TERMINOLOGY FOR THE TERRIFIED

When a horse is moving, specific terminology is used to describe that movement. Terms used in the equestrian world are often not precise enough for scientific use and so scientists have defined a set of terms to give a common language. These bear repeating here, as many scientific papers can be difficult for one using equestrian terminology to understand.

A **gait** is defined as a limb coordinating pattern used in locomotion. Each limb shows a **stance phase** and a swing phase. During a stance phase the limb is in contact with the ground and during a swing phase the limb is traveling through the air. Each stance phase and swing phase is made up of a **protraction** and a **retraction** phase, the former when the limb is moving forwards and the latter when the limb is moving backwards.

A **step** is the stance phase and swing phase for one limb, and a **stride** is a complete cycle of four limb steps and any periods of suspension. A stride is said to commence with the impact of the hind limb after the period of suspension. The **lead leg** is defined as the last leg of a limb pair to leave the ground prior to the period of suspension, and therefore, a stride is said to start with the impact of the **non-lead hind limb**. **Diagonals** are named by the **hind limb** of the pair; the **ipsilateral pair** of limbs are the front and hind limbs on the same side and the **contralateral pair** of limbs are the front pair or the hind pair.

These are fairly standard definitions, but I think one can see that for the equestrian trained person there are areas for confusion. It is important to understand that these terms are for convenience of researchers and scientists and do not necessarily have any training or riding context.

Measurement of stride characteristics demands even more definitions so that other scientists may follow precisely the protocol laid down in a paper. **Stride length** is the distance traveled by a given point of the horse, e.g., the center of mass, in one stride cycle. **Stride duration** is the time required to complete one stride cycle. **Stride frequency** is the number of strides in a given time. Therefore, **velocity** is stride length multiplied by stride frequency, so a horse can either lengthen stride to go faster or increase the rate of striding.

SWINGING THROUGH THE AIR

Protraction comprises the **flexion** and **extension** of the limb with the distal limb moving faster than the trunk into the extended, braced position at the full extent of the forward swing. Using 2 D and 3D motion analysis cameras, markers placed on given joints can be traced through a given gait. These cameras generate a map reference for each marker at least 50 times a second. These numbers are stored in a computer and later used to produce maps of that marker's movement against time, distance or height. Joint angles can also be plotted. This technology is often used in conjunction with a treadmill for horses. This enables running conditions to be accurately reproduced and many repetitions of a given movement to be collected without the horse moving with reference to the camera. A treadmill locomotion differs from over ground locomotion, and this should be borne in mind when looking at the subtleties of gait. Over ground locomotion analysis, especially of elite performers in competition, suffers from only being able to capture one set of data which may not be representative and certainly not repeatable.

The nature of the joint flexions during protraction is gait and speed specific. Left and right limb component joints should show an equal range of movement but it is entirely feasible that the joint maxima and minima may be different. Indeed, this is the way a horse can accommodate limbs of slightly different total bone length and yet the same limb height. A lame horse will show a different range of movement. The patterns of movement in space are also gait and speed specific. The asymmetric nature of the canter is readily identifiable by the path described by the lead and non lead limb markers, especially carpus and tarsus.

Retraction commences at the point at which the **extended** limb starts to move backwards reducing forward velocity to match ground speed prior to impact. It is important to note that retraction commences in a swing phase.

HITTING THE GROUND

At **impact** the foot first touches the ground. The limb is in retraction and is not fully load bearing. At this point the forces acting on the foot are **concussive**, the degree of concussion or vibration set up in the structures of the limb will influence the long term soundness of the horse. Correct **medio-lateral** and **cranio-caudal** foot balance will minimise the degree of concussion experienced at impact. The horizontal forces acting at this point are decelerative.

As the body travels over the grounded limb, the vertical forces experienced by the component structures of the limb increase until **mid--stance** is reached. Mid-stance is characterized by the metacarpal/metatarsal bones in the vertical position. Forces acting at this point are compressive, acting down the limb from above and eliciting peak vertical ground reaction forces. During retraction, the tendons and suspensory apparatus of the lower limb **store energy** that is released at heel-off in order to **catapult** the lower limb forward at the velocity required for protraction. The extension of the fetlock joint reaches its maximum around mid-stance. Once mid-stance is passed, the horizontal forces are accelerative. **Flexion** of the component joints of the limb commences as the body weight passes in front of the limb and the heels lift off the ground at **heel-off** followed by the toe at **break-over**, thus completing **lift-off.**

The pattern of force generation during a stance is again dependant on gait and speed. These forces are measured by allowing the horse to move over a force plate that is hidden under a rubber matting or riding surface. This device uses piezo-electric crystals at each corner of the metal plate to detect the ground reaction forces acting on the hoof as it strikes the plate. This information is passed to a computer for storage. Sophisticated software will convert this information to a series of graphs showing the vertical, horizontal and medio-lateral forces acting on the hoof.

The horse is ridden or led over the plate at the required speed and gait. Only a fore and hind limb can be recorded at anyone pass of walk and trot. At the canter, at times, it is only possible to record one limb. The precise limb sequence on the plate must be visually confirmed. At least six repetitions of each limb strike are used in order to produce an average reading for that limb. Using these traces, the scientist can tell how much a limb is loaded during that step, which limb has the most decelerative action, and which limb or limbs are accelerating or pushing the horse forward.

BACK CHAT

The contact with the ground may be the hoof, but the contact with the rider/patient is the horse's back or whatever we put on it to make that contact more comfortable for the passenger. The collective actions of the limbs move the seating area in a characteristic way dependant on the gait. The walk is unique in that the movements measured here, in all three planes (horizontal, vertical and lateral), are roughly equal. Care must be taken in reading the literature on this to ascertain exactly where measurements were taken.

The front limbs have the effect of raising and lowering the seating area from left to right. The hind limbs have the effect of pushing the seating area forward and back from one hind limb to the opposite fore limb. The four beat sequence of the walk results in a complex interplay of these movements depending which combination of limbs is on the ground.

The long muscles of the back are thought to help stabilize the spine, allowing efficient transmission of power from the hind limbs. The seating area involves intimate contact with these muscles. Symmetry of movement through the horse's back demands even contact with these muscles. As a result, the quality of the seat contact may well determine the quality of the gait. As it improves or equalises, the gait of the horse will subtly change.

The rider will further complicate matters as the seat contact area becomes active and as the rider influences the movement of the horse by accepted movements of the seat, legs, body weight and hands. As soon as this happens, the horse is rebalanced, for better or worse, and the movements of the back may be altered, especially in the relative timings with those movements of the horse.

THINGS THAT MAKE ONE GO "HMMMM"

Muyerbridge was one of the first scientists investigating the sequential movement of the horse using cameras triggered by the horse during its progress at given gaits. These sequential photographs elicited the sequence of footfalls during different gaits with and without a rider. Hildebrand worked along similar lines, postulating that the gaits shown by the horse were a continuum of movement patterns governed by speed of limb movement and efficiency.

Further detailed investigation has awaited the availability of technology to cope with problems of a moving target, variable range and different surfaces. This is without the imponderable of the effect of the rider on the horse. In scientific terms, the effect of the rider has been theorized, not investigated scientifically. By this I mean that there has been no controlled experiment to test a given hypothesis. As such, it is dangerous, as a scientist, to assume that a ridden experiment can be exactly reproduced. Research today falls into three groups:

- Those using motion analysis techniques to investigate performers during competition only getting one chance at collecting data.
- Those using such techniques as force plates and motion analysis techniques in controlled conditions, as far as possible, and obtaining many repetitions of a single task.
- Those using all available techniques to investigate the incidence of lameness and disease.

The latter two may involve the use of a horse treadmill which will eliminate the variables of ground contact and the target moving away from the camera. The downside of this is that the treadmill does not result in exactly the same characteristics as over ground locomotion and that horses have to habituate to the treadmill prior to collection of data. Habituation can occur in as few as three exposures to a treadmill locomotion at the required gaits.

The treadmill belt interacts with the hoof in a completely different way to a riding surface. The sand/rubber waste mix often found in riding arenas provides a firm but yielding surface, allowing penetration, rotation, forward and backward slippage. This movement is missing on a treadmill. As a result, it is thought that close attention needs to be paid to the foot balance of any horse used in such an experiment in order to minimize the effect of impact concussion and mid-stance compression on the limbs.

Each experiment should be carefully constructed to identify and standardize all known variables. This means taking into account such things as skin movement artefact when placing markers on the skin, reproducibility of marker placement, consistency of speed of gait, level ground, handler/rider effect, fatigue of horse/rider/handler, differences between horses and within a single horse with multiple attempts at a task; the list is endless. Using horses in experimental conditions is fraught with imponderables; using one or more riders as well is a nightmare!

Many research papers are available to the enquiring mind. They challenge the reader from an equestrian background, sometimes pointing up the vast gaps between the scientific and equestrian worlds, inducing frustration and fascination in equal quantities. Papers by Dr. Hilary Clayton of Canada, and more recently of Michigan State University ,are to be recommended, as are papers by Back, from the Dutch group. Those with good maths may enjoy Schamhardt and Merkens, while a fascinating insight into performance horse conformation may be gained by reading Magnussen. The knotty problem of the mobility of the spine of the horse is presented in the work of Jephcott and Townsend. A list of papers is appended to this chapter.

In terms of therapeutic riding and hippotherapy, definitions are most important. Is the person on the horse riding or sitting, passive or active, is the horse accommodating the balance of the rider during movement, is the handler influencing the gait of the horse, is the gait so slow that it is no longer a true walk? Herein lies the problem of investigating the effects of horse riding on the rider/patient. This does not mean that all research is invalidated by these imponderables. They just have to be identified, minimized and acknowledged in considering the results.

A standardized horse movement, the walk, is available to test hypotheses suggested by the real situation. Developed by a unique combination of Brunel University engineers, Bristol University equine scientists and ACPRD physiotherapists, this mechanical version of the horse at the walk can be used in the laboratory or physiotherapy situation to eliminate some of the variables already outlined. Measurements were taken in 3D of the seating area of the horse's back at the walk, with and without a saddle. Resulting data was used to programme the movement of the back of the mechanical horse (known by the nemonic BABS, Brunel Active Balance Saddle).

The frequency of the movement pattern can be altered by a hand-held control unit. Patterns made by the combination of the fore and hind limb action on the back showed left/right asymmetry in all horses tested. BABS was made symmetrical, so that any asymmetry of body movement observed could be ascribed to the body sitting on it. It has the advantage of not taking any notice of the rider or patient on its back, not reacting to or accommodating the responses to movement input. Used as a standard and repeatable movement pattern, BABS may have a powerful role in furthering research in the field of therapeutic riding. It can even be used as a "non-horse horse" to test the greater efficacy of the real thing!

UNDERSTANDING THE HORSE'S HISTORY

Science is a discipline, a way of thinking, constructing experiments and testing theories. Riding is a discipline, but an art when done well. Keeping a horse is helped by scientific advances in our knowledge of how the horse works and what to do when it goes wrong, but feeding every horse well and keeping it happy is a blend of art and science. Horses don't read nutrition books and, just like children, may turn their noses up at what's good for them. The study of the horse locomotion has not discovered anything new. It just shines a light on what already is.

There came a day when I thought I had a handle on the jumping horse. I had identified the questions, measured the levers and put forward a hypothesis and tested it. The theory stood up to this test. I then started to apply it to competitive horses that I came across, trying to see if they were in the correct discipline. I remember telling someone that the young horse in front of me would never three day event as it was a born show jumper. Then I saw it going around Badminton. I pondered the truth that horses are great levellers and went back to the drawing board. It was some time later that I heard of the same horse being extolled as an exciting new arrival on the showjumping scene. A good jumping horse is born and we have to spot it to make it!

Terri Richmond
United Kingdom

SUGGESTED READING

Back, W., van den Bogert, A.J., van Weeren, P.R., Briun, G. and Baneveld, A. (1993b) Quantification of locomotion of Dutch Warmblood foals. Acta. Anat. **146,** 141-147.

Back, W., Schamhardt,H.C., Savelberg, H.H.C.M., van den Bogert, A.J., Briun, G., Hartman, W. and Barneveld, A. (1995a) How the horse moves: 1. Significance of graphical representations of equine forelimb kinematics. Equine vet. J. **27,** (1), 31-38.

Back, W., Schamhardt, H.C., Savelberg, H.H.C.M., van den Bogert, A.J., Briun, G., Hartman, W. and Barneveld, A. (1995a) How the horse moves: 2. Significance of graphical representations of equine hind limb kinematics. Equine vet. J. **27,** (1), 39-45.

Barrey, E., Galloux, P., Vallette, J.P., Auvinet, B., and Wolter, R. (1993)Stride characteristics of over-ground versus treadmill locomotion in the saddle horse. Acta Anat 146, 90-94.

Buchner, H.H.F., Savelberg, H.H.C.M., Schamhardt, H.C., Merkens, H.W. and Barneveld, A. (1994) Habituation of horses to treadmill locomotion. Equine vet. J. **17,** 13-15.

Clayton, H.M. (1991) Advances in motion analysis. Vet. Clinics N. Am. - Eq. Practice **7,** (2), 365-382.

Clayton, H.M. (1993) The extended canter - a comparison of some kinematic variables in horses trained for dressage and racing. Acta. Anat. **146,** (2), 183-187.

Clayton, H.M.. Terminology for the description of equine jumping kinematics. Journal of Equine Veterinary Science, 9: No. 6, 341-348, 1989.

Clayton, H.M. and Barlow, D.A. Stride characteristics of four Grand Prix jumping horses. Equine Exercise Physiology, 3: 151-157, 1991.

Clayton, H.M. and Barlow, D.A. The effect of fence height and width on the limb placements of showjumping horses. Equine Veterinary Science, 9: No. 4, 1989.

Clayton, H.M. and Townsend, H.G.G. Kinematics of the cervical spine of the adult horse. Equine Veterinary Journal, 21: No.3, 189-192, 1989

Deuel, N.R. and Park, J. Biomechanical analysis of the jumping characteristics of superior Olympic showjumping horses. International Journal of Sports Biomechanics, 6: 198-226, 1990.

Deuel, N.R. and Park, J. Gallop kinematics of Olympic three day event horses. Acta Anatomica, 146: No.2-3, 168-174. 1993.

Essen-Gustavsson, B.Training effects on skeletal muscle. Proceedings of the International Conferance on Equine Sports Medicine, Stockholm, Sweden, 18-23, 1990.Editor: Kallings, P., ICEEP.

Fredricson, I., Drevemo, S., Dalin, G., Hjerten, G. and Bjorne, K. (1980) The application of high-speed cinematography for the quantitative analysis of equine locomotion. Equine vet. J. **12,** (2), 54-59.

Fredricson, I., Drevemo, S., Dalin, G., Hjerten, G., Bjorne, K., Rynde, R. and Franzen, G. (1983) Treadmill for locomotion analysis. Equine vet. J. **15,** (2). 111-115.

Hildebrand, M. (1956) Symmetrical gaits of horses. Science **150,** 701-708.

Holmstrom, M., Magnusson, L.-E. and Philipsson, J.Variation in conformation of Swedish Warmblood horses and conformational characteristics of elite sport horses. Equine Veterinary Journal, 22, No.3, 186-193, 1990

Jeffcott, L.B. Training effects on bone and joints. Proceedings of the International Conference on Equine Sports Medicine, Stockholm, Sweden, 14-17, 1990. Editor: Kallings, P., ICEEP.

Jeffcott, L.B. and Dalin, G. Natural rigidity of the horse's backbone. Equine Veterinary Journal, 12, 101-108, 1980.

Leach, D. and Dyson, S. Instant centres of rotation of equine limb joints and their relationship to standard skin marker locations. Equine Veterinary Journal, Supplement 6: 113-119, 1988.

Leach, D. and Ormrod, K. The the technique of jumping a steeplechase fence by competing event horses. Applied Animal Behavior Science, 12: 15-24, 1984.

Leach, D., Ormrod, K. and Clayton, H.M. Standardised terminology for the description and analysis of equine locomotion. Equine Veterinary Journal, 16: No.6, 522-528, 1984.

Leach, D., Ormrod, K. and Clayton, H.M. Stride characteristics of horses competing in Grand Prix jumping. American Journal of Veterinary Research, 45: No.5, 1984.

Magnusson, L.E. Studies on the conformation and related traits of standardbred trotters in Sweden. PhD. Thesis, Skara, 1985.

Merkens, H.W., Schamhardt, H.C., Hartman, W. and Kerrsjes, A.W. Ground reaction force patterns of Dutch Warmblood horses at normal walk. Equine Veterinary Journal, 18: 207-214, 1986.

Merkens, H.W., Schamhardt, H.C., van Osch, G.J.V.M., and Hartman, W. Ground reaction force patterns of Dutch Warmblood horses at the canter. American Journal of Veterinary Research, 54: No.5, 670-674, 1993

Muybridge, E. (1957) Animals in Motion, New York.

Richmond, T.M.. Bone length ratio analysis of the appendicular skeleton of elite jumping horses. Diplomate thesis, University College Dublin, 1990.

Scamhardt, H.C., van den Bogert, A.J. and Hartman, W. (1993) Measurement techniques in animal locomotion analysis. Acta. Anat. **146,** 123-129.

Seeherman, H.J. (1991) The use of high speed treadmills for lameness and hoof balance evaluations in the horse. Vet. Clin. N. Am. Equ. Pract. **7,** (2), 271-309.

Sprigings, E.J. Sport biomechanics: Data collection, modelling and implimenting stages of development. Canadian Journal of Sport Science, 13: 3-7, 1988.

Townsend, H.G.G., Leach, D.M. and Fretz, P.B. Kinematics of the equine thoracolubar spine. Equine Veterinary Journal, 15: 117-122, 1983.

Tokuriki, M., and Aoki, O. Neck muscles activity in horses with and without a rider. Equine Exercise Physiology, 3: 146-150, 1991 Editors Gillespie and Robinson, ICEEP

van Weeren, P.R., van den Bogert, A.J. and Barneveld, A. (1990a) Quantification of skin displacement in the proximal parts of the walking horse. Equine Ex. Physiol. Suppl. 9, 110-118..

Vasko, K.A. The equine athlete: Structure and function. Hinkley, OH., 1983.

CHAPTER 7
TEMPERAMENT, CONFORMATION, MOVEMENT OF THE HORSE: AS THEY RELATE TO THE RIDER IN A THERAPEUTIC RIDING

The horse in a therapeutic riding program is the noblest of horses for he has a special mission to fulfill. He will be helping that population with whom some find it awkward and difficult to communicate. A well-chosen horse will give of himself, accept the rider without judgement, and willingly acknowledge the love bestowed upon him.

THE NATURE OF THE HORSE
Lita Hughes

WHY IS ONE CONCERNED WITH THE BEHAVIOR OF THE HORSE?

Humans have an attraction to a horse--a bonding as strong as with a dog. Yet humans want to command this beast that is eight times the size of a human but with a brain that is one-eighth as big as man's brain. The modern horse has had to adapt to our domestic patterns of living. The horse's brain has had little or no change during the past five thousand years (Smythe, 1965). The change that one might recognize in his behavior is the distinction between intelligence untutored and the same degree of intelligence awakened by education (McCall, 1975).

There is a difficulty in separating intelligence from the tangled skein of characteristics that determine an animal's ability to get along in the world puts a crimp in the human's wish to stereotype.

- ❏ If intelligence is the ability to create patterns from the hundreds of stimuli that strike the senses and use this understanding to manipulate the environment--then horses possess a moderate allotment of this ability.
- ❏ If intelligence is the ability to solve problems--more than the simple trial and error of getting the gate open-- horses are not terribly well-endowed.
- ❏ If intelligence is understanding and dealing with new and trying situations, then horses' brains are poorly endowed; their "fight or flight" response (the primitive response to stress) predominates.
- ❏ If intelligence is the capacity to think abstractly, then the horse is lacking in this ability.

Horses learn to discriminate very well. Tests were performed to determine the equine abilities in the following areas by providing food rewards (McCall, 1975):

- ❏ The equine ear can distinguish between 96 and 100 beats of a metronome; 1000 and 1025 cycles per second; 67-70 decibels.
- ❏ The equine eye can distinguish between 87 and 90 watts.

Domestication favors animals that adjust to human lifestyles and needs. Horses and other domestic animals learn from repetition and adjust their behaviors to achieve and avoid (Smythe, 1965). Even adjustments differ within the species. Not all horses are created equal. Fillies may outshine geldings, and geldings may outshine colts in learning quickly. Quarter horses learn faster to discriminate grain in pictures than thoroughbreds; however, the thoroughbred shows more fine tuning in initial body response (McCall, 1975). Training has taken advantage of these particular specialties allowing the quarter horse to use his eyes somewhat like a sheep dog and the quick muscle twitch of the thoroughbred to enable him to race.

Many of the activities that one observes in horses are not acts reflecting intelligence but rather patterns of behavior. All horses exhibit nine behaviors (McCall, 1975):

1. Ingestive behavior (feeding).
2. Eliminative behavior (urination & defecation).

3. Contactual behavior (protective and bonding).
4. Epimeletic behavior (giving care and attention).

5. Et-epimeletic behavior (calling for care and attention).
6. Investigative behavior (sensory environmental inspection).
7. Sexual behavior

8. Allelomimetic behavior (mimicry).
9. Agonistic behavior (fighting or conflict).

INGESTIVE BEHAVIORS

All living creatures need to eat and drink (ingestive behavior) in some manner. This is strong instinctive behavior. Horses are grazers, and their digestive systems are anatomically adapted to accommodate small amounts of food at frequent intervals. Therefore, they must be fed small amounts frequently. Hay is a natural food and should be given before graining, with as much pasture or free foraging as possible. If there is enough balanced nutrition in a pasture, the horse will need grain only according to his "work" load. If he eats his food quickly, put large rocks in his tub to help slow him down. Bad feeding habits start from boredom, lack of roughage or nutrients, lack of exercise and/or can be learned from a companion.

In the horse's natural environment, the leader takes his herd to the best streams and grasses. Food can also be effectively used to train or distract a horse and change his responses in unpleasant or frightening situations. A trainer giving food reward is much appreciated by the horse but not necessarily associated with having done a task correctly. A horse will only associate an immediate prior action to receiving the food. For example, if a handler regularly rewards a horse for stopping by going into his pockets and giving his horse a carrot, the horse associates this reward with the sound or motion of going into the pocket, not necessarily the act of stopping. However, a horse that gets treats and plenty of positive attention from his handler is inclined to do new things more quickly than one who receives nothing. Proper reward depends on timing.

ELIMINATIVE BEHAVIORS

Horses will eliminate when they have to or as a result of activity, anxiety or marking their territory. Marking, often exhibited by the "flehmen position" with extended neck, head and a curled upper lip may define territory as well as a means of communication among equines. Urinating patterns define dominance among a herd; stallions urinate over a mare's fresh urine when she is in heat to diminish her attraction to other stallions. Defecation may also be related to stress. As part of the fight or flight response, the body eliminates and shuts down much of the digestive system, directing blood flow to skeletal muscles. Male horses, if slightly alarmed, will stop to smell dung. Their body's response is then to defecate. Horses establish a elimination area if enough space is available. Horses will not graze in the elimination area until all other grazing areas are gone. A horse's tendency to be clean rather then dirty is a characteristic learned from the dam. A barn manager can train to preferred elimination areas by cleaning the paddock areas where hay is fed outside, leaving one pile where the elimination area is wanted. In summer, feed the hay in a clean area that has morning sun and may be shaded in the afternoon. Horses will want to stand in the shade in the summer and in the sun in a non windy spot in the winter. They will move to the periphery of these areas to defecate as long as the areas are otherwise clean.

CONTACTUAL BEHAVIORS

Contactual, also known as herd behavior, begins at birth. The mare and foal establish contact immediately after birth. Once the foal is up, the mare will touch, nuzzle and attempt to keep herself between the foal and any other horse. The first half hour of imprinting will allow the foal to differentiate between his dam and the other smells and shapes his new systems are receiving. The olfactory system (sense of smell) is quite active immediately after birth and becomes extremely acute. Immediately after birth, the new foal will follow any shape until he learns what shape and smell offers him protection and food. His search for food is most immediate and somewhat clumsy, resulting in some nipping or walking off by the mare. Finally the foal suckles, drawing the colostrum and again developing a nurturing reaction from the dam. As the foal develops, his ability and desire to run and play becomes contagious with other foals. This encourages group behavior to develop and the foal learns how to act in a group or alone with his dam. The primary benefit of herd behavior is mutual protection and affection; one herd member may alert others to predators allowing the entire herd to escape.

Contactual behavior can cause training difficulties. Some horses are "sour" about leaving the group. A trainer can use this behavior by furnishing reassurance that usually comes from other horses. The horse then learns to rely on the trainer for decisions, confidence and ultimately protection in situations where he is unsure.

Riders and trainers must become Alpha (the leader), the number one protector, watching and thinking what the horse needs, and a lot of physical and emotional contact must be provided. One must judge how the horse behaves naturally before he is placed in strange and different riding situations.

EPIMELETIC BEHAVIORS

Epimeletic behaviors are nurturing or caring behaviors that encourage a bond to develop between equines. This behavior is also enjoyed by many handlers and disabled persons with their horses. These behaviors start between the mare and foal and are often seen throughout the horse's lifetime. Horses are commonly involved in mutual grooming of the withers or hindquarters. Certain body postures show signs of friendship such as one horse's head over another horse's neck or back.

To create a caring relationship, a person may brush the horse at least one-half hour daily. Reward him by scratching and use a soothing tone of voice as a reward immediately after, or if possible during a task well done. Reward the horse after the hardest part of the activity by giving the inside rein or scratching the neck and then finish the exercise. It is important to remember that the reward must be given contingent to the response so that the horse learns by association. This kind of a reward system can be an active part of the any rider's responsibility in keeping his mount interested and responsive.

If one has ever noticed the nurturing between children and ponies, it is no wonder that some ponies will act almost dog-like and bond so easily with children. Older riders should take the time to stand with or just walk beside their horse, putting their arm over his neck or back, scratching his withers to establish a caring relationship. Enjoy him! His responses to nurturing makes all the attention worthwhile, and he will reward one with better performance.

ET-EPIMELETIC BEHAVIOR

Horses signal their desire for nurturing or call out stress signals. These behaviors are identified with vocalizations and movements. Individual owners have described twelve to thirty individual vocalizations. Think of the basic vocalizations of the horse:

1. The whinny: It is amazing that a foal responds to the dam's whinny when it comes into the world. Horses will call to a handler when returning to the barn to feed or call to another horses from whom they have been separated.
2. The nicker: A "come closer" sound. The nicker is often directed toward companions including cats, dogs and goats.
3. The squeal: A sound of introduction between new animals and horses displaying battle and mock battle rituals. It is most often heard while one horse smells another's flanks and is often accompanied by pawing or striking out with the forefoot.
4. The shriek or snort: A sound most often associated with the fight or flight response. It is often directed toward a stranger or intruder by the lead horse.
5. The sigh: A sound associated with contentment, the sigh actually occurs when the horse clears his nostrils.
6. The blow: A sound of alarm created by filling the "false nostril" with air and immediately exhaling emitting an incredibly loud and alarming sound. The snort may be a sound of mock battle to develop the hierarchy or it can be heard when a stallion is smelling dung.
7. The growl: This is a sound made deep in the chest of the stallion. In the wild, stallions growl when near dung. In the human's environment, stallions are heard growling when they enter a quiet barn.
8. Allelomimetic behavior (mimicry).
9. Agonistic behavior (fighting or conflict).

Instructors and handlers are aware that horses respond to human sounds. They must recognize the horse's ability to communicate and their highly developed sense of hearing. One is reminded that talking in a quiet voice is more pleasing to the horse than a loud voice which may disturb him!

INVESTIGATIVE BEHAVIOR

Investigative behaviors are displays of curiosity and inspection of the horse's environment. Horses may be curious because of fear, insecurity or the need for leadership. Horses' sensory systems are very well developed. When they are investigating something new, they may use all of their systems - smell, touch, hearing and sight. The slightest sounds and movements can frighten the horse. Often the display of investigative behavior is a redirection behavior, "An activity that is shifted from the stimulus that elicited a motivational conflict to a more neutral substitute object" (Alcock 1976). While being alerted by one stimulus (a new horse in the arena, for example), a paper blows over the fence and makes an unusual noise. This second stimulus causes the horse to divert his attention from the initial stimulus. Instead of fighting or fleeing from the horse, the activity is directed toward the second problem, the paper.

Dealing with these responses can be unsettling. While being alerted by an unfamiliar object, all other sensory systems are distorted to receive the information from the stimulus. If you talk to the horse, he may not "hear" you. If you touch him , he may perceive that he is being hit. Punishing a horse at this time may only reinforce his "suspicion" that something was there to hurt him.

The handler should redirect the horse's activity or attention to what is expected of him and stay calm. Investigation can result in mischievous accomplishments which can be misinterpreted as learning. A horse rubbing at a stall latch resulting in the door swinging open is accidental. Some horses can associate getting the door open and getting out with getting a nibble of grass as a reward. Some only get the immediate reinforcement of the handler's attention as reward and go no further.

SEXUAL BEHAVIOR

Sexual behaviors of horses include all activities associated with courtship and breeding. Sexual patterns are also displayed by geldings. This is because these behaviors are both neurally and hormonally controlled. Sexual behavior plays a role in the dominance hierarchy. Dominance with horses is determined by the temperament of the animals in the group and their tendencies toward sexual displays. Once a hierarchy has been established, threats rather than harmful acts are likely to occur. Even after the hierarchy has been established, problems and reshuffling can still occur. Geldings as well as mares can become the lead horse, driving the herd to and fro.

Estrus periods of mares may negatively affect their learning patterns. When the mare in a therapeutic riding program has a shorter attention span, it may help to change her training schedule to increase her attention.

Flehmen, an olfactory response, is associated with stallions "testing" a female's urine to see if she is in heat. This is the strongest stimulus associated with the flehmen response, although it is also seen at other times. The horse raises his neck, and then compresses and lifts his lips to direct the air molecules toward the roof of his mouth to the Jacobson's organ. This organ may send information to the brain about the percentage of estrogen in the mare's urine. Foals will also do flehmen smelling of their own afterbirth.

ALLELOMIMETIC BEHAVIORS

Allelomimetic behaviors are mimicking behaviors. Horses do imitate or mimic the behaviors of other horses and other animals. Think about horses that are bored. Some may learn bad habits from their stall or pasture mates. Other horses never pick up bad traits such as chewing, cribbing or weaving because they have never been exposed to these vices. This copying behavior can be used to the riders' advantage. One may want to train with other horses that have accomplished the specific task, even if the task is to stand still! Horses will jump an obstacle more willingly when following another horse. To counteract the mimicking behavior, it is good to teach a horse to stand while another horse is working. Watching this mimicking behavior in the field can relay information about the herd hierarchy. Watch which horse rolls, which one imitates on the outskirts (lower in the hierarchy), and which one waits to roll in the prime spot.

AGONISTIC BEHAVIORS

Agonistic behaviors in the horse are the fight or flight response, threat displays and aggressive or submissive behaviors. Most horses' aggressive tendencies are chandelled into non-lethal activities to reinforce the hierarchy. Flight is more important to grazing animals than fight. At first it might seem that nature has drastically erred by introducing aggression into the physiological and psychological make up of the grazing animal. However, aggression is often the basis for motivation, and an aggressive animal is normally a better provider for and protector of his subordinates.

Handlers may see the quiet postures: ears laid back, head down, one ear back with head raised and shaking, a down curved mouth with twisted muzzle and head. These quiet postures may make humans laugh, yet send another horse a totally different message. These displays can signal peaceful intentions with some minor changes: head up, both ears splayed, eyes squinted with ears at rest or forward, head sideways, teeth clapping with head down. Threats displays include biting, and kicking that can develop into driving, stomping, lunging and running. Eye rolling, a very quick posturing that draws the eye protectively into the eye socket, is accompanied by threats of head swinging.

Aggression has its limits. Personality should affect how individual horses are chosen and the tasks they are directed to do. Stallions and/or horses with stallion-like tendencies are not appropriate for therapeutic riding programs. Often, even herd leaders are not well suited; middle-of-the-hierarchy horses are better suited to this activity. Aggression will also affect the way training proceeds. A young horse that has established a high-ranking position among his peers may view training as another dominance struggle and often require a firmer, more demanding training program. This program should include lots of reward and establishes the trainer as the leader by keeping the horse busy. Once the dominant horse accepts the supremacy of his trainer, he may show more brilliance and aptitude in learning.

Be sure, however, not to subdue the aggressive horse; this results in lack of natural boldness. If one uses an aggressive animal, learn to control the flow of energy. A submissive animal, on the other hand, needs a calm, perhaps more intermittent program. He may allow himself to be drilled, but beware, he is not often in need of it! Horses learn more quickly if the same lesson is not repeated daily.

CONCLUSION

It is essential to regard all equines as individuals, one never truly fitting into the mold of another. While they all exhibit the same general characteristics (the above presenting only the major behaviors of adult horses), different combinations of these traits may result in many entirely different types of personalities.

Watch the horse. Take time to get to know him. He is truly remarkable.

Lita Hughes
USA

References
Alcock, J. (1976). *Animal Behavior, An Evolutionary Approach.* Sunderland: Sinauer Associates, Inc. 199.
Kilby, E. (1981). How Smart is Your Horse. *Equus* 46, 22. Gaithersburg: Fleat Street Corporation, MD.
Hamilton, S. (1978). Man's Impact on Behavior, *Equus* 9, Gaithersburg: Fleat Street Corporation, MD.
Equus Staff. (1981). Attitude: The Winning Edge, *Equus* 49. Gaithersburg: Fleat Street Corporation, MD.
Houpt, K. (1980). Two is a Herd. *Equus*. 35 Gaithersburg: Fleat Street Corporation, MD.
McCall, J. (1975). Horse Management - Course notes. College Park, Univ of Maryland.
Smythe, R.H. (1965). *The Mind of the Horse.* Lexington: Stephen Greene Press.
Vavra, R. (1979). *Such is the Real Nature of Horses.* New York: William Morrow & Company, Inc.

THE HORSE'S REACTION TO HIS ENVIRONMENT

Barbara T. Engel, MEd, OTR

It is important for handlers, helpers and riders in therapeutic riding programs to have an understanding of the horse's senses in order to be able to understand and communicate effectively with this large animal. "The instinctive reactions of horses must be known and understood in order to anticipate trouble and then work around horses safely" (Lyles 1980).

THE ABILITY TO SMELL:

The horse's sense of smell is generally believed to be well developed. A horse will greet another horse by sniffing. Different emotional states give off different odors (Williamson 1980). He uses smell to identify food, other horses, people, and places. A horse will remember another horse or a person years later from their smell (Ainslie & Ledbetter 1980). He can smell things one-half mile away and smell a trail to find his way home (Rees 1985). At times, a strange smell can cause a horse great anxiety.

THE ABILITY TO HEAR:

A horse's hearing is more highly developed than in humans. It has been an important element in his historical survival. He can hear frequencies higher than man and from distances further away (Evans 1990). The horse's ears move independently of each other and, with the ten muscles that control the ear, they can swivel to pick up environmental vibrations for danger cues or for communication. A horse can judge the distance of an object from the vibrations it receives from sounds. He may snort to hear the vibration returning from a nearby wall. He can hear steps or voices and where they come from before humans can hear them. He can tell the difference between people and individual horses through sound (Kiley-Worthington 1987).

Soft, soothing sounds help the horse to relax. Playing music helps to wipe out distracting sounds and therefore helps to calm a horse during stabling or during a lesson (Liebermann 1980). Loud noises can be painful to a horse. When sounds make him apprehensive, he may swing his entire body in the direction of the sound. Sharp, loud commands punish a horse. Low, drawn out commands tend to slow a horse down. A firm, fast command will make the horse go faster. Importantly, the horse can hear and remember words for different exercises (Podhajsky 1965).

The direction a horse points his ears indicate where he has focused his attention. One ear can point forward to where he is going and the other toward the rider to pick up cues (Williamson 1974). Ears pricked straight forward indicate interest ahead, and when he continues to keep them forward for long periods, it may indicate a sight or hearing problem. Flicking an ear back slightly while being ridden indicates that the horse is attending to the rider. The horse also indicates emotions with his ears. Stiffly pricked ears indicate interest. Drooping ears indicate relaxation, exhaustion or serious illness. Flattened ears indicate anger, threat, fear or rage. Ears flicking back and forth indicate attentiveness or interest.

THE ABILITY TO FEEL:

A horse can easily feel a very light sensation such as a fly on his body or a leg touching his side. He can respond to the tension in a rider's leg. His muzzle and nostrils are especially delicate and the long whiskers increase sensation for more accurate perception of food sources in his environment. The lips of the horse respond to heat, cold, pressure and pain. A horse "processes" tactile sensations with its mouth as humans do with their hands (Williamson 1980). Somebody areas of the horse are more sensitive than others such as the mouth, ears, shoulders, lower leg, flank and neck. Awareness of pain has protected the horse from danger or injury throughout its evolution. A horse's sense of touch when compared to humans is more acute and sensitive. A horse feels and responds to changes in touch more than to continuous touch such as steady pressure from the leg or saddle. Susceptibility to touch varies from horse to horse and changes with its emotional state. A drowsy horse is less likely to react to touch than an alert horse and will be less responsive to aids. An anxious or temperamental horse has increased sensitivity. Anger or fear may decrease a horse's awareness or response.

THE ABILITY TO SEE:

A horse is probably able to see colors and movement much as humans do (Kiley-Worthington 1987). He can see quite well both at night and at distances, but his depth perception and focal adjustments appear to be slow and poor. Perhaps this is why a horse may startle or stare at a strange object, especially when seen at the edge of his visual field. The ability of the horse to focus clearly begins to blur at one and one-half feet from the horse's nose (Liebermann 1980). His ability to focus both eyes together is poor since the eyes are located at the side of the head and not in front of the face as in man. Although a horse has difficulty seeing at a distance, he can notice the most subtle movement. He may also see a slightly different image with each eye (Williams 1976). A horse can judge the height of an object such as a jump fairly well but has difficulty with perceiving width (Hedlund 1988). Horses can learn to recognize patterns and shapes.

A horse has a visual field of about 215 degrees (Evans 1990), and has several blind spots. He cannot see directly behind his rump and directly in front of his nose. When a person stands directly in front of the horse with the horse's nose at the person's waist, the horse sees two pieces of a person. At four feet away, the horse can see a whole person. When a horse leader stands in front of the horse, the horse sees only a left shoulder and arm and a right shoulder and arm and nothing in between. When the horse has his head forward, he is unable to see underneath himself, between his feet and behind his tail. Sharp, quick movements within his blind spots may frighten him since he can feel but not see the action. (Culbertson 1969; Williamson 1974; Hedlund 1988).

THE ABILITY TO LEARN AND REMEMBER:

"It is generally agreed that the memory of a horse is a very remarkable thing" (Williams 1976). When training a horse, one can see how strong his memory skills are by the use of the effectiveness of reward and discipline. The horse is quick to learn habits and retains them well (Museler 1984). A horse will *learn* to *learn* (Evans 1989), and remember certain events for years (Rees 1985). He has the ability to discriminate and remember patterns and remembers simple tasks longer than difficult ones (Evans 1989). He will learn the wrong thing as easily as the right thing, and therefore, it is important to reinforce good behavior and punish incorrect behavior. Evans points out that fear inhibits learning in the horse in the same way that humans cannot learn under threat and fear.

THE HORSE'S ABILITY TO INTEGRATE HIS SENSES:

The horse has a sophisticated nervous system which enables him to coordinate and learn in a remarkable way. He integrates his senses to his best advantage for safety and social behavior (Evans1990). He will point his ears in the direction he looks. He will use his nose to smell and his eyes to look at an unfamiliar object. His sense of balance is influenced by the position of his head with the help of the neck muscles (Hedlund 1988). A horse's desire to please, his willingness to adapt to human needs, and his excellent memory and athletic ability makes him a valuable partner in therapeutic riding programs. As he adapts to these new situations, he has proven to be a good-natured, trusting and reliable friend.

Barbara T. Engel
USA

RREFERENCES:
Ainslie, T., & Ledbetter, B. (1980). *The Body Language of Horses*. New York: William Marrow & Co.,Inc. 34.
Culbertson, (1969). 4-H Project
Engel, B.T., et al. (1989). *The Horse, The Handicapped and the Riding Team*. Pasadena, CA 91105. 83-86.
Evans, J.W., et al. (1990). *The Horse*. New York: W. H. Freeman & Co. 119-126.
Evans, J.W. (1989). *Horses*. New York: W. H. Freeman & Co. 43
Hedlund, G. (1988). *This is Riding: Dressage, Jumping, Eventing in Words and Pictures*. Middletown: Half Halt Press. 62-63.
Kiley-Worthington, M. (1987). *The Behavior of Horses: In Relation to Management and Training*. London: J.A. Allen & Co. 24-27,32.
Liebermann, B. (1980). The Sense of It All. *Equus*. Farmingdale: Fleet Street Publishing Corp. 34-39, 57.
Lyles, L.L. (1980). *Horseman's Handbook*. Santa Rosa: California State Horsemen's Assoc. 28.

McBane, S. (1980). *Keeping a Horse Outdoors*. North Pomfret: David & Charles Inc. 13-17.

Museler, W. (1984). *Riding Logic*. Arco Publishing, Inc.

Podhaisky, (1968). *The Complete Training of Horse and Rider*. Garden City: Doubleday. 21, 31, 69.

Rees, L. (1985). *The Horse's Mind*. New York: Prentice Hall Press. 27, 125.

Williams, M. (1976). *Practical Horse Psychology*. No. Hollywood: Wilshire Book Co.

Williamson, M.B. (1977). *Applied Horse Psychology*. Houston: Cordova Publisher Inc. 2-42.

TRAITS OF THE THERAPEUTIC RIDING HORSE

Barbara T. Engel, M.Ed, OTR

KEY WORDS

> **ACCEPTING**
> **TRUSTWORTHY**
> **PREDICABLE**
> **FOCUSED**
> **WILLING TO LEARN**
> **ATHLETIC**
> **WELL-BALANCED**
> **FORWARD MOVER**

Conformation of the therapeutic riding horse is important for several reasons. The therapeutic riding horse has a difficult job since he must carry riders with poor balance and delayed reactions to movements. A horse with good conformation can perform this task easily and remain sound more readily than a horse predisposed to muscle strains and lameness. He will work several hours carrying two to four different riders with varying problems and weights. This requires a strong, well balanced and a healthy back with good leg support. The horse must be strong and supple with forward movement and a rhythmic, balanced gait. This is necessary to provide riders with the appropriate stimulation which in turn, will teach **them** balance. If a therapeutic riding horse is to be used to facilitate physical changes in riders, both in the general program population and in equine-assisted therapy, then conformation becomes very important. Faults or lameness can affect riders in a negative way instead of encouraging balance, coordination and symmetry. The therapeutic riding horse is a horse whose conformation should not predispose him to lameness **nor should he be annoyed by the imbalance or stiffness of his or her rider**.

The horse must be able to perform various skills to meet the needs of many riders. He should accept longeing in both directions. His health and age should allow him to give many years of useful service. His big eyes should show a keen interest in people. He must be kind, steady and willing to learn. He should be free of disruptive traits, enjoy attention and not mind being handled by different people and several people at a time.

The selection process of this horse can best begin at the donor's site. Here you will see him in his familiar surroundings. Plan to spend plenty of time with him so you can gain a true picture of his qualities. Check his conformation for areas which may predispose him to lameness. His size and gait must meet the needs of the population he will serve. Lead him with a rider and sidewalkers and hover over him and confine him. Bring crutches and a wheelchair. Remember that not all horses will immediately accept these devices on the first visit but should show some willingness to accept them readily with further training. Lead him away from his stable mates to see if he is will to leave them behind.

People will say to you, "My children can ride this horse with no difficulty." A child with normal reactions to changes in movement, even a young child, may handle a horse well. This same horse may not be suitable for a person with a disability whose reactions are poor, who has little or no balance on the horse, who presses too hard on the horse's side, or whose movements are too uncertain. In addition the horse must learn to work with many people. Can he tolerate all these changes?

Once you feel the horse would be a good candidate for your program, he can begin his initial training at your center. The most important qualities in a therapeutic riding horse are that he is a trustworthy, predictable and responsive animal. These qualities must be present regardless of who handles him. Safety is always of primary importance, especially when working with people who have disabilities.

The following articles deal with the effect of conformation and soundness on the horse's performance and how that performance influences the rider with disability. Experts from the fields of hippotherapy and dressage give their viewpoints on the effect of different levels of training on both the horse's and the rider's physical performance.

Barbara T. Engel
USA

References
Bennett, D. (1988). *Principles of Conformation Analysis, Vol I.* Gaithersburg: Fleet Street Publishing Corp.
Bennett, D. (1989). *Principles of Conformation Analysis, Vol II.* Gaithersburg: Fleet Street Publishing Corp.
C.A.R.D. (1987). *The Therapeutic Application of the Horse's Movement.* Video. C.A.R.D. Toronto, Ontario
Evans, J. W., Borton, A., Hintz,H.F., Van Vleck, L.D. (1977). *The Horse.* New York: W.H Freeman & Co
Green, B.K. (1988). *Horse Conformation as to Soundness and Performance.* Northland Press.
Gonzales, T. (1986). *Proper Balance Movement, A Diary of Lameness.* Manassas, Va. REF Publishing.
Harris, S. (1993). *Horse Gaits, Balance and Movement.* New York: Howell Book House, Macmillan Publishing House.
Heipertz, W., Heipertz-Hengst, C., Kroger, A, & Kuprian W. (1977). *Therapeutisches Reiten* [Therapeutic Riding]. Stuttgart, Germany: Franckh'sche Verlagshandlung.
Reide, D. (1988). *Physiotherapy on the Horse.* Delta Society. Renton, Washington.
Rooney, J.R. (1974). *The Lame Horse: Causes, Symptoms and Treatment.* Cranbury: A.S. Barnes.
Schusdziarra, H., Schusdziarra, V. (1985). *An Anatomy of Riding.*Briarcliff: Breakthrough Publications.
Smythe, R.H. (1972). *The Horse, Structure and Movement.* Sec. ed. London: J. A. Allen.
Tellington-Jones, L. (1988-1991). *T.E.A.M. News International.*

CONFORMATION AFFECTS RIDER COMFORT

Eleanor Kellon, VMD

When choosing a horse for beginner lessons, or for handicapped riders, a primary consideration (after disposition) is how the horse will feel under the rider. While there are no hard and fast rules for predicting how easy a horse will be to sit, there are a few identifiable factors that play a role.

First, to be comfortable, level and even, the horse must be sound. Front-end lameness will have the most dramatic effect since a horse with an obvious front-end lameness will be trying to protect the sore (or most sore) leg, resulting in an uneven gait. Shortening of stride is also likely, and gait changes will be rough.

While hind-end lameness will not make the horse particularly rough as a rule, it does lead to uneven impulsion. The rider will feel off balance without knowing why and certainly without being able to correct this feeling by any changes in his own body position.

A common problem with hind-end lameness, and usually one of the most easily felt, is that there will be an obvious difference in how easy it is to post from one diagonal to the other. Exactly how this affects the rider will vary depending upon the precise source of the lameness.

One common problem, however, is that the decreased thrust on the painful side makes it more difficult to leave the saddle. The rider's leg opposite to the lame side may have the sensation of having to "reach" for the stirrup. This will usually happen when the sore hind leg is working to the inside of the ring, which exaggerates most lameness.

Almost everyone has heard it said that a long-pasterned horse will have a smooth and cushion-like ride while the short, upright pastern produces a choppy, rough ride. If this were the only determining factor, it would certainly be true. While pastern length does have an influence, it can be modified profoundly by the slope of the shoulder and how long a stride length the horse has.

The horse with a long, sloping shoulder will naturally have a much longer, freer stride in front than one with an upright shoulder. This is one of the things that, to many people, makes a horse "comfortable." The reason for the smooth ride is simply that the feet do not contact the ground as often when the stride length is long. Also, the farther out in front of horse the foot is when it contacts the ground, the less direct jar the rider will feel.

The angle of the horse's feet is also an important consideration in how comfortably he will ride. Feet that have very short toes and high heels, with the extreme being a club foot, result in shorter stride length regardless of shoulder conformation and poor shock absorption in the fetlock, giving the rider a jolt each time the foot contacts the ground.

The opposite of this, short underrun heels and long toe, contributes greatly to adding length to the stride, reinforcing the effect of the long, sloping shoulder mentioned above and making even a fairly straight shouldered horse more comfortable.

Both extremes, however, place excessive strain on the lower joints of the leg (fetlock and below), which can quickly result in lameness, negating any benefits and making these horses ones to avoid unless the defect can be corrected.

Perhaps the most important consideration, particularly to a beginning or handicapped rider, is how secure the rider feels astride the horse. There are many Thoroughbred types that meet the ideal requirements for front leg conformation and have long, flowing strides. The combination of a long back, prominent spine and relatively narrow body type, however, will still leave the rider feeling perched off balance every time the horse moves.

This is particularly true for riders that have not learned to relax completely through their lower spines, or can't do so for physical reasons. The immediate result is that a rider will curl forward, elevating himself further out of the saddle and off balance.

When choosing mounts for beginner or handicapped riders, lean toward the horses with very broad backs, short backs and a generous rib cage. The rider's seat on this type of horse will feel much more secure, encouraging relaxation.

It is also true while horses of this type might lack the "daisy-cutter" stride of fancier horses, they are extremely easy to sit, even at a rapid trot. Their canters, however, may be another story entirely, tending to have a great deal of roll that riders may find a little disconcerting. All in all, however, this type of horse is a good choice since the most important lesson-that of developing a secure, relaxed and independent seat-is easiest obtained on this horse.

Withers can also interfere with a rider's seat and balance, either when too high or too low, pitching the rider back or forward, respectively. This is a fairly minor problem, however, compared to the others mentioned and can be easily corrected by additional, strategically-placed padding.

Finally, while it might seem logical that a rider, particularly a small one, would feel more secure on a small mount that is close to the ground, many ponies are unsuitable simply because their stride length is so short that the ride is too bouncy. Ponies also tend, by their nature, to be a little too quick in their movements for the novice or impaired rider. There are certainly exceptions, either by virtue of the individual pony or by rider preference, however.

Use the guidelines to identify likely candidates for students, then proceed to try them. The most important factor is always to remember how a beginner feels, the things that make him or her comfortable or fearful, and evaluate all potential lesson horses with that important consideration in mind.

Eleanor Kellon
USA

Printed by permission - Chronicle of the Horse and Eleanor Kellon

THE SELECTION OF THE CORRECT HORSE FOR A SPECIFIC RIDER

Barbara T. Engel, M.Ed, OTR

In order for an instructor to select the appropriate mount for a specific person, he or she needs to evaluate the rider to determine the rider's needs. He or she also needs to understand what effects certain attributes of the horse will have on specific disabilities of a rider, such as the movement patterns, the size, shape and the strides of the horse. For example, a person with poor balance gains more security from a horse with a broader back which provides a larger base of support. A person with spasticity will relax more easily on a horse with good impulsion, long stride, rhythmic gait and smooth transitions. Evaluating a horse's conformation and characteristics, along with one's understanding of a disability and what qualities in the horse best meet the needs of a particular problem, will allow the rider to gain more from the therapeutic riding process (see Figure 1).

Questions one may consider in selecting the horse:

❑ Does the rider need a wide [ ] moderate [ ] or narrow base [ ] of support?

❑ Does the rider need smooth [ ] average [ ] or rough   [ ] transitions?

❑ Does the rider need movement/flexibility from the horse that is strong [ ] moderate [ ] or little [ ] mild/subtle [ ]?

❑ Does the rider need a horse with a quiet [ ] moderately loose [ ] or flexible back [ ]?

❑ Does the rider respond best to short [ ] medium [ ] or long strides [ ]?

❑ Does the rider sit best on a short [ ]   medium [ ] or tall horse [ ]?

❑ Does the rider need a horse very responsive [ ] moderately responsive [ ] or no need for response [ ] to aids?

Many therapeutic riding programs may not have the range of horse selection available to allow this process. Nonetheless, evaluation will point out areas of need and will help to accurately assess the soundness of the horse and determining appropriate training needs. With few horses, it is still best to select the most suitable mount from those in the program, even if the choice is not ideal. The use of an evaluation process, and understanding its significance, can help develop a stable of suitable horses for the program's population and skills. If programs educate the horse society in the type of horses needed for a successful disabled riding program, they are more likely to get these horses donated or at a reasonable price. There are many sound eventing, dressage and reining horses who have out lived their competitive lives but are ideal for therapeutic riding programs.

ANALYSIS* OF THE THERAPEUTIC RIDING HORSE FOR PROGRAM RIDERS

Name of Horse:_____ **Age:** _____ **Color:**_____

Breed or Breed Type:_____ **Height: Hands**_____ **Weight**_____**lbs.**

Identifying Marks: draw in white markings/ or other:

FRONT   HIND
LEGS FROM FRONT

FRONT   HIND
LEGS FROM HIND

PHYSIQUE:

HEAD LENGTH	AVERAGE/BALANCED	LONG	SHORT	
THROAT LATCH	AVERAGE/CLEAN	THIN/LONG	SHORT/THICK	
NECK	AVERAGE/BALANCED	THIN/LONG	SHORT/THICK	
NECK SET	WELL SET INTO SHOULDERS	LOW	HIGH	
SHOULDERS	AVERAGE/45 DEGREES	STEEP	FLAT	
WITHERS	AVERAGE	HIGH	LOW	
LOIN	AVERAGE	VERY STRONG	WEAK	
CROUP	WELL ROUNDED	FLAT	SHORT	FLAT
BELLY	FIRM/MUSCLED	SAGGING		
BACK-POINT OF POLL TO POINT OF CROUP	AVERAGE	LONG	SHORT	
TOPLINE-POINT OF POLL TO POINT OF DOCK	SMOOTH CURVE	WAVY	SAGGING	FLAT
BARREL/GIRTH-POINT OF RIDER'S PELVIS SPAN	WIDE	AVERAGE	NARROW	
SYMMETRY-RIGHT TO LEFT(TOP VIEW)	STRAIGHT	BEND TO THE RIGHT	BEND TO THE LEFT	
ANGLE OF HIND LEG-IN LINE WITH	RUMP	BEHIND THE RUMP	IN FRONT OF RUMP	

THIS FORM IS INTENDED TO ASSIST THE INSTRUCTOR IN EVALUATION A PROGRAM HORSE FOR THE PROGRAMS' CLIENTS. TRANSITIONS SHOULD BE OBSERVED WHILE THE HORSE IS BEING RIDDEN BY STAFF AND THE HORSE IS FREE MOVING.   B. ENGEL 1997 ©

MOVEMENT					
WALK	RHYTHM	SMOOTH/FLATFOOTED	REGULAR	IRREGULAR BEAT/ROUGH	
	TEMPO	AVERAGE	10 STEPS PER 12 SECONDS	FAST	SLOW
	STRIDE LENGTH	AVERAGE	SHORT	LONG	
TROT	RHYTHM	SMOOTH/STEADY	REGULAR	STIFF	ROUGH
	TEMPO	AVERAGE	FAST	SLOW	
	STRIDE LENGTH	AVERAGE	SHORT	LONG	
CANTER	RHYTHM	SMOOTH/STEADY	REGULAR	IRREGULAR /ROUGH	
	TEMPO	AVERAGE	FAST	SLOW	
	STRIDE LENGTH	AVERAGE	SHORT	LONG	

GAIT TRANSITIONS	VERY SMOOTH	GOOD	ROUGH
HALT TO WALK			
WALK TO TROT			
TROT TO CANTER			
CANTER TO TROT			
TROT TO WALK			
WALK TO HALT			
HALT TO BACK			

LEVEL · SKILL OF THE HORS'S TRAINING · PAST EXPERIENCE					
1. GAIT TRANSITIONS	GOOD	MODERATE		POOR	
2. GAIT AIDS: VOICE	GOOD	MODERATE		POOR	
LEG	LIGHT	MODERATELY LIGHT		STRONG LEG AIDS	
LEADING	ON LOOSE LINE	WITH MODERATE CUES		WITH MAXIMUM CUES	
3. FORWARD MOVEMENT/STRAIGHTNESS	GOOD	MODERATE		POOR	
4. FORMAL SCHOOLING	GOOD	MODERATE		POOR	
5. DRESSAGE LEVEL	TRAINING	1ST LEVEL	2ND LEVEL	3RD LEVEL	4TH LEVEL
6. GROUND DRIVING	FORWARD/STRAIGHT	LATERAL MOVEMENTS		SHOULDER/HAUNCHES IN	
7. LONGEING	BASIC	TRAINING METHOD		BY VOICE COMMANDS	
8. DRIVE TO CART	YES	NO			
JUMPING	BEGINNER NOVICE; 2 1/2' FENCE	NOVICE; 3' FENCE		TRAINING ABOVE 3FT	
EQUINE ASSISTED THERAPY	HIPPOTHERAPY	PSYCHO - EDUCATIONAL		PSYCHO-SOCIAL INTERVENTION	

THE HORSE

TEMPERAMENT - CHARACTER						
POSITIVE	KIND	PATIENT	GENTLE	PEOPLE ORIENTED	BONDS WELL	ATTENTIVE
	INTELLIGENT	RESPONSIVE	FOCUSED	STEADY/RELIABLE	DOES NOT SPOOK EASILY	
NEGATIVE	TEMPERAMENTAL	INATTENTIVE	LAZY	STALL BOUND	MEAN TO HORSES	SPOOKY

RIDER /CLIENT				
LEVEL - SKILLS OF THE RIDER FOR THIS HORSE				
CHILD	ASSISTED	BEGINNER	INTERMEDIATE	ADVANCED
TEENAGER	ASSISTED	BEGINNER	INTERMEDIATE	ADVANCED
ADULT	ASSISTED	BEGINNER	INTERMEDIATE	ADVANCED

HORSE'S RANGE OF DISCIPLINE AND TRAINING					
BASIC	LEADING RIDING	DEPENDENT RIDING WITH ASSISTANT		DRESSAGE/ WALK ONLY	
BEGINNING SKILLS	INDEPENDENT WALK/ TROT	TRAINING LEVEL DRESSAGE	LUNGEING RIDER	BACKRIDING	
INTERMEDIATE SKILLS	RAIL EQUITATION	1ST LEVEL DRESSAGE	WALK/TROT THROUGH POLES	EQUINE ASSISTED THERAPY	
	TRAIL EQUITATION	VAULTING	DRIVE TO CART		
ADVANCED SKILLS	2ND LEVEL DRESSAGE	3RD LEVEL DRESSAGE	HIPPOTHERAPY	REINING	JUMPING
COMPETITION EVENTS	DRESSAGE	WESTERN EQUITATION	VAULTING	ENDURANCE	
	GYMKHANA	DRIVING	STADIUM JUMPING	EVENTING	
MAXIMUM WEIGHT OF RIDER FOR THIS HORSE WITH TACK:			LBS.		
MAXIMUM WEIGHT OF THIS RIDER WITH TACK AND BACKRIDER:			LBS		

OVERALL IMPRESSION:
_____
_____

RECOMMENDATIONS:_____
_____

EVALUATOR_____ DATE:_____

THE ROLE OF DRESSAGE FOR RIDERS WITH A DISABILITY AND FOR THE HORSE

Barbara T. Engel, MEd, OTR

A horse trained by classic dressage methodology (**dressage means training**) offers the therapeutic riding program and its riders many advantages. Dressage is work on the flat for the **horse and rider**. The English style dressage methods train the horse to perform the same general skills that a Western reining or cutting horse performs. After all, who were the first "North American Western Cowboys?" They were those trained by the Spaniards. The Spanish brought the original horses to the American continent. They also brought along the classic riding techniques. Have you heard of the Spanish Riding School? The Spanish riding school teaches by the classic methodology. The bases of training a horse in English and Western riding are the same since they came from the same culture. The saddles have changed to accommodate the task the horse and rider are to perform but the training logic is not different. **Classic methodology** was developed over centuries and based on the skill needed for the horse and rider to perform well in battle and later in high school dressage. These techniques have survived over thousands of years and through out the world because they have produced excellent results. This is what is know as the classic theory of equestrian This is the only true theory of horsemanship. There are many approaches used to teach these principles which should not be confused with theory.

Dressage is much like the training we develop in primary school. For example, in order to develop the coordination system that we will need to write quickly and legibly in high school, we first learn to print, and to print on a straight line. Then we learn to make curves and a combination of curves and straight lines. This is followed by writing words with curves, straight lines and "0s" and connecting them in words and maintaining a level line from one side of the page to the other. We learn to do this at times when our neuromuscular system is ready to do each step. We then develop the fine muscle coordination and strength in our wrist and fingers to move and write in a coordinated way.

This is what the horse learns in riding dressage patterns - at the correct time and in a 'developmental' manner. Each level of dressage (introductory, training, first, second, third, and fourth) focuses on specific skills in a developmental level. The horse must be ready physically and mentally to move from one step to the next. The rider also develops his or her coordination in a sequential manner. The rider must develop a sense of self, be able to locate a specific limb or movement, and coordinate movements to give different messages with each part of the body. The hand aids must be softened or released when the seat and leg aids tell the horse to go. Otherwise, the rider tells the horse to stop/go. The horse is moved between ones legs, by use of leg aids, and also between the subtle movements of the fingers. This can be a complicated process but not above the abilities of therapeutic riding program riders.

The rider, whether with or without a disability, also learns to develop a balanced seat, to coordinate specific movements, and to "listen" to the horse through feeling and responses and develop systematic movements as coordination is developed. The point of dressage is to make riding more comfortable for both the *horse* and the *rider*. Such training teaches the horse to move in balance which is more pleasant and comfortable for both. Dressage is gymnastic exercise for the horse that develops its natural possibilities and prepares it for all possible purposes. The exercises are performed in a careful, educational, and affectionate way. The horse and rider work together in this method to teach the horse to carry the rider in *balance* thereby increasing his willingness to be obedient and submissive to the rider. It also preserves the horse's physical well-being and longevity. This training develops the horse's suppleness and responsiveness, allowing the rider to control it with light aids. The softness of the horse, its suppleness and flexibility, is transferred to the rider and this helps to normalize the rider's muscle tone and increases his ability to balance. A horse that can be ridden with light aids is a big advantage to the rider with a disability as it is an advantage to all riders of all levels.

Riders at all levels, can gain from a horse trained by the dressage technique. All riders can learn to ride using the principles of dressage. **Dressage and reining techniques train the rider to coordinate his or her movements with those of the horse. The**

horse and rider learn to work as one. For many riders with movement coordination problems, learning to coordinate specific body movement in very subtle ways will be a new experience. Body awareness will develop, and selective movements (specific muscle movements) will be refined for increased function of the rider. Though many riders in therapeutic riding programs may not be able to fully "train" their horses, they can perform dressage exercises when their horses are routinely trained by skilled trainers to maintain the horse's flexibility, suppleness and sensitivity to aids. A well-trained horse accepts the rider's aids and will guide the rider with constant feedback, helping him or her to stimulate and adjust his movements.

Riding is a dynamic exercise as the horse and rider move together in a relaxed manner. S von Dietz [see von Dietz "From External to Internal Posture" in *Therapeutic Riding II strategies for Rehabilitation*] states that balance is movement - that one cannot maintain balance without movement. Sally Swift also maintains that in balance the spinal column maintains the body with no effort. Swift and von Dietz base their riding knowledge on the classic dressage techniques where balance and softness come together. Dressage encourages the rider to be in balance with the horse; to move in a dynamic balance with the horse. Static positions of the rider will inhibit the horse's movements (Cummings- 1996 NARHA Conference, Cummings' clinic 1997).

In equine-assisted therapy, the use of horses trained by dressage methods becomes a necessity since the manipulation of the movement of the horse produces the therapeutic effects. The dressage horse is trained to be balanced. Through improving balance, the weight can be shifted to the hindquarters of the horse, thus increasing the collection and engagement of the hindquarters and the proper use of the back. This improves the horse's ability to carry the rider well and move correctly through various gaits. It will also help him to compensate for any imbalance in the rider, an important consideration for this field.

Dressage training or well developed flat work training encourages:
- ❏ The development of a flexible and supple horse that is comfortable to ride.
- ❏ A horse that is obedient and willing, making it easy for the rider and handler to control.
- ❏ The horse's acceptance of the rider's aids willingly.
- ❏ The rider to "feel" and respond to the horse's movement.
- ❏ A deep, mobile and secure seat which allows the rider to follow the horse's back movements.
- ❏ Balance and security of the rider.
- ❏ Body awareness, body control and suppleness of the rider.
- ❏ Self improvement with measurement against self.
- ❏ The development of timing and rhythm of human movements.
- ❏ A systematic method of developing riding techniques.
- ❏ Concentration of the rider and the horse.
- ❏ Bonding between horse and rider.
- ❏ Challenge and confidence.
- ❏ Discipline of both rider and horse.

The levels in dressage address skills. Each level can relate to a school grade. Introductory level - preschool, Training level could be kindergarten, 1st level - 1st grade and so on. When competing in dressage one may say "I am training at first level but showing at training level." I have perfected my training level skills and developing my first level skills.

WHAT SKILLS ARE STRESSED IN TRAINING LEVEL, FIRST AND SECOND LEVEL DRESSAGE SKILLS?
Training Level:
- → The rider encourages suppleness, willingness, obedience and responsiveness of the horse to aids and bit
- → The rider asks for free forward movement of the horse and stretching **into** the bit--not on the bit
- → The rider moves the horse from behind with a long and relaxed frame
- → The rider maintains correct hands; hands remain still with soft fingers → The rider asks for precision and straightness of the horse on the long side of the ring

→ The rider performs accurate one gait transitions up and down, halt to walk
→ The rider performs correct lead in the canter
→ The rider bends the horse through the corners and on the circle, rhythmically and in balance
→ The rider maintains a true, rhythmical 20 meter circle at a working trot and canter
→ The rider performs a trot, rising
→ The rider begins a working trot, sitting
→ The rider performs a working canter--left and right and trot-to-canter in corners
→ The rider performs a flowing downward transition using seat
→ The rider performs rein changes (changing directions)

Training level does stress a balanced horse and a secure seat, but not as deep as higher levels. It does not stress "on the bit" or collection, but rather acceptance of the bit.

FIRST LEVEL:
→ The rider puts the horse "On the bit"
→ The rider demonstrates a supple, independent seat and quiet hands of the rider
→ The rider supples the horse with increased balance
→ The rider performs a degree of collection
→ The rider brings the horse to a square halt
→ The rider performs a working walk, trot and canter
→ The rider performs lengthening of stride in all three gaits
→ The rider performs 10 and 15 meter circles at a working trot and canter
→ The rider performs beginning lateral work with leg yielding, shoulder-in
→ The rider performs serpentine and preparatory work for the flying change

SECOND LEVEL:
→ The rider deepens his seat to ride "in" the horse rather than "on" the horse
→ The rider rounds the back of the horse and elevates the topline
→ The rider performs collection at the medium gaits, not working gaits
→ The rider performs a precise rein-back
→ The rider performs half-turn on the haunches
→ The rider performs the traverse (haunches-in)
→ The rider performs counter-canter
→ The rider's seat must be so secure that the hands are separate from body influence

Barbara T. Engel

References
Burton, R., Sordillo, D. (1985). *How to Ride a Dressage Test*. Boston: Houghton Mufflin Co. 1-89.
Von Dietz, S. (1997). From External to Internal Posture in Engel, *Therapeutic Riding II Strategies for Rehabilitation*, Barbara Engel Therapy Services, Durango CO .
Hayes, R.O. 1997. *Hazardous habits*. Equus 239, September, Fleet Street Publishing, MD.
Museler, W. (1985). *Riding Logic*. New York: Arco Publishing Inc.
Podhajsky, A. (1965). *The Complete Training of Horse and Rider*. Garden City: Doubleday & Co., Inc.
Swift, S. (1985). *Centered Riding*. North Pomfret: David & Charles.
Traditional Equitation School. (1990). Dressage. Los Angeles.
Wanless, M. (1987). *The Natural Rider*. New York: Summit Books.

CHAPTER 8
STABLE MANAGEMENT

BARN MANAGEMENT FOR THERAPEUTIC RIDING FACILITIES

Donn Taylor

INTRODUCTION

Management of a therapeutic riding program barn is not a great deal different from the managing of a regular riding facility. Whether it is a large 30 or more horse facility with an indoor arena, barn, stalls and two hundred students, or a small two horse facility with a small horse shed and pasture areas as an arena, and a handful of students, the basic horse care and responsibilities are the same. The areas of responsibility are:
1. Feed management
2. Medical care
3. Daily routine procedures
    a. Grooming
    b. Inspection and checking physical condition of horses
    c. Turn out and/or exercise of horses
4. Facility care
    a. Stall maintenance
    b. Arena, riding area, trail care
    c. Grounds upkeep
5. Equipment (tack) maintenance

There are always exceptions that must be taken into consideration when dealing with therapeutic riding programs that regular riding facilities may not need to address:
1. Selection of suitable horses
2. Training and exercising of horses
3. Continual evaluation of horses for serviceable use
4. Special facilities needed for clientele
    a. Ramps and/or mounting blocks and their condition
    b. Fenced-in riding areas
    c. Easy access, free of barriers that could hinder those with wheelchairs or crutches
    d. Distraction-free areas to ride

Next we will be looking into the key areas of facility management. Areas will vary depending upon the location of the facility. Medical or health issues will need to be discussed with the program's veterinarian. Horse evaluation and facility care will be stressed here.

Therapeutic riding programs are unique in the horse world because of NARHA. Most regular types of facilities do not have standards of operations. NARHA (North American Riding for the Handicapped Association) Operating Center Standards and Accreditation Manual provides explicit guidelines. Whether one plans to become an accredited center or not, these guidelines provide excellent standards to follow. The topics discussed in the following paragraphs reflect the standards found in the NARHA manual, the *NARHA GUIDE*.

FACILITY

Before a program can have horses, it must have an appropriate place to keep them and have a place where they can be ridden. There are no limited rules to follow. The facility may simply have a pasture in which to keep the horses, a confined area to ride in and a small shed for storage of equipment, supplies and tack. On the other hand, the program may be blessed with a facility that has a large barn with stalls, wash racks, an indoor arena, an outdoor arena and riding trails. Each program must judge geographic requirements, the needs for their clients, and most important, what the budget allows.

PASTURE

Keeping the horses in pastures is the most economical and natural way of taking care of them. Horses are naturally herd animals and graze together. The pasture places them in an environment that is best suited for them. How the pasture is managed will determine its value. Key areas that need to be considered are:

1. Is there adequate space to keep the number of horses the program needs?

   Each horse needs two to three acres of forage in order to provide it with the required amount of nutrition. (Based upon a 1000 pound horse - Horse Industry Handbook)

2. Are the horses compatible with each other?

3. Does the program have a waste management program?

   Manure must be controlled and managed, both in the pastures and paddocks and in the stalls. It must be picked up daily or dragged on a regular basis in order to control:

   a. Worms. Worm eggs stay alive for a period of time in the manure and can be transferred to the grass leaf and re-entered into the horse's system.

   b. The fly population.

   c. The quality and quantity of grass. Manure that is left in the pasture causes lack of uniform grass growth and spottiness.

4. Are the pastures free from hazardous objects that may cause injury or illness to the horses? These may include weeds, trees, fencing, equipment, holes and creeks.

5. A watering system needs to be in place so there is adequate clean water at all times for the animals. Water containers must be kept clean and free of algae.

6. There must be shelters in case of inclement weather. These need to be kept clean and well maintained. Fencing and gates must be checked routinely.

7. Feeders for supplemental feedings should be cleaned and maintained in good condition.

8. Are appropriate measures taken to provide enough feeders for each horse and are they spaced to avoid fighting over the feed?

9. Does the pasture maintenance include fertilization, watering and seeding to provide a healthy stand of grass and weed control. Does the turnout schedule prevent overgrazing?

One must remember that quality pasture management is essential and requires a great deal of work.

The program needs to have some kind of shed or building that can be used to store equipment, tack, feed and other necessary materials. It is important that all items be kept in an orderly, clean and accessible manner. Rakes and manure forks need to be placed so they do not cause a hazard. Grooming tools need to be accessible but not in one's path. Staff and volunteers need to know where the equipment is and to return items to their proper places.

THE ARENA OR RIDING AREA:

The areas set aside for riding must be maintained to assure the safety of program riders, staff, volunteers and horses. Maintenance of the riding arena or field will include:

1. Footing must be maintained regardless of its composition. It can be composed of Fibar, wood chips, sand, shredded rubber, dirt or grass.

      a. All foreign objects or equipment that is not used must be removed.

      b. Manure should be picked up to keep the area clean, free from odors, and to help with insect control.

      c. The area should be level to allow easy movement for horses and persons. There should not be any hole, ruts or mounds to trip over.

      d. Dust must be controlled.

      e. If dust becomes a problem, one may need to add such material as Arena Saver, salt or fine grade oil to help control the problem. These products help to keep moisture in the footing and dust down.

      f. Replenish footing material to keep the ground consistent and workable. Over a period of time, all materials will break down and will need to be replaced.

    2. Fencing must be continually inspected, and gates checked to make sure that they are in good working order.

No matter what type of facility you have, you want to make sure you have an area that is confined, away from other horses, quiet, with minimal distractions, a good riding surface and a good barrier around the area. It does not have to be fancy, just workable and safe.

THE STABLE AND BARN AREAS

All programs may dream of having a barn with stalls, wash racks, tack room, offices and waiting room. It is a lot easier working with our horses and keeping everything where it belongs when these facilities are available. The following areas will need our attention:

    1. BARN AREA:

      a. There should be a plan for rodent and pest control.

      b. A regular maintenance routine should be in effect to assure that all facilities, buildings, grounds, activity areas are in good repair, clean and sanitary. Walkways shall be smooth, for both horses and people, and must be kept clear of all obstructions, and equipment.

      c. An inventory should be kept on all equipment, maintenance supplies, horse care supplies. All such items must be kept in the proper places.

      d. There must be a good ventilation system throughout the barns and indoor arena areas.

      e. Routine checks, replacement and maintenance must be carried out on all safety equipment, fire extinguishers and first aid supplies for horse and humans.

    2. STALLS:

      a. Each stall needs to be kept clean of all manure and urine. Stalls should be cleaned several times a day.

      b. Bedding material should be kept thick enough to give the horse comfort when lying down and be absorbent enough to keep the horse dry and clean. When some is removed while cleaning, enough should remain for adequate care or bedding replenished. Most facilities will strip the stalls at least once a week and put in all new bedding.

      c. Check the water containers on a regular basis for cleanliness and to ensure the containers are full of water.

      d. Feeders must be kept clean and rodent free.

      e. Stalls need to be checked for any broken material, sharp or foreign items. Make sure any tie up lines and hardware are safe and in good working condition.

      f. Insect and fly control equipment needs to be maintained and checked for effective use.

The bedding for the stalls can be of various materials. The most common materials used for bedding are: (Horse Industry Handbook)

    1. Straw: Attractive in the stall, very absorbent, comfortable for horses, high in labor cost to clean, maybe more difficult to dispose of dependent on were one lives, not as plentiful as other material in some areas, affects cost. Some horses eat the straw. Straw is a high fire risk.

2. Wood shavings: Highly absorbent, keeps down odors, requires less cleaning and saves on labor costs. It is not as flammable as straw. Initial cost may be higher but less labor cost. More room is needed for storage. May cause dust, must make sure no hardwood such as black walnut is used since this can cause a sudden case of laminitis.

3. Recycled, shredded newspaper: A rather new product. Fairly dust and pollen free, weighs comparatively less than other bedding products, may not be available everywhere. May cut back on stripping the stalls if properly picked daily. Does not blend in with soil as well when spread in fields, highly combustible, tends to rub off on horses.

4. Other crop materials: Corn stalks, ground corncobs, chopped hay, peat moss. Availability and cost are factors to consider. Handling and storage expenses must be considered. Horses may eat this type of bedding.

Make sure that the choice of material is absorbent, dust free, readily available, easily disposed of, unpalatable, and most important, affordable. Labor cost must be considered.

THE MOUNTING/DISMOUNTING AREA:

It is imperative that the mounting areas are checked on a regular basis for cleanliness, are free of obstacles, and that they are in good working order.

Mounting is a crucial part of any riding session. The safety of everyone concerned must be taken into consideration while mounting and dismounting. Clients or students are at a vulnerable state while mounting or dismounting. The staff must make every effort to make sure there are no surprises or accidents waiting to happen. All staff and volunteers must be well trained in the mounting and dismounting procedures. All persons will remain alert and watching for anything that could cause a threat to the process.

THE HORSE EVALUATION:

Once the facility is ready and organized, the staff can begin to select horses for the program. Without proper horses, our programs are useless. The horse evaluation, or the selection process, is the most important link to a successful operation.

There are three questions to ask when considering a horse for the program:
1. What clients will be able to use this horse?
2. Will the staff and volunteers be able to work safely with this horse?
3. Will the cost of the horse offset the hours that it can be used?

Conformation of the therapeutic riding horse is a vital factor to consider. One should become well acquainted with information on conformation so that one can evaluate a horse adequately for the purpose it will be used for.

LETS LOOK AT EACH CONSIDERATION FOR A MOMENT.

A. THE CLIENT:

What clientele or group of riders will best benefit from this horse? How many different riders will be able to use the horse? Consider the size one will need in height and weight. Look at the barrel size: is it narrow or wide? How is the gait of the horse? Slow, fast, smooth, or short strides? Look at the skill level of the program riders and what their needs are in order to challenge them.

B. THE STAFF AND VOLUNTEERS:

When looking at a horse for the program, one must take into consideration the training it has had. For instance if one acquires a Grand Prix level dressage horse, it may be difficult to work this horse to its fullest potential if the staff members have no dressage training.

Remember the personnel, especially volunteers, are changing from class to class or day to day. Consequently, one needs horses that will tolerate much change, different people working with them and several people (side walkers) working at the same time. The so called "one man horse" may not fit into the program.

C. THE COST FACTOR:

What will it cost the program per hour to use this horse? Consider how much money will be spent for feed, medication, supplements, special equipment, normal routine care such as shots, farrier, worming, etc. compared to the number of hours or lessons the horse will be used.

When you have established a need for a new horse, a good procedure must be in place to evaluate the horse. Without this procedure one can end up with a horse that will not be usable, or trainable, and cost more for upkeep than its worth. With a good evaluation, everyone is looking for the same thing. It gives one something in writing to show the person who is selling or donating the horse to the program what is expected. If the horse doesn't make the program one can show the owners why this horse will not work out. This is very important, for when a horse is donated, the program must keep it for a required period of time before they can sell it.

THE EVALUATION PROCEDURES

In the evaluation process one wants to find out everything one can about the horse. What can this horse do comfortably? In what areas will it need more training? Is it trainable or is it going to take more time than one has? Will the horse accept the facility? How about the toys, games, the ramps and all the other different things that may be involved in the program?

In order to find out about these things one needs to make sure that all procedures are covered in the evaluation. Break each area down into easy workable groups such as the following:
1. General barn analysis
2. Ground work analysis
3. Object screening analysis
4. Mounted performance analysis

Within each group list the areas that are pertinent to the barn and make sure to find out what the horse's reaction is to the area.
1. General Barn Analysis:
   This is where one finds out the basic care needs of the horse. Will it accept the daily routines, the facility or will the horse require special treatment?
   a. Housing: will the horse accept being in the pasture with other horses or does it need to be in a separate area? What is the best stall for this horse? Will he cross tie and what about the reaction to a wash rack area?
   b. Daily chores: Are there any bad habits displayed while grooming? Where can this horse be groomed? While cleaning the feet one can determine the reaction to the farrier. How does the horse react to clipping, vacuums, baths, mane pulling?
   c. Special Areas: Will he allow one to blanket him and will he let his legs be wrapped? Are there any problems giving him medication, wormer, or taking care of possible injuries?
2. Ground Work:
   In this phase of the evaluation, one wants to learn about the horse's movement, will he accept being led? What kind of a relationship is there between the staff and the horse? Next, test him in areas where he may be used with your students as well as with your volunteers.
   a. Round Pen: One wants to know if this horse will work without any kind of restraints. Can one get the horse's respect? Is it trainable or not? Start getting an idea of his motion and gait.
   b. Lead line: Will he accept being led? What cues are necessary to make him respond and will he do what is asked of him? How he will be led in classes is what one needs to test?

159

   c. Longe line: If you work your students on a longe line you'll need to know how this horse will respond, and, it's a great training or warm up exercise.

   d. Standing without moving: Since we do a fair amount of standing while doing exercises or games, or just making adjustments with equipment and our students, we must know if the horse stands quietly or does he get nervous and move around.

   e. Ramp and/or mounting block: How will this horse respond to the mounting procedures that you use? How about the special equipment: wheel chairs, crutches, student lifts? And what about the different mounts that are used: legs over the neck and total lifts?

   f. Mounted with leader and sidewalkers: Will the horse accept all those people working along side of him? What about the rider doing exercises or changing positions in vaulting movements?

   g. Dismounts: Can the horse accept the different types of dismounts, and again, all the different equipment? : wheel chairs, crutches, all the people helping?

3. Object Screening:

During this part of the evaluation you will want to see what the horse will accept and what objects seem to be a problem. For those items that seem to be a problem, you need to find out there is hope of change or if it is a definite no-way situation. Then, you must decide if you can live with that object not being used.

You will need to list all of the toys, game pieces, obstacles, everything that you use in your classes. Also consider the environment, traffic noise, tractors, music being played, crowd noises, clapping, and if you're in a neighborhood where police or ambulance sirens go off frequently. Remember, you may not know what the horse has been exposed to, and before it's too late you need to find out. Evaluate now.

An important key here is to make sure you give the horses time to get used to these items before you evaluate them. Give them the benefit of the doubt as to whether they should have been exposed to these things before or not. Even the more obvious things such as ground poles or cones may be new to these horses. In other words, don't throw a ball at them one time, watch them step away and mark them poor. Give them a chance.

4. The Mounted Performance

Again, in this section, as in the Object Screening, you want to list the areas that are important for your horses to do. Don't necessarily think of just your needs right now but also what future students you may have come your way. Some things to consider may be:

   A. Transitions: Not only gait to gait but within each gait.

   B. Circles: At the walk and trot and possibly canter.

   C. Figure 8: Serpentines.

   D. Halts, Starts, Standing.

   E. Lead changes, tracking left and right.

   F. What cues are needed as cues to make them perform.

   G. How they react with several horses in the arena.

   H. Trails and obstacles.

Make your mounted evaluation like a dressage test. Since we use the letters in our arenas, it was just natural to design the test as such. This way everyone rides the test the same way and does the same things.

SCORING:

The evaluation process will only be worthwhile if it gives you good answers. Good answers come from a good scoring table. Make your table workable for you. If you make it too hard, you will never keep any horses except maybe a Grand Prix level or World Champion. That is fine and dandy for those who get these kind of horses to look at and can wait till they come available. Unfortunately, most of us don't have that luxury. But, at the same time, don't make it so easy that every horse will pass. We can be selective and we must get good quality horses.

Our system is set up with four (4) categories;

1. Excellent: This is for the perfect maneuver - you couldn't ask for it to be better - the best you have ever seen - it's perfection. (Obviously not too many horses will be in this category.)

2. Good: Has handled the task well - not perfect - but very usable - room for possible improvement, but definitely can be used as is - shows positive potential.

3. Fair: Could be a lot better - may not be usable in this area at present - shows positive signs that they can be trained in this area - worth training.

4. Poor: Unacceptable maneuver - would take excessive training - no sign of accepting or understanding the procedure.

As we evaluate the horse we want to make sure that we see:
  A. Willingness to perform.
  B. Submission to the rider or handler.
  C. Relaxation through the work.
  D. Ease in transitions.
  E. Awareness of items and techniques we use.

Mike Richardson (horse trainer and clinician) states in his clinics that we don't want to desensitize a horse from something, rather make them aware of and assure them that it won't hurt them. To desensitize them to an object will make them dead to it or unaware of the item. We want them to be aware and not afraid of it, a point with which I agree.

CONCLUSION

A good horse evaluation is an essential part of every program. Not only do we use ours for all new horses but we also use it on all of our regular horses at least once (1) a year. During our leg-up process at the beginning of our season we will evaluate each horse to see if any changes have occurred during the off season. We would rather find out before an accident occurs.

Donn Taylor
USA

A HORSE WITH A HEART, NOT AN ATTITUDE: USING THE EQUINE EXAMINATION CHECKLIST

Kathleen E Harbaugh, M.Ed

Someone wants to donate a horse to your program. As usual, it is 12 yrs. old, sound, child safe and perfectly precious.

Can you test submission, trust and willingness?

Is this a horse with a heart or a bad attitude?

How do you use the Equine Examination Checklist to be sure "Perfectly Precious" (PP) is the horse you need?

1. Use the Telephone.

Call the Director or whomever will decide to accept the horse. With a red pen, circle the mandatory areas on the checklist and underline those with secondary priority. Call PP's owner and fill out the top of the checklist. (It's a wasted effort to test a 14.2 hand Arabian if you need a horse for backriding.) Make an appointment with PP's owner for you and another competent horse person to test her.

2. Prepare to **Test** the Horse.

Bring tack that is used in your program. If you must buy a new saddle to fit PP then she really isn't free after all. You'll need two or three saddles, bridles (find out if she uses a curb or snaffle), a halter, lead rope, longe line and whip, and crutches or walker. Collect a bell, whistle, white paper, a 12"x12" flag, poster board, and any other toy you use often. Bring carrots for the horse and a helmet for you.

3. Observe Horse in Pasture or Paddock

While the owner brags about her ribbons, watch PP for ten minutes with another horse. Ask about her position in the herd: is she top mare or an outcast? Take specific notes, i.e., "pins ears and kicks"or "wheels and runs." Ask the owner to halter and hold the horse while you test her reaction to noise and motion. Start 20 feet away and gradually move closer if PP shows little or no fear. If PP rolls her eyes and backs up, you've moved too fast. You should know in ten minutes if she is trainable.

4. Groom and Tack Up.

Ask the owner to tie up his horse. If he just loops the lead rope over the fence, suspect that PP has a well-developed sense of panic and often "sits back" when tied. Perform the rest of the grooming and tacking yourself.

5. Lead and Longe.

This section of the checklist is almost self-explanatory. Pressure on flank means: if a novice tries to clean a foot and accidentally gets stepped on, will PP move over when ask? While you longe, ask your helper to record stride length, rhythm, obedience to voice, etc. Pay attention to gaits needed in your program. If you plan to use PP only at the walk and trot, her disunited canter isn't important.

6. Mount and Dismount.

Complete the left side mount/dismount before you ride, and finish at the end of the ride when you are confident PP will safe for the off-side mount/dismount and exposure to crutches/walker test. You can test her ramp and wheelchair reactions later, at your own facility during PP's trial period.

7. Test Reactions to Rider Behavior.

    Be safe: use an enclosed area. Be gentle: walk PP for the first five minutes. Be patient: wait for her head to drop and try for a stretch down (or a nose blow) before testing.

8. Ride or Drive.

    If time is short, first test those movements you *know* you'll need for your clients.

SUMMARY OF BEHAVIOR

Do *not* fill this section until you and your trusted friend are alone. Tell PP's owner, "Our Board will make the final decision and call you." While driving home, discuss each section and fill in the blanks. Overwrite your original pencil comments in pen. Finally, agree on the recommendation.

If you have, indeed, discovered that PP is a horse with a heart, not an attitude, then note that you have found a grey mare that is just what Billy, Bob, and Bubba need as they learn to trot, and she is Perfectly Precious.

Kathleen E Harbaugh

EQUINE EXAMINATION CHECKLIST

Kathleen E. Harbaugh, M.Ed

Horse's Name: _____

Owner: _____ Address: _____ Telephones:_____

Breeds: _____ Color:_____ Sex:____ Ages:____ Height: _____ Width; _____ Back Lengths: _____

Health History Wormed: _____ Coggins: _____ Rabies: _____ Flu/Rhino: _____ Tetanus: _____

Encephalitis: _____ Teeth: _____ Veterinarian: _____ Farrier: _____

Soundness: Wind: _____ Limbs: _____ Vision: _____ Hearings: _____ Back: _____

Reason selling/donating and cost: _____

In Pasture or Paddock
1. General Disposition   Quiet: _____ Nervous: _____ Aggressive: _____
2. Reaction to Other Horses: _____
3. Catching and Haltering: Easy _____   Difficult_____
4. Reaction to Distractions: Noise - Bell/Whistle/Clapping:_____Motion -Paper/Flag/Poster:_____

Behavior: Acceptable_____   Trainable:_____ Unacceptable_____

Notes:

Grooming and Tacking-up	Calm	Nervous	Resists/Pulls	Flinches	Kicks
Grooming					
Picking up feet					
Saddling/Harnessing					
Bridling					

Behavior: Acceptable:_____   Trainable:_____   Unacceptable_____

Notes:

Leading and Lunging	Calm	Nervous	Resists
General leading			
Leading over poles			
Backing			
Standing/Ground Tie, one minute			
Pressure on flanks			

Longe 20 meter circle:	Rhythm/stride	To the right	To the left
Walk			
Trot			
Canter			
Halt			
Response to Voice/Whip			

Behavior: Acceptable_____ Trainable _____ Unacceptable _____

Notes:

Mounting and Dismounting	From the ground	From the ramp
Mounting - left side		
- right side		
Dismounting - left side		
right side		
Reaction to crutches/walker		
Reaction to wheelchair		

Behavior: Acceptable_____ Trainable _____ Unacceptable _____

Notes:

Reaction to Rider Behavior	Calm	Nervous	Notes
Hands on head/neck			
Hands on hindquarters//tail			
Arms in circular motion			
Legs on barrel/flanks			
Rider off-balance			
Rider lying forward/back			

Behavior: Acceptable_____ Trainable _____ Unacceptable _____

Notes:

Riding or Driving	Calm	Nervous	Notes
Walk	_____	_____	_____
Trot	_____	_____	_____
Canter	_____	_____	_____
Halts	_____	_____	_____
Back	_____	_____	_____
Stand (full minute)	_____	_____	_____
Leg Yield (walk)	_____	_____	_____
Around Barrels			

Summary of Behavior Ratings	Acceptable	Trainable	Unacceptable
Pasture or paddock	_____	_____	_____
Grooming and tacking-up	_____	_____	_____
Leading and longeing	_____	_____	_____
Mounting and dismounting	_____	_____	_____
Reaction to rider behavior	_____	_____	_____
Riding or driving	_____	_____	_____

A horse may be accepted into the Triple H Equitherapy program with a minimum of three acceptable behavior ratings and no unacceptable ratings. This horse is: Accepted_____ Rejected_____

Signature_____ Date_____

BASIC HORSE CARE FOR THE THERAPEUTIC RIDING HORSE--A REVIEW

Margaret L. Galloway, MA, BHSAI

Horse care is based on a combination of sound daily practices, the prevention of problems and accidents and good routine care of the therapeutic riding horse. The ability to observe any change or difference in a horse's appearance or behavior may mean the difference between a small problem or a crisis. A horse should be examined carefully on a daily basis for cuts, bruises or any abnormalities. A good time for checking would be during feeding or grooming. *KNOW EACH HORSE*. Note the general signs of his health and investigate any deviations from his normal condition. Hintz and Lowe (Evans 1977), identify five major areas of horse management that must be addressed in a therapeutic riding program:

1. The ability to identify deviations from a horse's normal condition.
2. The maintenance of a complete record system.
3. Being knowledgeable and up-to-date in equine diseases and their causes.
4. The development and maintenance of a vaccination and worming program.
5. Being knowledgeable about situations that could place the horse at high risk for disease or injury and avoiding such conditions.

It is beyond the scope of this book to provide a <u>complete reference</u> on stable management. Instructors, trainers and therapists should obtain good reference books on diseases, psychology, conformation and health care of the horse.(Refer to the bibliography.) In addition, they should keep up with current information by reading and attending short courses in horse management.

The Healthy Horse Should Have:
- ❏ Bright eyes without excess tearing.
- ❏ A shiny coat with hair lying down: in cold climates the hair stands up.
- ❏ Securely fitting shoes with properly clinched nails--no tenderness in the hooves.
- ❏ A normal appetite--all feed is eaten.
- ❏ Normal droppings--droppings must be firm but moist, and break when they hit the ground.
- ❏ No mucus in the droppings.
- ❏ Normal weight--one should be able to feel the ribs but not see them.
- ❏ Adequate hydration--skin that does not "stay up" when pinched but returns immediately to it's previous position.
- ❏ Legs devoid of swelling, tenderness, or heat--the feet should feel cool. Both front and hind legs should appear and feel the same. Many horses have benign swellings, known as wind-puffs or windgall in lower leg joints. Swellings caused by synovial joint fluid are blemishes and are of little concern. Once a horse develops these, they rarely disappear. If they do change, they should be examined (Adams 1972).
- ❏ Good balance at rest. The horse should stand evenly on all four feet. Resting a hind leg is normal but constant advancement of one front foot (pointing) is usually a sign of pain. The weight should be equal on both front legs.
- ❏ Sound legs. When walking or trotting, the horse should take strides of even length with equal sound of the footfall. The lame side may have a shorter stride.
- ❏ No head bobbing. If a horse is lame in the front, he will raise his head when the lame foot hits the ground.
- ❏ Urine--light yellow to yellowish-brown in color and "slimy" (mucous) in texture passed several times a day.
- ❏ No signs of sweating at rest except in unusually hot weather.

According to a poll surveying both horse owners and veterinarians, the following were the top ten health problems (in order of the most numerous)(Underhill 1989):

1. subtle lameness	6. incapacitating lameness
2. colic	7. respiratory diseases
3. wounds requiring sutures	8. eye injuries
4. puncture wounds	9. skin diseases and allergies
5. breeding/foal matters	

IDENTIFICATION OF HEALTH SIGNS

Taking measurements of the horse's temperature, pulse and respiration (vital signs) will provide objective criteria with which to evaluate any change in a horse's bodily functions (King 1990). It is a good idea to take vital signs when the healthy horse is at rest to determine a baseline for the horse. A record should be kept of these normal readings for future reference. Learning to take the temperature, pulse,and respiration is a simple skill to acquire. It will provide the veterinarian necessary information for acute care and emergencies.

How to Monitor Vital Signs

Temperature: The normal temperature of the horse is 99.5 to 101.4 degrees Fahrenheit (internally). Using a rectal horse thermometer with a string attached, shake the mercury down so that it reads below 98 degrees. Gently raise the tail and insert the thermometer gently into the horse's rectum until one-half inch the thermometer is showing. Tie the string at the end of the thermometer to the horse's tail to prevent the instrument from disappearing into the rectum. Using a clip at the end of the string holds it to the horse's tail and is easier than tying it. Adding petroleum jelly to the bulb end helps it to slide into the rectum. Leave it in the rectum for one and a half to two minutes before reading the temperature.

Pulse: The normal pulse rate is between 26 and 40 beats per minute. The pulse can be taken in several places but there are two common ones: at the *maxillary artery* where it runs over the underside of the jaw bone on the horse's left side, or on the artery as it curves into *the tail.* Use the first and middle fingers to locate the artery in either place. In the tail there is a groove in the middle of the fleshy underside of the tail bone. Using very light pressure, feel the pulse for several beats before starting to count. Then, count for thirty seconds; then multiply your count by two to get the per minute rate. The secret of getting an accurate pulse is not pressing too hard on the artery.

Respiration: Normal respiration is eight to sixteen breaths per minute with the horse at rest. Watch and count for 30 seconds each expansion of the flank as the horse inhales, then multiply that figure by two to get the per minute rate.

HOUSING THE PROGRAM HORSE

A horse needs to be housed in a well ventilated and dry stall to stay healthy. Good ventilation without drafts reduces the chances of sweating or getting chilled and also helps to remove urine and ammonia odors. A *stabled horse* needs to have his stall cleaned once or twice a day. If urine and manure are not removed, the horse's hooves will become damaged from dampness and toxins. Thrush, the bacterial infection of the frog, is likely to develop. The odor of ammonia from urine is unpleasant for horses and humans alike. To clean the stall, remove all manure piles, then begin forking through the bedding to find urine spots. Replace wet spots with dry bedding. Build up bedding material around the edges of the stall to reduce the chance of the horse being cast (rolling in such a way that he cannot move). All stalls must have an adequate supply of fresh water.

Pasturing a horse puts him in a natural environment, in which far less attention is required. "If the pasture is properly managed, many horses thrive on it and there are considerable savings in time and money" (Hadfield 1989). Horses in pasture need a form of shelter, such as a shed, to get out of wind and rain. The pasture needs to be picked clean of manure regularly. Cleaning up the manure is important because it can be a source of worm eggs; if horses are on a well maintained deworming program this should not be a problem. A weekly clean up may be necessary to avoid flies. Algae need to be cleaned out of water troughs. Some people keep algae-eating fish in troughs to help keep them clean. Pasturing is the most economical way to keep a horse, as little daily maintenance is needed. It is possible for a pasture to provide a mainstay of a horse's diet, but the area must be big enough to maintain healthy grass. In most cases, supplementary feed will be needed.

A major advantage of pasturing horses together is that it places them in their natural herd environment and they can exercise themselves enough for health but not for fitness (Hadfield 1989). The disadvantage of pasturing horses is that it can cause them to be wet and dirty if the fields are not maintained. There is some possibility of a horse being kicked, but the advantages usually outweigh the disadvantages. Feeding horses separately usually eliminates the problem of kicking.

Horses may be kept in *small corrals or paddocks*, either alone or with other horses. The footing may be of decomposed granite which drains well, eliminating mud. Sand is also used in many areas, as it provides good drainage. However, it may be ingested which can lead to colic. Feed placed in a large container on the ground that cannot be overturned helps reduce this problem. Dirt is often used for footing. It has the disadvantage of turning to mud when it rains. Paddocks should have a shed, or at the very least, a sturdy tree. Horses kept together in paddocks need to be monitored.

BATHING
In warm weather, a horse with a short coat can be bathed by being hosed or sponged off, but it is not necessary to completely bath the horse for his health, and this should not be overdone. The main disadvantage of excessive bathing is the loss of natural oils in the hair. Sweat from tack should be removed after riding to prevent sores and infections. The horse can be bathed by running water over all the sweaty areas and then using a sweat scraper to remove the excess water. Be sure to wash between the hind legs and also the poll. When washing the poll, remove the halter and buckle it around the horse's neck first; never tie or leave a horse with a halter around his neck since he can injure himself if he should pull back. Another important factor is to have sufficient traction in the wash area so the horse does not slip. In cool weather or in the evening, rub the coat of a horse with a towel. A heater lamp or a blower can be an asset.

BLANKETING THE HORSE
Blankets are used to keep a horse warm and help to keep a shorter coat in winter. Conversely, a horse left out most of the time develops a long winter coat. If he is blanketed, the hair is flattened, thus actually inhibiting the hair's natural insulating effect. Many horses never need to be blanketed, even in very cold climates. A horse in good condition that is fed properly does not need to be blanketed unless he shows signs of being cold, such as shivering. An older horse that requires extra feed in winter to maintain his body weight may not need as much feed if he is blanketed since the insulation of the blanket conserves his energy. Blanketing with a light sheet may be necessary for white and grey horses, who are more sensitive to the sun, to prevent sunburn and other effects from the sun's rays. When the riding session is over, a blanket can be put over the horses to keep them from catching a chill and allow them to cool down gradually.

Several varieties of blanketing can be used under various conditions. The summer sheet is a cotton or canvas blend with no lining. It offers some protection and may be used alone on cool nights or under a heavier, lined blanket. It is advisable to have two belly straps, which are criss-crossed diagonally underneath to prevent the horse from getting his feet and legs caught in the straps and pulling the blanket off. The most common blanket is the lined or quilted type. It may have an outer shell of cotton, canvas or nylon. Although all lined blankets are efficient, nylon usually lasts somewhat longer. A third kind of blanket is the waterproof type, of which the New Zealand Rug and the Gore-tex are the best-known brands. This is made of waterproofed canvas with a sewn-on surcingle and leg straps. It provides the maximum protection. The blanket may rub the shoulders of the horse causing friction burns and hair loss (Kilby 1987) and lameness. Satin or fleece can be sewn into the blanket at the withers, shoulders and hips to reduce friction. Blankets must fit the horse well in order to stay in place and to avoid injuring the horse.

Blankets must be washed when dirty. A dirty blanket can injure the horse and will not last. To keep a heavy blanket clean on the inside, a lightweight blanket can be used under the heavier blanket. The lighter blanket can be easily washed and kept clean, therefore protecting the horse's skin. If washing is a problem at the program stable, this can be resolved by using three lighter-weight blankets that are layered. Because of their light weight, they can easily be washed in standard washing machines, and the triple layer provides ample warmth. The other advantage of using a tier of blankets is the ability to adjust to varying temperatures.

CLIPPING AND TRIMMING THE HORSE

Horses should be clipped when their long coat presents a problem. Program horses may need to be clipped to remove long hair for the following reasons:

- ❏ To keep the horse clean and free of dust for riders who are allergic to animal dust.
- ❏ To prevent the horse from becoming sweaty after work.
- ❏ To keep him cool in warm southern climates.
- ❏ To speed drying time after bathing.
- ❏ For aesthetic purposes for shows.

Clipping should be done before November in North American climates by a person who is knowledgeable and experienced. It should be noted that horses should be clipped only to the extent needed as this removes the horse's warm coat and may necessitate the use of a blanket. Clipping a horse's muzzle and face hair takes away his sensors to feel for food and foreign objects and should be avoided. The style of clipping chosen depends on the workload and the type of stabling of a horse. When horses need to be clipped, they should be clipped when they have full coats and become sweaty after a workout. This can be a special problem when it is cold and a long time is needed to dry a horse. Horses can get chilled and this can lead to colds and pneumonia if they are not allowed to cool gradually after working. Because their protection is limited, pastured horses should be clipped minimally, if at all (Watkins 1986).

TYPES OF CLIPS:

HUNTER CLIP

TRACE CLIP

BLANKET CLIP

HORSE CARE SCHEDULE

A therapeutic riding program relies on healthy, strong and fit horses. In order to keep a horse strong and healthy, a daily schedule of horse care is necessary.

Daily activities include:
- ✓ Cleaning (mucking) stalls to remove manure and urine-soaked bedding
- ✓ Feeding a minimum of two times daily; three to four is preferred
- ✓ Checking water supply and condition twice a day
- ✓ Grooming and cleaning feet
- ✓ Checking for heat, swelling, injury or changes in vital signs
- ✓ Turning-out and an exercise program
- ✓ Warming up and cooling down routine
- ✓ Blanketing as needed

Periodic scheduled care:
- ✓ Shoe or trim every four to eight weeks depending on each horse's needs. A regular schedule should be set up with the farrier.
- ✓ Worm every two to four months. A schedule should be drawn-up with the veterinarian to meet the program's needs
- ✓ Vaccinations given routinely to prevent disease and disease-related physical problems such as colic. Vaccinations for influenza, rhinopneumonitis, tetanus, rabies, botulism, anthrax, Potomac horse fever, Venezuelan equine encephalomyelitis (VEE, E.E.E., W.E.E.), strangles; equine viral arteritis (EVA) may be included. A schedule should be drawn up with the veterinarian to meet the particular needs of your location, as not all diseases are present in all areas of the country.
- ✓ Semi-annual dental care--watch for problem teeth in the older horse, and an annual check for all horses.
- ✓ Sheath cleaning for geldings.

Margaret L. Galloway USA

HEALTH AND EMERGENCIES WITH A HORSE

Barbara T. Engel, MEd, OTR

Good stable management includes the knowledge of routine health care practices and vaccinations, as well as the knowledge of problems and how to prevent or minimize them. Health problems include lameness, colic, injuries, wounds, respiratory difficulties, eye irritations, allergies, internal diseases and skin diseases (Underhill 1989).

Know what to do for these signs of equine illness:
1. Swelling, heat and pain
2. Fever
3. Hard, labored breathing, cough or choking
4. Secretion from the nostrils, mouth, eyes or rectum
5. Tremors, shivering, sweating
6. Diarrhea, hard manure, no manure
7. Restlessness, rolling, discomfort, absent gut sounds
8. Changes in urine color, no urine
9. Loss of weight
10. Dull coat, loss of hair
11. Difficulty swallowing, abnormal gum color, foul breath
12. In-coordination, lameness, unusual stance, scuffing gait, muscle soreness
13. Big belly, along with other health related signs
14. Depression
15. Eats less then usual or does not eat at all
16. Excessive salivation
17. Increased water intake
18. Blisters, ulcers in and around the mouth
19. Unusual postures
20. Departure from usual routine and behaviors

Knowledge of the characteristics of the major horse diseases and problems can avoid the loss of a horse or can prevent serious illness. One also needs to know when to call the veterinarian and what to tell him or her.

Before the veterinarian comes be sure that there is a clean and safe examination area. Its should be free from distraction such as other horses and readied before the veterinarian arrives. Additional area requirements include good lighting, a supply of clean water - possibly hot water, and clean towels. A non-slip floor is ideal with a rubber mat. Information regarding the horse's vital signs should be available.

The following conditions require veterinarian attention or advice:

.DISORDER	SIGNS	CAUSE & EFFECT
Azoturia	Severe spasms--especially hindquarter paralysis that brings a horse to a standstill. Spasms can close the blood vessels.	Believed to be a bio-chemical imbalance. Strenuous exercise after days of rest. Can be threatening!
Colic	Rolling, horse looks or bites at flank, sweaty flank, kicking, restlessness, not eating, not passing manure, dried manure indicating dehydration, groaning, agitation, pawing the ground.	A dysfunction of the gastrointestinal track caused by inflammation of the small intestines, obstruction, muscle spasms, gas, blockage of blood vessels or displacement - causing pain in the abdomen. **Can be very serious and life-threatening!**
EPM (equine protozoal myelitis)	Cranial nerve signs-head tilt, ears in strange positions, changing eye sight and other in-coordination of head muscles, gait abnormalities, abnormal sweating, muscle spasms, doing poorly, difficulty chewing.	By a parasite produced through the feces of a opossum. It can be transmitted in the pasture, contaminated water or grain and hay that has been contaminated.
Equine Infectious Anemia (EIA)	Loss of appetite, paralysis, poor gait, weakness, depression, fever, sweating, increase urination.	A blood disease caused by a virus which is transmitted by mosquitos or flies. It can be a fatal disease with no cure. Horses may be carriers but not show illness but can pass the disease to other horses.
Heaves	Chronic cough, lack endurance and can not work hard.	A chronic cough caused by living in dusty areas, eating moldy hay, or allergies.
Influenza (flu)	Loss of appetite, runny nose with white mucus, cough, fever.	A respiratory disorder caused by a virus which is spread through the air.
Laminitis/Founder	Lameness, stance with weight on heels of front feet, feet hot, body sweats.	Inflammation (of the laminain) in the wall of the hoof. The pedal bone in the foot can rotate and cause permanent damage. **Can be very serious**.
Muscle strains and spasms	Pain or stiffness.	Poor conditioning and exercise habits, asking more from the horse than his condition allows, stepping into a hole or taking a bad step. If not attended to can lead to serious injuries.

DISORDER	SIGNS	CAUSE & EFFECT
Rabies	Difficulty eating and drinking, in-coordination, depression, aggressive or unusual behavior and paralysis. Site of bite may be inflamed. Signs may not appear for several months after the bite.	A viral disease that is transmitted in saliva by a bite from an infected animal. Can be prevented by shots.
Ringworm--a very contagious skin disease.	May cause hair loss. Can be transmitted to riders or handlers. Can be transmitted from grooming tools or other objects used in contact with ringworm.	Fungi. Veterinarian can provide medication to eradicate it.
Strangles	Swelling in the lymph glands in the head and neck, cough, nasal discharge, elevated temperature, difficulty in swallowing. An abscess develops and finally bursts.	Streptococcus infection, which can be carried in the air from horse to horse. **Highly contagious to other horses, so isolation is required.**
Tetanus (lockjaw)	Muscle spasms or muscle rigidity, "saw-horse" posture, difficulty walking, prolapse of the third eyelid.	Bacteria (Clostridium tetani) enters the body through deep wounds. Very serious, fatal if not treated. Even when treated the horse may not survive.
Tying up	Stiffness that affects the hindquarters during a workout. Similar to Azoturia but less severe.	Seen after a workout with a horse who stands idle for several days, in out-of-shape horses, or those on heavy grain diets.
Thrush	Smell and inflammation of the frog of the foot.	Due to poor care of the foot, degeneration of the frog due to lack of contact with the ground causing decreased circulation, dirty conditions of the stall or pasture areas.
Wounds, punctures or cuts	Any injury, cut, swelling to any part of the body. Needs to be attended to immediately or can develop into a serious condition.	Being cut on an object or fence, kicked by another horse, stepping into a hole or on an unsafe object.

EMERGENCY CARE:

Wallace (1991) divides emergency care into three categories: crisis care, urgent care and prompt care.

Crisis care--when life-threatening--is given immediately by the person who is present at the time of the injury or the one first observing the impairment in a life-threatening situation. Care cannot be put off until the veterinarian arrives. **Urgent care** involves situations that require intervention to prevent a life threatening condition. **Prompt care** reduces the likelihood of the worsening of an injury.

Crisis care is needed when the horse is:
1)   bleeding severely
2)   not breathing regularly (obstruction to nostrils or unable to breath)
3)   unconscious
4)   suffering from shock or trauma to internal organs or to the head
5)   colicky

Urgent care is needed when the horse has:
1)   heat prostration (severely over-heated) or hypothermia (subnormal body temperature)
2)   continuous bleeding
3)   fracture/dislocation
4)   open joint injuries
5)   puncture wounds to vital organs

Prompt care is necessary when the horse has:
1)   deep cuts and puncture wounds to non-critical areas
2)   sprains or severe swellings
3)   eye injuries

Emergency care of humans and horses is similar in many ways (Wallace, 1991). It is certainly similar in the immediate attention required. Instructors, therapists and horse managers must know how to deal with emergency first aid to both humans and horses in all areas mentioned above. Your veterinarian can advise you in special emergency medication you should have on hand. These are in addition to a complete first aid kit. Check the common problems likely to be seen and note what is needed to deal with them. Have your veterinarian help you with this.

MEASURING THE WEIGHT OF A HORSE
Measuring the weight of your horse(s) accurately can have a critical effect when giving medications. *WEIGHT OF THE HORSE*: a measurement of weight can be obtained with a tailor's measuring tape [(girth)^2 x body length] divided by 330 = body weight in pounds. (ASHA Horse Show)

A simpler method is to use a weight tape that can be bought at most tack shops. The horse is measured around the girth. Regular measurement will show weight loss or gain, if any. The measuring tape is meant for the "average" horse being the American Quarter horse type. Other horses will not show an accurate reading due to their differences in conformation. (ASHA Horse Show). This method if good for routine care BUT NOT FOR THE USE TO DETERMINE MEDICATION.

CARRYING WEIGHT: Generally a horse who is fit and in athletic condition can carry 20% of his body weight.

For example: Rusty's measurements are 65 x 57 = 240,825 divided by 225 = 1070 pounds of body weight (Perrault, 1987). Rusty is 14 years old, is on a regular training program and has no conformation faults. He should be able to carry a rider weighing 214 lbs.

Dr. Harman and Susan Harris (1997) state that the horse's maturity, his confirmation, his soundness and fitness enter into his ability to carry weight. A horse who is stocky with a short-back and well sprung ribs, well-built cannon bones and well-muscled loins can carry more weight then a longer backed horse with thin legs. Another consideration mentioned is the condition of the rider. A well conditioned, balanced and agile rider weighing 250 pounds exerts less pressure on the horse than a stiff, unbalanced

140 pound rider. This is certainly an important consideration since most riders in therapeutic riding programs fit into the latter category. The saddle-fit will also influence the ability the horse has to carry a rider since a poorly fitting saddle will cause discomfort and decrease the ability to carry weight.

Features that one must consider when matching a horse to a rider and its task..

❑ One must consider the condition, conformation and the age of the horse.

❑ The muscle tone and agility of the rider that will effect the horse's ability to carry a rider. A rider with low muscle tone will "feel heavier" to the horse because he/she is "dead weight"--(body muscle mass does not resist gravitational pull). A rider with physical involvement, especially if he/she is more involved on one side than the other, will require more work from the horse as it must compensates for the rider's lack of balance.

There are a number of good books on horse care, veterinary problems and preventive medicine. Each program should have one or two books on hand which deal with health care. A good reference book on "First Aid to Horses" could be worth its weight in gold, that is, if it is well read.

References

Adams, O.R. (1972). *Lameness in Horses*. 2nd ed. Fort Collins: Lea & Febiger. 340

AHSA. Horse Show 1996.

Blazer, D. (1982). *Horses Seldom Burp*. San Diego: A.S. Barnes & Co, Inc.

Equus. (1980). "Cleaning the Sheath". 32.

Evans, J.W. (1977). *The Horse*. New York: W.H. Freeman and Company. 555

German National Equestrian Federation. (1987). *Horse Management*. Gaithersburg: Half Halt Press.

Hadfield, M. (1989). *The Manual of Horsemanship*. British Horse Society and Pony Club. London: Threshold Books. 108.

Harman, J., Harris, S. (1997). In Practical Horseman, vol 25, no 1, pg 15.

Harris, S.E. (1977). *Grooming to Win*. New York: Charles Scribner's Sons.

Kilby, E. (1987). Where Weather is always Front Page News. *Equus*. 110. 40-41, 62.

Kinnish, M.K (1988). *Healthy Hooves Their Care and Balance*. Gaithersburg: Fleet Street Publishing Corp.

King, P.A. (1990). "Your Horse's Vital Signs". *Horseplay*. 18, 26-27.

Lyon, W. (1984) *First Aid Hints for the Horse Owner*. Glasgow: William Collins Sons & Co Ltd.

Pascoe, E. (1986). *The Horse Owner's Preventive Maintenance Handbook*, New York: Charles Scribner's & Sons.

Perrault, G. *The New Horse Owner Illustrated Manual*. Ottawa: Editions Grand Prix Reg'd. 22,

Smallwood, P.(1988). *The Manual of Stable Management: Care of the Horse*. Middletown: Half Halt Press.

Thompson, D. (1979). "They Kill While You Wait". *Equus*.

Watkins, V. (1986). *Trimming and Clipping*. London: Threshold Books.

Summerhays, R.S. (1988).*Summerhays'Encyclopaedia for Horsemen*. Rev. ed. London: Threshold Books. 29, 68, 159, 231, 270, 283.

Underhill, L.J.P. (1989). *The Wellness Movement*. Equus. 145. 44-45.

Wallace, M. (1991). Emergency Care. *Equus*. 166, 52-55 95-97.

MINIMIZING STABLE VICES IN A THERAPEUTIC PROGRAM HORSE

Margaret L. Galloway, MA, BHSAI

Horses can remember events that are either the first, the most frequent or most recent. They also remember negative events well (Sumner 1976) since these pose a threat to them. Bad habits (vices) may develop from bad experiences, fear, boredom, excessive energy, stress, curiosity, nutritional deficiencies or bad temperament (Borton 1990). They may be maintained because the horse seeks a way to relieve stress, and thus gets a rewarding response from the vice. Some behaviors are so subtle it is difficult to tell the place and time for a reward to be given. The job of a handler is to prevent negative behavior and reward behavior that is *desirable*. It is important to find ways to keep the horse happy and avoid vices or stereotype behavior.

"In work with a variety of animals, B.F. Skinner . . . found that punishment is less effective in behavioral control than positive (rewarding) reinforcement" (Sumner 1976). This suggests that in correcting problem behavior, ways should be found in which the horse can be rewarded. One should correct a problem when it occurs and then reward the horse for giving the right response.

STABLE VICES

Stereotypic behavior or repetitive behavior, frequently called stable vices, arises from the release of stress hormones in the body. Such behavior is more likely to occur if one or both of the parents show this behavior. (Marsden 1996.) Stress results when a horse faces unresolved conflict which can relate to the lifestyle imposed on the animal. Stress may be caused by any of following imposed restrictions which are unnatural to the nature of a horse. Exercise routine, diet and limited feeding time, turn out schedule, stabled alone, being with a horse with stressed behavior, or change of location and pasture mats. Confinement is unnatural for horses and threatens their physical, mental and emotional well-being. Therapeutic riding program horses need to be attentive, social and happy to provide their riders with the most beneficial results. Stereotypic behavior is possibly easier to prevent than to cure.

A person can help avoid stereotype behavior or reduce stress by:

1. Turning horses out in paddocks or pastures to allowing the horse more movement, to run and buck.
2. Being with and around other horses to meet their social needs. They need to see, hear, and smell their peers.
3. Being sure all horses have some form of exercise daily.
4. Feeding them bulky hay instead of pellets or cubes may help alleviate boredom. Changing feeding from twice a day to three times a day or more. Place the hay in hay bags so they have to spend more time pulling the hay out and increasing their feeding time. (This will provide a more natural feeding routine.) Adding carrots, potatoes or other succulent feed can be beneficial.
5. Making sure the horses get enough work and that it is varied.
6. Providing a good daily grooming to provide for tactile needs.
7. Talking to them while handling them also helps alleviate their boredom.
8. Another method of making the confined horse's life more interesting is to provide him toys (an old barrel, tire, balls, cones) and music.

Dodman of Tuft University and McDonnell of U of PA (Horse! 1996) state that you should not feed a horse with stereotype behavior or prone to stereotypic behavior grain since grain tends to increase this tendency. Also, aerobic exercise tends to reduce this behavior. They also note that each horse has his own agenda and while confinement may cause one horse stress, it may relieve another horse's stress.

Cribbing: Cribbing is the act of a horse grabbing a surface with his mouth, arching his neck and swallowing air. Swallowing air may lead to colic or gastric upset. It may be copied from other horses. The most effective way to restrain this behavior is with a Miracle Collar™ that places pressure on the larynx during cribbing. It does not prevent eating or drinking.

Weaving: Weaving is a repetitive ritualistic pattern in which the horse stands in one spot but shifts his weight from one side to the other. He almost always does it in the door of his stall. "This suggests that the habit may have its origin in the horse's attempt to find a way out of confinement" (Sumner, 1976) or is copied from a stable mate. Weaving can cause lameness, weight loss or physical exhaustion (Borton, 1990). Regular exercise and time spent turned out usually help this vice. Smaller feedings given more frequently may decrease the boredom. Some people hang safe objects, such as soft wood or a plastic container, from the top of the stall door so that the horse hits them if he weaves.

Mane and Tail Rubbing: Mane and tail rubbing usually results from itching. Mane itching is often from dirt or an allergy. Tail itching may be from worms. Worming should be performed according to the schedule and method suggested by your veterinarian. Both the mane and tail may be washed with an anti-bacterial or fungicidal soap such as Nolvasan®, or Phisohex®.

Stall Walking: A horse who may be high-strung or does not get enough exercise may develop stall walking. This is a nervous habit that wastes energy (Evans, 1990). Regular exercise will work off excess energy, and companionship, grooming, soft music and challenges of exercises in the arena and on the trail will help to prevent boredom.

OTHER PROBLEMS AND SOLUTIONS

Aggressive vices: Horses who kick, strike, bite, bolt, buck, rear or charge their handlers or other horses, are unsuitable for therapeutic riding programs as they may cause injury. If the problem cannot be corrected, the horse should not be used in a therapeutic riding program. When a horse with a history of negative behavior causes an injury in a therapeutic riding program, a lawsuit could easily follow. The program "knew" that the horse might be dangerous yet "continued to use it."

Hard to Catch Horses: Horses may become hard to catch because (1) the horse associates being caught with boring work; (2) they may not want to leave the other horses; (3) they may associate being caught with pain or punishment. The horse needs to associate positive rewards with being caught. Some horses may be cured by being fed carrots or grain every time they are caught or just being given a good rub and attention. The handler may be able to find a way to feed horses their usual ration after catching them. Catching the horse to take him out for grazing or other pleasurable treats is another solution.

Pulling Back: Some horses panic and pull back when tied. These horses should never be tied in the usual way. The best way is to tie them in their stall, where they have a wall behind them and less incentive to pull back. If they must be tied outside, just looping the rope several times around a hitching rail is safe. The best method for handling tying problems is to teach the horse to ground tie or use the TT.E.A.M. method to retrain this horse from his bad habit

UNDERSTANDING THE HORSE

There are numerous books which will educate the reader in understanding the horse. When the instructor, trainer, riders and volunteers understand the horse, they will have more insight into resolving problems and avoiding negative behavior.

Margaret L Galloway USA

Reference

Borton. A. (1990). In Evans, J.W. el al *The Horse*. New York: W.H Freeman & Co.

Blazer, D. (1982). *Horses Seldom Burp! How to Keep Them Happy and Well*. La Jolla: A.S. Barnes & Co. Inc.

Condax, K.D.(1979). *Horse Sense*. Causes and Correction of Horse and Rider Problems. New York: Prentice Hall Press.

Evans, J.W. (1889). *Horses*. 2nd ed. New York: W.H. Freeman & Co. 49.

Marsden, D. , McDonnell. (1996). Repetitive Behavior in Horse! Vol, no 2, February, Tuft University school of Veterinary Medicine.

Schramm, U. (1986). *The Undisciplined Horse*. London: J.A. Allen.

Sumner, D.W. (1976). *Breaking Your Horse's Bad Habits*. Millwood: Breakthrough Publishing.

NUTRITION OF THE THERAPEUTIC PROGRAM HORSE

Robin R. Koehler, MS

Basic Anatomy and Function of the Digestive System

The feeding of horses has become more scientific in recent years. Research has enabled horse owners to formulate the best diet for their animals to meet their nutrient requirements at the most economical costs. The old cliche, "we are what we eat," holds true for the horse as well as humans. A good understanding of the horse's digestive system is needed to promote the importance of proper nutrition and to appreciate it in selecting a balanced diet.

Being a nonruminant herbivore, the horse possesses a single stomach and consumes plant material as the bulk of its diet. Through evolution, a continuous eating behavior developed allowing the horse to eat small amounts of food frequently. This explains the small capacity of the stomach compared to the horse's size (2.1 to 4 gallons) and the recommendation to feed confined horses at least twice daily.

Digestion begins in the mouth with the mastication of the feed and the production of saliva by three pairs of glands to moisten it. From the mouth, the food bolus travels to the stomach by way of the esophagus. Because of the stomach's limited capacity, gastric secretions offer little digestive assistance to the food particles. The stomach does, however, provide a constant supply of food to the small intestine where most digestion and absorption of nutrients takes place. The small intestine is the primary site of protein, carbohydrate and lipid digestion and absorption, along with the fat-soluble vitamins (A, D, E and K), dietary B vitamins and some minerals.

From the small intestine, the food passes to the large intestine, which includes the cecum, colon and rectum. Here digestion is dependent on microbes, similar to those found in ruminant animals such as cattle and sheep. The cecum initiates the breakdown of fiber through microbial fermentation producing volatile fatty acids, an important energy source. Significant amounts of the B-vitamin complex are also produced in the cecum by the bacteria. These vitamins contribute to the requirements of the animal. Fiber digestion continues through the colon, along with water absorption. Finally, the remaining waste products are excreted from the rectum.

Nutrient Requirements

Horses require six nutrients to sustain normal health: carbohydrates, fats, proteins, minerals, vitamins and water. The amount of nutrients vary with the class of horse and depend on age, level of work, reproductive duties and the status of the individual animal.

Carbohydrates and Fats

Carbohydrates and fats provide the main energy sources. Energy is the fuel of life that enables the horse to perform work. The soluble carbohydrates, such as starch, maltose and sucrose are primarily absorbed in the small intestine. Insoluble carbohydrates, or the fibrous fraction of the diet, are digested in the large intestine and absorbed as volatile fatty acids. These acids are produced in the cecum from microbial fermentation and are used as energy. Dietary lipids are digested and absorbed in the small intestine. The horse does not have a gall bladder, but the absence of one does not appear to hinder the digestion of fat. The requirements for energy vary with each horse and its activity. The maintenance requirement of a nonworking horse is the amount of energy needed to sustain a constant body weight during normal activity. This requirement is based on body weight, and additional energy must be fed to compensate for performance, environmental factors, health and individuality. Energy content of feeds is often expressed as digestible energy (DE) designated in calories. DE is the total energy content of the feed minus the energy lost in the feces. Both forages and concentrates supply energy. The grains such as corn, oats, barley and wheat are the primary energy sources fed to horses. Consuming excess energy makes for a fat horse, whereas symptoms of insufficient energy intake are loss of weight and tiredness.

Protein

Protein is composed of building blocks called amino acids, the major components of lean body tissue, enzymes and several hormones. The amino acids are complex substances, which contain a fairly constant amount of nitrogen. They are divided into essential and nonessential groups. The nonessential ones are synthesized by the body and the essential amino acids must be supplied in the diet. The essential amino acids are arginine, histidine, isoleucine, leucine, lysine, methionine, phenylalanine, threonine, tryptophan and valine. The exact amino acid requirements of the horse are not known. However, the quality of protein and the digestibility of that protein are important to ensure that the horse is getting the proper amino acid compositions. A good quality protein has the same levels of amino acids as are present in the body. Poor quality protein lacks one or more of the required essential amino acids. The feeds most commonly fed are usually of a good quality protein that is readily digested by the horse.

The small intestine is the primary site of protein digestion and absorption in the horse. Protein requirements are referred to as crude protein (CP) or digestible protein (DP). Crude protein is the percentage of nitrogen in the feed, but all nitrogen therein is not available to the horse. Digestible protein is the amount of available protein in the feed. Mature horses have a much lower requirement for protein than young, growing horses, since their requirement is for maintaining existing tissue, not growing new tissue.

Excess protein in the diet can be used as an energy source, but feeding excess is not recommended due to the costliness of it. Protein-deficient animals exhibit poor growth, weight loss and general lack of thriftiness. Although both forage and grain provide protein, the quality of hay or pasture will determine the amount of protein needed in the concentrate. Hay will supply 7 to 18 percent CP depending on the type and quality, whereas cereal grains range from 8 to 12 percent CP. If additional protein is needed, a protein supplement can be added in the diet. Soybean meal is one such protein supplement commonly used in horse rations.

Minerals

Minerals serve many functions in the body including skeletal components, muscle contractions and electrolyte balance. Seven macrominerals include: calcium, phosphorus, potassium, sodium, chloride, magnesium and sulfur. The eight microminerals are cobalt, copper, fluoride, iodine, iron, manganese, selenium and zinc.

Calcium and phosphorus make up about 70 percent of the mineral composition of the horse's body. Not only do they need to be supplied in adequate levels, but the proportions of calcium to phosphorus are important for normality of bone development. The ratio should not be less than 1:1, but should be fed at 1.2 to 1.6:1 of calcium to phosphorus, respectively. With either a high level of dietary calcium or a high level of dietary phosphorus relative to the calcium, the digestibility and absorption of calcium are decreased. Salt (sodium chloride) should always be available to the horse. Usually, a trace mineralized salt block or granules are available free choice. The horse procures most of its mineral needs from pasture, hay, and grain.

Vitamins

Vitamins are a group of unrelated organic compounds that are necessary in trace amounts for normal metabolic functions of the body. Vitamins are classified as either fat-soluble or water-soluble vitamins. Fat-soluble vitamins include A, D, E and K, while the B-complex groups, vitamin C and others belong to the water-soluble group. Vitamin supplementation is not a recommended practice, if the horse is receiving a balanced diet of good quality ingredients. In fact, vitamins fed in excessive dosages can be harmful to the horse. Most high quality forages contain adequate levels of vitamins. The B-complex vitamins are synthesized by the microflora in the cecum. They are also present in forages, so consequently additional supplementation is not usually needed.

Water

Water requirements are dependent on several factors, such as air temperature, physical activity, reproduction and diet. Pregnancy, lactating mares, hot weather, high intensity work and a diet high in dry matter demand increased consumption of water. Fresh, clean water should be available at all times. A horse will drink 10 to 12 gallons per day during normal environmental and working conditions.

Feeding Management

Most horse rations are made up of hay or pasture (roughage) plus grain (concentrate). Many idle and light working, mature horses can meet their nutrient requirements on roughage alone. For the digestive tract to function normally, some type of roughage must be supplied in the daily diet. Roughage should contribute to at least half of the daily ration, by weight, in the form of either hay or pasture. A horse can consume 2.5 to 3.0% of its body weight per day in total feed. For example, a 1000 pound horse will consume between 25 to 30 pounds of feed per day and at least 12.5 to 15 pounds of that should be roughage. The higher the proportion of roughage to concentrate, the safer the diet. Feeding more grain than hay constitutes many digestive disturbances, including colic and founder.

There are two general types of hays fed to horses: grass hays and legumes. Grass hays include many species of grasses with the most commonly fed being timothy, orchard grass, bromegrass, coastal Bermuda grass, tall fescue and Sudangrass. Legume hays provide higher levels of soluble carbohydrates, protein, vitamins and some minerals than the grasses. Examples of the commonly fed legumes include alfalfa, lespedeza and red clover. Where both legumes and grasses are available, a mixed hay is an ideal roughage for horses. Forage quality will vary depending on soil type, climate, plant maturity and harvesting procedures. Hay should be soft, bright colored and free from weeds, molds, fungi, dust and debris to ensure good quality forage. When feeding a legume hay, look for leafiness and a lack of stems, as the leaves contain most of the nutrients and are also more digestible than the stems. Long stem hay is the form most commonly fed to horses, however processed forages are available in the form of pellets, cubes, chopped hay and haylage. Processed forages can be beneficial for horses that have difficulty chewing or have allergies to dust and molds. Horses consume processed feeds faster, which means more time for boredom. To alleviate boredom and minimize digestive upsets, it is advisable to feed horses at least 1% of their body weight in long stem roughage. Also, processing adds to the cost of feeding.

The term "concentrate" denotes the non-forage portion of the ration, predominately the cereal grains. After the roughage has been selected, the concentrate can be determined to guarantee that the total daily requirements are being satisfied. Grains provide more energy than roughage and they are a good source of phosphorus. Oats, corn and barley are three common grains fed to horses. Oats tend to be popular because they are palatable and are relatively high in protein and fiber. Corn is higher in energy and lower in protein than oats and barley. Other ingredients are commonly added to the concentrate portion, such as molasses, soybean meal and plant and animal by-products, to increase palatability and the nutrient levels. Additional vitamin and mineral supplements generally are not needed in the diets of most equine, as long as they are being fed a balanced diet with good quality ingredients. In fact, many vitamins and minerals can be toxic when fed in quantities above recommended levels.

Many therapeutic programs have access to pasture. Good management is the key for good quality pastures. Mixed pastures (grass/legume pastures) usually provide better nutrition and higher protein levels than just grass. Pastures should be mowed or grazed to keep plant height at 6 to 8 inches to optimize digestibility and growth of young plants. As plants mature, digestibility decreases. Manure should be spread out or removed to control parasites and promote more even grazing. Avoid overgrazing and if possible, rotate pastures to ensure ample vegetation. Fertilization and irrigation help ensure growth of desirable plants, especially heavily grazed pastures. Even if pasture is limited, a short turn out time of 1 to 4 hours is essential for healthy, happy horses. Horses enjoy grazing and exercising at will, not to mention the companionship of their stable mates. Because of their gregarious behavior, horses benefit by being turned out together. If the pasture is small, pairs are adequate.

Often times, the horse involved with a therapeutic riding program is an older individual. These geriatric horses may require special attention due to the general slowdown of body functions. Additional energy is needed by the older horse to perform physical activity, as compared to the younger or middle-aged horse. Concentrates may be needed to meet the energy needs, if the roughage alone is not adequate. If teeth are in a poor state, a more palatable diet is recommended to help insure proper nutritional requirements. Hay can be chopped and grain can be processed by crimping, rolling or crushing to make consumption easier thereby improving digestibility. When chewing is difficult, a mash can be made by soaking the grain in hot water before feeding. Pelleted feeds are also an excellent feed source as they are easy to chew and digest. Both alfalfa and concentrates are available in pellet form. Soaking pellets in water will result in a gruel, which is very palatable for horses with poor teeth. Older horses often benefit by being fed individually, rather than in groups, to reduce feeding competition and to allow them the additional time required to consume the feed that they often need.

Feeding horses successfully is not only the ability to formulate a balanced diet, but also the ability to adjust the diet according to individual needs. Because of variation in production and performance, as well as metabolic and behavioral differences, horses need to be fed as individuals. Experience and good judgment about feeding are key elements to insure the welfare and happiness of the horse.

The following feeding management guidelines are recommended for optimal feeding results.

1. Use top quality feeds. Since roughage supplies the bulk of the diet, select good quality hay.

2. Confined horses require a minimum of two feedings per day. Three or four feedings per day are better.

3. Feed by weight, and not volume. Have a scale in your barn, as weighing the feed provides consistency in the diet.

4. Provide fresh water and salt at all times.

5. Maintain a regular feeding schedule.

6. Allow horses one hour to digest meal before forced exercise.

7. Maintain a routine dental and parasite management program.

8. Determine each horse's ideal weight and maintain it.

9. Avoid sudden changes in feedstuffs.

10. Loss of appetite warrants further investigation of the health of the animal.

Robin R. Koehler
USA

References

Evans, J.W. (1989). *Horses: A Guide to Selection, Care, and Enjoyment.* New York: W.H. Freeman and Company.

Evans, J.W., A. Borton, H.F. Hintz, and L.D. Van Vleck. (1990). Second edition. *The Horse.* New York:W.H. Freeman and Company.

Lewis, L.D. (1996). *Feeding and Care of the Horse.* Second Edition. Williams & Wilkins.

Maynard, L.A., J.K. Loosli, H.F. Hintz, and R.G. Warner. (1979) *Animal Nutrition.* Seventh edition. McGraw-Hill Book Co.

Naviaux, J.L. (1985). *Horses in Health and Disease.* Second edition. Philadelphia: Lea and Febiger.

NRC. (1989). *Nutrient Requirements of Horses.* Fifth revised edition. National Academy of Sciences, Washington, D.C.

Robinson, D.W., L.M. Slade. (1974). *The Current Status of Knowledge on the Nutrition of Equine.* J. Animal Science. 39:6.

Wood, C.H., S. G. Jackson, (1988). *Basic Horse Nutrition.* Lexington: University of Kentucky Cooperative Extension Service.

THE HOOF AND ITS IMPORTANCE TO THE THERAPEUTIC RIDING HORSE

Barbara T. Engel, MEd, OTR

KEY WORDS

Health, Balance

The horse was created to roam over dry grass plains, and in his natural environment the hoof served him well without trimming or other special care. In the domestic environment, however, the hoof will need special care because:

- ❑ Most horses have limited space to wander. Lack of walking throughout the day decreases circulation because the pumping action of the circulatory system in the foot is not activated, therefore causing weakness of the hoof.
- ❑ Even in a well-cleaned stall, bedding harbors acids and solvents from urine and manure which are destructive to the hoof.
- ❑ Improper trimming can cause stress at certain points of the hoof. An unbalanced hoof will cause the horse to move unevenly and may lead to hoof problems and lameness.
- ❑ Standing in areas too wet or dry contributes to the destruction of the horse's hooves. (Kinnish, 1988)

The hoof is the base on which the horse stands. His four hooves create his points of balance. If the hoof surface is uneven instead of flat, it does not allow the leg to stand straight. One uneven hoof will cause the rest of the horse to be unbalanced. One can compare this to a table with one leg worn off at a corner. The table will not stand evenly. Anthony Gonzales demonstrated how trimming a quarter of an inch off the inside of one hoof can produce balance in the gait of a horse who walked unbalanced prior to the hoof trimming (Gonzales, 1991). A hoof that lands on one edge rather than flat, will cause stress at the point of impact and modify the leverage of the total leg with resulting complications, strains, and possible lameness. This demonstration showed the subtle changes that can occur due to the shape of hooves and how this can affect the delicate balance of the horse. The balance of the horse influences the rider as sensation is transmitted through the movements of the horse.

If the horse is not balanced, the rider will not sit straight on the horse, nor will the rider perceive smooth, rhythmic movements which are essential to the therapeutic effects of riding. Healthy, well-balanced hooves are therefore essential to productive therapeutic riding.

THE HOOVES

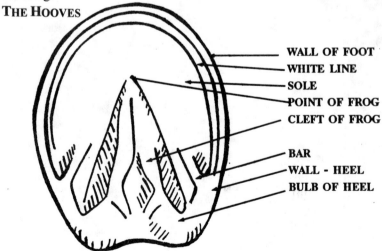

- WALL OF FOOT
- WHITE LINE
- SOLE
- POINT OF FROG
- CLEFT OF FROG
- BAR
- WALL - HEEL
- BULB OF HEEL

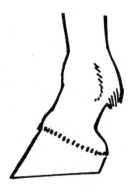

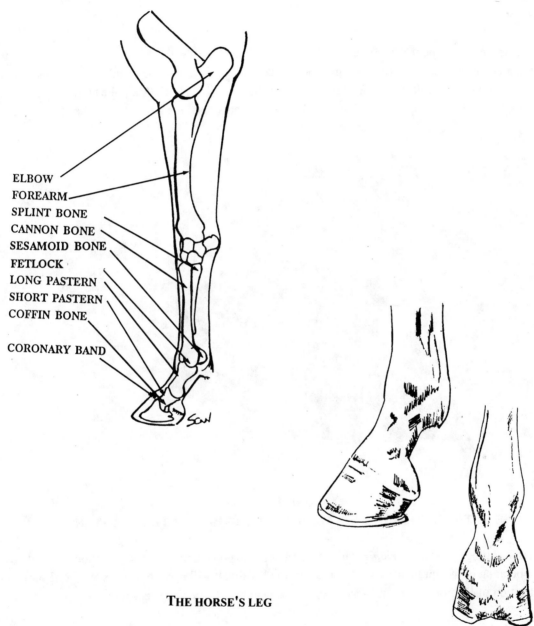

ELBOW
FOREARM
SPLINT BONE
CANNON BONE
SESAMOID BONE
FETLOCK
LONG PASTERN
SHORT PASTERN
COFFIN BONE

CORONARY BAND

THE HORSE'S LEG

References

Kinnish, M.K. (1988). *Healthy Hooves*. Gaithersburg: Fleet Street Publishing Corp. 10-11.

Gonzales, A. (1991). Performance Horse Symposium: Tellington-Jones, Swift, Gonzales. Clinic notes 2-1991, Pleasanton, CA.

Gonzales, A. (1986). *Proper Balance Movement*. Manassas: REF Publishing

THE HOOF: CARE AND RELATION TO BALANCE

Anthony Z. Gonzales

CARE Of THE HOOF

First I would like to introduce you to the technical term for the hoof wall, *epidermis*. Epidermis means skin, and in this case, outer skin. The hoof is an extension of the coronary band and the skin above it. It is made of tubular, hair-like substance, a protein that gets most of its nourishment from the blood supply inside the body (Figure 1). And, like human hair, it needs to be maintained with conditioners and moisturizers from the outside, and nutrients from the inside to stay healthy.

FIGURE 1.
SHOWS THAT THE HOOF WALL IS MADE OF HAIR-LIKE PROTEIN SUBSTANCE.

The outer hoof wall has a coating called the *periople*. This acts as a buffer to prevent moisture evaporation. It is only when there is a breakdown in the bonding of the epidermis and periople that the hoof wall will start to deteriorate. Feed supplements, as well as external application of hoof dressings, such as lanolin-based emollients, become very important parts of maintaining good solid feet.

OBSERVATION OF THE HOOF WALL SHOULD BE APPROACHED LIKE THIS:

Cracks are the first signs of breakdown of the hoof and generally indicate a rapid change in rate of moisture evaporation. The tubules of the hoof wall swell from moisture and dry out or shrink from evaporation. If this occurs too rapidly, cracks will appear. The second sign of hoof breakdown is a dry coronet. Cracking may occur here as well. Because it is in the coronet that most evaporation occurs, hoof dressing should be applied into the hairline of the coronet (coronary band) to keep it moist.

The frog is very important to the function of the hoof. In inspecting the frog, it is desirable that it be solid tissue but flexible to the push of the thumb. This indicates suppleness as well as providing adequate absorption shock from concussion. A wide frog generally indicates that the heels will be wide and flexible. The narrower the frog, the more chances for contraction of the heels, which may lead to lameness.

If a horse is shoeless, inspect the white line located between the sensitive part of the sole and the outer wall. Check to see that there are no crevices in which stones can be wedged since this condition will create a wall separation (Figure 2 & 3). If a stone is found wedged in the wall, a hoof pick can be used to take it out. *If the stone is allowed to stay in, it will move upward due to the weight of the body pushing down on the ground as the horse moves.* If this condition occurs at the toe, it is called *seedy toe*. It would be advisable to fill any holes with cotton if deep enough. This will prevent more stones from entering.

REMEMBER THESE THREE WORDS:
- ❏ **PROTECT**
- ❏ **PREVENT**
- ❏ **PRESERVE**

Protection of the horse's hoof is very important. Remember the saying: *"No Hoof, No Horse."* To help **prevent** damage, use hoof dressings both on the outer hoof and on the coronet band, frog, and sole. **Prevent** thrush, a fungus infestation which develops because of unclean conditions, and treat it if it occurs. **Preserve** the hoof by maintaining a committed series of hoof care procedures all year around.

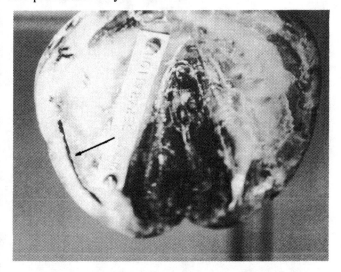

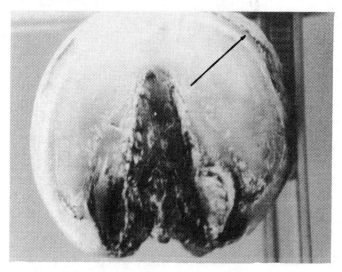

FIGURE 2. SHOWS WHAT A WALL SEPARATION LOOKS LIKE. THIS IS USUALLY CAUSED BY A GRAIN OF SAND OR STONE MOVING UP THE WHITE LINE

FIGURE 3. SHOWS THE BEGINNING OF A WALL SEPARATION ON THE LEFT HAND OF THE HOOF

HOW THE HOOF RELATES TO BALANCE OF THE LEG

First one must realize that the hoof has but a limited ability to stabilize the leg. The major elements involved with the leg's stability and balance are muscles, ligaments, tendons and skin. One must not be fooled into thinking that shoeing and trimming alone will give the horse a balanced leg. The hoof is a base and the leg a column. The base must be evenly balanced in order for the column to remain straight and upright.

By observation of the horse's leg, one will see that the pastern bones lie below the third metacarpal bone and that the column of short and long pastern bones, forming a straight shaft, will rest in the center of the hoof capsule. The pastern will normally tilt outward at the long pastern/cannon bone connection. When this straightness is not present, and the pastern bones tilt inwardly just above the hoof, the leg will appear pigeon-toed. If the tilt is outward right above the hoof, the pastern is dropped to the inside at the long pastern/cannon bone connection and the leg will appear splay-footed.

One must be aware of some of the conditions that can result from either type of unbalanced hoof:

- ❑ **Pigeon-toed feet**
- ❑ **Sidebone** on the outside above the coronary band. This is due to more weight bearing on the outside of the leg.
- ❑ **Outside splints** due to more pressure on the outside of the knee joint.
- ❑ **Sore shoulder muscles** on the outside of the leg due to the foot dropping inward toward the body, causing a paddling movement when the horse moves.
- ❑ **Splay-footed** due to the feet turning outward because of more weight being on the inside of the leg. Side bone may result on the **inside** of the top of the coronary band and splints. Splints will be due to more pressure on the **inside** of the knee joint.
- ❑ **Sore muscles on the inside of the shoulder** due to the body weight of the horse dropping through the chest onto the inside of the front legs instead of being equally balanced front and rear.

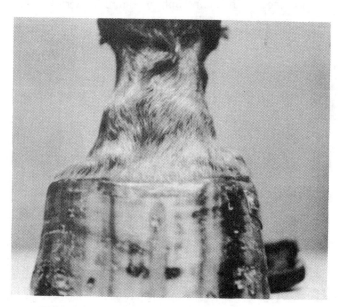

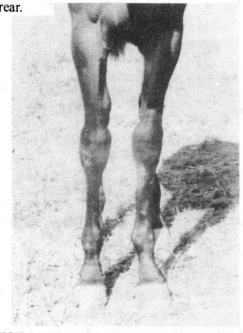

FIGURE 4. SHOWS THAT THE HORSE WILL DEVELOP "SIDEBONE" AS A RESULT OF UNEVEN BALANCE OF THE HOOF AND LEG.

FIGURE 5. SHOWS THE LEFT FRONT FETLOCK TURNED INWARD AND THE HOOF TURNED OUTWARD.

These are not the only problems with front legs, but they are the ones you should be readily aware of to make appropriate changes. The hind legs show similar stances to those of the front legs. A *pigeon-toed* condition in the hind leg is called *bow-legged*. A *splay-foot* condition is called *cow-hocked*. However, the hind legs show a totally different set of problems than those of the front legs to produce these anomalies. In the hind legs, both bow legs (hocks turned outward) and cow hocks (hocks turned inward) affect two main joints: the hock and the stifle. Either problem causes a twisting of both the hock and stifle and if this condition persists, it could lead to the stifle catching, arthritis of the hock or spavin. When the hoof is unbalanced from such conditions, the horse will have a hard time making smooth turns, or may resist taking the correct lead. The hoof must land flat as it strikes the ground for a gait to be correct and true.

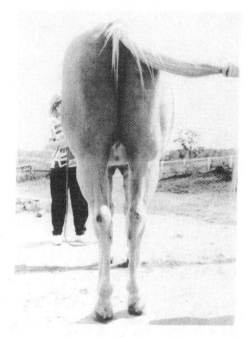

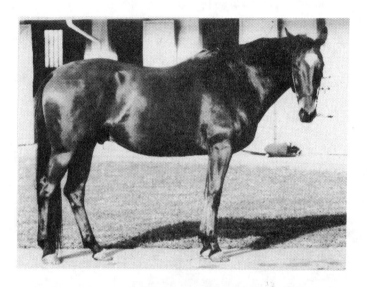

FIGURE 6. SHOWS THE RIGHT HIND LEG OF THE HORSE TURNED OUTWARD MORE THAN THE LEFT HIND LEG. THIS WILL CAUSE THIS HORSE TO PIVOT AT ITS STIFLES.

FIGURE 7. SHOWS HOW LOW HEELS WILL AFFECT A HORSE'S STANCE. THIS HORSE'S KNEES ARE PUSHED BACKWARD AND ITS TOES ARE TOO LONG. THE HIND HEELS ARE LOW AS WELL.

HOW HOOF ANGLES AFFECT THE UPPER BODY

One must remember that the hoof contains a "coffin" bone. The lower coffin bone and the short pastern bones form the first joint in the lower part of the leg. Other joints continue up to the shoulder blade. The first joint, however, affects and controls the angle of the hoof. When the hoof angle changes, so will the position of all leg joints. In other words, if the heels are too low on a horse, not only is the coffin bone joint affected, but also the knee joint and the shoulder. One tends to think only of the lower joints being affected. What is known, however, is that if the heels are low, the short pastern will put a lot of pressure on the navicular bone. But don't rule out that the knee could hyper extend producing possible tendon and ligament pulls. One can tell if a hoof has enough "heel" by looking at the coronary band. If the angle of the coronary band dips from the front of the hoof towards the heel in a sharp manner, (viewing should be done from the side) one sees the "reverse wedge" syndrome. Another way to tell if a hoof has too little heel is to look from the back of the hoof to see if the bulb of the heel is on the ground.

When low heels in the front feet occur, the joints all close with greater backward pressure. When this condition occurs with the hind feet, the joints all close with greater forward pressure. In both case it creates hyperextension of the knees.

Signs to look for to help identify how stance and angle of the hoof affect the upper body are:
1. An unbalanced front hoof is present when:
        a. the knee drops to the inside,
        b. one shoulder is lower and more forward than the other,
        c. the knee is straight or outward and the shoulder is higher and back.

2. An unbalanced hind hoof is present when the leg is "twisted." The more severely the leg is turned out or in, the more twisted it will be. The twist will cause one hip to rise higher than the other.

3. The lower the front heel, the more knee action, and shorter stride of landing the horse will have. This means there is an illusion of having a long stride, but in reality, the landing of the leg is on the backward swing thus shortening the stride. The shoulder will also drop in a downward motion.

4. The lower the hind heel, the straighter the hock and stifle will be, and the less action the fetlock will have. The hoof will travel closer to the ground, the hip will go up higher, and more weight will be transferred forward onto the front legs. Thus the horse will become heavy on the forehand.

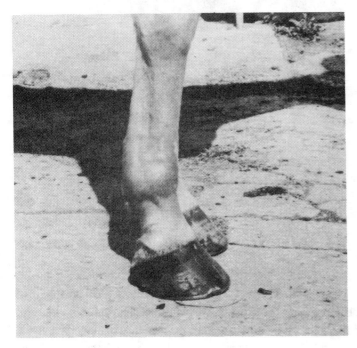

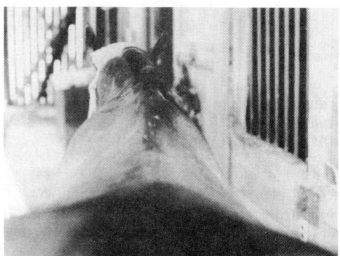

FIGURE 8. SHOWS A HORSE WITH "RUN UNDER" HEELS. IT IS EVIDENT THAT THE WEIGHT IS ON THE HEELS BECAUSE THE HOOF HAS GROWN OVER THE SHOES.

FIGURE 9. SHOWS THE LEFT HIP ON THIS HORSE IS HIGHER THAN ON THE RIGHT.

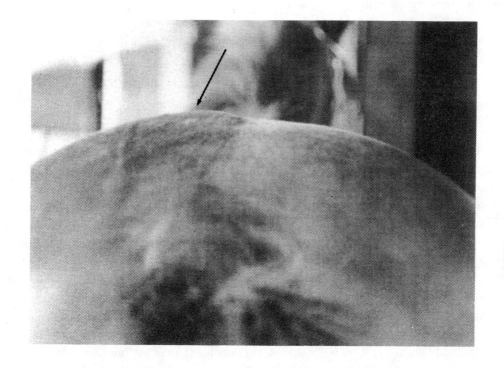

**FIGURE 10. SHOWS THAT THE LEFT SHOULDER ON THIS
HORSE IS WIDER AND HIGHER THAN THE RIGHT SHOULDER**

Anthony Z. Gonzales
USA

CARE AND MAINTENANCE OF THE OLDER HORSE

Jean S. Hoffman, DVM, BS Animal Science

The majority of horses used in therapeutic riding programs fall into the middle age to a senior citizen category. For most, therapeutic riding is their second career. Since the natural life span of the horse is 30 to 35 years, the geriatric term is generally reserved for those animals more than 20 years old.

The three main areas of special emphasis regarding the older equine are:
1. Nutrition for the older working horse
2. Veterinary and health maintenance
3. Conditioning in relation to athletic training and athletic restrictions

NUTRITIONAL GUIDELINES FOR THE OLDER WORKING HORSE

The first thing to be considered in nutrition is proper dental care. As horses get older, they need their teeth examined more often (around every six months). This is done to avoid rough edges and points on the lateral or lip surface of the upper cheek teeth and the medial or tongue surfaces of the lower cheek teeth. The upper first premolars should be checked for hooks and points also. The cardinal sign of abnormal tooth wear or other dental problems is "quidding" or dropping partially chewed food out of their mouth while eating. Thorough floating will take care of these problems. In geriatric animals the teeth, both incisors and molars, may wear down over time to the gum line, in which case the animal will have trouble adequately chewing coarse hay and grains, and consequently lose weight and condition. This can be alleviated by chopping the hay and/or feeding processed feeds such as pellets in a wet mash or a prepackaged alfalfa and molasses feed as the primary part of their diet.

The optimal weight desired in the older working horse can be seen when the ribs are not visible but little fat can be felt between the ribs and skin. It is highly recommended to put older horses on a broad spectrum vitamin-mineral supplement along with a half to full cup of vegetable oil daily. Most feeds are deficient in fatty acids and fat soluble vitamins, especially if processed by heat or stored for long periods of time. In addition, trace mineralized salt and plenty of fresh, clean water should be provided. Two to three gallons of a soupy bran mash every other day is a good way to help prevent impaction colic, especially in the winter when horses tend to drink less. Adding psyllium to their grain will aid in preventing sand colic. When adding psyllium to grain, don't add water or it will turn into a gelatinous clump of feed. If something is needed to help mix it into the feed, use vegetable oil.

Most horses will do well on a diet of primarily grass hay or grass hay cubes supplemented with a little alfalfa hay, an alfalfa and molasses mixture, or a pelleted supplement for the older horse such as Equine Senior to help them maintain their weight. A small amount (a half pound to two pounds daily) of some type of grain or sweet feed is okay to add to the ration as a treat. The trace mineralized salt can be added loose to the grain or pelleted supplement, or fed free-choice in a TM salt block. The vitamin-mineral supplement and vegetable oil can also be added into the grain or other pelleted supplement. Keep the amount of alfalfa in the diet to a minimum since horses do not need all the protein that is in it, and it will just force the kidneys to work harder to excrete the excess protein. In addition, stay away from using Bermuda grass hay as a main hay source since it has been theoretically linked with impaction colic and enteroliths. It is relatively inexpensive and may be helpful to send off a sample of the horses' hair for mineral analysis. This can bring up any deficiencies or toxicities of certain minerals, which may be due to the soil the feed is grown in. Certain feed changes or mineral supplements can then be recommended to balance the horse's diet. Be sure to specify on the lab form that the hair sample in question is of equine origin or it may end up being compared to normal human values rather than equine values.

HEALTH MAINTENANCE
Routine health programs for the older equine are similar to those for any other horse or pony.

I. Vaccinations
1. Yearly "five in one" or "six in one" combination: Eastern, Western and Venezuelan Equine Encephalomyelitis; Tetanus toxoid; influenza; in addition, or minus, rhinopneumonitis.
2. Influenza plus, or minus, rhinopneumonitis every three months.
3. Vaccinating against Strangles (Streptococcus equi) in adults is not recommended because clinical disease is uncommon and the risk of immune-mediated complications, namely purpura hemorrhagica, is greater.
4. Potomac Horse Fever (Equine Monocytic Ehrlichiosis) annually.

In areas where mosquitoes are present year-round, EEE, WEE, VEE and PHF should be vaccinated against every six months, i.e., spring and fall. Currently VEE is commonly vaccinated for only in states bordering Mexico. It is a good idea to vaccinate for PHF in any state where it has been reported, not just in endemic areas such as Maryland, Illinois and the Gulf States. Rhinopneumonitis is also known as EHV-1, or Equine Herpes Virus - 1, and is associated with abortions and upper rspiratory disease mostly. The related EHV-4 is only a respiratory disease. The available vaccines may incorporate either or both forms of the virus. Older horses are vaccinated for one or both in order to help prevent against outbreaks of either form at boarding stables and breeding farms and to keep overall herd immunity high. Neither rhinopneumonitis or influenza vaccines provide high levels of protection against disease, but it's better than nothing. Think of it like a flu shot in humans - the shot may or may not protect you, but the more people that are vaccinated, the less likely an outbreak will occur.

On continents other than North America, other vaccines may be advisable and the owner should consult with local veterinarians for recommendations.

II. Parasite Control:
1. Deworm every two to three months with a paste dewormer.
2. Rotating dewormer is still a good idea, but to kill bots deworm with Ivermectin in the fall after the first frost.

When rotating dewormers, rotate classes of dewormers such as benzimidazoles, organophosphates and avermectins. Examples of anthelmintics in each of these classes are fenbendazole, dichlorvos and ivermectin, respectively. A new dewormer on the market is a gel instead of a paste. The gel is moxidectin and is the only product other than ivermectin that kills worms and bots. Unlike other dewormers, this product has a residual action that lasts for three months, so it only needs to be given four times a year. It isn't known yet whether resistance to it will occur.

Another alternative to paste dewormers is over the counter Strongid C (pyrantel tartrate) which comes in the form of an alfalfa pellet base. It is fed to horses daily, so it kills larvae before they migrate through and damage tissues. This can especially benefit hard-to-keep older horses since they tend to need less feed while on this regimen. To eliminate a large number of a horse's parasite loads, give one dose of ivermectin on two consecutive days prior to starting on Strongid C. A potential side effect of this product is the development of resistance. To gauge the effectiveness of this or any other deworming program, it is smart to submit a fecal sample to a vet or lab for a fecal egg count occasionally. Few horses will be completely free of parasite eggs regardless of the deworming regime, but the strongyle egg count should be less than 100 eggs /g as a general rule for the program to be considered effective.

III. Preventive Dentistry

Have teeth checked at least once a year to see if they need to be floated. Special problems such as wave mouth and step mouth may need care more often. Make sure that each horse's dentition can handle the type and form of feed being provided. Signs of a possible dental problem include tilting the head while eating, eating only particular foods, dropping food out of the mouth, refusing to eat or weight loss. If a horse develops bad breath have his mouth checked for an abscessed tooth, or tooth root infection.

IV. Special Problems of Older Horses

This is just a brief list of conditions that may appear in older horses or that may be exacerbated by age:

- ❑ cataracts
- ❑ glaucoma
- ❑ periodic ophthalmia or "moon blindness"
- ❑ blindness
- ❑ tumors or cancer: lymphoma, malignant melanoma, lipomas, sarcoids, nasal polyps, squamous cell carcinoma, fibrosarcoma, ovarian tumorsand brain tumors
- ❑ colic
- ❑ abdominal abscesses
- ❑ bacterial endocarditis
- ❑ heart murmurs
- ❑ atrial fibrillation
- ❑ chronic obstructive pulmonary disease or "heaves"
- ❑ emphysema
- ❑ chronic infections
- ❑ laryngeal hemiplegia or "roaring"
- ❑ arthritis/degenerative joint disease
- ❑ navicular disease

Unfortunately there isn't room here to discuss each of these diseases, so the list is presented to make horse owners aware of problems their horse may currently have or develop in the future. An aged horse should have a geriatric work-up at some point, such as during spring vaccinations. This can help pinpoint problems before they interfere with your horse's activity. Depending on the horse and the suspected problem, the vet will start with a thorough history and physical exam plus or minus a complete blood count, chemistry panel, lameness exam, x-rays, eye exam, fecal analysis, urinalysis, electrocardiogram, or echo cardiogram. As with people, the sooner a problem is found the sooner treatment can begin. Age is not a disease, so give an older horse the same quality of health care as an up-and-coming two-year-old athlete.

CONDITIONING

Most of the horses in therapeutic riding programs are donated and/or retired from other fields of athletic endeavor, many with previous or chronic degenerative orthopedic disorders. Such maladies as arthritis of various joints (spavin in the hock, ring bone in the pasterns, osselets in the fetlocks) are very common, as is chronic lower back soreness (coldback) in the lumbar, sacral, and thoracic regions. Navicular disease and chronic laminitis are also common problems seen in aged athletes. In spite of these conditions, the majority of these individuals serve very functionally and enthusiastically.

The best approach to training and conditioning is to start with a long, slow warm-up period, and finish with the same. This simple strategy is the key to keeping the equine athlete sound, and thus can't be over emphasized. Start with ten minutes at a walk and trot on a loose rein both directions, no matter what kind of work the horse is doing during that day. End the session with ten to fifteen minutes of easy walking followed by five minutes of cold water hosing on the legs only (weather permitting). Many horses with chronic arthritic disorders will warm out of their stiffness with this approach. There is a definite place among these older equines for warming liniments, braces and leg washes such as Absorbine, Bigeloil, Vetrolin, isopropyl alcohol, and DMSO, used after workouts. DMSO (dimethyl sulfoxide) especially is effective for navicular and ringbone: massage it into and around the joints and coronary band before or after workouts, but always wear gloves when using it. It may help some horses to wear standing leg wraps on all four lower legs when not working to protect and support tendons and keep warmth and circulation within the lower limbs. The wrapping works by preventing lower leg edema or "stocking up," which inhibits circulation.

Stretching exercises are as important for equine athletes as for human ones. Carrots are tempting incentives for most horses, and can be used to teach them to stretch their neck and bend their body to the left and right, and stretch their topline by getting them to reach down between their forelegs in a pseudo-bow. It's great to do this every day before riding. Linda Tellington - Jones' TTEAM method has techniques for stretching legs, available in her books, videos and articles. Horse massage therapists can teach leg stretches also, as well as to give your equine a well deserved and soothing rub down. Both massage and acupressure can be used to help treat musculoskeletal problems and keep them in check.

If the horse has more progressive or severe degenerative disorder that liniments and stretching cannot completely control, oral nonsteroidal anti-inflammatories (NSAIDs) may be in order. Examples of NSAIDs are phenylbutazone, aspirin, flunixin meglumine (banamine) and ketoprofen. Consultation a veterinarian to choose the right drug for the horse's condition and to determine the dosage and length of treatment. Watch out for gastrointestinal upset with any NSAID or steroid. Like aspirin in humans, these drugs can cause ulcers and other stomach distress. Discontinue these drugs if the horse develops diarrhea. Also, do not use two or more NSAIDs together or a NSAID and a steroid together. Be especially careful with phenylbutazone (bute); while it is a very effective anti-inflammatory, high doses over prolonged periods can cause irreversible kidney damage. As a general rule, do not exceed a dose of greater than three grams per day for more than three weeks.

Other helpful therapies for arthritis and other joint problems are chondroitin sulfate and glucosamine. These agents protect and may help repair cartilage. They are sold either together or alone in feed supplements such as J-Flex, Flex-Free and Cosequin, and are often combined with vitamins and herbs which are, in theory, helpful in joint disorders. Another joint supplement, hyaluronic acid, is administered as an intramuscular or intra-articular injection and can be very effective. The effectiveness of the feed supplements, however, is still in question, but they are worth a try. In other words, no clinical studies have proven them effective but anecdotal evidence in their favor is building. It is okay to use these joint supplements in combination with an NSAID. Additional alternative therapies which are worth a try are magnets, acupressure, acupuncture, massage and the services of a chiropractor.

Never forget the benefits of therapeutic trimming and shoeing to assist the four-footed athlete. The farrier and vet together can figure out the best plan to keep the horse comfortable and active.

The most important thing is to keep the athletic equine active. If the horse gets injured, do not stop work completely unless absolutely necessary. It is harder for an older horse to regain condition, and often they will not get back to their previous level of conditioning if they are taken out of work for long periods. Light to moderate exercise is the best bet to keep muscles and joints flexing and circulation flowing. Maybe most vital is the effect exercise has on the horse's mind. As in humans and dogs, an old horse needs a job to feel useful. A completely retired horse can feel neglected and unneeded, and may lose his zest for life.

CONCLUSION

Just as broodmares are a blessed group of our equine population, so are these older, dedicated working horses. Let's face it, most of them have paid their dues to the horse society as runners, jumpers, working stock animals, show horses and so forth. Now that they have become integral parts of therapeutic riding programs, they deserve some special consideration and human insight. They need a little more time to get warmed up and get that circulation moving, require a little more individualized attention to diet and dentition, but they are very rewarding animals with which to work.

Jean S. Hoffman
USA

References:

Kellon, EM. (1986). *The Older Horse. N.Y.,*Breakthrough Publications

Kobluk CN, AmesTR and Geor RJ. *(1995). The Horse: Diseases and Clinical Management,* N.Y. WB Saunders Co.

Special thanks to Robert R. Johnson, VMD, who wrote the original article in the previous edition of this book, which was revised.

To witness the love and respect that occurs between horse and rider as each devotes itself to the other is to understand why this unique therapeutic riding technique works!

THE MEDICINE CHEST FOR THE THERAPEUTIC RIDING HORSE

Barbara T. Engel, MEd, OTR

Horses, like humans, have accidents and become ill. Stable personnel must be able to administer first aid until they can obtain help from a veterinarian. It is important to be prepared for such things as bruises, cuts, puncture wounds or sprains. Horse handlers should have basic knowledge of horse first aid. First aid with the horse should be part of any orientation. This should include the line of responsibility. For instance, if the stable manager is present, he /she should take charge of the sick or injured horse; The next in line may be the head instructor and so on. This process maintains an order of authority and keeps friction to a minimum. There may be times when the only person at the center is a volunteer who is feeding the horses and notices an injury. He/she must act quickly and, on such an occasion, this person must have the knowledge and authority to take charge.

The first aid supply kit must be kept in a clean chest such as a large cooler with a lid that seals, and the tools must be maintained in good condition. The chest should be kept in a central area that is easy to reach by the handlers, BUT AWAY FROM THE PROGRAM POPULATION. It should always be kept in the same location, and all staff handling the horses should know where it is. These items must be easily available for emergency use. The following list contains the major items that should be included in a horse first aid box. The contents should be checked frequently and replacement made promptly. Having a complete list of items in the chest will help to keep the inventory current.

A large center should include all items listed and any other items the veterinarian and staff may need. A center with one or two horses may not need all items listed. Regardless, make sure you have all the important items and know how to use them.

If you are fortunate to live in an area where your veterinarian can get to your center within fifteen minutes you may not need some of the medicines and items that a veterinarian normally carries with him or her. In large cities or rural areas your veterinarian may not be able to reach your center in case of an emergency in less then an hour, than you must be prepared to take care of your horse with the necessary equipment and supplies. Sometimes the veterinarian has two emergencies at the same time or maybe it is a holiday weekend and he or she must cover another veterinarian case load. In any case it is best to be prepared!

All the equipment and supplies are of little help if your staff lacks horse knowledge in such things as normal respiration, colic signs, what dark urine means, what it means when that yellow stuff comes out of the nose and so on. Have a good **First Aid Book** for **Horses** on hand and <u>read</u> it with the staff.

Be sure that phone numbers are clear and available to all staff members. List the name and address of the center including the cross roads or streets. Phone numbers should include the veterinarian(s), the barn manager, the head instructor and any other person who may be in charge. The phone number of the center should also be listed in case it must be left on a message machine.

It might be a good idea to post a RED ALERT LIST in a noticeable place. This would help out a volunteer who might be coming in on an odd day to feed the horses. While there, the volunteer observes a horse with unusual behavior. This person can check the list to determine whether this could be a serious condition. The RED ALERT list can easily be made by a volunteer or purchased from Equus.

THE RED ALERT LIST MIGHT INCLUDE THE FOLLOWING::

Stops eating - can't eat or swallow	Chills
Does not drink	Gums other than pink
Does not urinate	Dehydrated
No bowel movements	Leg stance- stiff, sawhorse stance
No gut sounds	Will not stand
Sweats	Staggers or falls
Unusual rolling	Depressed, lowered head, dull eyes
Wet cough	In-coordinated
Difficulty breathing or unusual sounds	Bleeding anywhere in heavy flow
Fever above 102○ F	Puncture wounds
Irregular pulse or greater than 60 beats per minute	Hives
Appears to be in shock	Convulsions
Bleeding from the mouth	Eyes closed, oozing, bleeding
Unusual behavior for that horse	

THE MEDICINE CHEST FOR THE THERAPEUTIC RIDING PROGRAM

First Aid Book for **Horses**
adhesive tape, 1" or wider
alcohol, rubbing
bandage, roll non stick, 1", 2" 2½"
bandage, 2" squares - sterile sponges
bandage, elastic, crepe, Vetrap™,stretch
bandage, 4" square surgical pad dressing
bandage, triangular
bandage, 6" ace
bandage pins
bentadine solution
blood coagulant
cold pack, chemical- several pkgs
cotton roll, sterile absorbent
cotton, wool roll-2
clorax
dressings, Melolin™, Fucidin Tulle™
dressing, wound- nitrafutazone, Nolvasan™,Betadine™
iodine
leg wraps, cotton or diapers, track bandages
leg brace (PVC pipe cut in half)

Drugs (with advice from your veterinarian recommended)
  antibiotic, oral
  antibiotic- mitrofurazone*
  antihistamine
  anti-inflammatory
  antiseptic ointment
  acepromazine*
  aspirin
  Banamine™ *
  phenylbutazone (bute)*
  dimethyl sulfoxide liquid (DMSO)-medical grade
  dressing antobotic
  eye ointment
  epineprhine
  fungus cream
  eye wash
  epson salts
  liniment or body wash pads, pressure - sanitary napkins
  mineral oil
  paper towels
  saline solution, sterile - bottle of
  pail and pan for washing
  petroleum jelly

* prescription drugs from your veterinarian

Tools

bucket, large for leg soaks, water/ice treatment
duct tape
hack saw
hammer
hoof knife
hoof pick
flash light with batteries
lights, electric bright
pliers
rasp
scissors
screwdriver
shoe puller-spreader combination
towels, clean
tweezers
utility knife
wire cutters
tourniquet, latex tubing
towels, clean-
twitch, humane
vaseline or glycerine
weight and height tape (gives a general estimate for the "average" horse such as the quarter horse.)

Horse equipment(extra)
halter
lead rope
stud chain
sun screen

clean sheets or towels
fly bug spray
forceps, straight
gauze rolls, Kling™ - 2 ½" to 3"
gloves, latex or vinyl examination
pill smasher
plastic bags
plastic wrap
plaster casting rolls - 2-3
poultice, powder or paste - cold or hot
saline solution, sterile
scissors, blunt nose bandage
shampoo, iodine or medicated
sheet, a sterile bed sheet
sponges
splint, leg (PVC 3" length-6" wide cut ½ length wise and close cell foam pad) [backpackers]
stethoscope
surgical soap
surgical sponges
Swat™
50 cc syringe in sterile pack/ needles-18 gauge, 1½" long
syringe - irrigating
thermometer, veterinary

THE GROOMING TOOLS FOR THE THERAPEUTIC RIDING HORSES

Barbara T. Engel, M.Ed, OTR

Grooming is the daily attention that stabled horses need for the animal's health --to maintain healthy coats, prevent disease and sustain cleanliness. A daily grooming routine gives the handler the opportunity to check the horse for any problems. The grooming process also provides the contact needed to maintain the human-animal bond.

It is preferable that each horse has his own grooming kit--this prevents the possible spread of disease. Tools must always be kept clean by frequent washing.

The following tools are necessary for proper grooming:

BODY BRUSH is a soft, short bristle brush used after the dandy brush to remove finer dirt.

BRUSH CLEANER CURRY COMB a brush used to clean the brushes while brushing the horse. Hold the metal curry comb in the free hand and run the brush over the metal teeth several times to remove the dirt. A dirty brush cannot clean a horse's coat. A rubber curry comb can also be used if a metal one is not available.

CLIPPERS are used to shear the coat in warm climates, to prevent the horse from over heating and to trim the whiskers for a horse show and possibly when a horse is injured.

DANDY BRUSH is a stiff-bristled brush used to remove the large dirt particles brought up by the rubber curry comb and is used on the large muscle areas of the horse. This brush is used with short wrist strokes; brush in the direction that the hair lays.

HOOF BRUSH is used to paint the hoof with dressing to prevent the hoof from drying out. This is especially important in dry, sandy climates.

HOOF PICK is used on all parts of the hoof, to clean off mud, manure; to remove stones and or foreign objects. Keeping the hoof clean prevents disease, injury, hoof separation and problems before becoming a serious problems.

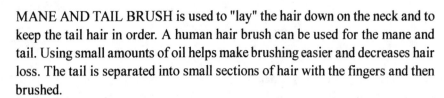

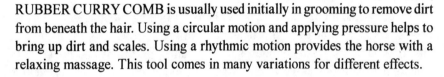

MANE AND TAIL BRUSH is used to "lay" the hair down on the neck and to keep the tail hair in order. A human hair brush can be used for the mane and tail. Using small amounts of oil helps make brushing easier and decreases hair loss. The tail is separated into small sections of hair with the fingers and then brushed.

METAL CURRY COMB has a spring action. It is usually used in the winter to remove dirt from heavy coats. Care must be taken not to hurt the horse with the metal edges.

RUBBER CURRY COMB is usually used initially in grooming to remove dirt from beneath the hair. Using a circular motion and applying pressure helps to bring up dirt and scales. Using a rhythmic motion provides the horse with a relaxing massage. This tool comes in many variations for different effects.

RUBBING CLOTH OR TOWEL is used, either damp or dry, to remove the remaining dirt and hair from the horse and to wipe sensitive areas. This is especially important to do for individuals sensitive to dust who will be riding the horse.

SPONGE OR MOIST CLOTH used to clean the eyes, nose, muzzle, rectum and genitals. Always use a clean sponge for the front and another for the rear areas.

SHEDDING SCRAPER OR BLADE is a flexible metal blade with teeth on one side. The teeth are run over the coat in the same direction as the hair grows to loosen and remove hair. This process aids the removal of hair during the shedding season.

SWEAT SCRAPER is a long metal or plastic tool used to remove excess water from a horse after bathing or sponging off.

SPECIAL TOOLS FOR SMALL AND DISABLED HANDS can be adapted from standard tools with straps, velcro, long handles and wooden blocks. Hand brushes and dog brushes can be used for small hands.

TRAILERING THE PROGRAM HORSE

Jean Hoffman, DVM, BS, Animal Science

One of the many skills a horse person needs to know is how to trailer a horse safely. Traveling with a trailer and horses always has many variables, such as time, weather and road conditions, so planning ahead is key for the horse's safety and the owner's sanity. This guide will cover basic safety tips for trailer maintenance, loading and unloading and traveling. In addition to these hints, remember to use common sense, obey the traffic laws and try not to travel alone. It is also wise to belong to an organization such as an auto club that provides emergency roadside assistance. The best way to avoid needing such assistance is to maintain your vehicles.

TRAILER MAINTENANCE

A safety check should be done on a trailer before traveling, whether you own the trailer or are borrowing one, and before buying a used one. Look at the biggest problem areas first, starting with the metal shell. Check for rust everywhere: exterior, wheel-wells, floor supports, ramp, hinges, springs, chains, partitions and hooks. While rusting hooks or hinges may not look like a problem, they can stick at the worst possible moment and be dangerous. Next, examine the flooring on the ramp and inside the trailer. The floor is usually made of wooden planks. Look for problems such as dry rot, termites, worn spots and water damage (especially under rubber mats). It may help to seal the floor with a wood preservative.

Lastly, inspect the electrical wiring, lights (bulbs and covers), wheels and bearings, brakes and tires, including the spare. A professional inspection of these major areas should be done about once a year. In addition, the trailer and towing vehicle should be checked about once a month in the applicable areas: tire wear, air pressure, headlights, brake lights and signals, oil and fluid levels, brake wear and hitch parts. In other words, all parts that move or slide should do so easily, all stationary parts should be strong and sturdy, and every component should do its job. Finally, make sure all vehicle registration and insurance is up to date, all horses have up-to-date health certificates, Coggins test papers (within a 6 month period), when necessary, brand inspection cards and that the horses are not sharing their traveling quarters with hornets or wasps' nests.

LOADING AND UNLOADING

The most important part about loading is this - don't wait until the travel day to try it. Loading horses into a trailer requires practice and patience. The time spent at home quietly teaching a horse to walk in and out of a trailer will pay off. It seems that every horse show has a scene at the end of a long day where a desperate owner and several onlookers spend hours prodding an animal back into the trailer for the ride home. A bad struggle or injury at a time like this is enough to keep a horse from ever going back in a trailer. Make sure your trailer is big enough for your horse to stretch his head and neck to help balance and feel comfortable.

In order to protect the horse from injury while traveling, the following pieces of equipment are recommended:
- ❑ Head bumper.
- ❑ Fleece-covered halter, tail wrap or padded tail chain or bar on trailer.
- ❑ Day sheet or light blanket (optional).
- ❑ Non-skid rubber floor mats.

There is a fine line between restraining a horse for its protection and releasing it in an emergency. For instance, leather halters, panic snaps or quick-release knots allow a horse to escape when in danger, yet strong lead ropes with sturdy snaps keep the creature from leaving whenever he pleases. Likewise, the animal should be tied loosely enough so he can raise and lower his head enough to eat and maintain balance, but tight enough so that he cannot get himself into trouble or bother his traveling companion. When the horse is properly outfitted for travel, prepare the trailer for him. The trailer should always be hitched to the towing vehicle before the horse is inside, to provide stability. Park the vehicle on level ground and away from possibly dangerous obstructions, such as fence posts and machinery. If possible, try parking the trailer in an aisle so that the horse is more likely to go inside than around it. Since horses do not like dark holes (and who can blame them), turn on the lights inside the trailer and open the windows and escape doors. If the horse is being loaded for the first time, practice without the partition in the trailer. Also, keep onlookers away from the trailer entrance and the horse to keep from scaring him away from the vehicle. When ready lead him in by walking in front of him (for trailers with escape doors) or standing beside him as he enters. Always secure the tail-chain or bar behind the animal before tying his head. Likewise, untie the horse before releasing the tail chain when unloading. Terrible accidents can occur when a horse runs backward, finds his head is tied, and panics.

Once horses and equipment are loaded safely, the trip begins. To ensure the animals' comfort, drive as if in slow motion. That is, all maneuvers such as braking and turning should be done slowly and smoothly, as if one's self were in the trailer. It may help to pull an empty trailer to practice. Slant load trailers also help the horses to balance themselves. In fact, many experienced horse people claim that horses will most often travel standing diagonally or backward rather than forward when given a choice. In any case, they are safer when tied with a lead rope or in crossties than untied. If a horse is traveling alone in a two-horse trailer, most horse people will load the animal on the left side, since roads tend to slant to the right. As for choosing a ramp-loading or step-up type trailer, personal preference is the only rule. Horses can be trained to load either way. When it comes time to unload, common sense dictates that the same basic rules apply as for loading. Most importantly, always untie the horse's head before undoing the tail bar or chain. Other hints include:

❑ Back the horse out slowly and toward the center of the ramp, so he does not fall off the side and scare himself.
❑ Be cautious when unloading the first horse, so the second horse does not try to back out at the same time or panic, thinking he will be left behind.
❑ Walk the horses to help their circulation before putting them back in their stalls.
❑ Remember to put blocks behind the trailer wheels when the vehicle is disconnected and parked.

Equipment:
Traveling can be made safer and easier by carrying the appropriate equipment. What is actually taken on a trip depends on space allowances and, again, one's belief in Murphy's Law. Each horseman must decide what is best for his situation, but here are some recommendations.

1. Tool kit, including:
   ◦ Swiss army knife (to cut lead ropes in an emergency)
   ◦ Crowbar
   ◦ Screwdriver
   ◦ Pliers
   ◦ Hammer
   ◦ Wrench
   ◦ Work gloves
   ◦ Flashlight
   ◦ Spare batteries
   ◦ WD 40 or grease
2. First aid kit--for horses and humans
3. Jumper cables
4. Bucket
5. Sponges and towels
6. Spare tire jack for truck and trailer.
7. Flares
8. Plastic bottle of water (for car or/and animals)
9. Extra lead ropes and halters
10. Hay and other feed for trip
11. Maps and necessary phone numbers
12. Tools
   • rake
   • shovel
   • broom
   • plastic bags for cleaning trailer

This list will help you deal with minor emergencies on the road until the veterinarian arrives. These items are included to help you take care of minor hoof injuries, wounds or colic. Have your veterinarian and farrier show you how to use anything on the list you have not used before.

FIRST AID KIT FOR TRAVEL

Sterile, non-stick gauze
Clean (non sterile) 4"x4" gauze
Roll cotton
3" or 4" wide cling
Vetrap™ or similar product
Betadine ™ solution
Bottle of sterile saline
Duct tape
Sanitary napkins (maxipads & roll of Elasticon for pressure bandage)
Suran Wrap

Furain ™ointment
Bute™ (phenylbutazone)
Banamine ™ (flunixin meglumine)
Acepromazine (do not use on stallions)
Betadine ™ or Nolvasan™ scrub
Hoof pick
Hoof knife
Hoof nippers
Shoe pullers

Happy Trails!

Jean Hoffman
USA

CHAPTER 9

SCHOOLING AND MAINTENANCE OF THE THERAPEUTIC RIDING HORSE

HORSE PRE-TRAINING SCHEDULE FOR OWNERS OF HORSES TO BE USED PART TIME OR DONATED TO A PROGRAM

Jean M. Tebay, MS, MCTRI

KEY WORDS

> **SUITABLE**
> **TRAINED**
> **SAFE**
> **HEALTHY**
> **SOUND**

In therapeutic riding, one may be approached by a well-meaning individual wishing to donate a horse, most often for a tax write-off. Perhaps the youngster, who owned the horse, has gone off to college and the family no longer wishes to keep it, or perhaps the horse is elderly and unable to jump, hunt or do upper level dressage. It is important to assess immediately if the horse is sound, healthy and temperamentally suitable, before considering it for therapeutic riding. Once this has been determined, then training the animal for specific roles in therapeutic riding can begin.

This training can be conducted by the owner wishing to donate the horse. The therapeutic riding program can say: *"Here is a training schedule. Once this has been completed, we will be willing to evaluate the horse for the use by our program."* Or perhaps the horses being used in the therapeutic program are brought by Pony Club or 4-H members. In that case, this training schedule, under the direction of the therapeutic riding program instructor, can be used by owner or rider to ready the horse for participation in the program.

Basically, this form (HORSE PRE-TRAINING SCHEDULE on the next page) is intended to upgrade the performance quality of the horses used in therapeutic riding programs. In addition, Jan Spink, MA, has published a comprehensive book titled *The Therapy Horse* , A Model for Standards and Competencies, available from New Harmony Institute, RR #5, Box 272, Charlottesville, Virginia 22901.

Note: The **Horse Pre-Training Schedule** on the following page has been printed by permission - B.T. Batsford LTD, UK., 1991, in Britain., Riding for the Disabled

HORSE PRE-TRAINING SCHEDULE

Horse's Name: _____   Trainer's Name: _____

Training Started: _____   Date Training Completed: _____

Areas completed in training	Completed	Date
1. Accepts Being Led, Both Sides.		
2. Accepts Side-Helpers, Both Sides.		
3. Accepts Rider Movements.		
4. Accepts Rider Noises.		
5. Accepts Ramp.		
6. Accepts Mounting Dismounting from the Ground and at the Ramp.		
7. Accepts Wheelchair On Ground.		
8. Accepts Wheelchair On Ramp.		
9. Accepts Wheelchair Transfers.		
10. Accepts Crutches, Canes, Walkers.		
11. Accepts Balls, Rings, Games.		
12. Obeys Voice Commands - Halt.		
13. Obeys Voice Commands - Walk.		
14. Obeys Voice Commands - Trot.		
15. Obeys Voice Commands - Canter.		
16. Obeys all Voice Commands On Longe.		
17. Longes Both Directions - Walk.		
18. Longes Both Directions - Trot.		
19. Longes Both Directions - Canter.		
20. Performs Smooth Transitions, Led.		
21. Performs Smooth Transitions, Longe.		
22. Accepts Special Adapted Equipment.		

This animal has been reviewed and is ready for service in a therapeutic riding program.

Signature - Evaluator_____   Date Reviewed _____

Tebay © 6/1990

Margaret L. Galloway, MS, BHSAI

NEW PROGRAM HORSE RECORDS

Horse's name:	Date of birth/age:
Past Owner :	Date Obtained:
Address:	Phone/fax:
Breed/Identification marks :	Hands:
Sex:	Past training/ work history:
When last worked:	
Type of last work:	
Temperament considerations:	
Vices:	
Likes:	Dislikes
Shoeing considerations:	
Medications:	
Feeding considerations:	
Drops weight in cold?	Blanketing: Clipping:
Tying problems:	Trailing:
Normal weight: Temperature:	Pulse: Respiration:
Vet Check: Date: Findings:	
Teeth: Soundness:	
Condition:	
Heart: Eyes:	Respiration:
Work Schedule:	

Margaret L. Galloway, MS, BHSAI

MAINTENANCE RECORD

Horse's Name:	Year born:
Veterinarian:	Phone: Cellular:
Farrier:	Phone: Cellular:
Body weight: Hands: Work Load- pounds:	
Daily Exercise Program:	
Feed Ration:	
Medical Problems:	
Hoof Problems/Program:	
Special Considerations:	
Medication: Schedule:	

SHOEING DATES	WORMING DATES	IMMUNIZATION	Notes/Medical

MAINTAINING THE THERAPEUTIC RIDING HORSE

Max Read, CEF Level 1, CTRI, CanTRA Examiner

Healthy, sound, happy and well-behaved; four things your horses must be if your therapeutic riding classes are to run smoothly. In many ways, keeping horses healthy is the easiest of the four. Make sure the barn and surroundings are safe, keep shots and worming up to date, follow a carefully monitored individualized feeding programme and consult your vet early on if any problems arise. Remember that the horse's age must be considered when deciding what to feed; hay high in alfalfa may have higher nutrient content but it is also harder for older horses to digest. Overfeeding horses can be as bad as under feeding, particularly with ponies who will founder more quickly than horses.

Probably the commonest health problem in horses is lameness. While we all agree that our horses should be completely sound, it is a fact that many programmes use horses who are technically unsound. Few of the horses in our barn would pass a vet check, yet they are all functionally sound and have solid, even movement. The importance of a good farrier cannot be overestimated; over time, he or she can get to know the horses, spot potential problems before they develop and sometimes prevent them through corrective or preventive shoeing.

Keeping horses happy is sometimes harder than keeping them healthy and sound, as it involves consideration not only of their physical state but of their mental state as well. Physically, therapeutic riding can be very demanding as horses often carry unbalanced, uncoordinated or deadweight riders and can develop back problems or muscle soreness. Sometimes, a horse who suddenly turns cranky is only trying to tell you that it hurts somewhere. There are a number of things you can do to prevent or relieve back problems or soreness. To start with, some sort of guideline for maximum weight of riders is essential - the quickest way to ruin a horse's back is repeatedly to ask it to carry excessive loads. Someone once said that structurally speaking, cows are better suited to carrying heavy riders than horses are! At our therapeutic riding programme, we use the following guidelines: For active riders, maximum weight is 175 lbs. For inactive riders, who cannot follow the movement of the horse properly (for instance, those with balance problems or low muscle tone), the rider's weight plus up to 30 pounds will be less than 175 lbs. If a rider needs sidewalkers for support, and must therefore have a mount less than 15 hands high, the rider's weight plus up to 30 pounds will be less than 150 lbs. We adhere very strictly to these guidelines which, with TTEAM work, have virtually eliminated back problems in our programme - at least, among the horses!

The weight limits are based on the assumption that the horse will be wearing an English general purpose saddle or a back pad and surcingle. If the horse is wearing a particularly heavy saddle (such as a heavy Western saddle or Australian stock saddle), you should take the weight of an average English saddle and subtract that amount from the weight of the heavy saddle, and then reduce the maximum rider weight figure by that amount - in other words, by the amount of extra saddle weight the horse is carrying.

What if the rider is using a surcingle and pad which weigh less than a saddle? A rider on a pad is harder on a horse's back than a rider on a saddle, as the pad does not distribute the weight on either side of the horse's spine like a saddle does. Thus, the weight of the rider will fall directly on the spine, and in the case of an unbalanced rider, the rider's seat bones may press directly on the horse's backbone which is very uncomfortable for the horse. Hence, we don't make any allowances in the weight limits for riders on back-pads; if anything, we're inclined to be more strict because the risk of injury to the horse's back is actually greater.

Of course, these weight limits are just some guides; you must let the animal's build, age and fitness level guide you as well. It is not true that the larger the horse, the more weight it can carry. This may be true up to a point, but ponies and short-coupled horses (with short, strong backs) are stronger for their size than large horses or horses with long backs or sway backs. A horse that is young (or at least not old) and more important, fit and well-muscled, can carry more than an older one or one who is only led at a walk or occasionally at a trot. It's a good idea to go through your barn with a vet or knowledgeable horse person, who can give you some idea of the condition and strength of each horse's back, and then be guided by their opinion. In some cases, your horses will tell you that they're uncomfortable with the amount of weight they're being required to carry, and it's important to pay attention to this and not just dismiss it as "bad behaviour." An uncomfortable horse is a grouchy horse - just like humans!

It is important to give the horses regular exercise in order to help their backs stay in shape outside of the therapeutic riding programme. Longeing horses correctly or riding them in a long, low outline encourages them to round and stretch their backs. This will help develop the long muscles on either side of the spine, which supports the saddle and the bulk of the rider's weight. Of course, this means that your horses must be young enough and sound enough to be able to do this extra work, but if they aren't able to do it you need to think seriously about their value to the programme. You can also help their backs by teaching your leaders to encourage the horses to lead with lowered head and neck (within reason) instead of carrying their heads high and hollowing their backs.

A well-fitting saddle is of paramount importance. I don't have space here to describe how a saddle should fit; see the section on saddle fit, but the best method is to get hold of a saddler or knowledgeable tack shop owner and ask him or her to look at your horses and saddles with you. To check the fit, try putting your hand between the horse's body and a girthed-up saddle and feel what the horse feels. There must be no contact between any part of the saddle and the horse's spine, and the top of the horse's shoulder blade must not be pinched. Check that the saddle seat level on the horse's back and that the panels are in contact all the way from the pommel to the cantle. Compare different saddles and different horses; hands-on is the only way to learn about saddle fitting. Once you know how a saddle should fit, your problems are just beginning. Ideally, each saddle should be stuffed to fit a specific horse - but who has that kind of money? The next best thing is to find a saddle that fits reasonably well, and then fine-tune the fitting with careful padding until you can afford to have it reshuffled. It's important to remember that thicker padding is not necessarily better padding - like the Princess and the Pea (go read your fairy tale books) an ill-fitting saddle with lots of padding merely becomes an ill-fitting saddle perched on a lot of stuff. The idea is to use padding to adjust the fit of the saddle in the same way that you would do if you were reshuffling it - by filling in a hollow here, creating more space there, and so on. The fit of each saddle must be rechecked frequently as horses and saddles will both change shape over time, and a combination that works through the winter may not work by next summer. Remember, too, that unless a pad is made of fairly firm material, any effect it has will be removed once the rider sits down unless the rider is very light, indeed.

Then, what happens if you want to put a rider on a specific horse (Copper), but want to use another horse's saddle? Willy's, for example, as it's an Ulster (synthetic) and this rather slippery rider needs the extra grip. It's back to square one - find a way to make Willy's saddle fit Copper, or find an alternative. A badly-fitting saddle is not only uncomfortable for the horse but can also be uncomfortable for the rider if it does not fit right, or dangerous if it slips.

One of the best things you can do for your horses to keep them happy is to make sure they get turned out as often as possible. The paddocks need not be enormous, but there should be room for a few horses to run a little, roll a little, and be part of a herd each day without feeling crowded. Running free and rolling are underrated pastimes. The running and bucking horse will stretch its muscles and make minor chiropractic adjustments to its body, while rolling improves circulation.

Then there's the mental state of your horses to consider. (First make them comfy then send for the shrink.) Taking them out on hacks when the weather's nice (yes, even in winter!) can do wonders for a horse who's getting grouchy because he's bored with seeing the same four arena walls every time a rider gets on his back? Make sure you pick sensible, experienced, tactful riders from among your volunteers to help hack the horses, as the last thing a horse needs is another beginner on its back when it's supposed to be having a break.

Good volunteer training can make a big difference to your horses' lives; after all, they spend a lot of time being handled by volunteers of all shapes and sizes. Emphasize the importance of not yanking a girth up quickly, but instead doing it up so it's just snug and then inching it up gently one hole at a time, only tightening it fully after the horse has walked around the arena a few times. This gives the horse time to adjust to the pressure of the girth, and the walking moves the skin and hair around so that it doesn't end up getting pinched.

Be prepared to spend a lot of time teaching volunteers how to put on a bridle correctly. Sometimes even "experienced" volunteers will have difficulty bridling our horses, as they bang the bit repeatedly on the horse's top or bottom teeth or push it hard against its gums. Naturally, the horse gets cross. Instead of allowing this to turn into a wrestling match, show volunteers how to hold the bit where the teeth meet and ask the horse to open up by putting a thumb gently in the corner of its mouth, where there are no teeth. If bridling is always done this way the horses quickly learn to open their mouths as the bit touches their lips - we even have one horse who will pick the bit out of your open palm!

Leading is one of the commonest things we do with horses in therapeutic riding, so it's worth spending time on. Both volunteers and horses must be taught to lead well. **When the horse is being led, the lead rope should be slack with the leader's hand six to eight inches from the horse's mouth. If the lead-rope is held any closer, the horse will be restricted from nodding its head up and down as it walks**, which will affect its movement as well as its temper. Horses must be trained to follow willingly with the lead rope slack, and must never need to be pulled along. If you find your volunteers pulling or leading with a tight rope, take time to demonstrate that it's not necessary. But, know your horse; if you find that pulling is necessary to get the horse to walk out, then a little reminder training for the horse is in order!

When a horse is brought up to a mounting block or ramp, make sure that the helper on the horse's off side doesn't push the horse over. If a horse is suddenly pushed off balance, it can't pick its feet up quickly enough to move, so all that happens is that the horse's joints, particularly the hocks, are stressed sideways. If this happens often, the nicest-natured horse will become sour at the ramp. Instead, ask helpers to put a hand on the horse's side as it is walking the last few steps into position; this indicates to the horse that it should move closer to the ramp. A horse that doesn't want to get close to the ramp, is far too heavy for a human to push anyway, but with practice, a horse will quickly learn that a gentle press means, "move over, please," and will usually oblige. If not, then it's your responsibility to work with the horse outside of classes until it understands and becomes more responsive.

It's important to remember that although your volunteer training must be detailed and your expectations of performance high, you will only have happy volunteers if you treat them as gently and tactfully as you do your horses. Always remember to praise, appreciate and reward!

Many programmes rely on donated horses, as ours did until very recently. But, good horses have become harder to get as gifts, at least in Canada, for several reasons. The tax benefits of a donated horse are not as good as they were a few years ago, meat prices are higher, and horse prices generally are higher as a result. Thus, people are less inclined to donate a usable horse as they can probably sell it for greater value. Our programme has recently changed its approach to the acquisition of horses, and it has resulted in a strengthening of the programme and an improvement in the quality and reliability of our services. The following is an excerpt from the Programme Committee's report and recommendation to the Board of Directors:

"In the past and at present, we obtain horses for the programme primarily by donation. This means that the majority of our horses are older (+ 17 years) and are not able to maintain the same workload as a younger horse (eight years and up). It also means that we must wait for a suitable donation to come along before we can replace a horse in the programme, and sometimes we have had to retire a horse before a replacement has been obtained. Unless the programme can have younger horses and the freedom to replace them quickly as needed, it is impossible to guarantee consistent quality or to increase the capacity of the programme without risking having to cancel classes and students later on if one of our horses is injured or ill."

"We need to change our attitude to the horses, without whom the programme does not exist. Horses must be regarded not as donations, but as essential programme equipment, as indeed they are. As with other essential equipment, the programme must be able to purchase horses which suit its needs exactly, and can then choose animals with a view to replacing some of the older horses we have at the moment. We should be soliciting donations of money from major corporations or service clubs which we can then use to purchase horses. As long as we continue to obtain our most important programme equipment by waiting for suitable donations, we cannot rely on consistent quality in our programme or expect to increase programme capacity."

These recommendations were adopted by the Board of Directors. As a result, we have two new programme horses. We were able to choose exactly the size and type of horses we needed, and they are both sound, fit and well-trained, and old enough to be sensible and young enough to handle the workload easily (10 and 12-year-old). Purchasing ideal horses, which once seemed a dream, has now become a necessity as we've realized what a tremendous difference it makes to the programme. There is a small tradeoff; younger horses may take longer to work into the programme as they may not have seen and done as much as older, seasoned campaigners, and they tend to require more ongoing schooling and training to keep them sane and sensible under beginner riders. But it's worth doing, believe me!

If your horses are healthy, sound and happy, they'll quite likely be well-behaved too. Regular riding and handling by your tactful volunteer riders will help prevent problems from developing. If there is a problem, first make sure that there isn't a hidden reason for it; if a horse is grumpy it's usually because it's uncomfortable somewhere. Check the horse for pain, especially legs and back, and find out if something happened in a class to create difficulties. If you can understand why a problem is occurring you're halfway to solving it. (For example, one of our horses recently, and without warning, began stamping and snapping when his saddle was put on. A little investigation revealed that the day before he had been carrying a heavy rider who sat tipped very far forward whenever possible, putting all her weight on the forks of the saddle. This, coupled with a saddle pad erroneously placed too far back, had actually bruised him just behind the withers on each side. After a couple of days the swelling went down, and he returned to work with no further saddle problems.) Once you've eliminated all causes of discomfort, you need to spend some time with the horse reviewing the area that was causing difficulty. Enlist the help of your volunteers, if necessary, since the more volunteers understand your horses, the better things will be all round. Good luck with your healthy, sound, happy and well-behaved horses!

Max Read
Canada

TT.E.A.M. AND ITS APPLICATION TO THERAPEUTIC RIDING

Linda Tellington-Jones

The Tellington-Jones Equine Awareness Method, (TT.EA.M.) The double T stands for <u>T</u>ellington - <u>T</u>ouch — is a multi-dimensional method for training and healing horses. The methodology, developed by Linda Tellington-Jones, divided into three: parts: body work, ground exercise and riding awareness. The TT.E.A.M. training was inspired by Linda's training with Moshe Feldenkrais, known for his development of Functional Integration and Awareness through Movement (Feldenkrais, 1984).

TT.E.A.M methods are applied in a systematic program that promotes learning, aware behavior and willingness in both humans and horses. Therapeutic riding and TT.E.A.M seem to work with a similar mind-body processes and goals; thereby, TT.E.A.M provides great value to therapeutic riding. TT.E.A.M is useful for:
1. Preparing, steadying, rewarding and rehabilitating a horse.
2. Adding safety, order and structure to training sessions.
3. Educating and empowering staff and volunteers.
4. Enriching and directing the experience for the rider.

DEVELOPMENT OF TT.E.A.M.
A 30 year pursuit of traditional equine training techniques revealed to Linda that those methods did not always provide satisfactory solutions for horses' behavior and physical problems. After studying with Dr. Moshe Feldenkrais for four years (at the Humanistic Psychology in San Francisco), Linda has integrated this education and methodology with her lifetime experience in riding, world-class competition, teaching training and years of research at the Pacific Coast Equestrian Research Farm. The cumulative result is TT.E.A.M., an internationally renowned organization using these techniques.

Feldenkrais believed fervently that learning is a process which has to occur within the learner (Feldenkrais, 1984.) Knowledge cannot be poured into the animal or human like water into a pail, nor can training be injected like some information transfused. Instead of "teacher" or "trainer," the job title should be "learning facilitator." Deep insights learned from Feldenkrais are that, in addition to creating an external environment which facilitates learning, the teacher/trainer can alter the learner's inner "environment" in ways which radically enhance learning (Feldenkrais, 1984). TT.E.A.M. follows principles by using tactile and kinesthetic stimulation to connect the house with his "environment" of mind, nerves and body (Feldenkrais, 1984.)

TT.E.A.M. TEACHING TECHNIQUES INCLUDE THREE AREAS:
1. BODY WORK
Specific body touches (the TTOUCH) and manipulations of head, ears, neck, legs0 and tail. The horse learns to move his body in a more efficient, pain-free manner. Tension and muscle tightness are lessened. Range of motion, suppleness and flexion are increased.

2. GROUND WORK
The horse is led through a prescribed set of positions, non-habitual exercises, exercises and obstacles. The animal is taught coordination, balance, rhythm and a sense of his own body. He learns to listen to specific signals, and a line of communication is developed between horse and handler. The horse learns to respond to a given set of circumstances, rather than react to them (as in fight or freeze).

3. RIDING WITH AWARENESS
While riding in a saddle, TT.E.A.M. ground exercises and body work are carried into the "mounted experience."

CONCEPTUAL MODEL
Consideration of the following assertions is useful in conceptual modeling when working with TT.E.A.M.

A prerequisite to relating to the horse is to learn his method of communication, mainly his body language.

1. Fear, pain, and anxiety block most equine learning. Most equine behavior is automatic reflex-like reactions triggered by fear, pain or anxiety. Pain or tension is often a "holding pattern"--a neuromuscular response to present **OR** past experiences.

2. The nervous system organizes habitual patterns for handling inputs, sensations, actions and behaviors. When the nervous system is functioning below optimum awareness, "unaware" habitual patterns govern the animal's usual responses. These patterns persist until they are changed. TT.E.A.M. allows new patterns to be introduced in a non-threatening, non-painful way.

3. The introduction of appropriate non-habitual touch and movement changes habitual patterns. At this level, the habitual inscriptions tend to be broken and replaced by more effective movement.

4. Non-habitual challenges must also be non-threatening. Failure of a horse to understand creates a threatening, anxious and confusing situation. Divide tasks into small, sequential components. If the horse is intimidated or balks at a new lesson, return to a level that was easily understood and accomplished.

5. The circular TTOUCH profoundly alters the mental and physical state. The circles effectively activate the nerve connection between the area worked on and corresponding brain centers. Changes include calming, relaxation, focus and acceptance of humans. Brain wave monitoring suggests activation of both hemispheres into patterns analogous to what is termed the "*Awakened State*" by some biofeedback workers (Wise, 1984; Tellington-Jones 1985). Petting, stroking and massaging DO NOT evoke these changes. The state produced by TTOUCH is a "*learning*" state that connects the experience to the brain, enabling the body to adopt new information such as relaxation, release of pain or tension and positive behavioral patterns.

6. Aided by TTOUCH and non-habitual TT.E.A.M. exercises, the animal can correct unwanted behavior, enhance performance and amend resting-state body-mind health. Results often occur after one or a few sessions. The modifications are often permanent.

7. Repeated use of TT.E.A.M. to challenge un-aware automatic functioning moves the animal toward operating routinely in the aware mode.

8. The TT.E.A.M. worker experiences changes which mirror the changes in the animal. These include calmness, awareness, openness to learning, connectedness and changes in brain wave patterns (Wise, 1984; Tellington-Jones, 1985).

9. TT.E.A.M. has positive effects on behavior. This means more than simply adjusting the animal to our human standards of decorum for horses. The term "behavior", in its larger sense, refers to "the manner in which a thing acts." With TT.E.A.M., pronounced changes are observed in the mental state and in neural, muscular and cardiovascular behavior. Discoveries in psychoneuroimmunology (the science of dealing with specific neurological and psychological systems) and biofeedback (Newsweek Magazine, 1988; Borysenko, 1987) are providing a paradigm (model) which indicates that changes in neurological and psychological systems result in changed glandular and immunologic behaviors as well. Results observed with horses give the impression that such complex changes are, in fact, occurring.

SOURCES OF INSTRUCTION:
TT.E.A.M. is both simple and capable of seemingly infinite development. Those naive to both horses and TT.E.A.M. can obtain positive results with only a few minutes of instruction; yet, those who have studied for years continue to learn daily.

TECHNIQUES:

A dozen varieties of touch, ten specific leading positions, numerous obstacles and more, are included in the TT.E.A.M. "tool-kit." This variety does not represent capricious elaboration; each technique has been developed to fill a specific need. Selected techniques which have proved most useful to therapeutic riding centers are illustrated.

Touch and leading positions have animal names. In addition to being mnemonic (developing memory), the imagery inspires visualizations which help activate the right brain with its strengths in rhythm, dimension, intuition and creativity. These names often provoke humor which helps in the extremely important task of putting aside ego-driven win or lose thinking. Such thinking loads one's esteem on the animal's behaving "correctly" and diminishes ability to "hear" what he is communicating.

Two training aids are employed extensively in TT.E.A.M., a wand and a chain. They are never used to punish or inflict pain. The wand, to some what might be called a whip, is used to conduct thoughts to the animal. A chain shank is employed as a *chain of communication*. This chain allows the handler to transmit subtle signals between horse and human with the use of light pressure. Such imagery again is to denote function. Through use and testing, a specific model of wand and shank have been selected as most useful for TT.E.A.M..

APPLICATIONS:

The following is a general outline to introduce the horse to TT.E.A.M.(This might be for a horse being adapted to therapeutic riding or a horse who needs to be adapted to new activities.) First, begin with two or probably three sessions of complete body work and selected ground work. At the first session, use TTOUCH to establish connection; work the body all over to locate tense and sensitive areas. Determine which movements and activities are performed poorly or cause discomfort or fear. Start to establish the TT.E.A.M. leading positions and perhaps start a little obstacle work. Some specific problem solving may be done, but the paramount goal of this initial session is learning. The human learns about this horse; the horse learns to operate in a calm-focused mode with trust in the human and trust in his new way of relating. Start the next session with body work to establish connection and get the horse's mind and body into a relaxed, aware state. Concentrate more on specific problems. Work more on leading positions and introduce more obstacles.

There can never be one set formula because the horse's responses determine the program. Later, TT.E.A.M. sessions may become shorter and fit into the daily routine. Subsequently, TT.E.A.M. should seep into and color all activities with the horse since the method helps to improve handling in areas such as approaching, catching, touching, leading, grooming, trailering, saddling and riding. Introduction of any experience new to a horse may cause it to react in an unpredictable manner. TT.E.A.M. is extremely gentle, but one must be conservative. Introduce any new TT.E.A.M. techniques to the horse before the rider with a disability is aboard or in proximity.

TERMS IN TT.E.A.M.

There are many words used in the teaching of TT.E.A.M.--to define hand movements, leading positions and other training techniques (unfamiliar to those individuals new to the TT.E.A.M. approach). The various Tellington Touches and leading positions are named after some of our friends in the animal kingdom and to bring some humor into our lives. We have given each position an animal name which helps attach a visual picture to the technique.

TOUCH TECHNIQUE

TTouch: TTouches are single, random clockwise circles with the thumb and little finger resting on the animal and the middle three fingers starting at 6 o'clock and pushing the skin around in a circle and quarter, then pausing and releasing before starting another circle at another spot. The TTouch method has been expanded into a variation of hand-finger movements to gain specific results.

Wand: A 120 cm (4 ft.) stiff, white whip with a hard plastic "button" on the end. The wand (imported by TT.E.A.M. from Germany) is well balanced and easy to use. It is used as an extension of the arm to stroke, give reassurance and to convey signals.

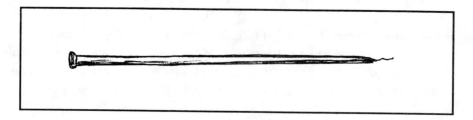

FIGURE 1.WAND

Half Walk: An exercise that asks the horse to step half the length of the normal stride for 4 or 5 steps, and then to walk on; **repeat** several times. This exercise influence the rider's balance by giving new sensory input. Both rider and horse must focus on the signals, and both learn steadiness and precision.

Lead: A *30 inch chain* sewn to a 6 foot, light, flat and soft nylon lead is attached to the halter in a specific manner so that the **CHAIN GOES OVER THE NOSEBAND** of the halter. The chain is an essential tool of the TT.E.A.M. work. Purpose: to get the horse's attention, to give specific signals and for control. It is a tool for teaching subtle signals and is **never** used to *shank* the horse. The position of the chain is shown here.

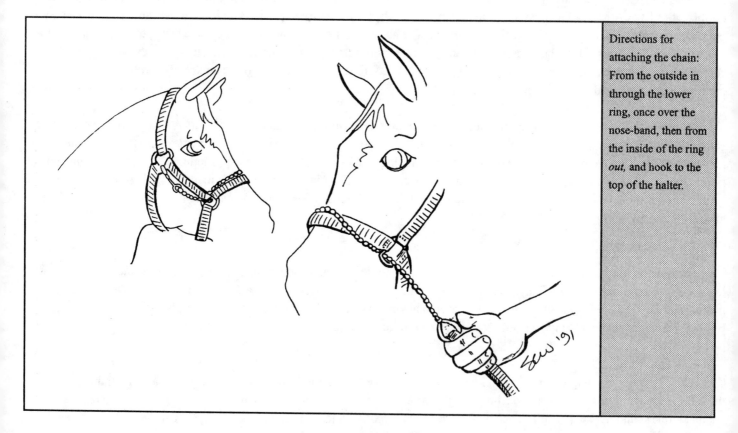

Directions for attaching the chain: From the outside in through the lower ring, once over the nose-band, then from the inside of the ring *out,* and hook to the top of the halter.

FIGURE 2 - LEAD

216

Ribbon Lead: A second loop is added when using the Dingo (see page 219.) Using the folds is safer because line is not wrapped around the hand. It is also much smoother as one slides away from the horse as in the **Dolphins Flickering Through the Waves**.

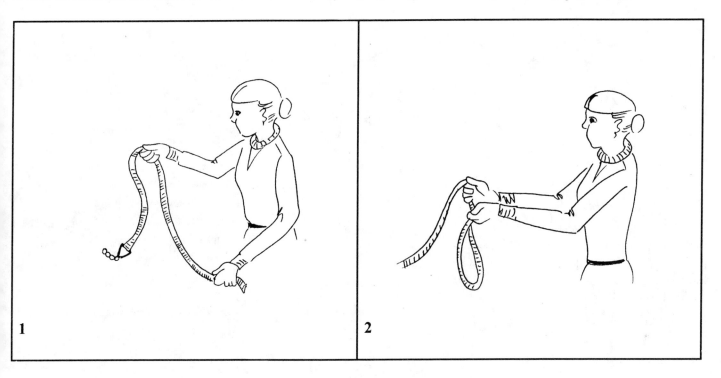

FIGURE 3A. RIBBON LEAD

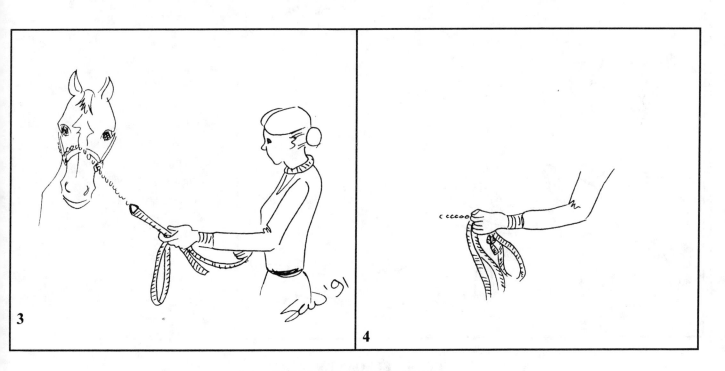

FIGURE 3B. RIBBON LEAD

217

Elegant Elephant*:* The basic TT.E.A.M. leading position is the safest and strongest way to lead a horse. The leader stays even with the horse's nose and uses the chain for clear signals and the wand as a focus point for the horse.

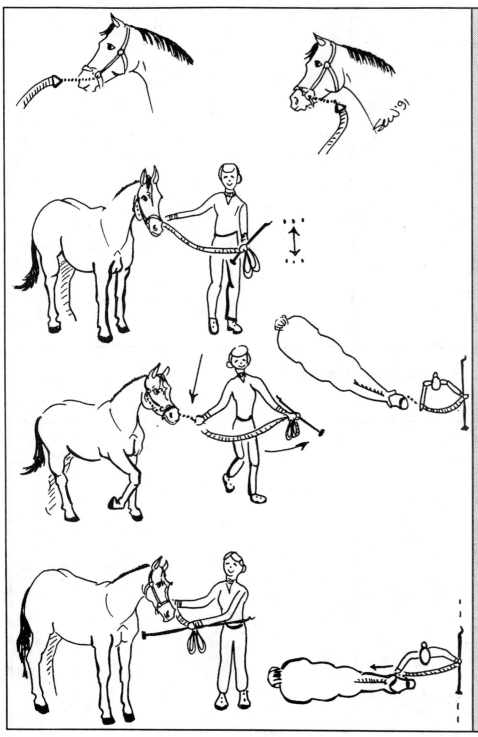

☛Use *chain*, as well as *voice* to teach horse to move The *chain* is held in the other hand (at the triangle of the chain) with a straight line from the horse to the hand Use the *chain* (lightly jiggle back towards neck) while asking horse to <u>stop</u> by combining *voice*, *wand* and chain signals.

☛Prepare for transition from halt to walk by moving the wand softly to focus the horse - use the *chain* to steady and maintain halt.

☛To walk, use the *chain* in <u>forward position</u> with **CONTACT, release, CONTACT** rhythm. Use *the wand* to *open the door*-- (move wand from in front of the horse to in front of handler).

☛Use the *wand* movement to *close the door* (in front of horse) and stopping signal on *the chain* (straight line back to windpipe), along with verbal "whoa" to halt horse. The *wand* moves in front of the horse clearly up-down, up-down. If the horse is just learning to respond, **tap** chest with the *knob* of *wand*. Then bring the *wand* back out to 2½" in front for final single movement to indicate STOP. Then stroke the horse's chest with the wand.

☛To prevent making a loop around your hand with the lead line, use the traditional method of holding a longe line. When leading from the left side of the horse, hold the end of the line between your index and middle fingers. Slide your right hand up the line toward the horse.

FIGURE 4A. ELEGANT ELEPHANT

FIGURE 4B. ELEGANT ELEPHANT

Dingo: The leading position used to teach a horse to go forward from a signal from the wand. The lead is held as described below in the "ribbon". The Dingo leading position is also helpful in teaching a horse to come forward when loading into a trailer. The wand is held in the right hand (when you are on the left side of the horse) and the lead in the left hand; use the wand in a firm stroke tap motion along the top of the croup following a clear signal to go forward from the chain. The exercise <u>teaches the horse to wait for the signal</u>, <u>overcome nervousness about contact with the back</u>, <u>teaches the horse to come forward from a signal on the chain</u>, <u>reinforced by wand signal</u> behind.

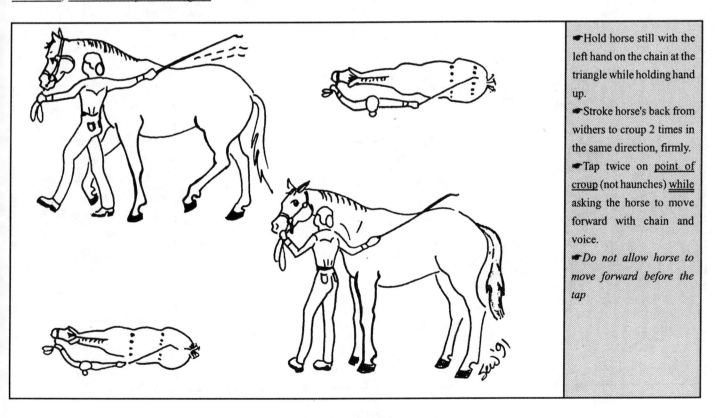

☛Hold horse still with the left hand on the chain at the triangle while holding hand up.

☛Stroke horse's back from withers to croup 2 times in the same direction, firmly.

☛Tap twice on <u>point of croup</u> (not haunches) <u>while</u> asking the horse to move forward with chain and voice.

☛*Do not allow horse to move forward before the tap*

FIGURE 5.

Dancing Cobra: A position to improve balance, focus, obedience and self control. It teaches a horse who tends to rush forward, or who pulls back when tied, to move forward when signaled.

☞ The handler will organize the horse's movement so that he will respond to the signal of the chain and the wand **NOT just to follow you.**

☞**WAIT**. A light handed connection is kept with the right hand while the wand signals **"_wait_"**. The handler's upper body will be inclined slightly towards the horse with hips and knees bent to stay balanced.

☞**GET READY TO MOVE.** The handler's upper body is shifted to upright with about 70% of body weight over the back right foot.

☞Bring the wand toward handler to "_open the door._"

☞**NOW COME.** Signal **COME** (using smooth flexion of knuckles to tighten the line, then release slightly) with the right hand on the lead.

☞Step back with left foot **AS** the right hand <u>asks</u> for the forward movements.

☞With the Wand, in the left hand, signal the horse to **COME SLOWLY** by moving wand toward horse's head.

☞**WHOA**. Wand forward.

FIGURE 6.

Dolphins Flickering Through The Waves*:* A method used to teach a horse to stay out away from the handler. It is also used when teaching a horse to longe. This exercise is useful to accustom the horse to signals being applied to different parts of his body. It also helps to overcome sensitivity associated with fear about being touched in these areas.

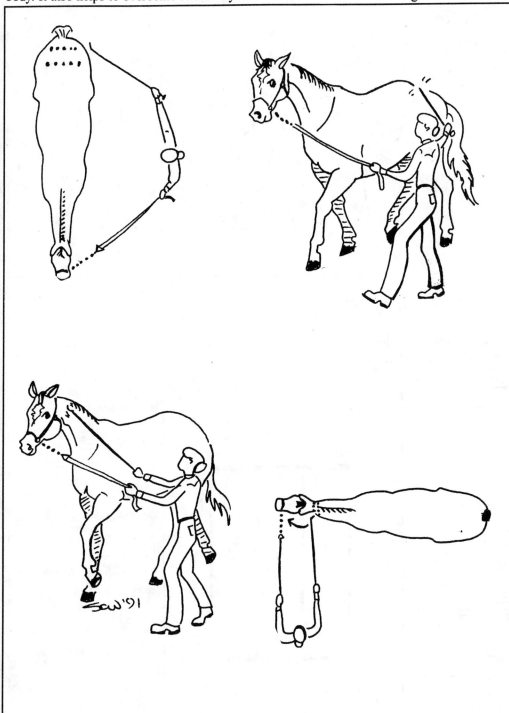

☛Begin in <u>Dingo position</u>, ask horse to go forward. Start in a straight line before asking for a circle.

☛When horse is moving <u>forward</u>, slide the hand down line to the knot (end) as you step away from the side of the horse.

☛To keep horse moving in a forward motion without drifting into your space, use flicking action, a quick moment of contact; avoid pushing with the tip of the wand.

☛As the horse understands staying away from the handler, slide the hand further down the line until reaching the end of the line.

☛Specific points signal the horse to do specific movements: on the croup asks the horse to go forward; on top of the scapula signals the horse to bend; a tap a few inches behind the ears on the neck indicates the horse should give rather then push in towards the handler.

FIGURE 7A.

The handler stays even with the horse's shoulder.

If the horse steps in toward the handler, flick him again on the neck while stepping away to maintain the desired distance.

FIGURE 7B

Labyrinth: A maze set up with a minimum of 6 poles which is used to teach obedience, balance, self control, focus, patience and precision for horse, horse handler and rider.

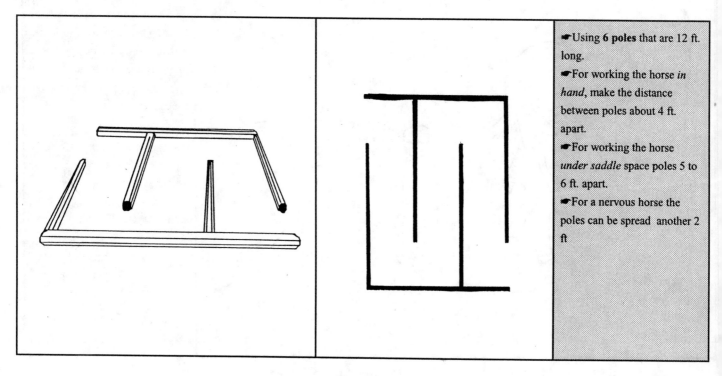

Using **6 poles** that are 12 ft. long.

For working the horse *in hand*, make the distance between poles about 4 ft. apart.

For working the horse *under saddle* space poles 5 to 6 ft. apart.

For a nervous horse the poles can be spread another 2 ft

FIGURE 8

Journey of the Homing Pigeon: A way of leading which is the quickest way to override a horse's instinct of flight. The horse learns to focus. Balance and self-confidence are improved. This method teaches a horse to keep its distance from the handler. It gives a horse a sense of containment. It prepares a horse for riding and driving, and teaches the handler to lead from the right

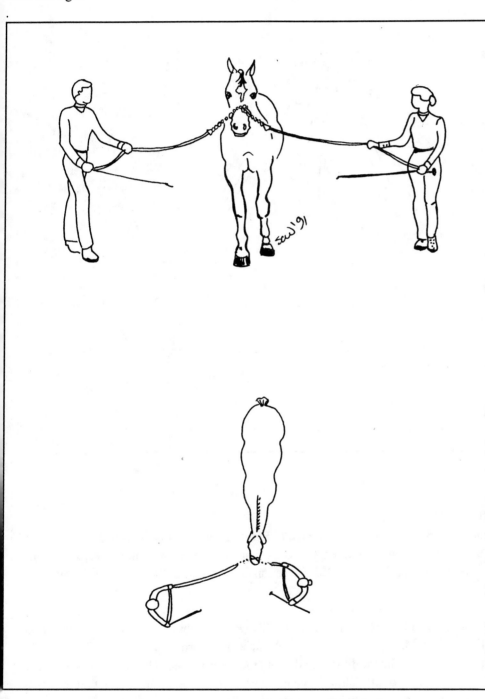

☛Two chains with leads are used for this exercise.

The chains are placed over the noseband to form an **"X"**. This helps to balance the horse.

☛The handlers stand on each side of the horse. The handlers hold the lines in both hands at least 18" from the chains, the *wand* is held at the button end with the end of the lead line.

☛Decide which person becomes the lead person and maintain communication with each other.

☛Slide the hand nearest the horse up the lead line so that the space between the hands is slightly wider than the shoulders.

☛The handlers should stay far enough in front of the horse so they can always see each other.

☛In this position, it is not the lead that stops the horse but rather a signal from the *wand*.

☛~One handler stays in this position while the other moves forward.

☛To go forward, stroke the horse's chest with the *wand* and bring the wand forward toward where you want him to go, like showing the horse the way.

☛*One must stay 3' in front of the horse for him to see the wand.*

☛To stop the horse, use the *wand* 3' in front of him at shoulder height, flick the end of the *wand* twice in front, then at the shoulder, then in front of him to stop.

FIGURE 9.

Star: One end of each of four 12 foot poles is raised onto a straw bale, tire or other object. The other ends of the poles are spaced on the ground about 4 feet apart in fan shape. The height of the poles is gradually raised and the distance between them is changed, depending on the skill of the horse. The idea of this exercise is that the horse can be successful in walking over the poles with full alertness.

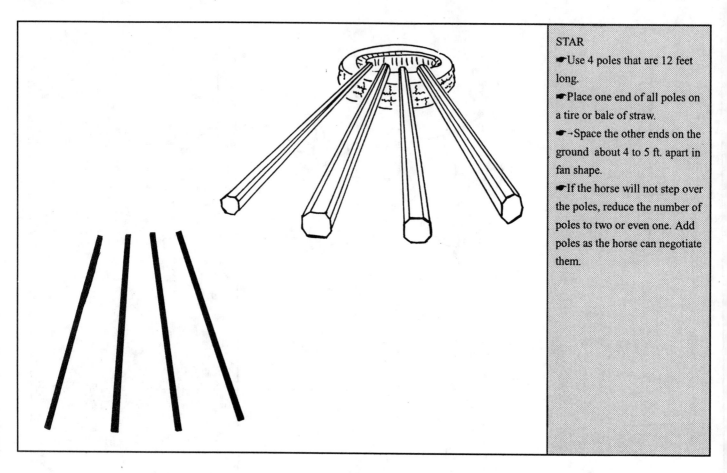

STAR
- Use 4 poles that are 12 feet long.
- Place one end of all poles on a tire or bale of straw.
- →Space the other ends on the ground about 4 to 5 ft. apart in fan shape.
- If the horse will not step over the poles, reduce the number of poles to two or even one. Add poles as the horse can negotiate them.

FIGURE 10.

THERAPEUTIC RIDING CENTER EXPERIENCES

TT.E.A.M. has been integrated into the care of horses at *Winslow Therapeutic Riding* in N.Y. All horses have been schooled using TT.E.A.M. leading positions and obstacles. The most frequently used techniques are *Elegant Elephant, Dingo* and *Dolphins Flickering Through The Waves*. Even though the horses are led conventionally in sessions, they retain the balance, self control and responsiveness gained in schooling.

Handicapped Equestrian Learning Program in Austin, Texas, is using the TT.E.A.M teaching techniques to achieve the program's desired results. For example, the TT.E.A.M. labyrinth and other obstacles have proved to be versatile tools. The process of negotiating a narrow defined area not only benefits the disabled rider, but the horse as well. The labyrinth is extremely adaptable. For the adult, the labyrinth is a challenging and difficult task requiring concentration, constant attention to details, changes of speed and direction, and constant processing and sequencing of information. "Where the body is in space" and changes in proprioceptive information elicit continuous balancing and coordination adjustment. For the child, the same labyrinth can become a "house" with a little "friend" awaiting the rider. No matter what the disability, its severity, or the age of the rider, that labyrinth now becomes a challenge to conquer and an opportunity for achievement. The labyrinth has become a solid base of learning for all of the program horses and all of the riders: One which can be adapted for almost any circumstance or condition. The labyrinth is a multi-effect tool; it forces riders and horses to receive optimum levels of mental, physical and emotional stimuli. The labyrinth can be tailored to provide such a variety of challenges that it seems without limitation.

At *C.A.R.D.* (Canadian Association Riding for Disabled), the physiotherapist and the TT.E.A.M. practioner worked with a 5 year old boy with cerebral palsy and poor muscle tone who required two side-helpers for him to maintain balance. The TT.E.A.M. practitioner worked with the horse while the physiotherapist worked with the child. The physiotherapist wanted slow transitions to help the rider gain balance. The practitioner, using the lead rope with a chain shank, applied in the usual TT.E.A.M. manner, helped steady the horse's head carriage. This stopped the horse from looking side to side with associated lateral body movement. The practitioner was able to give a clearer signal to the horse with the lead rope and chain shank since this lead provided a more direct connection to the horse's head. The horse was then able to move on in balance. Using a wand in front of the horse's head, a slow halt was performed with the horse maintaining his head position.

Since the rider's head was not staying centered, and this was affecting his balance, the physiotherapist walked along side the rider and at the same time put the wand on the abdominal muscles of the rider to improve front to back and side to side balance. The TT.E.A.M. practitioner switched to the *Dancing Cobra* position. In this way, the horse became very focused and the rider was able to focus on the physiotherapist and gain more control over his balance.

Marci is a 26 year old lady who has multiple sclerosis. She uses a wheelchair and has lost her hearing. She works at R.E.I.N.S.(Riding Emphasizing Individual Needs and Strengths), helping however she can. On a recent visit she noted that one of the aged ponies, who has chronic laminitis, was extremely lame. He was unable to stand without help when one of his feet was lifted. The pony was given TT.E.A.M. work once and a farrier trimmed the feet. A one gram dose of phenylbutazone was given to the pony the following day. Marci has a great affinity for animals. She wanted this pony as a TT.E.A.M. project. She was guided through the TTOUCH and ear and tail work and began to work on the pony daily. Three days later, the pony was relaxed and free from pain. When the pony was brought to Marci, he lowered his head for her to work on it. Then, as she moved to the body and tail he made small movements to make himself accessible to her hands. He even put his hoof on her wheelchair footrest so she could reach him. The pony is now back in the program.

CONCLUSION

TT.E.A.M. is a discipline that can be learned through demonstration and clinics through out the states and in other countries. Demonstrations provide an observer with simple techniques, while two-to eight- day clinics provide intensive hands-on training. Videos and literature are available for the continuous learning process. TT.E.A.M. techniques provide instructors and the therapeutic riding teams with valuable methods to handle the program horse.

Given the time and manpower demands at therapeutic riding centers, some directors may object that there is not time to learn and do the TT.E.A.M. program. Since time spent on TT.E.A.M. is invested in a systematic program of intense communication with a high rate of success, it is hardly surprising that TT.E.A.M. actually saves time, and therefore, the investment of time in learning the technique is justified:
  1. Less time to adapt horses to the program.
  2. Less time wasted circumventing horse's idiosyncratic behavior.
  3. Shortened warm-up times.
  4. More flexible use of horses for various riders and activities.
  5. More flexible assignment of workers to horses.
  6. Less time spent training volunteers.

7. Less lay-up time and longer retention of trained horses.
8. A benefit of healthier, sounder and safer horses.

In addition to time-savings and convenience, TT.E.A.M. can add to the quality of a program. Safety margins are increased with aware, connected horses and workers. Horses are more comfortable and involved as real partners. Clients and workers are empowered and enriched by the connection TT.E.A.M. provides. It would seem that from these utility features and from a shared interest in neuromuscular--mind learning, TT.E.A.M. and therapeutic riding are natural partners.

Linda Tellington-Jones
USA

References:
Tellington-Jones, L., Hood, R,, *T.E.A.M. News International*, Edmonton, Alberta, Canada.
Humanistic Psychology Institute: Moshe Feldenkrais Center. San Francisco, CA
Newsweek Magazine. (1988). Can Animals Think. May 23,1988. 52.
Pacific Coast Equestrian Research Farm, Badger, CA
Tellington, W., Tellington-Jones, L.(1979) *Endurance and Competitive Trail Riding*. New York: Doubleday. Wise, A. (1984). Biofeedback. *TTEAM New International*. 4,5, 13-15.

TEACHING THE THERAPEUTIC RIDING HORSE TO GROUND-TIE

Margaret L. Galloway, MS, BHSAI

KEY WORDS

SAFETY
TRAINING

Ground tying the therapeutic riding horse is a safe, effective way to keep him standing still. Ground tying means you simply take the lead line or reins (untied) and drop them to the ground without tying them to anything. The horse is expected to remain in place.

A well-trained horse can be safely ground tied even in fairly large areas, such as arenas. It is a method with many advantages: One has no ropes to deal with; the horse has nothing to pull against; the horse is obedient to voice command and remains still until the command to move; there is never a problem finding a place to secure the horse. Some therapeutic riding programs require ground tying as it makes horse handling much easier.

To train a horse to ground tie, one needs a halter and lead line and a bridle with split reins, such as a western bridle, or reins that can be unbuckled after the horse has responded well to the halter. No gimmicks, such as hobbles, are necessary. To start the training, use a halter and lead line in an area relatively free of distractions. Stand in front of the horse. Take the lead line and give a quick pull toward the ground, saying "Ho," then drop the lead line. Walk several steps away. If the horse moves, walk back and firmly tug again on the lead line, repeating "stay." If there are other horses around, who already ground tie, it sometimes helps to have them ground tied nearby as horses may imitate each other. When walking back to the horse, who has successfully stood still, reward him verbally and with patting. Repeat the process of a pull, drop the lead-line, and walk away. Gradually increase the distance moved away while the horse stands. Be sure to reward him if he is successful. *Teaching a horse to ground tie is much like teaching a dog to **stay and carries the same type of safety factor**.*

The next step is to move the horse to another spot and repeat the performance. Finally, repeat the process with reins. Use unbuckled reins to begin with to prevent the horse from getting his leg caught in them. Be aware that a horse can step on the reins and become frightened during his early training and break the reins. One should practice with a halter and a bridle, equally, until both are easy for the horse to understand. If, after time, the horse becomes "sloppy" and wanders, he may need to be retrained and reminded to stand. Always emphasize good behavior and use lots of praise.

Advantages: Ground tying is indispensable in controlling the animal. The horse learns to respond to commands. The handlers and riders avoid becoming tangled in ropes. There are no ropes for the horse to "pull back" on or step on. Ground tying is safe for grooming because the horse remains still. The degree of safety is dependent on the degree of training. If the horse is completely submissive to this technique, he will be reliable and safe.

MAKE SURE THE HORSE IS ABSOLUTELY TRAINED IN "GROUND TYING" BEFORE USING THIS TECHNIQUE WITH BEGINNING, UNSTABLE RIDERS AND YOUNG PROGRAM RIDERS.

Margaret L. Galloway USA

LONGEING A THERAPEUTIC RIDING HORSE

Margaret L. Galloway, MS, BHSAI

Longeing the horse means the horse works at various gaits on a longe line in a circle around the handler. It is a training technique that teaches the horse to respond to the handler's commands and balance himself on a circle; it can be used for exercise. *"All tack used when working with a horse on the longe should be light but well made, well cared for and very strong, as it is often subject to sudden strain"* (Inderwick, 1986). It should be noted that horses with soundness problems (We don't use unsound horses anymore, do we?) may not be longed. Ask your vet regarding longeing a horse with leg problems - some other forms of exercise may be less stressful to their condition. Frequent turnouts are excellent for these horses since standing in a stall tends to make any horse stiff.

TACK USED IN LONGEING (Figure 1)

- ❑ A halter, a bridle with a snaffle bit or a longeing cavesson
- ❑ A longeline of 23 to 33 feet, light-weight but strong. Cotton gives a better grip than nylon
- ❑ A longe-whip long enough to *touch* the horse with the lash
- ❑ Side-reins
- ❑ A saddle, surcingle or a longeing roller
- ❑ Brushing boots, bell boots or wraps are used when horses tend to overreach and injure themselves
- ❑ Gloves

A halter provides less control than a bridle or longeing cavesson and should only be used on horses well trained to longe for limited exercise only - not for training. *Use only a snaffle bit* when using a bridle for longeing. A horse that is light in hand, balanced and that lets itself be driven forward can have the longeline attached to the inside bit ring. For more control, the longeline can be brought through the inside bit ring, over the poll to the outside and attached to the outside bit ring.

When using a **bridle**, use a regular or drop noseband. The noseband must be at least four fingers above the horse's nostril and not too tight [two fingers between nostril and noseband.] Bring the end of the longeline through the near bit ring and over the horse's poll (Richter, 1986). Snap the longeline to the far side of the bit ring. The reins are removed or secured to the head stall by twisting them and running the throat latch through them. Be sure to unsnap the longeline and change the direction of the line when longeing in the opposite direction.

The **longeing cavesson** can be used over the snaffle bridle or alone. It provides secure control with a lighter touch, is better fitting than a halter, and, with the longeline strapped onto the center nosepiece attachment, the horse may be longed on either rein without further adjustment. The longeing cavesson must be strong and well fitted so there is no shifting. **Podhajsky (1968) suggests that longeing should only be performed with a longe cavesson because he feels that attaching the longeline to the bit destroys the soft contact with the horse. Soft contact gives the handler a more obedient and responsive horse.** Practice with the cavesson before putting a rider on the longe horse; it affects the horse very differently from a line attached to the bit.

The use of a saddle, a training surcingle, a vaulting surcingle or a longeing roller depends on the purpose of longeing. The saddle is used in preparation for riding or with a rider. The surcingle or a longeing roller is used in training or exercise. The vaulting surcingle is used for sports vaulting, therapeutic riding or improving a rider's seat. Side-reins are attached to the surcingle, saddle or roller.

PURPOSE AND FIT OF SIDE-REINS

The side-reins attach to the snaffle bit and to the saddle, longeing roller or training surcingle on each side of the horse. The side-reins prevent the horse from turning his head around. They teach him that if he does not pull at the rein, the rein will not pull at him, and they restrain the bit from moving about too much in the mouth. The side-rein should never be so short as to restrict the movement of the horse (Richardson, 1981). When first introducing the horse to longeing, one should not use side-reins, but have all the other equipment in place. Side-reins should not be used until the horse goes forward obediently. When first using side-reins with a horse, they should be longer so that the nose is just beyond the vertical as the horse becomes more supple. Podhajsky (1968) suggests that the side-reins be of equal length on both sides. A German technique teaches that the inside rein is one hole tighter than the outside rein when going in a circle. It is important to let the horse reach his head down and seek the contact of the bit, shortening his neck by tight side-reins. Lowering the head allows the back to raise (TT.E.A.M., 1990). The side-reins should be adjusted so that they are comfortable at the halt. As the horse develops a bend, the inside rein might have to be tightened in order to maintain even contact.

AIDS AND POSITION OF HANDLER

The longeing whip is an essential piece of equipment that urges the horse forward with more energy than can be done with other methods. It is used as an aid, for the same reason the rider's legs are used, never as a means of punishment. The handler must learn where to stand in relation to the horse in order to use the whip correctly (Figure 2). The handler, the longeline, and the whip form a triangle with the horse making up one side. The handler stands approximately at the horse's croup, so he or she can drive the horse forward with his or her body position. The whip is held in the hand nearest the horse's hindquarters. The handler moves the horse forward and out and develops a consistent circle. The handler needs to become ambidextrous to manage both the whip and the longeline in a coordinated manner. A horse must not be frightened of the whip, but must learn to respect it. The whip reinforces the voice command and the slight tugs or message on the longeline.

When longeing, *"one of the most important aids is the voice....It may be soothing or exhorting. It is important that the word and sound remain the same for the same commands"* (Podhajsky, 1968). Stand quietly and use a quiet tone. Strengthen the voice command as needed. Avoid shouting. A sharp "no" may occasionally be appropriate, but this sound can easily be confused with "oh," "good," and other exclamations from the student, and should be avoided. The German prrrr, or some reasonable approximation, is better.

The longe session is a good time to teach voice commands. The first command a therapy horse should know is "ho." There may be times when a rider becomes unbalanced and the horse needs to be collected or halted, and a promptly responsive horse is very valuable. To teach the horse "ho," gently give and take with the longeline and say "ho or "whoa"." "Ho" is said in the same tone, usually a deep, drawn-out verbalization. If the horse turns in toward the handler, step back toward his hindquarters and point the whip, saying "walk." "Walk on" is said in a brisk, energetic voice. After a few minutes, repeat the gentle give and take until the horse stops correctly on the circle facing forward. Walk up to him, **gather the longeline in a figure eight** while approaching the horse. Praise him heartily, stroking his neck. Reverse and repeat the process. After reversing the horse, re-adjust the side-reins so that the new inside rein is shorter by one hole than the outside rein.

TECHNIQUE

Most adult horses know the basics of longeing. Those that do not need to be trained, unless your veterinarian has requested it, need not be longed. In initial training, an assistant is very helpful. The handler should hold the longeline in his or her near hand and the whip in his or her far hand (Figure 3.) He or she should stand near the horse's head, stepping back toward the horse's hindquarters, keeping a very light contact with the longeline. At the same time, an assistant stands on the horse's far side and begins to lead him forward. The handler stays behind the horse's girth area and uses the whip judiciously to encourage the horse forward. The assistant can step back and away from the horse's head as the horse begins to understand that he must circle the handler (Inderwick, 1977).

It is important to note that, as in leading, the longeline should never be wrapped around your hand, wrist or arm, as this can lead to serious injury. Rather, the line should be folded so that a little can be let out at a time. The longeline should never drag on the ground since the instructor will no longer have direct contact with the horse's mouth. The leadline is held in the same way as one would hold the reins. The upper arm is held next to the body and the lower arm is held in line with the longeline, making a straight line from the elbow to the bit, cavesson or halter (TT.E.A.M., 1990). The walk and trot are the first gaits in which to work the horse while longeing. Once these gaits are mastered, cantering may begin. Begun too early, the horse may not be balanced or may canter with his hindquarters to the outside (Podhajsky, 1967).

EXERCISING THE HORSE

Exercising the horse can be done on the longeline. The basics of longeing remain the same. Be sure that the horse is warmed up at the walk, and then the trot, before attempting faster work. If the horse plays by bucking, use a soothing voice and give and take on the longeline. The horse must learn that longeing requires a working attitude with or without the rider. Play must never be tolerated. Under no circumstance should the horse be allowed to race around the handler as he can injure himself, get loose, or destroy the 'working attitude.' Try long trotting periods for those horses who need to expel energy. Work in a quiet area so that extraneous stimuli are kept to a minimum. One should work equally in both directions, just as one should ride equally in both directions (Equus, 1989). One should also maintain contact with the longeline; do not let it get slack. The horse should learn to maintain contact with the longeline but not pull or lean on it nor come in to cause a slack in the line. Use the whip consistently and effectively as an aid to drive the horse forward and keep him out on the ring. Never use it to punish the horse.

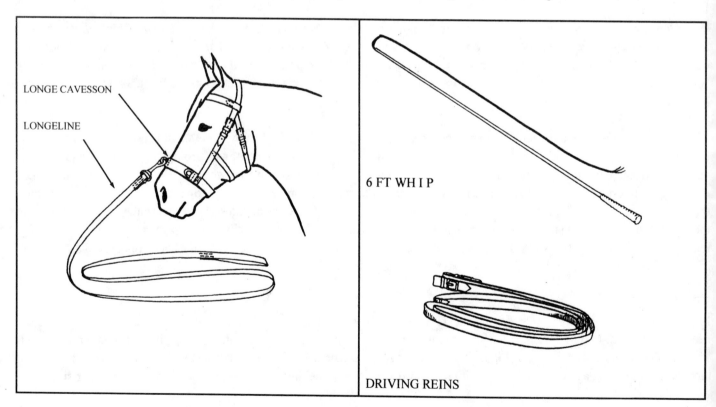

LONGE CAVESSON

LONGELINE

6 FT WHIP

DRIVING REINS

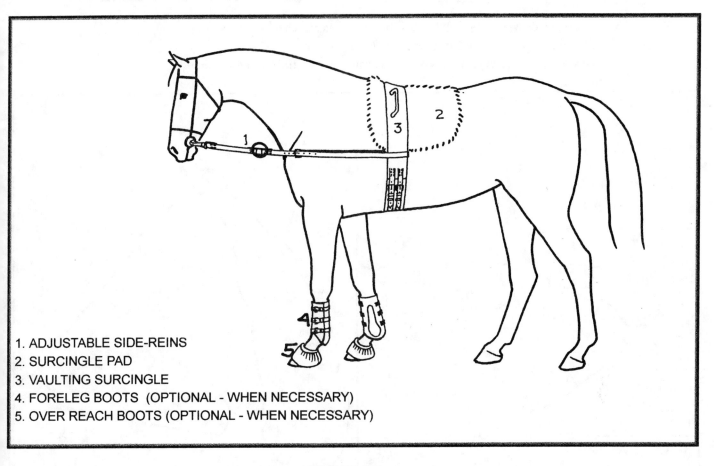

FIGURE 1.
LONGEING TACK AND THE HORSE

1. ADJUSTABLE SIDE-REINS
2. SURCINGLE PAD
3. VAULTING SURCINGLE
4. FORELEG BOOTS (OPTIONAL - WHEN NECESSARY)
5. OVER REACH BOOTS (OPTIONAL - WHEN NECESSARY)

LONGEING BASICS

- ❏ The horse must maintain a working attitude at all times.
- ❏ Work equally on each side, just as one would ride equally in both directions.
- ❏ Keep a sensitive contact with the longeline. It replaces the reins and should be handled accordingly.
- ❏ Use a well-fitted longeing cavesson or halter for training and exercise. Longeing with the snaffle bit is hard on the horse's sensitive mouth. The cavesson may be put over the bridle. In vaulting, the snaffle bit is used. The snaffle bit can also be used when longeing with a rider. This, however, requires a very well-trained horse and an experienced longer.
- ❏ Hold the upper arm close to the side, with the elbow bent, so that a straight line is maintained from the elbow to the horse's cavesson, halter or bit.
- ❏ Always longe on soft and level ground.
- ❏ Wear gloves to protect the hands.
- ❏ Be consistent with voice commands, using a different inflection for each command.
- ❏ Use protective boots or wraps and bell boots if the horse overreaches or brushes.
- ❏ Stay at or behind the horse's girth. Never get ahead of the horse.
- ❏ Stress relaxed, calm work. Let each session be pleasant for both trainer and horse

- ❏ Use protective boots or wraps and bell boots if the horse overreaches or brushes.
- ❏ Stay at or behind the horse's girth. Never get ahead of the horse.
- ❏ Stress relaxed, calm work. Let each session be pleasant for both trainer and horse

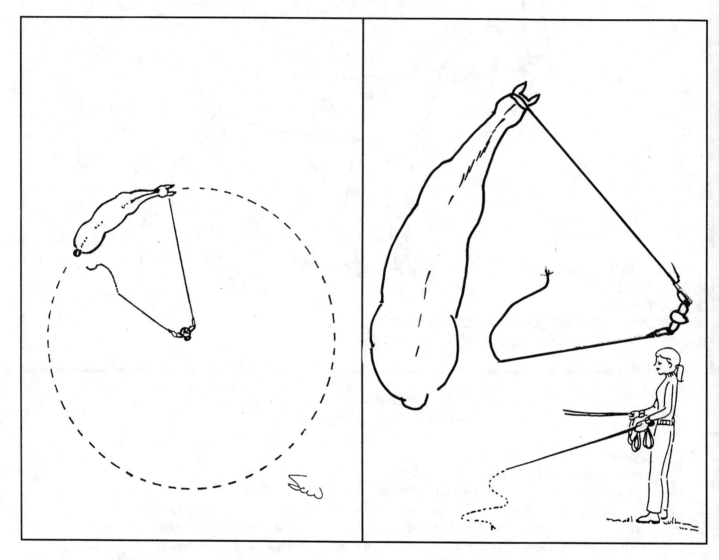

FIGURE 2.

POSITION OF THE HANDLER TO THE HORSE.

FIGURE 3.

POSITION OF THE LONGELINE AND THE WHIP

References

Equus Magazine, Editorial. (1989). 69. 137.

Hood, R. (1990). *TT.E.A.M. Clinic.*

Inderwick, S. (1986). *Lungeing the Horse and Rider.* David and Charles Press. 11, 21-23

Podhajsky, A. (1968). *My Horses, My Teachers.*, Garden City: Doubleday and Co. 14, 79

Podhajsky, A. (1967). *The Complete Training of Horse and Rider.* Garden City: Doubleday & Co. 82.

Richardson, J.(1981). *Horse Tack.* New York: William Morrow & Co, Inc. 22-25.

Richter, J. (1986). *The Longeing Book.* New York: Prentice Hall Press. 17

CONDITIONING A HORSE FOR A THERAPEUTIC RIDING PROGRAM

Margaret L. Galloway, MS, BHSAI

Let's imagine your therapeutic riding center has been given or acquired a twelve-year old, 15 hand, sound, quarter horse gelding. He had been shown as a four, five and six year old in jumping and dressage. Later he was ridden for pleasure and for trail riding. For the last several years, he has been left unworked in the pasture. How would you get this potential "gem" into condition for therapeutic riding and then maintain it?

Every horse is an individual and should be treated as such. If you are in doubt about a horse's capability, you can ask your veterinarian. A suggested schedule for evaluation and training is as follows:

The first step is to have him checked by the veterinarian for soundness and health. He should be wormed and his teeth should be floated as necessary. Next his feet should be checked by the farrier. He should be placed on an appropriate feeding program. If he is fat, he should be placed on a diet; feed should be added if he is too thin. It is also important to establishing a bonding relationship with the animal. After his basic needs are met, strength, muscle, and endurance should be built up gradually. Walking, with only a little trotting, is the primary gait for very out-of-shape horses. For all out-of-condition horses, the warm-up is very important. A correct warm-up and cooling-down period helps prevent injuries and azoturia, or tying up.

By the second or third week, longer periods at the trot help develop endurance. Work should not last longer than thirty or forty minutes, half of which should be a brisk walk with long strides.

By the fourth week, the horse can be trotted 15 minutes within the 40-minute exercise period. Cantering can begin between the fourth and fifth weeks. For the next several weeks, the work-out should be lengthened, or preferably, long walks (one half hour), ideally on a hilly trail, should be added or alternated with the workouts. Begin to work on dressage exercises to develop, balance, suppling, self carriage, gait transition and forward movement. After seven years without a rider on his back, it is important to strengthen both back and belly muscles in order to carry the weight of a rider.

After six to eight weeks, the horse should be fit enough to be used in a busy therapeutic program. To maintain fitness, some trail work, with hills if possible, as well as schooling at all gaits, should be sufficient if carried out at least twice a week. In general, long slow work is better than strenuous short workouts.

Margaret L. Galloway
USA

INITIAL TRAINING OF THE THERAPEUTIC RIDING HORSE

Barbara T. Engel, MEd, OTR

KEY WORDS

TRAINING
SAFETY

In the average equine environment, there is always concern with the safety of the horse and rider but not to the extent that is required in a therapeutic riding setting. The horse must have additional training to be virtually spook-proof to all elements in his environment and to meet the many obligations required of him in his new venture. The better the horse is trained, the more successful the instructors, the therapists and the volunteers will be with their riders. The therapeutic riding horse must respond immediately to the voice command of his/her instructor in all gaits. He must learn to stand still upon command for grooming, tacking, mounting, or while being ridden until he is signaled to move forward. This skill can help to avoid many difficult and dangerous situations. Voice command may be necessary for longeing and other riding exercises. When the instructor or handler has verbal control of the horse, a rider may be allowed more independence in the development of his/her riding skills.

One may say that no horse is **spook-proof.** That may be so but, under certain circumstances a horse can be *essentially spook-proof.* Horses are fundamentally cowards. If there is nothing to be scared of and nothing that they consider new coming into view, then they will not likely spook. Also if their attention is maintained to the task at hand, they are unlikely to be distracted and spook. Initially, the horse is carefully selected. The horse must be well cared for and maintained in a beneficial environment to avoid pressure, stress and fatigue. The instructor/trainer must be knowledgeable in horse behavior so that vices can be minimized or avoided. Adequate diet, training and exercise are essential in maintaining level attitude, and must be planned to meet "this horse's" needs, not just that of the "average" horse. Nor can this plan be based on **the needs of the staff.** It is important to know that the horse understands what is expected of him and is physically trained and able to carry out these expectations. The instructor and/or horse handlers must understand the steps involved in the development of balance, gait and collection, and be able to work with him to develop the necessary skills. The horse handler needs to work with the horse to develop trust. The horse must trust the handler in order for him to carry out commands given to him in a safe manner . Some horse as so dull and tuned-off that they just go along with whatever they are asked to do. More alert horses may question your ability to handle them or may be unclear about your command.

Volunteers and staff must understand that the routine and method of training that THIS center has implemented will be the way THESE horses are handled. Horses like a routine and regularity. If everyone handling them in the same way, the horses will know what to expect and will be a happier and cooperative partner. This is no place to show off "your" horse skills. Stick with the center's methods.

Saddles must fit well to avoid pain or discomfort. What may be the most important factor, to avoid the possibility of the horse spooking, is to **know** the horse. This must include knowing his likes and dislikes; what disturbs him or makes him uneasy? Does he have some vision problems that cause him to shy at an object or at dusk? Does the wind cause him discomfort or does perfume bother him? Does he need another horse in the arena? Do some personality types bother him? Be sure that the horse's likes, dislikes and needs are both known and met by all leaders or horse handlers. When one really **knows** the horse and works **with him,** one may really have **a spook-proof horse.** When this horse does spook, how does he move - a quick step and halt, a side hop, or does he stop and display nervousness? Knowing how he might spook will help the handler manage him. **But,** now that one feels the horse is virtually spook-proof, a word of caution is appropriate. A horse reacts when his environment presents something that is unknown to him. This may include a new smell as a perfume he is unfamiliar with, a new volunteer or a new horse at the stable. At a horse show away from his stable, he may be exposed to many unknown elements. Always remember that the horse hears and smells things a human cannot. Be alert to his anxiety and ready to calm him. Many horses will respect your "its OK."

This chapter has focuses on basic and advanced training techniques for the therapeutic riding horse, as well as how to design an ongoing program of schooling to reinforce that training. Useful ways to record information on a new horse are given - a maintenance record to help keeps track of the horse's health and work load. A pre-training checklist is there for use by donors to use at home to ensure the horse is suitable, or by owners whose animals are "used part time" in a therapeutic riding setting. Information has been provided by several authors on the same topic. This will help a center customize their plans to meet their needs by reading various opinions on a subject.

A willing horse, regardless of age, can be trained in safety methods by a knowledgeable instructor. Ray Hunt (Hunt, 1978), Tom Dorrance (Dorrance 1987), and John Lyons (Lyons, 1991) and others who are using these methods, gives insight to the instructor in handling a horse in a safe manner with good communication and kindness. Linda Tellington-Jones has developed methods to train horses to be handled with safety and ease. It is important to use training techniques that foster the human-animal bond as bonding is acknowledged as a major therapeutic feature of riding programs. A safe way to groom and tack a horse is offered while he is ground tied; that is, a horse who has been trained to stand still when the lead rope is dropped to the ground. One will not need to be concerned with tie ropes, cross ties, or pulling back, nor will the horse move about. Ground tying is not difficult to teach a mature horse but requires patience and time. It is commonly taught to Western style horses but can be taught to any horse.

The horse requires an exercise, training and suppling program to develop cadence and general conditioning to carry out the tasks of therapeutic riding. A therapeutic riding horse needs to move smoothly from one gait to the other. As most riders with disabilities have difficulty with balance, in order to allow the riders to begin with some sense of stability, the horse needs to move from one transition to the other smoothly. The horse needs to be able to maintain balance under all circumstances. The horse must be physically fit and possess a flexible, strong back and underline. When a horse is used in *equine-assistive therapy,* he will be used for his movements in a very specific way. Therefore, his requirements exceed those of the therapeutic riding horse. He must, in fact, be trained in a collection and movement equal to or beyond that required in first and second level dressage. If he becomes stiff from working or being stalled too much, he may need the skill of an equine massage therapist or stretching, as described by Nancy Spencer in Therapeutic Riding II Strategies for Rehabilitation.

The qualities and skills of the therapeutic riding horse will depend on the work he will be required to do. Regardless of his task, he must be in good condition to carry on the strenuous work of a therapeutic riding horse. People may think that carrying disabled riders is an easy job. Though horses seem to enjoy their work with these special people, it is not an easy job working so many different people with numerous disabilities; it requires continuous conditioning and training. A way to use volunteers to keep animals fit and happy is also discussed, later in this chapter.

When the horse has learned all the basics and gained the traits required, he is ready to learn the tasks involved in therapeutic riding. Requirements that are unique to the therapeutic riding horse include being able:
- ❏ To tolerate people on each side of him as well as someone leading him and one on top.
- ❏ To tolerate people over him and on each side while confined at the ramp.
- ❏ To tolerate the `noise' from several people walking on the ramp above him.
- ❏ To lead willingly, with balance, from the near or far side.
- ❏ To stand for long periods of time while he is groomed, tacked and mounted by unstable and uncoordinated riders.

- ❑ To walk up to and stand motionless next to the ramp while several people hover over him to assist the rider in mounting.
- ❑ To learn to tolerate on his back different sizes and weights of riders.
- ❑ To carry imbalanced riders on his back who may jerk or have spasms against his sides.
- ❑ To walk and trot at varying paces with a handler leading him or next to him.
- ❑ To tolerate longeing with a rider and sidewalkers in both directions.
- ❑ To accept crutches, canes, wheelchairs and other objects against his side.
- ❑ And to accept all the hugs and kisses that a good therapeutic riding horse receives.

Prior to being used in an actual therapeutic riding session, the horse may be exposed to many activities and objects he has not previously encountered, such as a ball thrown around him, rings or toys placed on his rump and head, or placed on poles or into buckets, walking through obstacles or stopping facing signs. Some horses may not tolerate such activities but do very well with adult riders who are more concerned with developing balance or riding skills. The horse must also learn to adjust to the special riding tack needed for some riders. After the horse has learned to adjust and accept his new environment, he is ready for a rider from a wheelchair, with crutches or a walker. He needs to learn to expect jerking movements, sudden changes of pressure on his back, or possibly two people riding together. He may experience riders placed in unusual positions on his rump or shoulder. The riders may move from one position to another while the horse is walking. The horse needs to adjust to noises, a possible scream from a student or various kinds of music.

Many programs now participate in horse shows. Additional training for the horse will be needed to advance to this stage of riding. Trailering a horse has its own specific training and hauling problems. To keep the horse's confident, the staff and students going to the show must be well prepared and confident. Three to six weeks of daily training, beyond the initial introduction to program activities, is probably needed to develop a well-trained and safe therapeutic riding horse - a partner in the therapeutic riding team. A checklist of training goals is provided for you. The amount of training time depends on the horse, the skill of the instructor/trainer and the techniques used. Some horses may not be suited for disabled riders and must be returned to their donors or previous owners.

Therapeutic riding program horses are frequently handled by many people. Because there can be changes in horse managers, it is vitally important to maintain accurate records from the time the horse enters the program to the time the horse is retired. These records serve as a plan for management. A *HORSE HISTORY* that includes an analysis of the horse (page 148), the results of a pre-training schedule (page 206) and the new horse record (page 207), should be initiated when a horse enters the program. Information can be obtained from the previous owner, the vet check and observations. A *MAINTENANCE RECORD* (page 208) should be kept continuously, with all pertinent information regarding the horse. These forms provide the instructor with examples they can use or adapt.

References

Dorrance, T. (1987). *True Unity*. Tuscarora: Give-It-A-Go Enterprises.

Hunt, R. (1978). *Thinking Harmony with Horses*. Fresno: Pioneer Publishing Co.

Lyons, John; Browning, S. (1991). *Lyons on Horses*. New York: Doubleday

TT.E.A.M. News International, Edmonton. 1987-1990.

WHY IS REGULAR SCHOOLING OF THE THERAPEUTIC RIDING HORSE NECESSARY?

Barbara T. Engel, M.Ed, OTR

According to Dr. Nielsen of Michigan State University and Dr. Potter of Texas A&M, horse bones change through the years in size and shape. One understands that bones of a young horse change as they grow older. But bones of the older horse change too. Nielsen and Potter's research showed that stall-bound horses showed weaker bones. The stall-bound horse endures less stress that builds strength than the pasture-bound horse. They felt that horses asked to walk, trot and canter at slow speeds are also at risk. Some fast sprints are needed to stress the bones for horses to maintain the strength of their legs.

But, one might say therapeutic riding horses are not sport horses and do not endure heavy work. If you were to carry an unbalance load on your back while your partner carried a balanced load, who would be the first to tire on a trek through the wood? Our therapeutic riding horses carry many unbalanced riders during the day. Most persons with head injuries or neurological problems are asymmetrical and cause stress to the horse. It is generally agreed that any imbalanced rider causes an imbalance to the horse. Therapeutic riding horses are not light workers. They work hard at their jobs - some work many hours in one day at difficult tasks.

For horses to remain healthy, they need an experienced instructor/rider to rebalance and work them for short periods with faster gaits. This can be done both through riding and longeing. Longeing needs to be done in a training mode - not racing the horse around a circle, as frequently seen, and off balance. Lungeing in the field on an incline helps strengthen and rebalance the horse. During regular schooling, the horse is given a tune-up. He is relaxed, rebalanced, and allowed to stretch out and use his muscles at full strength. He needs to have his aids re-tuned since most riders are not experienced enough to use aids in a correct and light way in all three gaits. Lateral work is also important to maintain suppleness.

With correct schooling horses will stay healthy, responsive and enjoy their work. They will not become stiff from lack of balance and exercise, tuned out due to boredom and lack the ability to "read" their riders (by this, one means that horses can sense their riders' needs, rate of speed, lack of balance or need to rebalance. Some can even read the skill level of their rider.)

Regular schooling must be apart of any good therapeutic riding program. It is the good qualities of the horse's movements that transfers these qualities to the rider and produce the therapeutic effects which the person with disabilities seeks. This is especially true with horses used for physical or occupational therapy. If the therapist/horse has poor skills, the therapy will not be affective.

There are many ways this can be accomplished through the use of a Pony Club, a 4-H group or college students, or including intermediate riders as volunteers whose job it is to condition horses.

Reference:

Nielsen, BD., Raymond C. (1997). Help Your Horse Build Better Bones. *Horse Show,* July/August 1997 issue.

SCHOOLING THE THERAPEUTIC RIDING HORSE HOW TO USE ABLE BODIED RIDERS TO HELP PROGRAM ANIMALS STAY FIT AND HAPPY.

Sunny Pfifferling, BS

Many of us became acquainted with therapeutic riding because of our passion for horses. Often, in the course of carrying out treatment, we become so focused on the progress of our riders that we lose sight of the progress and maintenance of our horses. Those wonderful creatures that originally drew us to this field require ongoing schooling to keep them balanced, fit, responsive and mentally healthy.

How often and how much schooling really depends upon your program, your staff, and the level of training of each individual horse. The majority of horses in our program (Loveway*) work an average of one to four hours a day, five days a week. Most are in walk/trot classes; in therapeutic riding classes, they canter and jump on a limited basis, usually one to three classes a week. Not all of our horses are capable of, or are permitted to canter, or jump. Be realistic about your horse's physical condition, as well as their ability to carry your students safely. Not all horses who canter and jump make suitable therapeutic riding horses. Conversely, not all suitable therapeutic riding horses need to canter or jump.

We try to keep our horses schooled by competent riders twice a week. Some horses need less. Newer program horses require more. I feel it is most beneficial to alternate a schooling session in the arena with a relaxed hack outdoors. Methods of schooling will vary with your resources and your horse's needs: longeing, long-reining, ground driving and ponying can be utilized as well as work under saddle. This is especially beneficial for ponies too small to be ridden by an adult. I will not go into "how" to school the therapy horse, because you know the type of work and needs of all your horses. Each animal will need to be schooled individually. Basically, the purpose of schooling is to maintain the horse's fitness, responsiveness, obedience, balance and mental health. A horse that is properly schooled should be easy to handle by any of your students and volunteers.

TRAINING SCHEDULE

Sundance--FITNESS GOAL: 20 minutes of trot and canter with normal respiration

SCHOOLING GOALS:

1. Eliminate behavior problems during grooming, tacking and mounting
2. Eliminate head yanking while ridden
3. Maintain steady, slow trot rhythm
4. Developing a slow, balanced canter

Muri - FITNESS GOALS: 30 minutes of trot and canter work with normal respiration.

SCHOOLING GOALS:

1. Softening to rider's hand on turns and transitions
2. Voice response to walk on, whoa, trot and canter
3. Steady and quiet over cavalletti and small jumps

FIGURE 1.
HORSE NEEDS AND GOALS

Your methods will vary according to your program's goals as well as your horse's individual needs - there is no formula. It is valuable to keep a chart listing each horse's needs and training goals (Figure 1), and to update it annually as these goals are met.

Often a horse may develop an inappropriate behavior due to boredom, and you will need to indicate a short term goal of eliminating that behavior. Every schooling rider should be given a chart of "Horse Needs and Goals" (Figure 1); we also post one in the tack room. Schooling should be done at times when there are no therapeutic riding classes in session, unless it can be accomplished without distracting your program students. If your program is anything like ours, we never have the staff or time to keep our horses schooled adequately. Our first rule is never, never advertise that program volunteers can ride the horses for recreation. Allowing that to occur will undoubtably do damage to your horses. In addition your program's reputation for professionalism, not to mention your liability, may be threatened. You will find "volunteers" crawling out of the woodwork who would do you the great favor of exercising your horses. Usually these volunteers are of the teenage variety and are not interested in benefitting the horses as much as their own pleasure, and more than likely, cannot ride at all. PRINT IN YOUR VOLUNTEER TRAINING MANUAL THAT VOLUNTEERS ARE NOT PERMITTED TO RIDE, AND STATE YOUR REASONS. Make your position clear, and do not make exceptions. Volunteers are more easily replaced than ruined horses (Figure 2). It is most advisable to recruit competent schooling riders from outside your program. Adults are preferable for their reliability, judgement, and understanding of your program's needs. A good source is lesson barns - inquire if there are any intermediate or advanced students who would like additional riding time.

As you get to know your program volunteers, you may discover that some may be competent riders; find out what experience they have, and what their current level of riding is. If you feel confident that a volunteer would be a suitable schooling rider, talk to him or her privately about schooling for you and arrange a try-out session to evaluate his or her riding ability.

You may also submit an article to your local horse publications explaining your need for schooling riders, and the criteria required for acceptance. The more organized you portray your schooling rider program, the more serious and dedicated schooling riders you will attract. Be realistic with yourself: a novice rider, no matter how nice, is not going to be an effective schooling rider. They will usually do damage to your horses that you will need to un-do yourself.

Set up a time for try-outs; we use a combination of riding and written tests not only to weed out the unsuitable candidates, but also to evaluate riding styles so that our schooling assignments assure the best match-ups. Above all, make it clear to your potential schooling riders that they are doing a job that is vitally important to your program's success. They should be trained and monitored as extensively as your program volunteers. They also need to be understanding of how special your horses are, as well as of the type and amount of work they do.

Another schooling option that has worked for us is to recruit advanced level Pony Clubbers or 4H-ers to ride as a group in a weekly **supervised** schooling session. We found the advantages to be:
- ❑ Many of these children are small enough to school your smaller ponies
- ❑ The class will simulate an actual therapeutic class; problems that your program students encounter, such as a horse not staying on the rail while the others are parked in the middle, can be dealt with successfully by competent riders
- ❑ You can get a good number of horses/ponies schooled in a small amount of time
- ❑ Your program instructor should oversee each schooling session--and stress that it is not a riding lesson

You may find that there are some wonderful and dedicated people who are interested in being schooling riders, yet lack the necessary riding capabilities. As well as encouraging them to obtain riding instruction, you can still use these people in various functions, such as:

1. Ground work with horses:
   a. Body work, such as TT.E.A.M. work
   b. Schooling on the lead line
   c. Introducing new horses to wheelchairs, games, balls and so forth
   d. Ground driving, longeing
   e. Grooming, clipping, mane-pulling

2. "Under saddle" work at the walk only, such as:
   a. Teaching the horse to stand immobile while being mounted
   b. Teaching the horse to respond to verbal cues, such as walk on, whoa
   c. Teaching a horse to neck rein
   d. Assisting the instructor when introducing backriding, vaulting positions on the horse

---

SCHOOL RIDING POLICY

1. To help in decreasing Loveway's utility costs, and to give the horses and ponies a break from being ridden
   a. The barn will be closed at 9 pm in the evening
   b. The arena heaters are to be used by Loveway classes only
   c. The barn will be closed on weekends to all volunteers, students, and community service workers --some exceptions with prior board approval
2. Regarding Hartwood Pony Club:
   a. Hartwood PC shall not hold its monthly meetings at Loveway.
   b. Pony Club members shall be considered volunteers at Loveway, and agree.
      - That all schooling be done in supervised lessons under the instruction of Sunny or Marcia
      - That Pony clubbers agree to school Loveway horses/ponies specifically for Loveway's purpose and needs
      - That the supervised lessons be conducted every Monday night from 5:30 to 6:30pm
      - That all members wear boots and Pony Club approved helmets
      - That all members will school only the horses/ponies selected by Marcia and Sunny
3. Regarding Schooling Riders

   Definition: A schooling rider is a competent equestrian chosen by the Loveway staff to school and exercise Loveway horses/ponies selected by the Loveway staff. Schooling riders work to maintain the horses'/ponies' fitness, obedience, responsiveness, and to correct behavior problems:
   - That Loveway utilize Pony Club members as schooling riders on Monday night supervised lessons only.
   - That schooling riders must school, on staff-selected horse/pony each time they school, with the option of working with other horses if they desire in the time following on that day.
   - That schooling riders school at Loveway a minimum of once a week.
   - That Loveway staff increase or decrease the number of riders, depending on the need and subject to prior Board approval.
   - That any schooling rider may be dropped from the program following the disregard or written rules or endangerment to Loveway animals, facility or property.

FIGURE 2. SCHOOLING POLICY

Depending upon the number and types of horses and schooling riders you have, you may want either to assign riders to horses, or post a weekly list of horses to be schooled in priority of needs.

The ideal situation for schooling is to have your program's staff school the program horses. Since most programs do not have the time or staff available to accomplish this, it is vital to your horses' physical and mental health to keep them conditioned, responsive, and happy. Your staff, particularly the instructors, should work more extensively with the newer program horses. This is important for understanding their moods and movement, finding any hidden "holes" in them, and to prepare them specifically for their job as a therapeutic riding horse. Recruit as many schooling riders as you see the need for--realistically look at each horse's age, ability, level of training, fitness and workload and assign your schooling riders accordingly.

SCHOOLING RIDER LOG

Week of January 23-29

Horse	Name	Day	Time	Method	Place
Chantel	Marcia	1-23	12"30-2:00	hack	road
Cosby	Kelly	1-23	30 min	schooling	inside
Sundance	Sunny	1-24	7:00-8:00	longe	inside
Choker	Brace	1-24	5:30-6:30	lesson	inside
Ginger	Chris	1-24	5:30-6:00	schooling	inside

FIGURE 3

LOVEWAY SCHOOLING RIDER AGREEMENT

1. That the horses/ponies schooled be worked for Loveway's therapeutic riding program, and not for individual recreation.

2. That the schoolers work with the horse(s) listed in order first, and work option horse(s) afterward

3. That all schoolers wear Pony Club approved helmets, boots or shoes with heels at all times when riding.

4. That the horses are not ridden beyond the rider's capabilities unless properly instructed in a lesson.

5. That the priorities in schooling be:

   a. Maintaining safe and appropriate behavior (no nibbling, dragging, pushing leader or walker while being mounted)

   b. Maintaining obedience and responsiveness to voice aids before using physical aids (legs and hands).

   c. Maintaining the horse's responsiveness to turning, keeping steady pace, staying on the rail without using undue force (so that Loveway students can handle them easily).

   d. Correcting any habits or behaviors indicated (neck yanking, aggressiveness, not keeping pace).

   e. Reporting to the Loveway staff any problems, questions, or noted progress.

   f. Horses/ponies shall not be jumped any higher than 2 ft, and then only with prior consent.

I have read above agreement and understand it is my privilege to school the Loveway horses/ponies.

Signed_____

Parent/guardian if under 18 _____Date_____

FIGURE 4

The results of a successful schooling schedule will be evident in your therapeutic riding lessons: your students will be achieving their goals with the help of capable horses that are willingly doing their job. Good luck, and may you always have happy horses!

Figure 1, 2, 3, and 4 are samples of the paperwork use with our schooling riders. You will obviously want to adapt them to fit your individual program's needs.

LOVEWAY SCHOOL RIDING RULES

1. All schooling must be carried out at times when there are no classes in session at Loveway.
2. Schooling must be completed by 8:00 p.m.
3. Any schooling rider under age 18 must have a parent present at all times while at Loveway.
4. A commitment of once a week is requested.
5. Schoolers must work horses listed in order of priority.
6. No weekend schooling without prior board (Director's) approval.
7. No solo riding off Loveway premises.
8. No cantering or galloping outside of the arena, i. e., roads.
9. All horses schooled must be logged-in on the clip board.
10. All horses must be ridden in saddles and their own bridles.
11. All horses/ponies schooled must have at least 5 minutes of warm up and cool down at the walk.
12. All horses must be worked according to goals posted.
13. When schooling in the arena, plan on 20-60 minutes per horse.
14. Schooling riders are requested to make note of any lameness or problem discovered.
15. All schooling riders must wear Pony Club approved helmet with harness attached, long pants, boots or shoes with a heel.
16. All schooling riders must leave the barn, arena and tack room as they found it. When you are the last to leave the barn, please:
   1. Make sure all doors and gates are latched
   2. All lights are out except entrance floodlight
   3. Tack room door is locked
   4. Loveway front lobby doors must be kept unlocked

FIGURE 5.

SCHOOL RULES

* Loveway Inc, Bristol, IN

Sunny Pfifferling
USA

PART III
HUMAN DEVELOPMENT AND BEHAVIOR

CHAPTER 10
DEVELOPMENT

HUMAN GROWTH AND DEVELOPMENT

Barbara T. Engel, M.Ed, OTR

KEY WORDS

NORMAL
   FUNCTION
      DEVELOPMENT

In order to gain a good perspective of various disabilities, one needs to understand normal human function and development. This knowledge provides the background needed to understand the difference between normal and abnormal function. It provides the instructor with the framework required to understand parts of the body involved in a disability and helps the instructor to assist persons with the disabilities to work toward more normal skills. Part III will help provide the reader with an overview of normal function and development and the terms involved, followed by a brief description of many disabilities in (Part IV) that are seen in therapeutic riding programs.

Part III will cover:
- Growth and development
- The skeleton
- Anatomy as it relates to riding
- The central nervous system
- The integration of the nervous system
- The psychological systems.

It is not the intent here to give a course in anatomy and physiology. This manuscript would be unable to cover the in-depth subject due to limited space. This is not to say, however, that an understanding of normal human function and movement is not important when working with any rider. Sally Swift (1985) and Mary Midkiff (1996) have explained in detail the importance of understanding the human structure and its relationship to riding: how the human body is positioned in order to balance and be in rhythm with the horse. In addition, it is especially important to understand the anatomy of riders with disabilities so that one can help and not hinder the rider. To provide the instructor and staff the technical information regarding a particular rider and his or her specific disability, occupational and/or physical therapists are included as consultants, or full time members of therapeutic riding programs, for they have the knowledge to assess a client with various disabilities.

Areas of the anatomy which riding relates will be briefly covered. Any instructor must have an understanding of the anatomy of the rider (along with the anatomy of the horse) in order to achieve the harmony of horse and rider. The instructor must be able to *"communicate to the student what should be felt on the horse. It is a problem of recognition and understanding. Accurate and useful images can then be developed"* (H.Schusdziarra, V. Schusdziarra 1985.) In addition to the general knowledge of the structure of the human body, one must be aware of areas which are directly related to the populations who are "at risk" or "physically fragile."

It is also important to have a basic knowledge of those growth and developmental aspects which relate directly to the learning process, to neurological disorders and to developmental disabilities. This knowledge helps the instructor to connect appropriately to riders with various sorts of psychological, neurological involvement or developmental delays.

Growth refers to the increase in size of the structure of the human body. This would include the size of the head and body bones, height of the structure and weight of the body (Banus et al1979). Growth can be increased by good nutrition, bonding, stimulation, and exercise or it can decrease by internal or external causes, such as disease, malnutrition, lack of nurturing, trauma, drugs, abuse, or other factors (Banus et al 1979).

Progression of growth and development occurs on two basic levels.
1. **Phylogenetic** (inherited) development involves structural changes such as cell division to develop into a complex multi cell organism, dependent on its genetic pool or species origin as in all more primitive creatures.
2. **Ontogenetic** development is the progressive and sequential behavioral change that occurs by the individual's experiences within his or her environment and by his or her cultural inferences (Banus et al 1979).

The central nervous system (CNS) receives, assimilates and responds to information it receives. Maturation and myelination of the nervous system increase the speed of messages transmitted and the resulting action of the transmission. The function of the CNS gives the human the ability to move and perform skills while maintaining one's posture and equilibrium against gravity (K. Bobath 1980). *"There is thus a continuously changing environment with a continuously changing organism, a closed loop of four elements: skeleton, muscles, nervous system, and environment,"* with feedback and feed-forward throughout all systems (Feldenkrais 1981). The nervous system needs to be stimulated to develop. Development is dependent on the ability to move. *"Only active movement can give the sensation essential for learning voluntary movements and skills"* (K. Bobath 1980). Movement stimulation needs to be purposeful in order to be registered by the brain for an adaptive response since the brain only *learns* with meaningful activities (Masuda 1988, Oetter 1987).

Recent research has found that the brain develops microscopic connections in response to specific stimulation. In the first month of life, the number of synapses will increase 20-fold, to more than a trillion, in response to stimuli in the infant's environment. Each experience - rocking, being read to, cuddling, visually following a simple object, being spoken to makes a microscopic connection in the brain. Experience wires the circuits. Researchers report the difference of a healthy baby's brain scan to deprived Romanian orphans - many areas of their deprived brains are not developed and these children will later suffer both emotional and cognitive problems. (Newsweek Special Edition, Spr./Sum 1997). The brain's basic structure develops within the first three years. Research has found that development lessens with age and areas not stimulated wither away. By 12 months, the auditory map is formed. The amount of language a child hears from another person will influence his/her own language. It was found that the spoken words on TV come across more like noise. If the experience is not related to an event that involves emotions and meaning the brain's connections are not as strong. The feedback the infant gets - she smiles and gets a smile back - develops synapses. The brain is also affected by trauma. Trauma produces hormones that can cause damage to brain cells or scramble connections.

Functional movement stimulation evokes more alertness and provides more comfort to the child than contact without movement. Movement increases motor behavior, visual and auditory alertness (Korner 1984). Movement increases the respiratory capacity which in turn increases alertness (Oetter 1987). Movement may be necessary to enable all living things to form their exterior object world (Feldenkrais 1981). Feldenkrais point out the need to be *AWARE* of one's movements in order to learn and make choices, *"by shifting our attention to the means of achieving instead of the urge to succeed, the learning process is easier"* and alternative choices can be made.

If the nervous system has not developed to a certain point, a given skill will not develop and cannot be taught. For example, an infant will creep only when his or her nervous system has developed to the point that this can occur. Skills develop in a sequential manner: rolling, sitting with hand support, sitting with hands free to play, kneeling, standing holding on, walking holding on, then standing free with good balance. Though **skills cannot be taught to an immature nervous system**, the nervous system in a fostering environment can be stimulated to help it to adapt and mature (Lawther 1968).

Early handling of infants and the bodily contact of caregivers are necessary for the development of touch and emotional bonding in children. This give and take interaction between mothers/caregivers and infants is also the beginning of language development. A mothers/caregiver, who talks a lot to the child, produces a child with increased language of similar sentence structure. Touch and proprioceptive feedback begins four months after conception at which time fetuses suck their thumbs, touch their bodies and presses against the uterine wall (Almi 1985). After birth, the babies put their fingers into their mouths and progressively touch all parts of their bodies as mobility increases (K. Bobath 1980). The infants begin to touch and move, to see and explore their environment, as they begin to become more proficient in mobility.

As infants move their arms, their hands come into their visual field which climaxes at three months of age, and the beginning of *eye-hand connection* begins. As they feel their body parts, they develop *body perception* or "a feeling of themselves as a unity separate from their environment" (K. Bobath 1980). As *body perception* is developed, infants begin to relate themselves to the environment around them and *spatial orientation begins*. *Body images* develop when infants develop a visual image themselves which are separate from the environment. From the research of the institutionalized Romanian babies, this development does not develop at a normal rate without the stimulation and interaction of others.

Development and learning are dependent on maturation of the CNS. Learning and development can be differentiated as follows (Banus et al 1979):
DEVELOPMENT:
  a. Development results from genetic endowment with experience in the species milieu
  b. Developmental tasks, such as self feeding, are dependent on the maturation of the CNS in a sequence
     from simple to complex movements
  c. Development attempts to maintain a stable internal condition (self preservation)
  d. Development requires action on the environment such as maintaining sitting balance when tilted off balance
  e. As development progresses, performance increases to more difficult tasks such as walking rather than creeping.

LEARNING:
  a. Learning is dependent on environmental influences which guide the individual's potential such as eating with a spoon
     and fork
  b. Learning involves coping with requirements of the external environment
  c. Learning is knowing that certain surfaces will require balance--learning from past experience
  d. Learning is watching others and copying their actions
  e. Learning can be forgotten. Knowledge is not permanent.

Maturation of the Central Nervous System (CNS) is influenced by:
  ❑   WHAT INFORMATION THE INDIVIDUAL TAKES IN.
  ❑   HOW INFORMATION IS INTEGRATED.
  ❑   WHAT OCCURS WITH THE INFORMATION TAKEN IN.
  ❑   WHAT ACTIONS THE INDIVIDUAL MAKES ON HIS ENVIRONMENT.

The CNS synthesizes feedback from actions from both internal and external sources and coordinates appropriate data from memory of prior experience. Synthesis and coordination lead to development of perceptual skills and learning. Ayres has noted that input through the touch system increases arousal and the ability to *motor plan* one's actions (the active performance of a skilled task with one's limbs) (Sensory Integration International, 1990). Affolter (1990) states that touch sensation must be felt accurately, registered and interpreted by the brain to be useful in the adaptive process in response to the environment. Feldenkrais cites an experiment in which a group of people used eyeglasses which inverted the image on the brain so all the participants saw everything upside down. Everything they touched began to look normal, but what they did not touch continued to be inverted (Feldenkrais 1981). THERE IS CONSIDERABLE EVIDENCE SUGGESTING THE IMPORTANCE OF TOUCH, AS IT IS FULLY INTERPRETED BY THE BRAIN, IN THE DEVELOPMENT OF MOVEMENT, LEARNING AND INTERRELATIONSHIPS OF THE BODY TO THE ENVIRONMENT.

Changes in posture produce changes of the body's relation to gravity. The body must adapt to changes in the environment by making fluid changes of postural tone of groups of body muscles in order to prevent falling. This is called *dynamic equilibrium* since the body is never totally still. There is an interaction of muscle groups which causes one group of muscles to flex and others to extend. This, for example, allows us to walk. There must be enough tension in the muscle tone to allow the body to stand or sit against the pull of gravity of the earth. The tension must fluctuate to allow for intended and controlled movement.

Body postural reflexes and reactions are automatic mechanisms which allow groups of muscles to react together to maintain *equilibrium* in posture. "The reflexes were found to contribute to maintaining the characteristic orientation of the body in space with respect to gravity (labyrinthine reflexes) and with respect to the interrelationship of the body parts (tonic neck and righting reflexes) (Capute 1978)." These body reactions are present throughout normal life and may be easily observed during physical exertion. These reactions differ in characteristic from "primitive reflexes" which are observed in normal infants' development through the first six months of life. "The persistence of **primitive reflexes** beyond the newborn period has long been a classic sign of a central nervous system dysfunction (Capute 1978)."

Some postural reflexes and reactions which are commonly known are:
1. *Protective reactions* are active in all directions to protect the body from injury. For example, placing the hands out front of oneself to prevent falling forward after stumbling or losing balance forward.
2. *Neck righting reactions* help to maintain head control and an upright body position against gravity. The body follows where the head goes.
3. *Tonic neck reflex*--there are two:
    Symmetrical tonic neck reflex is present when the head is brought forward, causing the upper extremity to bend and the lower extremity to straighten.
    Asymmetrical tonic neck reflex is present when the head turns to the side (to look), the arm and leg on the chin side straighten, the arm and leg on the hair side, bend
4. *Body righting on the head occurs when* the body aligns itself with the head against gravity.
5. *Optical righting* assists upright posture against gravity using the eyes as the main control.
6. *Equilibrium reactions* are automatic responses to the change of posture and movement to maintain balance against gravity using any or all of the above reactions to maintain balance.

Postural reactions mature and integrate in the normal person though they always remain present. These responses do not interfere with voluntary movements as they can be inhibited at will and support intentional movements. Maturation of the CNS and the consequences of growth in all areas of human development during the infant and childhood ages are a major focus by many investigators, but not so for the older age groups. Assuming normal growth and development continues through adolescence, the body continues to grow and refine its abilities to respond to its environment. It was once thought that growth and maturation of the CNS were completed at the time of adolescence, and there was a general deterioration of the nervous system in later years. Evidence indicates that this is not the case. There is reason to believe that constructive changes may occur in the brain into the seventies (Oppenheim 1981). Man has enormous adaptive capabilities to adjust to injury or illness, but one must understand, as an instructor, what the functional implications is that result from such trauma.

References
Affolter, A. (1990). *The Use of Guiding as a Perceptual Cognitive Approach*. Course notes. Santa Barbara.
Almi, C.R. (1985). Normal sequential behavior and physiological changes throughout the development arc: in Banus, B.S.; el al *The Developmental Therapist*. 2nd ed.Thorofare, Charles B. Slack, Inc. 1-163.

Begley, S. (1997). How to Build a Baby's Brain. NewWeek Special Issue, Spring/Summer.

Bobath, K. (1980). A Neurophysiological Basis for the Treatment of Cerebral Palsy. In *Clinics in Developmental Medicine No 75.* Philadelphia, J.P. Lippincott Co. vii, 1-2, 5.

Brunnstrom, S. (1972). *Clinical Kinesiology.*3rd edition. Philadelphia, F.A. Davis Co. 242-250.

Capute, A. J.; Accardo, P.J.; et. al., (1978). *Primitive Reflexe Profile.* Baltimore: Univ Park Press.

Erhardt, R.P. (1982). *Developmental Hand Dysfunction.* Laurel, Ramsco Publishing Co.

Feldenkrais, M. (1981). *The Elusive Obvious.* Cupertino: Meta Publications.

Knobloch, H, Stevens, F. Malone, M. (1980). *Manual of Developmental Diagnosis* Hagerstown: Harper & Row.

Korner, A.F. (1984). *National Center for Clinical Infants.* "Zero to three". V,1. Sept.1-6.

Lawther, J.D. (1968). *The Learning of Physical Skills.* Englewood Cliff: Prentice-Hall Inc.

Masuda, D.L. (1988). Integrated Approach to Treatment. In *Rehab '88, The Moment of Truth*, Abby Medical Conf. Los Angeles.

Midkiff, MD. (1996). *Fitness, Performance and the Female Equestrian.*New York: Howell Book House.

Oetter, P. (1988). Las Vegas NM. Sensory System Course Notes.

Oppenheim, R.W. (1981). Ontogenetic Adaptions and Retrogressive Processes in the Development of the Nervous System and Behavior: A Neuroembryological Perspective. in Connolly, K.J. & Prechtl, H.F. ed: *Maturation and Development: Biological and Psychological Perspectives*

Piaget, J. (1963). *The Origins of Intelligence in Children.* New York, W.W. Norton & Co.

Pulaski, M.A.: (1980). *Understanding Piaget.* New York, Harper & Row.

Schusdziarra, H., Schusdziarra, V. (1985). *An Anatomy of Riding* Briarcliff, Breakthrough Publications. 2-35.

Sensory Integration International. (1990). Sensory Integration Treatment Course notes. Los Angeles.

Shortridge, S.D. (1985). The developmental process: prenatal to adolescence. In Clark, P.N.; Allen, A.S. *Occupational Therapy for Children.* St Louis, C.V. Mosby Co. 48-63.

Swift, S. (1985). *Centered Riding.* North Pomfret: David & Charles. 32-49.

Umphred, D.A., editor: *Neurological Rehabilitation.* St. Louis, C.V. Mosby Co. 61-63.

A BIRDS EYE VIEW OF THE PHYSICAL DEVELOPMENT OF THE INFANT

Barbara T. Engel, MEd, OTR & Stephanie C. Woods, BFA

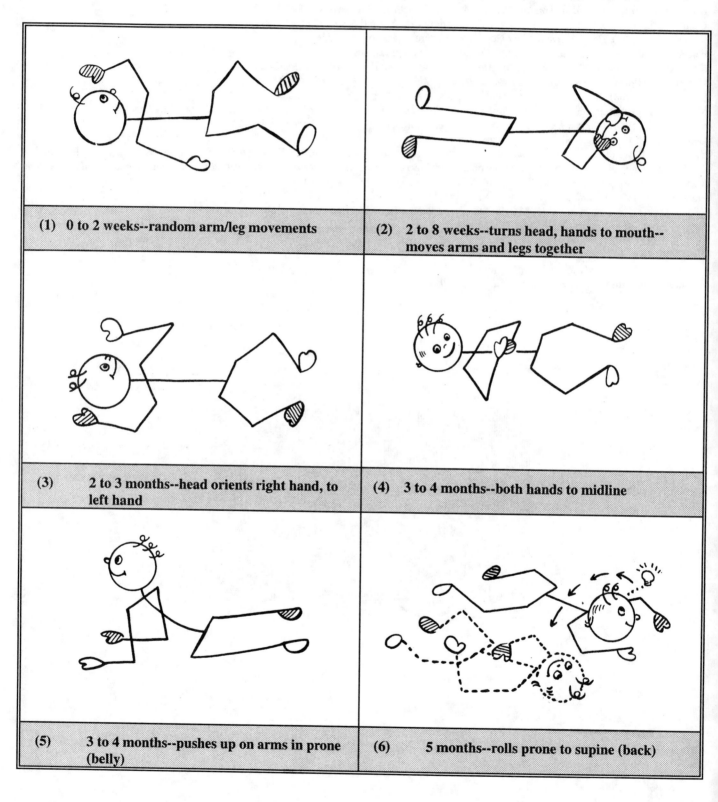

(1) 0 to 2 weeks--random arm/leg movements

(2) 2 to 8 weeks--turns head, hands to mouth--moves arms and legs together

(3) 2 to 3 months--head orients right hand, to left hand

(4) 3 to 4 months--both hands to midline

(5) 3 to 4 months--pushes up on arms in prone (belly)

(6) 5 months--rolls prone to supine (back)

(7)   6 month--sits with support of hands

(8)   7 months--pivots in prone position

(9)   7 months--hand-eye connection develops

(10) 8 months--protective support reaction develops

(11) 7 to 9 months--crawls on belly or hands and
       knees

(12)   9 months--pulls self to stand holding on

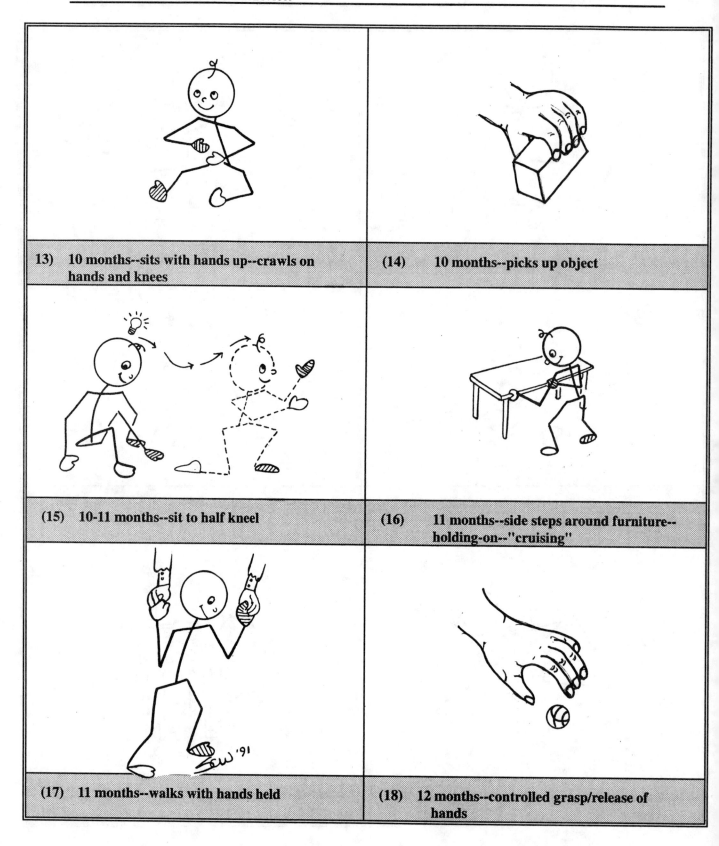

13) **10 months--sits with hands up--crawls on hands and knees**

(14) **10 months--picks up object**

(15) **10-11 months--sit to half kneel**

(16) **11 months--side steps around furniture-- holding-on--"cruising"**

(17) **11 months--walks with hands held**

(18) **12 months--controlled grasp/release of hands**

(19)   12 to 13 months--takes a few steps alone

(20)   15 months--walks well

(21)   18 months--up stairs--holding on

(22)   19 months--get up to stand alone

(23)   23 months - climbs into chair

(24)   2 years - runs well

(25) **2 years - kicks ball**

(26) **2½ to 3 years - walks up/down**

(27) **3-4 years - jumps well**

(28) **5 years - stands on one foot**

CHAPTER 11
HUMAN ANATOMY

HUMAN SKELETON

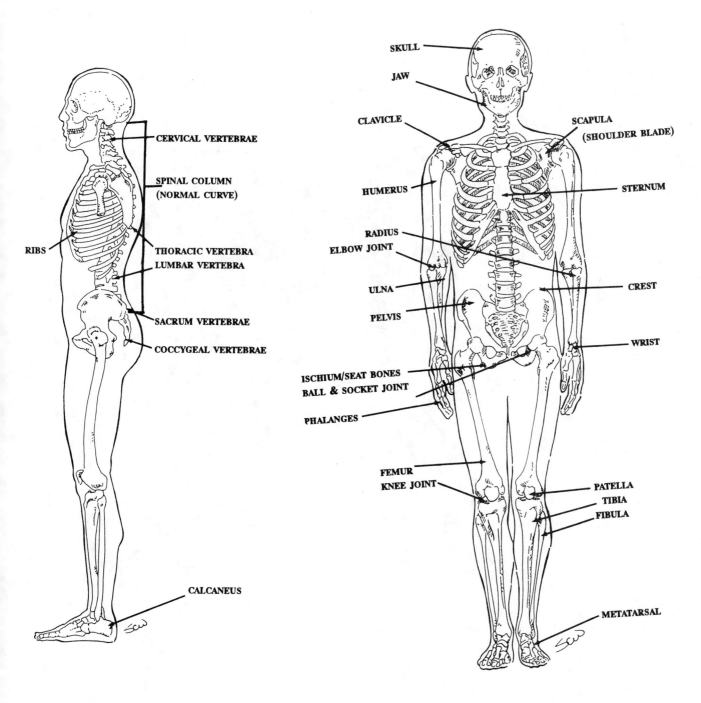

CERVICAL VERTEBRAE

SPINAL COLUMN
(NORMAL CURVE)

RIBS

THORACIC VERTEBRA
LUMBAR VERTEBRA

SACRUM VERTEBRAE

COCCYGEAL VERTEBRAE

CALCANEUS

SKULL

JAW

CLAVICLE

HUMERUS

RADIUS
ELBOW JOINT

ULNA

PELVIS

ISCHIUM/SEAT BONES
BALL & SOCKET JOINT

PHALANGES

FEMUR
KNEE JOINT

SCAPULA
(SHOULDER BLADE)

STERNUM

CREST

WRIST

PATELLA
TIBIA
FIBULA

METATARSAL

HUMAN SKELETON ↔↔ HORSE SKELETON
Understanding how one relates to the other-

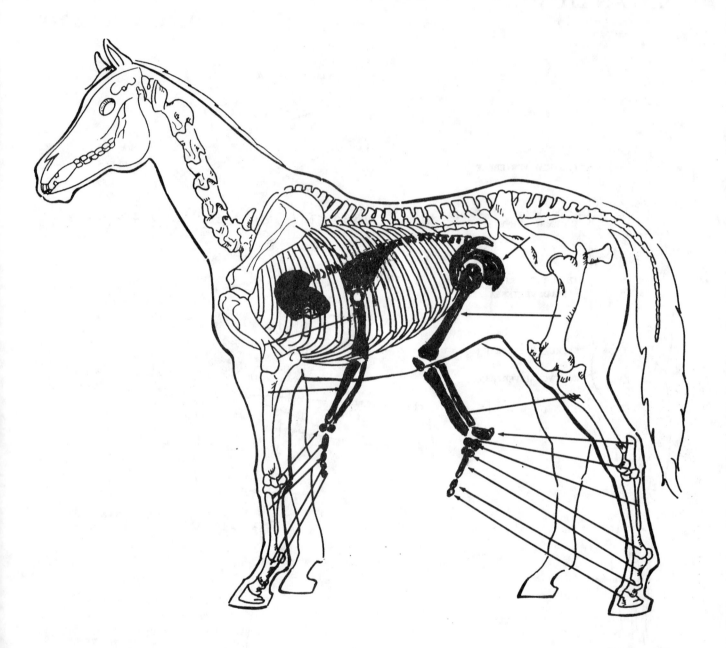

HUMAN ANATOMY AS IT RELATES TO THERAPEUTIC RIDING

Barbara T. Engel, MEd, OTR

The description that follows relates to the adult skeleton. The skeleton of the infant and child changes as the child grows. One must be careful to address the infant - less than three years, the child and adult skeleton in proper perspective.

The spinal or vertebral column is the major supporting part of the skeleton and is composed of 33 vertebrae: seven cervical vertebrae form the neck; the chest area has 12 thoracic vertebrae; the lower back has five lumbar vertebrae; and the sacrum five (fused) vertebrae, and four (fused) coccygeal vertebrae that makes up the tail bone. Looking at the skeleton from the side-view, the spine curves forward through the neck and waist region where it is more flexible. It curves backward at the upper back and the tail bone or sacrum. In a resting or neutral position, the normal spine does not curve from side to side. Between each vertebra, there is a disc which acts as a buffer from jolts received from movement. There is a balance and flexibility to the normal spine which allows for support and a spring reaction (H. Schuszdziarra; V. Schusdziarra 1985). It also allows for stability, mobility and movements in all directions of the torso. Mobility includes rotation, lateral bending, extension and forward flexion. Muscles are attached to the bones by tendons. Ligaments attach bones to bones, holding the spine together, and allowing the spine to move with other parts of the body. Additional stability is provided by the rib cage as ribs are attached to the vertebral bodies by ligaments and muscles. Bones are held together at the joints with ligaments.

The shoulder girdle consists of the clavicle (collar bone) and the scapula (shoulder bone). The humerus (upper bone of the arm) is joined by tendons and ligaments to the scapula. The clavicle attaches to the scapula at one end and the sternum at the level of the 7th vertebra. The shoulder can move up-down, forward-backward, and rotate in a circle.

The sacrum is joined to the pelvis by strong ligaments. The ischial tuberosities (seat bones) of the pelvic bone can be felt through the buttocks and form, along with the pubic bone, the bones that carry the body weight when a person is correctly sitting in the saddle. The bridge of the pelvis between the spine and seat allows a cushioning, springy effect between the two (Swift, 1985). The top edge of the pelvis can be felt below the waist and is the iliac crest.

On each side of the pelvis, below the iliac crest is a round hollow. The ball-like head of the thigh bone (femur) fits into this hollow. The joint is called a ball and socket joint. The weight of the entire body is distributed into the pelvis through these two joints while a person stands. In sitting, the pelvis can tip to the front or to the back, rocking on the seat bones which are rounded. The seat bones are further apart when rocking backward, allowing for extension of the hip joint and a deeper seat in the saddle. When the seat bones rock forward, the hip joint flexes and the legs come together causing the seat to become shallow. The structure of these bones allow the pelvis to rock side to side or back and forth (H. Schusdziarra & V. Schusdziarra 1985).

The male and female skeletons are different and this affects how each sits in the saddle (Figure 1 & 2), and the fit of a saddle to the female and male seat. The size of the twist of the saddle for the male may be different than for the female and will affect how the thighs hang along the side of the horse. This difference in anatomy is due to the manner in which humans bear their children. The female pelvis is naturally wider and deeper with a more circular pelvic outlet. Female seat bones (ischia) diverge to the rear and the tail bone (sacrum) and tends to tip toward the back. The position of the seat bones inhibits the female pelvis from rocking back and forth freely. The male pelvis is narrower with the seat bones nearly parallel allowing them to rock back and forth with ease. These differences make it easier for a man to sit with his seat "under" him as his pelvis naturally wants to tilt to the back. The female pelvis naturally wants to tilt to the front causing her to sit more on the pubis rather than the sacrum, making women more likely to sit a "crotch" seat. The "crotch seat" tends to throw the female forward and she must learn to compensate for this natural tendency and sit back to place her spine in a nurtural and balanced position in line with the center of gravity of the horse. Due to these differences, men tend to have less and women have more of a lumbar curve (Bennett

1989; Harris 1985). Walsh (1996) points out that the female's hormonal changes will cause changes in the joints, increase pain and laxness of joints.

The more the pelvic bones, the spine and other parts of the skeleton are in balance; the more relaxed the muscles that cover them (Swift 1985). This allows a person to move dynamically with the movement of the horse. "With the decreased tension of the muscles, the rider sits more at ease on the moving horse, the pelvis accommodating itself to the swaying up-and-down motion of the horse's back" (Schusdziarra & Schusdziarra, 1985). It can then follow the motion of the horse. Bones come together at the joints. Most joints are sites of movement. The degree of movement is determined by the combined structure of the joint, ligaments, tendons, muscles and connective tissues. The legs hang from the ball and socket hip joint to the side of the body. The femur (thigh bone) protrudes from the socket joint out to the side (the "neck") like an upside down "L" before it drops down toward the knee joint.

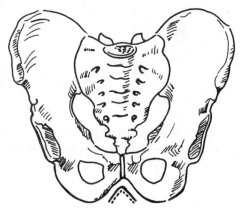

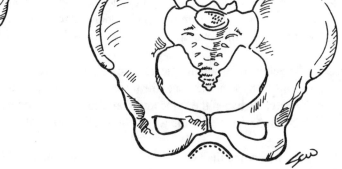

FIGURE 1. MALE PELVIS   FIGURE 2. FEMALE PELVIS

The neck of the femur forms a 125-degree angle with the shaft in men, less of an angle with the shaft in women (Brunnstrom 1972). The neck of the femur, which is two to three inches in length, give the legs an increased ability to straddle the horse (Swift 1985). Because of the different structure of the pelvis and the change in the angle of the neck of the femur, the leg of the female hangs with the knee pointed out more than the male, while the male foot hangs flat and the female foot is angled inward (Goss 1966; Bennett 1989). Prior to and during the middle of the menstrual period the woman may experience more pain and laxness of the joints due to the increase in her hormone level. These changes may affect the woman's seat and her ability to "put the leg on" (Walsh 1996).

The spinal or vertebral column houses the spinal cord extending from within the skull bones to the first or second lumbar vertebrae. The spinal cord is a part of the central nervous system (CNS). The central nervous system is a communication system that includes the brain as the main computer, the spinal cord as the main trunk line and a system of nerves through which the brain communicates with the muscles and vital organs. The central nervous system relays information through sense organs: receptors of the skin, bones, joints, muscles, eyes, ears, nose, tongue, inner ear and the internal organs. All systems are interrelated to some extent, some more than others. The CNS distributes impulses which activate muscles and cause movement patterns. Movement produces change in the entire organism (Feldenkrais 1981).

The skeletal system begins to develop as the fetus grows and progresses as the human body gains size. Major maturity begins between 14 and 15 years in girls and 15 and 16 years in boys with complete maturity occurring at about 25 years. <u>Bone formation in the early years is incomplete; it is composed of cartilage and can be fragile</u> (Raney & Brashear 1971). Normal children under four years may not have joint unions in areas of their body which could be affected by their position on the horse. Children who are affected by problems in development of any kind may have the completion of their bone structure delayed (Royer, 1974).

Instructors must be aware that the angle a joint assumes could be affected by positioning and by stress against the horse, which could have a lifelong influence upon the individual. Instructors must consult with a therapist or physician, who is both knowledgeable in the use of the horse and its effect on small children, prior to putting a small child on a horse. In addition, the size and the gait of the horse becomes an important consideration with a young rider, especially one with any kind of orthopedic disorder or delayed development whose *bone age* may be younger then his or her chronological age. REMEMBER that THE RHYTHM OF A CHILD IS DIFFERENT FROM THE RHYTHM OF AN ADULT. CHILDREN, GENERALLY, CANNOT ACCOMMODATE THE LONG STRIDES OF AN AVERAGE TO LARGE HORSE. IN GERMANY, SWITZERLAND, AND AUSTRIA, ONE FREQUENTLY SEES THE USE OF SMALL HORSES - SUCH AS THE NEW FORREST, CONNEMARE AND HAFLINGER. (See Dr. Ingrid Strauss's book *Hippotherapy 1995* where one can see the majority of children being treated are on Haflingers.) These breeds are horses, but small, and with a good over-stride; their strides accommodate well to a child's rhythm. They are not ponies in the sense of their structural conformation. **One must also remember that horseback riding is not for everyone.**

CONCLUSION

When the instructor has a visual image of the skeletal form of his or her student on the horse (Figure 3), he or she will be better able to understand how to manipulate the horse to gain a balanced seat. Remember, bones are connected by ligaments, tendons, and connective tissue, and muscles are the movers of the bones. Some preparation is necessary to prepare the ligaments, tendons and muscles for the exercise they receive while horseback riding. Persons who are out of physical condition, getting limited exercise, having more than average high tonal or low tonal qualities are more in need of warm-ups and stretching than the average person. Preparation is always necessary in any athletic endeavor. As in all riding, from a simple trail ride to competitive sports, the first and most important point to consider are the ability of the rider to sit in a relaxed frame on the horse. Without the relaxed frame, the rider will not gain the essential benefits from the horse - be this an able-bodied rider or one of our riders in a therapeutic riding setting.

References:
Bennett, D. (1989). Who's Built Best to Ride. in *Equus*, 140, June. Equus Magazine. Boulder, Co. 58-63,112-115.
Brunnstrom, S. (1972). *Clinical Kinesiology*. 3rd edition. Philadelphia: F.A. Davis Co. 227-228.
Feldenkrais, M. (1981). *The Elusive Obvious*. Cupertino: Meta Publications.
Goss, C.M. (1966). *Gray's Anatomy of the Human Body*. ed 28. Philadelphia: Lea & Febiger. 222-245.
Harris, C. (1985). *Fundamentals of Riding*. London: A. J. Allen.
Keim, H.A., Hensinger, R.N. Spinal Deformities. in *Clinical Symposia*. West Calwell: Ciba-Geigy. 3-4.
Midkiff, MD. (1996). *Fitness, Performance and the Female Equestrian*, NY, Howell Book House.
Raney & Brashear. (1971). *Shands' Handbook of Orthopaedic Surgery*. St. Louis: C.V. Mosby Co. 2-7.
Royer, P. (1974). *Scientific Foundation of Paediatrics*. Philadelphia: W.B. Saunders Co. 376-399.
Schusdziarra, H., Schusdziarra, V. (1985) *An Anatomy of Riding* Briarcliff, Breakthrough Publications. 2-35.
Swift, S. (1985). *Centered Riding*. North Pomfret: David & Charles. 32-34.
Walsh, MB. (1996). The Female Rider in Midkiff, *Different in Fitness, Performance and the Female Equestrian*, NY., Howell Book House.

**RIDER ON HORSE
FIGURE 3.**

CHAPTER 12
THE CENTRAL NERVOUS SYSTEM

INTRODUCTION TO THE CENTRAL NERVOUS SYSTEM

Barbara T. Engel, M.Ed, OTR

Most people have experienced, either by themselves or by those that serve them, what happens when "the computer is down." Nothing! Communication is lost. Whatever one was working on, or wished to order, could not be done. Yet, those persons operating the computer are intact. The operator is much like the heart. When the heart goes, all function ceases. But, if the computer goes, the ability to function is still there, but the method to send messages is gone. The computer is much like the central nervous system. This text will only present an <u>overview</u> of the central nervous system to give the reader a general idea of how these systems function. A working knowledge of the central nervous system involves extensive study and is best obtained through university courses on the subject. Occupational and physical therapists with a strong neurological background have knowledge on these subjects.

The nervous system has been divided into two sections: The central part which lies within a bony structure; the peripheral section that reaches beyond the bony structure. We can compare this to the computer, the hardware (central nervous system) and the Internet (the peripheral.) To use the computer to interact with others, both systems must work well.

THE CENTRAL PART OF OUR NERVOUS SYSTEM CONSISTS OF:

THE SPINAL CORD	**THE CEREBELLUM**
☞ CERVICAL LEVELS- C1,C2,C3,C4,C5,C6,C7	THE BRAIN STEM
☞ THORACIC LEVELS- T1,T2,T3,T4,T5,T6,T7,T8, T9,T10, 11,T12	☞ MEDULLA
☞ LUMBAR LEVELS- L1,L2, L3,L4,L5	☞ PONS
☞ SACRAL LEVELS- S1,S2,S3,S4,S5	☞ MIDBRAIN
☞ COCCYGEAL LEVEL	

THE CEREBRUM - THE BRAIN
☞ TWO HEMISPHERES (EACH HAS SIX LOBES)
- ☞ FRONTAL LOBE
- ☞ PARIETAL LOBE
- ☞ OCCIPITAL LOBE
- ☞ CENTRAL
- ☞ TEMPORAL LOBE
- ☞ LIMBIC

Each section and part of the nervous system addresses specific functions but also influences other functions. In other words, there is a great deal of interrelationship of all parts of the nervous system. To function well, all parts must work well together. The spinal level produce primitive levels of function. They elicit primitive protective responses. The brainstem involves regulatory of muscle tone, gravitational and postural muscles adjustments, righting reactions, and voluntary and involuntary motor activity. The cerebrum deals with the higher levels of function.

Function at each level interacts with levels both above and below and through the peripheral nervous system. In this way, one part of the central nervous system influences the function of another part.

Each spinal nerve is distributed to a specific region of the body. An injury to a level of the spinal cord will reduce or eliminate function below that level. For example, a complete spinal cord injury at the C5-C6 level causes paralysis below the nipple level of the body and eliminates the ability of the hand to move.

The peripheral nervous system resembles a cable of connecting telephone lines. They are composed of cranial and spinal nerves and their branches. The function of the nervous system is to receive, assimilate and act on information. The nervous system picks up stimuli or stimulate muscles. Damage to a part of the peripheral nerves will result in weakness, decreased reflexes, and/or sensation. The streams of impulses conveyed by the peripheral nerves from both internal and external environments are the sources of information that is fed to the central nervous system. It is through these systems that we feel and react to such senses as touch, sight, sound, smell and taste. Interpretations may include warmth, cold, pain, itching, wetness, tickling, malaise, well-being, and position. These sensations can have many variations. Individuals with injuries to the nervous system and with nervous systems that have been poorly developed for numerous reasons can misinterpret such sensations as touch - soft can be hard, warm can be cold or painful. The lack of appropriate interpretation has nothing to do with "knowing what is right," the interpretation is occurring within the nervous system.

The following articles will give the reader more detail, though still very basic knowledge, into areas of importance for therapeutic riding instructors.

THE BRAIN

John H. Brough, OTR
Edited by B. Engel

KEY WORDS

Right hemisphere
↕ Integration of hemispheres
Left hemisphere

A person would find it inconceivable to go to a lawyer who had never studied law, or to a dentist who had never studied the anatomy of teeth. Unfortunately, children are sent to school and are taught by people who have never studied the brain or its function in academic learning. It is not necessary for a teacher to be a neurosurgeon. He/she does need to have a basic understanding of the brain's function, such as how integration of fine and gross motor input, perception, long and short term memory is accomplished, and the methods for getting this information back out so that it is useable. This absence of basic understanding of the brain's function is due in part to the schism between the medical and educational communities. The result of the work that has been done in brain research has been reported in technical terms that may not be familiar to teachers and parents resulting in a lack of understanding. Yet, it is a fundamental need!

The brain is essentially a small but highly a sophisticated computer. It responds to stimuli that are presented to it and by making choices. These choices are decided by the kind of information being fed in. This information is compared to that already stored and accessible. The information enters the brain through the various sensory channels which include, but are not limited to; touch, taste, sight, hearing, movement and smell. In actuality, there are eight major pathways to the brain with at least 23 smaller routes. All of these feed information to the "computer" which during the first three years develops new wiring in the brain. Most of these paths travel to the brain via the **spinal cord**, enter the **brain stem,** or enter the brain through sight and hearing mechanisms. As they ascend to the highest levels of the brain, they pass through three basic brain levels. These levels originated as the brain developed through time. The first level is essentially the same as the brain of a reptile, the **brain stem**. This area is concerned with protecting the organism, maintaining respiration and heart beat and is complete at birth. The second level of the brain through which the information passes is the filtering mechanism called the **medulla oblongata**. It decides which information needs to go to the higher brain centers and which information can be dealt with at lower levels. The highest level of brain function is the **cortex (cerebellum)**.

This area receives messages from the sense organs, thinks, and among other things, sends messages to the muscles. Located here is control of conscious movement, speech, writing, and thoughts and feelings. Synaptogenesis of the motor cortex begins during the second month after birth. To learn, the individual needs a small amount of challenge or emotions otherwise, the individual would sleep, eat, and only exist. During the third month, the visual cortex peaks. At eight months, the hippocampus becomes functional allowing indexing and memory to develop. When the individual has a challenge and accepts it as nonthreatening, learning takes place. It takes the right and left hemispheres of the cerebrum to look at problem-solving possibilities.

Research and the brain's mapping is presently going on at many universities. With the use of the positron-emission tomography (PET), researchers are able to determine actual function of the brain in progress and the site of specific function. One needs to keep up with the new research which is made available to lay persons in our modern society. Since there is an abundant year-to-year change occurring in information, some of the present paper may quickly become out dated. What seems to remain the same is that major development of the brain's wiring occurs during the first three years of life when stimulation has its greatest effects on the nervous system. Those of us who have worked with youth, adults and seniors do know that even though change occurs at a slower pace, it does occur in more then in the first three years and stimulation needs to continue. The changes that occur in later years are different from the early development of the brain. If the early brain structures have not developed, certain functions will be lost.

At the cortical level, the **right** and **left hemispheres** deal with information differently. The **left hemisphere** function is believed to be more highly specialized in women. The world of education emphasizes the left hemisphere functions. The left hemisphere is believed to have the following characteristics (Clark, Florey & Clark, 1985)(Sensory Integration International, 1986):

LEFT HEMISPHERE FUNCTION:
    IS MORE CRITICAL AND INVOLVES:
- analytical thinking
- logic
- skills in the association of verbal and symbolic material involved in auditory-language skills discrete sound discrimination)

    IT IS MORE INVOLVED IN:
- abstract thinking
- task sequencing
- details
- concrete thought
- inhibition

The **right hemisphere** (Clark, Florey & Clark, 1985)(Sensory Integration International, 1986) is believed to be more highly developed in men. Creative and artistic individuals predominantly use the right hemisphere of the brain (Clark, Mailloux, Parham, 1985). The right hemisphere is believed to have the following characteristics:

RIGHT HEMISPHERE FUNCTIONS:
- deals with math symbols
- are involved in visual-spatial tasks
- are intuitive
- are involved in the sensory system
- are involved in the non-verbal areas
- are involved in affective reactions
- are aesthetic
- are uninhibited
- are abstract
- are non-linguistic
- are involved in holistic aspects
- emotional

For a person to perform adequately, each area of **each** hemisphere must develop fully, and, there must be effective communication **between** the **two sides**. According to Ayres (1972), this requires brain stem intercommunication. Reading requires the use of both hemispheres; the **right hemisphere** for visual recognition and perception of the whole and **left hemisphere** for language skill and specific details. Some researchers (Umphred 1985) have found that children with learning disabilities are more "right brained" and seem to have more difficulty with left hemisphere tasks. They have some of the same difficulties seen in persons with left hemisphere injuries. They function more with the right brain. An instructor with right brain tendencies has a great imagination, BUT his or her organization and ability to handle specifics are poor.

Right hemisphere:

☞ Relation of self/horse to environment - holistic relationship ☞ Visual skills ☞ Non-verbal responses ☞ Visualization (Swift's "soft eyes")	☞ The feeling or awareness of balancing on the horse ☞ Absorbing the feel of a learned "position on the horse" ☞ Body image development ☞ Bonding with the horse ☞ Ability to follow visual demonstration

Left hemisphere:

☞ Relation of self/horse to instructor - specific focal localization ☞ Listening to instructions ☞ Interpreting instructions ☞ Sequencing given instructions (turn your horse, walk on rail, stop at A, make circle at walk) ☞ Maintaining rhythm	☞ Following visual demonstration to verbal meaning (interpretation) ☞ Learning of aids ☞ Identification of letters (dressage letters) ☞ Making a circle or other specific shapes--analyzing shapes ☞ Stopping or changing transitions at specific points

Have you experienced the riding instructor (right brained) who can really guide you through all the minute body changes that ones need to develop and expedite aids ---- but cannot organize a lesson? It must always be remembered that to function adequately, one need **BOTH hemispheres** that integrate well together, but there are individuals whose hemispheres do not.

When any individuals are confronted by more stress or challenge than they can easily handle, their **autonomic nervous system** function is activated. Severe stress or trauma during the early development of the brain - during the first three years - can cause irreversible damage to brain cells by hormones emitted which act like an acid like washing of some cells. The more stress applied to the human the more downshifting in brain level functioning occurs. As stress mounts due to various interfering factors, an individual may not function at a cortical (**cerebellum**) level, but starts functioning at the next level down (**medulla oblongata**). Complex behavioral choices, commonly associated with humans, are then limited. The mammalian brain is capable only of elementary problem solving, such as finding food, nurturing young, and seeking comfort. Additional stress creates further downshifting, so that the reptilian brain (**brainstem**) takes over control of internal organs. The **autonomic nervous system** is centered in the brainstem and on down the spinal column. Behavioral options are then limited to basically self-protective choices. The individual will choose to fight or leave (the fight or flight reaction) a common reaction we see in horses.

Understanding these brain levels and their importance as to how they alter behavior, makes work with people more effective. Those individuals working in therapeutic riding centers with children and adults who have disabilities need to have the necessary understandings of brain function, especially if they are attempting more than teaching recreational riding. Particularly if they are actually trying to make changes in functional behavior. Individuals who are mentally disabled may appear low functioning due to the stress the environment imposes on them. What may appear as a WONDERFUL environment to the instructor or therapist, may be very unfamiliar and stressful to the student. When the stress is eliminated or reduced, this individual may function at a much higher level. One must always take into consideration the functional aspects of the CNS before possibly interpreting "that bland look" as a severely defective mind. To do this, one must have knowledge and the ability to patiently observe in-depth.

John H. Brough USA

References:
Ayres, A.J. (1972) *Sensory Integration and Learning Disabilities*. Los Angeles: Western Psychological Services.
Banus, B.S., et, al. (1979). *The Developmental Therapist*. 2nd ed. Thorofare, Charles B. Slack, Inc. 1-158.

Clark, P., et al. (1985). Developmental Principles and Theories. in *Occupational Therapy for Children*. St. Louis: C.V. Mosby Co.34.

Moore, J.C. (1969). *Neuroanatomy Simplified*. Dubuque: Kendall/Hunt Publishing Co.

Moore, J.C. (1973). *Concepts From The Neurobehavioral Sciences*. Dubuque: Kendall/Hunt Publishing Co

Sensory Integration International. (1986). *Sensory Integration Theory and Practice*. Course material.

Sensory Integration International. (1986). *A Neurological Foundation for Sensory Integration*. Course material.

Umphred, D.A. (1985). *Neurological Rehabilitation*. St. Louis: The C.V. Mosby Co.

THE TACTILE SYSTEM

John H. Brough, OTR
Edited by B. Engel

It is touch that provides children with their earliest awareness of whom and where they are. This tactile system is and remains a primary, sensory system. The infant touched by a parent, learned about security, warmth and love. Early touch and movement responses prepare and strengthen a child's muscles for later stages of normal development. Normal stimulation of this very important sensory system is necessary for the total brain's functioning. When there is a lack of tactile stimulation or some interference to the normal processing of sensory information, children may not behave as one would expect. Infants that are deprived of touch will crave stimulation. They demonstrate immature, fearful and even aggressive behaviors. Lack of experience or the inability to process this sensory information interferes with the child's developing awareness and organization of self. The areas of the brain that develop due to tactile stimulation may fade if not accessed.

Touch also alerts children to be aware of threats from the environment. This alarm system can be triggered by a touch so light that it barely brushes the hair. Touch that takes the form of deep pressure that cannot be quickly identified may also trigger the alarm system. Children with learning problems may be under sensitive or oversensitive to touch. The individuals who are under sensitive may not respond at all to touch. Knees can be cut or hands can be scraped without awareness. They may not be receiving important part of the information needed to identify their bodies. They may not receive enough information about objects in their hands to match this information with what their eyes and ears are giving them.

The individual, who is oversensitive to touch, lacks the ability to discriminate and determine which touch requires protective responses and which touch gives routine information about them and their environment. They may become tense and uptight, become tactilely defensive about being touched, and touching. Touch triggers a protective response. The behaviors that can interfere with the learning process will results in abnormal performances. Examples of the behaviors that interfere with learning may include any or all of the following:

a. Inadequate balance
b. Lack of flexibility of movement
c. Difficulty planning sequences of movements
d. Withdrawal from touch--resistive to touch--pulls away
e. Incorrect interpretation of touch--a light brush or touch may be interpreted as a hit, result in a fight
f. Exhibiting fear reactions to touch--screams in the barber's chair
i. Intolerance of crowds--becomes hyperactive, and whines
j. Dislikes being picked up, holding hands, having some one's arm on his shoulders
k. Makes tactile contact with others only if he initiates it
l. Compulsive cleanliness--avoids getting dirty
g. Exhibiting excessive scratching, rubbing, picking, or even self abuse
h. Negative verbal reactions

Without touch, learning is incomplete from the most elementary developmental step to the formation and organization of multiple concepts. Development of the tactile system and its integration with the other sensory modes contributes to the completeness of the individual. Tactile sensitivity must be an integral part of what every person brings to a learning situation. The information that the hands receive when they are touching the horse, not only supplies the rider with important information about the horse, but also aids in beginning a communication between rider and horse. The creation of this communication begins to development a bond and trust between rider and horse.

References
Ayres, A.J. (1972). *Sensory Integration and Learning Disabilities*. Los Angeles: Western Psychological Society.
Chaney, C. (1980). *The Tactile System*. Columbus: Charles E. Merrill.
Guyton, A.C. (1976). *Structure and Function of the Nervous System*. Philadelphia: W.B. Saunders Co.

THE VESTIBULAR SYSTEM

John H. Brough, OTR
Edited by B. Engel

The vestibular system of the brain (part of the proprioceptive system) is a source of sensory information said to be the second earliest appearing sensory input system (Weeks, 1979). Its prenatal maturation prepares each of us for the effects of gravity from the moment of birth. This special proprioceptive system enables individuals to ORIENT THEMSELVES IN SPACE and to make ADAPTIVE OR EXPLORATORY HEAD, LIMB AND EYE MOVEMENTS.

The vestibular system receptors are located in the inner ear on each side of the head and are composed of three connecting tubes called semicircular canals. These canals are filled with fluid that moves as the head moves. The moving fluid stimulates nerves which carry the information about head positions to the central nervous system. Through the semicircular canals, the central nervous system learns whether the head is vertical, horizontal or turned on its side. It also learns whether the head has started to move in any direction or whether it has stopped moving. This directional awareness and movement awareness includes rotation or spinning activities. The vestibular system is considered to be very important to the development of early motor skills such as balance, movement of the head, crawling, creeping, and walking. Information about the position of the head in relation to gravity is continuously being sent to the neck muscles, the muscles of the trunk and the muscles of the arms and legs where it is matched or integrated with the information being sent by nerves in the muscles and joints (kinesthetic awareness or proprioception). The eyes also receive information from the vestibular system and match it with what they see.

Adequate vestibular function and opportunity for stimulation of this sensory system have been shown by researchers to aid postural responses, visual attention and language development (Ayres 1972)(Norton 1975)(Gregg 1976)(deQuiros 1978). It is known to be directly related to a sense of well being. And, absence of stimulation shows a high correlation with emotional disturbance (King, 1978). This system appears to be critical to the integration processes of the brain. Chronic interferences from ear infections, allergy responses, and other internal stress factors appear to result in retarded development of the sensory motor milestones. Adverse behaviors which may result include the following:

   a.   Poor balance--static as well as dynamic
   b.   Abnormal postural adaptations such as head position, spine alignment
   c.   Difficulty with or avoidance of locomotion and movement tasks which require good balancing abilities, such as skipping, jumping, moving sideways or backward
   d.   Very rapid movement patterns--always moves fast, runs, is hyperactive
   e.   Sits in a slouch position--seem to "fold" into a chair
   f.   Fear or avoidance of rotation or spinning
   g.   Seeks out spinning activities with no dizziness resulting from prolonged activity
   h.   Always leans on something--does not stand up

Since everyone must live with the effects of gravity from the moment of birth, this sensory system is extremely important to normal development. Even temporary disturbances can cause disorientation and resulting discomfort. An ear infection can lead to dizziness, and enough dizziness can cause nausea. A moderate degree of interference can reduce learning. Vestibular stimulation is generally positive stimulation. It can be as calming as the porch swing or as exciting as an amusement park ride. Children will seek out stimulating activities. Adult responses do differ from those of children. They seem to require less intensity and less frequency of stimulation. As one matures, other sensory systems become dominant. In particular, the eyes are used to orient the individual in space and may dominate the vestibular system after the late teen years. This sensory system is primary to survival and does trigger responses of the autonomic nervous system. Because of the individualized nature of our central nervous system, it is difficult to predict how each of us will respond to stimulation of the vestibular system when that system may not be processing information as it should. Therefore, it is wise to be aware of certain behaviors which may occur as a result of spinning, rolling, bouncing, jumping, or even running on uneven surfaces.

Behaviors stimulated by the vestibular system may include the following:

1. Dizziness
    a. reported dizziness
    b. observable unsteadiness while walking
    c. an expressed desire to lie down
    d. an unnatural reaction to movement, unusual tilt of the head
2. Vertigo (severe dizziness)
    a. unusual pale color about the face and extremities
    b. sweating .. maybe a "cold" sweat
    c. vomiting
    d. depressed pulse
    e. nystagmoid (horizonal) movements of the eyes
3. Seizures
    a. any seizure behavior whether normal or abnormal to the child
4. Excitement
    a. increased hyperactivity
    b. destructive behavior
5. Depression
    a. withdrawal from environment

Remember, also, that these behaviors or symptoms may occur as much as two to three hours after an experience with vestibular stimulation. It is natural to seek and enjoy stimulation for this extremely important sensory system. Children and adults may need assistance in successfully participating in this area of sensory motor development to facilitate learning at higher developmental levels. An occupational therapist or physical therapist with extensive trained in the theory and practice of Sensory Integration may need to work with these individuals or guide the instructor in dealing with those who cannot tolerate vestibular stimulation.

(Editor's note: The editor of this manuscript has a moderate vestibular disorder. It can cause severe impairment to advancements in riding. Each change of movement of the horse or different movements of different horses becomes a critical issue. Every change must be carefully dealt with as one observes the stress reactions of the rider. It can be very humiliating to be fearful of going from the walk to a slow trot on a new horse. Be respectful of this unseen disability.)

References

Ayres, A.J. (1972) *Sensory Integration and Learning Disabilities*. Los Angeles: Western Psychological Services.

deQuiros, J.B., Scgrager, O.L. (1978). *Neuropsychological Fundamental in Learning Disabilities*. San Rafel: Academic Therapy

Gregg, C., Haffner, M., Korner, M. (1976). The Relative Efficacy of Vestibular-proprioception Stimulation and the Upright Position in Enhancing Visual Pursuit on Neonates. *Child Development*. 47:309-314.

Guyton, A.C. (1976). *Structure and Function of the Nervous System*. Philadelphia: W.B. Saunders Co.

King, L.J. (1978). Occupational Therapy Research in Psychiatry. *Am J Occ Ther*. 32:15-18.

Norton, Y. (1975). Neurodevelopment and Sensory Integration for the Profoundly Retarded Multiply Handicapped Child. *Am J Occup Therapy*, 29:93-100.

Weeks, Z.R. (1979). Effects of the Vestibular System on Human Development. AJOT: June-part 1; July-part 2. Rockville: *Am J of Occup Therapy*, 376-381, 450-457.

HUMAN REFLEXES

John H. Brough, OTR
Edited by B. Engel

Neurological reflexes: are reactions of an involuntary movement nature or exercise of function in a part excited in response to a stimulus applied to the periphery or viscera and transmitted to the nervous centers in the brain or spinal cord (Capute 1978).

❑ Primitive reflexes are essential in normal development.

❑ The response to reflexes prepares the child for progressive motor development such as rolling over, sitting, crawling or standing.

❑ In normal development, these primitive reflexes (which are initiated at the spinal and brainstem level) gradually diminish, in order that higher patterns of righting (the body's response against gravity) and equilibrium (balance) may appear.

❑ When inhibitory control of higher centers is disrupted or delayed, primitive patterns dominate.

❑ Levels of Reflex Development:

There are different levels of reflexive development.

a. **Spinal level reflexes** are the lowest level. These predominate with motor development when the child is **lying prone** (on the stomach) or **supine** (on the back) Example: flexor withdrawal. This is the pulling away of the foot when the sole of the foot is touched or stimulated.

b. **Brain stem level reflexes** cause changes in muscle tone in the body:
1. in response to change of position of the head and body in space (stimulation of the labyrinths).
2. in the head in relation to the body (stimulation of the neck proprioceptors). Positive or negative reactions to brain stem reflex testing may occur in the normal child within the first 4-6 months of life. Example: The **asymmetrical tonic neck reflex** (ATNR) can be observed when a child is lying or sitting and turns his or her head to one side resulting in extension of the arm on the chin side and flexion of the opposite arm. This has also been called the fencer's position. The **symmetrical tonic neck reflex** (STNR) is similar to the ATNR except that the flexion-extension axis changes to upper-lower instead of the right-left side of the body. When the head is extended, the arms will straighten and the legs will bend at the hips and knees; when the head is bent forward, the arms will bend at the shoulders and elbows and the legs will straighten. Both the asymmetrical tonic neck reflex (ATNR) and the tonic neck reflex (STNR) is present up to 6 months of life.

c. **Midbrain level reflexes** include the righting reaction. Righting reactions work toward establishing normal head and body relationship in space as well as in relationship to each other. These develop after birth and continue through the 10-12 months. Gradually, they disappear toward the end of 5th year of life. Example: Neck righting reflex occurs when the child is lying on his/her back, rotation of the head results in rotation of the body as a whole in the same direction as the head. This occurs from birth to six months and is what permit the baby to roll over. Other righting reactions entail tilting the child who will react to right him/ herself. It is that tendency toward keeping the body upright, the head upright and eyes level with the ground.

d. **The highest level of reflex** is that of mature equilibrium reactions. Equilibrium is balance. Development of mature equilibrium responses helps to bring the child to a bipedal stage of motor development. They occur when muscle tone is normalized and they provide body adaptation in response to change of the center of gravity in the body. Equilibrium reactions occur from six months on and remain throughout life.

Abnormal Reflex Maturation:

❑ Automatic reactions also reflect maturity of the nervous system. One which stays with us for life is protective extension. This is an automatic thrusting out of the arms when the body is suddenly thrown downward toward the floor. The body is protected from serious injury when one falls, as the first part to touch the surface is the outstretched hand or arm.

❑   In children with severe nervous system damage one may see a dominance of the early primitive reflexes and the child is "bound" by them. For example, a child with cerebral palsy may be so dominated by these early low level reflexes that the position of his or her head controls and demands a particular position of his or her arms. One can imagine how this may interfere with learning. Achievement of higher level motor patterns will not be possible because the child is rigid and controlled by these reflexes.

❑   In the learning disabled child, one needs to look at these early brain stem reflexes as well as at equilibrium responses. The ATNR and STNR may cause the child to be "bound" (totally involved) by the reflex or the reflex may appear to be exerting only minimal influence on him or her. If one sees that a child is still being influenced by a reflex, this shows immaturity of the nervous system and one need to look at how and when that reflex may interfere with his/her movements. Example: ATNR may prevent adequate bilateral use of the arms for coordinated activity. It may prevent complete crossing of the midline of the body and may contribute to decreased flexibility around the midline.

❑   Good flexibility around the midline is the ability to rotate around the midline and to return to that stable middle point (trunk rotation). If children are being influenced by a primitive reflex when their balance is threatened, that is, when they are pushed off their center or midline, they may be unable to respond normally.

Emotional impact of abnormal reflex integration is significant. If children have not developed normal balance reactions or protective extension, one can easily imagine how fearful they may be as they move through their environment.

In therapy, stability is provided, then positioning is utilized to inhibit primitive reflexes so that normal feedback is given to the nervous system. Vestibular stimulation can be also used because this type of information has an integrating, organizing influence on the nervous system. Vestibular input is provided through movement of the head through space (rocking, rolling, spinning are some examples). There is no substitute for integration that occurs at the lowest levels of the nervous system. Normal motor development depends on lower level organization and integration.

John H. Brough
USA

Reference:
Capute, A.J. et el. (1978). *Primitive Reflex Profile*. Baltimore: University Park Press.
Fiorentino, M. (1973). *Reflex Testing Methods for Evaluation C.N.S. Development*. Springfield: Charles C Thomas.

PHYSIOLOGICAL SYSTEMS AFFECTING THE RIDER

Barbara T. Engel, MEd, OTR

INTRODUCTION

When instructors of horseback riding teach able-bodied students, it is to the advantage of both the instructors and the students to understand how the human body functions, how the nervous system directs the students to understand directions, to coordinate their bodies' movements, to develop balance, and to "feel" the movements of the horse. The rider can then be more skillfully guided through the development of posture, movement and sensitivity in order to learn to manipulate the horse effectively and to understand how the horse responds to the rider's movements.

However, when instructing horseback riding to a population with special needs, this knowledge becomes fundamental! Abnormal behavior cannot be understood unless one understands normal behavior. Certainly, it is a big task to place a human on a large, mildly cooperative animal and teach them to work as one coordinated unit in a pleasurable way. When that human has numerous problems with coordination, learning problems, limbs that do not work well, bodies that are not sure where they are, vision or hearing difficulties, the task becomes enormous. For instructors to be successful with disabled clients, it is imperative for them to understand their students' disabilities.

For riders, it is frustrating not to be understood. People do not like to be told that if they would only pay attention, they would be able to understand what to do; or to hear that there is nothing wrong with them except for their negative attitude. How do they "put the heels down" when the muscles are tight or when they cannot "feel" the legs - what heel is the instructor talking about? When a student can do what one asks of him one day but not the next - does one say she's not paying attention, or does one understand that this is a common symptom of a learning disability or one with seizure activity? When an adult does not know right from left, it is certainly degrading to hear "I thought you were smart." Even a child with retardation is not so "dense" as to know where his/her abilities are. To be treated below ones abilities is degrading and stressful - even if you are retarded - these people have as sensitive feelings as any of us have. They may be different in some ways, but are definitely personalities in their own right and must be treated with consideration and respect. Some of the most rewarding children the author has worked with, have been children with Down Syndrome who were remarkably less retarded, after they had been worked with, then originally assessed. Half were one grade below average - even when they lacked spoken words.

Ayres (1979) describe two vestibular modulation disorders which involve intolerance to movement. First, she describes gravitational insecurity where an individual may experience a sensation of falling when in a stable, but threatening position, which causes anxiety and distress to movement. The second disorder of vestibular hyper-responsivity describes unpleasant movement activities, but not threatening to children, except for the secondary reactions of nausea and discomfort. The author experiences mild gravitational insecurity and a moderate vestibular hyper-responsivity. If one is standing by a high cliff looking down, though behind a fence, gravitational insecurity becomes severe. After not being able to ride for a year, due to knee reconstruction, she found that she had to begin anew to establish a tolerance to the movement of the horse beneath her. A year before, she was riding well at the first level dressage with no fear of movement. Now, she felt nausea and discomfort when the horse's gait changed or he made an unexpected or fast move at the walk or trot. An instructor, who is unfamiliar with this type of disorder, would quickly give up on such a student--"Look, she is scared of the horse--she cannot even ride!" Does one need that kind of reinforcement when one is having to struggle with "starting all over again--and I was doing so well?" It took a year to be comfortable with a gentle canter again.

Problems that are not visible are difficult to explain, especially to those who have no understanding of human function. They become even more difficult to understand if the person that is involved is above average or has gifted in intellect. An instructor will have less difficulty relating to a person who is physically disabled because that person is visually "different." The instructor may be unsure how to deal with a physical problem. He/she may ask "What am I going to do with this person?" The instructor must also separate out the physical problems from the mental and intellectual ones. A child with severe cerebral palsy may be gifted intellectually – but will the instructor be observant of this – for the child cannot <u>do anything.</u> How can that person learn to ride?" On the other hand, with a student with major learning disabilities, head injuries or mental problems, the instructor may feel socially comfortable because this person is not obviously "different"; but, **understanding** this rider may be more difficult.

CONCLUSION

Instructors, who have basic knowledge of anatomy and the physiological systems of the human body, will be able to gain an understanding of physical, mental and learning disabilities. This will permit them to request assistance from therapists or other professionals and will enable them to adapt their instructions to meet the needs of the rider who is "different." They will be more successful instructing and bringing out the talents of their students. Always remember that each person is a bit different from another - even with the same disability. Remember that each of us can not be everybody to the rider. We must rely on others with education in specialized areas to meet the rider's needs.

References
Ayres, A.J. (1979). *Sensory Integration and the Child.* Los Angeles: Western Psychological Services.

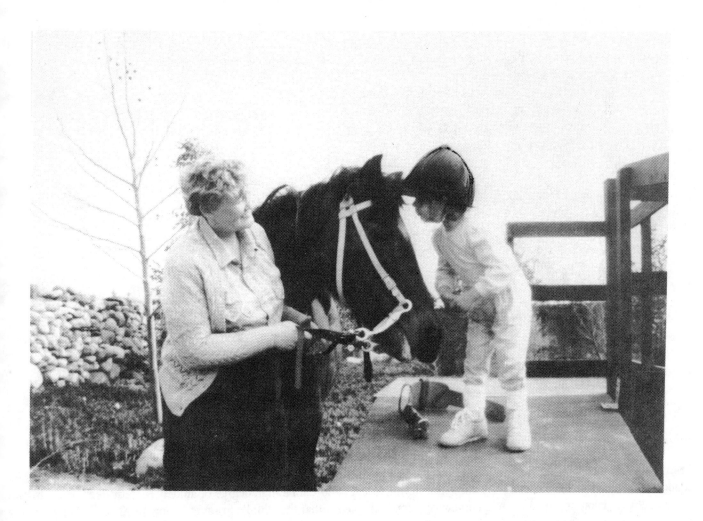

SELF CONCEPT IN CHILDREN AS IT AFFECTS LEARNING

John H. Brough, OTR

One of the most important and least understood areas of development is the affective area or *"the way I feel about myself"* (Piers). Professionals talk about self image, self concept and their importance, but little is really known about how such feelings develop. Self concept is a complicated system composed of many subsystems. The perception of self-worth is elusive and complex. The following breakdown, showing six factors, is taken from the **Piers-Harris Children's Self Concept Scale**. The six factors give a good view of the important parts of children's feelings about themselves.

The areas measured are:
- Physical appearance and attitudes
- Anxiety
- Intellectual and school status
- Behavior
- Popularity
- Happiness and satisfaction

In the areas of **physical appearance and attitudes,** the child is assessed on his or her feelings related to:
- General looks
- Does he or she see him or herself as strong?
- Is he or she important in class?
- How does he or she feel about his:
  - Eyes?
  - Hair?
  - Face?
  - Figure?

How does the Mary perceive her classmates think about her in the areas of:
- Ideas?
- Leadership?
- Popularity?

In the critical area of **anxiety**, the child is assessed as to:
- Shyness
- Perseverance
- Nervousness
- Amount of worry
- How well does he or she sleep?
- Test taking (how he or she feels about it)
- Feelings of fear

Testing these concepts gives one an idea about the degree of anxiety or stress to the body that can be caused by poor self concept, a perception that can radically change performance. A child with a high degree of anxiety is most likely ruled by the sympathetic division of the autonomic nervous system. This means that this child's brain has "downshifted" and he or she is basically working at the most primitive level. Cortical function is repressed and learning may not be possible.

272

The area of **intellectual and school status** is evaluated in the following areas:

Does the child feel that he or she is:

- ☞ Smart?
- ☞ Capable of creating good ideas?
- ☞ Liked by the teacher?
- ☞ Good at school work?
- ☞ Important?
- ☞ Popular with peers?

The area of **behavior** is evaluated in many ways. The child's **relationships** are rated in the following environments: school, family, home, with peers, with other people. The tester examines how well the child works and what the trouble areas are in the above situations. The behavior the child describes may or may not be the truth, but it is important to remember that the significance is how the child **feels** about him or herself and his or her behavior.

Popularity is rated on the child's relationships in school and peer group--with boys and girls. Popularity can also be looked at in the extended family.

Happiness and satisfaction is rated in all areas. Evaluation is made as to whether or not the individual feels happy, likes the way Jonny is, feels lucky and cheerful. Also examined is whether the child wishes that he or she were different, or wants to change. The most important fact to remember is that the relationship of how the child feels and what the truth actually is may be either erroneous or very accurate. The child's self-concept comes from how he or she feels, not necessarily from the truth. The self-concept is very important and may greatly influence the course of therapy. A positive and accurate self-image can speed the learning process. A negative self-image, whether accurate or inaccurate, can slow down or completely hinder the self-concept. To build a good concept, it is necessary to give the individual accurate and concrete feedback; help Johnny develop positive attitudes to replace his negative ones and tap any or all of his sensory avenues as aids in developing the necessary precepts upon which he build his self-concept.

John H. Brough
USA

References
Piers, E., Harris, D. *The Piers-Harris Children's Self Concept Scale.* (The Way I Feel About Myself). Nashville: Counselor Recordings and Tests.

SENSORY INTEGRATION DEVELOPMENT

Jill Standquist, OTR/L, NDT

The infant uses reflexes and information from his/her senses of:	To develop these senses motor abilities:	The infant uses sensory motor abilities to learn more concrete concepts and to develop:	The infant uses motor skills to accomplish an automatic level of function:
TOUCH	BODY SCHEME	EYE HAND COORDINATION	ACADEMIC LEARNING READING WRITING NUMBERS SPELLING
MOVEMENT	REFLEX MATURATION	OCULO MOTOR CONTROL	
GRAVITY	CAPACITY TO SCREEN SENSORY INPUT	POSTURAL ADJUSTMENT	ACTIVITIES OF DAILY LIVING
HEARING	POSTURAL SECURITY	AUDITORY LANGUAGE SKILLS	ABILITY TO CONCEPTUALIZE
TASTE	AWARENESS OF TWO SIDES OF BODY	VISUAL/SPATIAL PERCEPTION	INDEPENDENT WORK HABITS
SMELL	MOTOR PLANNING	ATTENTION CENTER FUNCTION	BEHAVIOR - ABILITY FORM MEANINGFUL RELATIONSHIPS
VISION		MASTERY OF ENVIRONMENT	

SENSORY MOTOR PHASE
0-12 MONTHS

PERCEPTUAL MOTOR PHASE
1-5 YEARS

LEARNING PHASE
COGNITIVE OR INTELLECT

Jill Standquist
USA

SENSORY INTEGRATION AS A FRAME OF REFERENCE FOR THE PRACTICE OF HIPPOTHERAPY WITH A PEDIATRIC CLIENTELE

Sandra L. Hubbard, MS, OTR/L

INTRODUCTION

A. Jean Ayres, an occupational therapist, was the pioneer of Sensory Integration Theory. It is a theory that has become an important frame of reference in the practice of occupational therapy, and a theory that continues to be expanded upon since her death in 1988. Sensory Integration is a frame of reference that can be used successfully in hippotherapy. The equine environment provides a sensory diet that can provide clients with an opportunity for successful interaction with their environment. Sensory Integration Theory provides one with means to understand and communicate how and why the horse and the equine environment can be a valuable therapeutic modality.

UNDERSTANDING SENSORY INTEGRATION THEORY

Jean Ayres defined Sensory Integration Theory as "the ability to organize sensory information for use" (Ayres, 1979). "Organization," "sensory information," and "use" are the key words.

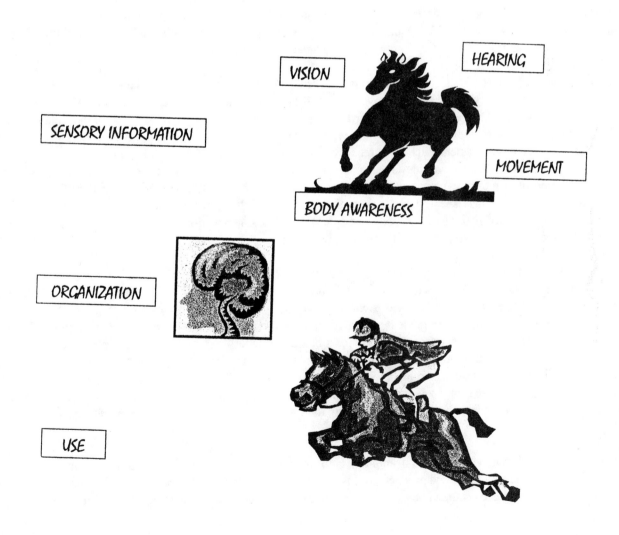

SENSORY INFORMATION

As sensory information is taken in, it is "organized" and "processed", and "used" and it is responded to by moving our bodies. We take external sensory information (external to our bodies) in through our eyes and ears. this information comes from the sights and sounds around us. Internal sensory input (within our bodies) is the touch and awareness of where our bodies are in space. With concentration and effort, we can become aware of how we take in sensory information. For example, you are riding in a group jumping riding lesson. You are warming up, focusing on your leg position, stacking your body blocks so your pelvis is over your ankles, your shoulders are over your pelvis, your head is suspended above the shoulders, and all of your body is over the horse (Swift.) You are checking your sense -- where your body is in space (proprioceptive information). You're focusing on your hands; how they feel in relation to the horse's mouth. Your hands are a part of your horse through the reins, in your hands and the bit in the horse's mouth. You are checking your sense of touch (tactile information). As you tune into your body, you begin to be aware of the horse's rhythm. You allow your body's rhythm to synchronize with that of the horse's body rhythm. Now, you are checking in with your sense of movement (vestibular information). This is the internal (somato-sensory) sensory information that most of us take for granted. Those of us taking riding lessons have to bring somato-sensory information into consciousness until we get our body movements just right, then we can let the somato-sensory information slip into unconsciousness, as we move onto the next skill level.

Think about riding your horse on the lounge line. You feel your pelvis relax into the saddle and move with the horse. Your pelvis dissociates its movement from your shoulders and moves with the horse's withers. You can feel your legs lengthen, and your trunk rising, as you begin to move in unity, with the horse. Have you ever jumped with your eyes closed, or without stirrups? How do you make your body stay on the horse? The somato-sensory information helps you stay with the horse. There are exercises that we as riders use to focus on internal or somato-sensory information.

How about our horses? Their bodies move easily for them when they are running with the herd through the fields, and gracefully jumping the fallen trees. They too, take their movement for granted, until its time for dressage. Then they, too, struggle with how to move their bodies. Their ears pricked forward telling us that they are trying to make sense of the feel of their humans' leg against their side as the rider pushes them forward with their legs and at the same time holds them back with still reins. The horse has to reevaluate his movement and his awareness of where his body is in space, based upon incoming tactile information (aids). The horse makes its body move sideways in a leg yield by crossing the front legs and crossing the hind legs. The rider's tactile and proprioceptive messages convey to the horse, how to move his body in this unusual and perhaps frustrating direction. How about the young horse that is learning to pick up the correct lead? It is interesting to watch him as he tries to figure out which leg has to go forward first, (focus on body and spacial awareness) so he does not fall over while cantering on a circle. Imagine us having four legs to keep track of rather than two.

While we are concentrating on synchronizing our movement with that of the horse, we are feeling the horse's mouth through the reins in our hands, and taking in visual and auditory information from our environment. For instance, we have warmed-up. We have been through the trot poles. The next exercise is two "X" jumps on a twenty-meter circle, one at 3 o'clock and one at 9 o'clock. We are using our eyes to guide the horse along a perfect 20-meter circle so we meet the jump at the apex of the "X". Perhaps we are in a dressage lesson preparing for a halt at the letter "X," we're using our peripheral vision to find the letter "B" (taking in external information to locate where to stop) and the letter "E", so that we can line-up our horse for a perfect halt. Auditory information is coming in too. Our instructor is pointing out that the halt is not square and asks us to do it again. Meanwhile, there are frantic whinnies coming from the barn. Our horse becomes much more attentive to the auditory information that he is getting from his buddies in the barn, than the tactile information he is receiving from our spur in his side.

ORGANIZATION

What you and your horse do with this (visual, auditory, tactile and movement) sensory information, that which happens between the seeing, hearing, feeling and the end products, the use, (the perfect jump or the perfect halt), is the middle-processing piece. This middle-processing piece occurs in our brain. We are unable to observe central nervous system processing so we make an assumption about what is happening, based upon evidence published in neuroscience. Because we assume the processing is happening rather than observing it, it becomes a theory - Sensory Integration Theory. (Fisher, Murray, 1991).

The processing piece is perhaps the most trying for instructors. It precipitates such comments as "That's not what I told you to do!" The same information entered into different brains (horse vs. rider, rider vs. rider, horse vs. horse) can yield different results due to the differences in processing.

How do we account for the same information entering different brains yielding different results? Brains process differently. Putting sensory information on a continuum is one way of demonstrating how processing differs. Hypersensitivity vs. Hyposensitivity is one continuum and hyper-responsiveness vs. hyporesponsiveness, another continuum.

What is loud to one person may not bother the next person. The person, who is irritated by loud, action packed movies on TV is more hyper (increased) sensitive to noise, in comparison to another who likes the volume loud and the radio and the TV on while they are reading. The one who likes the noise is on the hypo (decreased) sensitive side of the continuum because they are seeking more information. They seek more information because they need more information for their brains to process.

The hypersensitive horse spooks at every little noise. He's the white knuckle trail ride, the horse who's visually and auditorily attentive to everything on the trail. The hyposensitive horse manages quite a bit of sensory information without overreacting to it. He's Wyatt Earp's horse who gallops confidently across country amidst gunfire, coyotes and outlaws. Then there's the horse who three kids can pile on (hyposensitive), our therapeutic riding horse, and there's the horse who flinches when a fly lands on him (hypersensitive).

USE

"Irritation," "spooking," "turning the volume up," "flinching," "galloping confidently" are responses to sensory information that are expressed as movement. A horse may express "irritation" by tossing his head or pinning his ears back. "Spooking" is a quick, unpredictable movement that frequently dislodges the rider, which expresses fear. "Turning the volume up" is a human hand movement of the fingers when seeking more auditory information. "Flinching" is movement of the horse's skin to dislodge a fly. "Galloping confidently" is rhythmic, reciprocal movement of all four of the horse's legs. How your brain processes sensory information makes one respond or move in one's own unique way. Your response is your "use" so to speak.

The horse who spooks on the trail is hyper (more) responsive in comparison to Wyatt Earp's horse. The horse who is not bothered by gunshots on a hunting trip in the back-country is hypo (less) responsive in comparison to the horse who pricks his ears and lifts his head as he spins around on his front legs whenever he hears a gunshot or any other loud noise, (more response/same stimuli). The horse who fusses whenever he is brushed is hypersensitive/hyper-responsive to tactile input. The hypo-responsive horse on the other hand is the one that we may have referred to as "dead to the aids" or "hard mouthed."

The following diagram plots the white knuckle horse and Wyatt Earp's horse on the hypersensitivity vs. hypersensitivity and hypo-responsiveness vs. a hyper-responsiveness continuum.

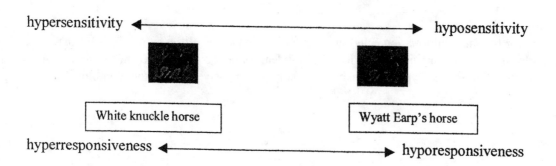

Where are you on this continuum? What type of sensory information turns your brain on? What type of sensory information sets you up for an optimal response?

Tactile information: Do you like oysters? Would you rather do needlepoint, paint flowers on porcelain or operate a jackhammer with your hands?

Visual information: Do you like bright lights, or do you like the lights off?

Auditory information: Do you like rock and roll concerts or the sound of a mountain stream?

Vestibular information: Do you like the rides at the carnival? Or do elevators scare you? Do the big jumps on horseback scare you?

Proprioceptive information: Are you a bull in the china closet? Or do you enjoy classical ballet with very precise movement through space?

How do you move your body through space? Can you tell who's walking down the hall by the sound of their feet? Do they clomp or do they tiptoe? The "clompers" have a system that needs more proprioceptive and auditory information for processing to take place (hyposensitive). More body pressure and more noise increases the amount of feedback one needs to process where one is in space. The "tiptoers," in comparison, require less pressure to feel where they are in space therefore are considered more sensitive (hypersensitive).

The fact that you are reading this article about horses, reveals something about your sensory system. We horse people must like movement, we do not mind dirt and dust. There is nothing like a good ride after a stressful day to reset our attitudes. The right kind of sensory information sets us up for an optimal interaction with our environment. Many of us would rather be here in this equine environment than in a lab researching how to split an atom, although we'd really prefer be on our horses.

The hypersensitivity vs. hyposensitivity and hyporesponsiveness vs. a hyper-responsiveness continuum is meant to be a way of understanding how your brain processes what it takes in, and what it puts out. Horse shopping is another sensitivity-responsivity dilemma: finding the right horse-human match. My ideal horse is medium sensitive-responsive. I like a horse that is responsive with subtle leg pressure that I can ride with light hands. I want a horse to move-out but not so responsive that he moves or responds to anything and everything. Breeders too, are trying to achieve this balance: not over responsive and not under responsive.

Unfortunately, we do not have the option of shopping for our children. We have to be happy with what we have: at home, in school and in therapy. Understanding Sensory Integration Theory not only provides occupational and physical therapists with an understanding of the normal range of sensory processing, it also provides them with guidance in how to intervene in hippotherapy with abnormal sensory processing that results in inappropriate behavior.

SENSORY INTEGRATION DYSFUNCTION

We all perform our best when we feel good. We're all trying to achieve the balance that makes us feel in harmony with our horses and with life. Think of that perfectly rhythmic dressage test where you and your horse were one, or how the jump with the perfect take off and landing felt. They made you feel on top of the world. Watch an Olympic jumper. The horse lifts his one thousand pound body into the air, tucking his legs to clear the poles of the jump with his hooves, judging the distance of where he needs to take off and land while at a gallop. As the poles are raised in three inch increments, the horse's hooves continue to clear them, sometimes by less than an inch, as if he knows exactly how high the poles have been raised. This horse takes in sensory information, processes it, and responds with precision. He is aware of where his body is in space, and tuned into the tactile input from his rider's aids. He is visually judging distances (how far away the fence is, how fast he is going ,and how high the fence is). By the time he's an Olympic jumper, the roar of the crowd (auditory input) only adds to his enthusiasm and his precision. This is a horse who is able to organize sensory information for use.

Wouldn't the classroom teacher like a room full of these perfect little children as organized as the olympic horse? These children would sit with correct posture at their desks all day long, attending to their lessons. Their behavior would be perfect. They'd remember everything they were told because they could process verbal information. They would copy information off the chalkboard correctly because they could process visual information. They could sit still and listen because they could integrate visual and auditory information with the postural security of knowing where their body was in space.

Many of the children referred to our therapeutic riding programs are not able to achieve this balance and as a result, they demonstrate inappropriate behaviors that have kept them out of riding lessons with their peers or have precipitated a referral to special education. Two areas of Sensory Integration Dysfunction we typically see are:
1. Arousal level that is inappropriate for the situation
2. Dyspraxia.

AROUSAL

In order to behave appropriately in various situations, to learn, and to develop language, we must be able to take in information of all kinds (visual, auditory, tactile, vestibular) and correctly process that information without overloading or shutting down. Our ability to attend, learn, and behave appropriately is dependent, in part, on our state of arousal or alertness (Trott, Laurel, Windeck, 1993). Children referred to occupational therapy for sensory integration dysfunctions have difficulty organizing sensory information for use. Their response are not adaptive. Ayres defined an adaptive response as an appropriate action in which the individual responds successfully to some environmental demand (Ayres, 1979).

Compare the two horses on the trail ride. . . my horse and Wyatt Earp's horse. Wyatt's horse was relaxed and enjoying life with his rider. My horse's ears were pricked forward ready to jump at any rustle of the leaves or rock on the trail. My horse's muscles were tense, listening for any sound that could indicate danger or an excuse to dislodge me from the saddle. This was the same trail, same ride, same sensory information, yet different responses, and different organization of sensory information.

Visualize a deer in a field in a stance that indicates "alert" and "ready to flee." He is still as a statue, his eyes are searching the environment, and his ears are upright trying to localize and identify the noise. Deer and horses are animals of flight. "Flight" is their first method of protection. Incoming sensory information is integrated and processed so a decision can be made: is it safe or do I flee? Their muscles are tensed in a readiness position, ready to flee. The sensory system, the motor system and the arousal systems are wired together at the central nervous system level. Visual and auditory information is alerting them which increase their arousal level and their attention. The increase in arousal level puts them on stand by for flight should it be necessary.

Some children referred for occupational therapy are in this high state of alertness/arousal all of the time, which interferes with their day to day functioning including their learning and their social interaction. Imagine hearing sirens that sound awfully close, then seeing fire engines zooming down your road and smelling smoke! Would you be able to sit calmly to study for the neuroanatomy test under these circumstances? No, in this high state of arousal your train is on the survival track, not the learning track: two different central nervous system tracks. Many SI children (children with sensory integration dysfunction) cannot get onto the learning track. The difference between these childrens' nervous systems and ours, is that when the danger is gone, you and I can readjust our arousal levels to be situation appropriate. We realize the fire is several blocks away. It is already under control, so we can go back to studying for the neuroanatomy test. We know how to get our train to the intersection where we can switch tracts to the learning mode track. Some of the children referred to occupational therapists for SI treatment can't switch tracks. They are stuck on the survival track. Their arousal level is stuck in protection ready to flee mode, which is a flight response. They may also demonstrate a fight or fright response. These are not the good little children who sit at their desks all day in a state of balance and harmony. These aren't the children that are like the horses that make it to the Olympics or become a "therapy horse." These are the children -- like the the pony that is running around in circles all day, kicking and biting the other ponies, bucking the rider off - same sensory information, different response.

Children with sensory integration dysfunctions can demonstrate a variety of sensitivity=responsivity patterns including hyper=hyper, hypo=hypo, hyper=hypo and hypo=hyper. Children who are hypersensitive to sensory information, can cause them to get stuck in a survival fright, flight fight mode, triggering an increase in arousal level or hyper-response (hyper=hyper). Examples were given earlier where hypersensitivity to sensory information caused a hyper-response and hyposensitivity to sensory information caused a hyporesponse (hypo=hypo). This is not always the case. It is not as simple as "A" causes "B." Children with Sensory Integration Dysfunction can also demonstrate hypersensitivity to information causing a hyporesponse (hyper=hypo). An example would be an autistic child who is hypersensitive to sensory information, and who shuts down in response. Sensory information, which would be considered in the normal range to some people, can cause an autistic person to lower their arousal level to a level, much lower than would be expected, or to activate a withdrawal response.

Many children with sensory integration dysfunction who are hyposensitive to sensory information demonstrate a hyper-response (hypo=hyper). If they are hyposensitive, then their threshold for sensory information is low. They need more information than usual to get enough neurons firing so to speak, to generate a response. Their excessive, hyperactive movement is this seeking of more information. These are the clumsy children who are bumping into things; they step on the cat because they didn't know it was there. They're touching everything they're not supposed to, and they're in and out of their seats - mostly out. They're squirming and their voices are way too loud. Their brains are saying "more information." Without this active seeking of more information, their batteries are too low to do their math, for example, unlike the "Eveready bunny" who can just "keep on going." These children's processing is ignited by movement, which in turn, ignites a more adaptive response. Movement is a natural stimulant like jogging as a natural stimulant. The horse can be the source of movement that these children need.

There is another group of hyposensitive children who rather than having a low threshold, put up a protective wall against sensory information, because their brains cannot make sense of it. Because they are not processing the sensory information, they respond with disorganized movement, or fright, flight, or fight, a protective response against sensory information they do not understand. With treatment they begin to process and organize the sensory information and actually crave it until they eventually find a happy medium, which is considered in the normal range.

280

The important concept here is that abnormal behavior can be the result of abnormal sensory processing. A child who appears to have a sensory processing disorder should be referred to an occupational therapist or one trained in Sensory Integration Theory to determine if the child is under-processing or over-processing sensory information so the correct sensory diet can be prescribed. Is this a child who needs more sensory stimulation, or less sensory stimulation for more purposeful and adaptive interaction with his or her environment? **"Sensory diet," as a foot note, is a term used to describe our total sensory experience.** An adequate "sensory diet" is related to the essential but changing need of all humans to have an optimum amount of organized and integrated sensation being registered by our central nervous system at all times (Pat Wilbarger, 1984). Prescribing a special sensory diet for a special child is the art of therapy.

A child who responds too much or too little, who cannot regulate his or her arousal level to be situation-appropriate has a self-regulation disorder (Greenspan). According to Greenspan, regulatory disorders are characterized by the infant or young child's difficulties in regulating behavior and physiological, sensory, attentional, motor or affective processes, and in organizing a calm, alert or affective positive state.

Sensory Integration Theory provides us with a frame of reference to modulate arousal level, by modulating sensory input, thus improve self-regulation. The rhythmic movement of the horse, and the unique sensory experiences the equine environment provides, can be a therapeutic sensory diet for children with Sensory Integration Dysfunction. It can help them organize sensory information, which in turn, helps them self-regulate their arousal level to be situation-appropriate.

PRAXIS

How we process sensory information not only affects our arousal level and self-regulation, but also can also affect the quality of our motor response. There is a category of children who have sensory integration dysfunction, who have good strength and coordination, who can climb a ladder onto the roof and can jump off anything, but cannot put a puzzle together and cannot play games with other children because they cannot follow the sequence. They tend to break their toys before they figure out how to use them. These children cannot figure out "how to do" a task. Figuring out how to do a task is referred to as "praxis." Children who have difficulty figuring out how to do tasks are referred to as "dyspraxic." When these children learn a task, they can usually do it quite successfully. Once it has been learned, it is a motor skill and no longer requires motor planning.

Think back to when you were learning to drive a car. There were so many things you had to do at once: steer, put your foot on the gas pedal or brake petal and hopefully not both at the same time, look ahead of you, look behind you, watch your speed, etc. It was important that all these things were done in the correct sequence. Putting your foot on the gas pedal while looking behind you, then steering would not work. It is times like this when you may talk yourself through the task: first I do this, then this. It does not do any good to bake a cake, then add the eggs. Planning is an important part of doing. After awhile, actions that have been repeated over and over, like cooking or driving a car become automatic. Most of us do not even remember driving to work or to the barn, unless something unusual happens that causes us to re-motor plan. Once a task no longer requires motor planning, it is a motor skill. Sitting in a chair and going down stairs are motor skills for most of us. We do it automatically, and every once in awhile, we miss. The chair or the step was not the height we expected it to be and we switch from motor skill to motor plan.

Ayres describes praxis as a uniquely human skill that enables us to interact effectively with the physical world. It requires the cognitive functions of ideation or concept formation; the integration of sensory input and planning that enables motor expression. Subhuman species often excel over man in some aspects of motor function, but not in praxis. A person can have adequate neuromuscular function and still be dyspraxic. Praxis is not strictly neuromotor function, but it uses the neuromotor system for execution of practice acts. In developmental dyspraxia, or children who never developed praxis, the problem lies mainly in all the neural activity that should take place before the motor execution is begun (Ayres, 1985). The neural activity Ayres refers to includes processing and integration of sensory information.

According to Sensory Integration Theory, we need to be able to put visual and auditory information together to direct our bodies' movement and we need to have adequate internal, somato-sensory awareness of where our body is in space to support our movement. Otherwise we stepped on the cat because we were not using peripheral vision to note the position of the cat and we did not know where our body was in space in order to navigate around the cat. All this sensory information must be integrated before we can come up with a plan for how to use our body to interact with our environment.

Visualize a horse entering the show ring and getting ready for a round of show jumping. The course is arranged in a certain way, with the jumps, a set distance apart, and the horse has to go through the jumps in a certain sequence. We now understand how the horse receives visual, auditory information from his environment, and tactile, proprioceptive and vestibular (movement) information from within his body. We understand how he is processing it, and, hopefully, organizing it for use. The horse has the coordination, the neuromotor control: he can contract and relax his muscles adequately to clear the jumps. What he does not know is where to begin or end, or in what order to go through the course of jumps. His rider positioned him so he could watch the horse ahead of him jump the course in hopes that he would memorize the course, in case the rider forgot.

Unfortunately, it is up to the rider to remember after all. The rider has the concept or the plan in her head and it is her job to use the horse's neuromotor skills to get them through the course. Without the concept or motor planning, the horse's neuromotor skills would not be useful. This concept and planning is "praxis." Praxis is figuring out what to do, which in this case, is to go through the jumps in the correct sequence with the correct timing and strides between jumps. According to Sensory Integration Theory, motor planning is dependent on processing and integration of sensory information. There is a category of children who may have good self regulation and a situation appropriate arousal level but are dyspraxic.

Sensory Integration Dysfunction is a continuum that range from mild too severe. We may see children anywhere on this continuum in hippotherapy and in therapeutic riding. A child with mild disorder might be a twice exceptional child who is both gifted and learning disabled. This boy reads and comprehends at the fourth grade level but writes (illegibly) at the first grade level. He is frustrated because he thinks faster than he can move the pencil with his hand to write. His writing is messy because he's trying to keep up with his thoughts. His desk is messy. He pushes too hard with his pencil and dips and smears the already messy paper. His thoughts are elaborate and full of fantasy but he cannot put a model together and he would not even consider competitive sports. He is very intelligent, but his body is not working for him. This child is like a pony who cannot pick up his leads no matter what.

On the severe disorder side of the continuum would be the autistic child. Autistic children typically have motor planning problems along with problems in social interaction and communication. The autistic child spins objects or moves them repetitively, stacks objects, or lines them up. Autistic children have extreme difficulty figuring out "how to" use objects adaptively to interact with their environment. They tend to prefer familiar, predictable sensory information. Although no two autistic children are alike, processing is typically difficult for them. They like routines so they will know what to expect, which keeps the amount of activity processing they have to do to a minimum.

Sensory Integration Theory provides us with a frame of reference to help children improve their motor planning skills by prescribing a sensory diet that increases their awareness of their bodies and environment so that they can use their bodies for more adaptive interactions. The equine environment provides not only a rich sensory opportunities, it has its own organizational structure that is part of caring for a horse that is beneficial to these children who have difficulty with organization.

CONCLUSION

Sensory Integration Theory is defined by A. Jean Ayres as "the ability to organize sensory information for use." Children referred to therapeutic riding and hippotherapy programs frequently demonstrate Sensory Integration Dysfunction. These children are not able to organize sensory information and, as a result, may have self regulation disorder or dyspraxia. The equine environment can be therapeutic for a child with Sensory Integration Dysfunction because of:

❑ Its rich visual, auditory, tactile, proprioceptive and vestibular sensory experiences.
❑ The structure and organization that are a part of caring for a horse.

It is important that an OT or PT trained in Sensory Integration Theory evaluate the child, so that an appropriate sensory diet can be prescribed.

It is interesting that Linda Tellington-Jones has come to some of the same conclusions about the importance of body awareness in her work as a horse trainer, that Jean Ayres has found in her work with dyspraxic children. By putting horses through a series of TT.E.A.M. exercises, she noted that:

❑ The horse's confidence increases as he develops a greater awareness of his body.
❑ His coordination and movements improve.
❑ His sense of balance improves.
❑ He obeys without constraint, and develops self-control and patience.
❑ He becomes a keen observer, paying exact attention to detail.
❑ The basis for mutual respect and rapport between man and horse is established.

The horses she trains are:

❑ Safer, because they do not run away or shy in unfamiliar situations.
❑ Safer, because they listen to their rider and seek solutions together with the rider.
❑ More of a pleasure, because they give the rider a feeling of being one of a pair, of having a partnership on which can be relied less stressful, because the horse does not have to spend his emotional energy fighting the commands of the rider and can instead focus this energy toward the pleasure of both.
❑ Better performers, because they can understand what is wanted of them and they are more willing to learn (Tellington - Jones 1995.)

Sandra L. Hubbard
USA

References:
Ayres, A. J. (1979), *Sensory Integration and the Child.* Los Angeles: Western Psychological Services.
Ayres, A. J. (1985), *Developmental Dyspraxia and Adult-Onset Apraxia*, Torrance, CA: Sensory Integration International.
Fisher, A. & Murray, E. (1991), *Introduction to Sensory Integration Theory, Sensory Integration Theory and Practice*, Philadelphia: Davis.
Greenspan, Stanley (1994). Diagnostic Classification of Mental Health and Developmental Disorders of Infancy and Early Childhooh, Washington DC: Zero to Three, 31.
Reide, D. (1988), *Physiotherapy On The Horse*, Riderwood, MD, Therapeutic Riding Services.
Tellington-Jones (1995), *The Tellington-Jones Equine Awareness Method*, New York: Breakthrough Publications.
Trott, M., Laurel, M., & Windeck, S. (1993), *SenseAbilities*, Tucson: Therapy Skill Builders.
Wilbarger, P. (1984), *Planning an Adequate "Sensory Diet" - Application of Sensory Processing Theory During the First Year of Life, Zero To Three*, Washington DC: Zero to Three, 113-117.

ZPART IV
DISABILITIES

CHAPTER 13
DISABILITIES ENCOUNTERED
IN THERAPEUTIC RIDING PROGRAMS

WHAT TO DO WITH A RIDER WHO HAS - - - -

Barbara T. Engel, M.Ed, OTR

The disabilities included in this section are those disabilities that may have been seen in clients involved in NARHA's 30 largest centers in the U.S.A. These disabilities were obtained by a survey of centers. Other centers may have clients with other disabilities not listed here. With the present increase of genetic identification, new syndromes will be identified. Once a syndrome is identified, there is a better understanding, and possible development of intervention, of the disorder. <u>Diagnoses are always made by physicians</u>. NEVER ATTEMPT TO CLASSIFY A CLIENT FROM THE DESCRIPTIONS GIVEN IN THIS PAPER. DIAGNOSING ANY CLIENT CAN CAUSE MANY PROBLEMS AND IS LEGALLY UNSOUND. ONLY PHYSICIANS AND SPECIFICALLY TRAINED SPECIALISTS ARE QUALIFIED TO DO SO. Do not attempt to set up an educational or therapeutic riding program based on this information alone. Always consult a physician, therapist, or seek additional intervention information from persons knowledgeable on the subject as well as the person or gardian to which the diagnosis applies.

The information on specific diagnosis was requested by instructors of therapeutic riding centers. With the advances in medical diagnostic techniques, many disabilities that previously were encompassed under such terms as developmental delays, mental retardation, neuropathy and so forth have been identified as specific disorders. The information given here is general and not intended as a model for intervention. New research instruments are rapidly discovering and changing information regarding a specific disability. As a consequence of the acceleration of information, facts mentioned here may be outdated as of this writing. The definitions are intended to identify a diagnosis that will appear on a referral record. A client may have several diagnoses. For example, a person may have arthritis, a congenital heart defect, cluster headaches and skin cancer. This information will only give a general idea of the problem involved. Why does this child compulsively have his/her hands in their mouth? Will the problem this client presents get better, remain generally static, or will it get worse?

A classic description of a disability or disorder is given in medical literature. It is not always the case that a person with a disability "fits" the classic description. One must be careful to consider all potentials of an individual before making a judgement of his/her abilities. For example, a child with Cri du Chat syndrome was a student at a developmental school. During a funding conference, the occupational therapist requested speech therapy for a severe tongue thrust which interfered with this child's ability to be understood and acquire additional educational skills to develop reading skills. She was told that the child already functioned way above the level expected of a child with the Cri du Chat syndrome. "What more do you want!" Her request was denied. This child did not "fit" the typical characteristics of the diagnosis; and, therefore, whatever potential the child had should have been pursued. Never let the diagnosis limit the functional abilities of the individual.

It must be remembered that each child or adult is an individual with individual genetic and environmental personality traits and characteristics. These traits and characteristics which may not be caused by the disorder but can be hereditary in nature, influence any disability. Consequently no two persons with the same disabilities are the same or should be treated the same.

It is inappropriate to say these "CP kids," "those strokes," or those "mentally retarded." There is a tendency to lump persons with certain characteristics together. The most current example is the "popular" group of ADHD or attention deficit hyperactivity disorder. Children with ADHD or ADA fall into many folds. Children can be hyperactive for many reasons - too little or too much stimulation, vestibular disorders or a low arousal system. Also, ADHD can be an early symptom of a developing disability such as bipolar disorders.

This section cannot be a "cookbook" of resolutions. That would cause more problems then be of help. If one wants specific information on how to deal with a specific client, one must consult a knowledgeable therapist, the client's therapist or the physician. Dealing with many types of disabilities requires years of study in many fields. Centers are encouraged to have a qualified occupational and/or physical therapist on their staff for this reason. Occupational therapists are not only trained in neuro motor dysfunctions but are trained in cognitive and psychosocial rehabilitation. Each therapist may have been trained in specific areas and have the background to deal with specific problems that present themselves within many disabilities.

A general section is included on syndrome seen in a variety of disabilities. **WHAT TO DO WITH A PERSON WHO HAS---** will help instructors plan their programs. Remember that these are not step by step directions for solutions. Only when an individual is throughly evaluated for his/her assets, deficits and goals, can they have well-conceived program developed for them. No matter whether the instructor intends to teach riding skills, initiate recreational riding, or develop an educational intervention program, a well-thought out evaluation must be performed and a plan must be developed. This format, for an instructor in a therapeutic riding environment, is not too dissimilar from one required of a good, responsible riding instructor at any given training stable. However, the therapeutic riding instructor needs to add the disability dimension to the evaluation process.

Instructors of therapeutic riding programs need to become familiar with the disabilities of clients with whom they will work. Instructors should know what is involved regarding function with each disability, and any special considerations, in order to guide the team (along with the physical or occupational therapy program consultant), in appropriate handling of all riders. When team members have this knowledge and understanding, a safer ride can be provided to the client.

THE FOLLOWING TOPICS WILL BE COVERED IN THE ~~ "WHAT TO DO" SECTION ~~

ALZHEIMER'S DISORDER	FRAGILE EMOTIONS	PARALYSIS
APRAXIA	HEARING IMPAIRED	PARESIS
ARTHRITIC CONDITION	HYDROCEPHALUS	PATHOLOGICAL REFLEXES
ATTENTION SPAN (SHORT)	HYPER-SENSATION	RANGE OF MOTION
BRACHIAL PLEXUS PALSY	HYPO-SENSATION	RESPIRATORY DISORDERS
BRAIN DISORDERS	LANGUAGE DISORDERS	SICKLE-CELL ANEMIA
DEVELOPMENTAL DELAY	LEARNING DISABILITIES	SPINAL DISORDERS
DOWN SYNDROME	LIMB LOSS OR DEFORMITY	SEIZURE DISORDERS
(MATERNAL) DRUG ABUSE	MENTAL RETARDATION	TRAUMATIC HEAD INJURIES
DWARFISM	MUSCLE TONE	VESTIBULAR PROBLEMS
BEHAVIORAL DISORDERS	NEUROMUSCULAR DISORDERS	VISUAL PROBLEMS

Following the "what to do" section is a section on psychiatric and emotional disabilities. The last section will described 212 conditions seen in therapeutic riding programs.

BODY PARTS INVOLVED IN DYSFUNCTION
   Monoplegia involves disability in one limb.
   Hemiplegia involves disability on one side of the body.
   Paraplegia involves both of the legs and lower trunk.
   Diplegia involves the trunk and 2 arms, or 2 legs with more involvement in the legs.
   Quadriplegia involves all four limbs and trunk.
   Triplegia involves the trunk and three limbs, usually leaving one good arm.

WHAT TO DO WITH A PERSON WHO HAS ALZHEIMER'S DISORDER

❏ The rider may have some ability to control his or her actions.
❏ Face the rider as you speak. Speak slowly and use simple language when indicated. Give only one instruction at a time.
❏ Focus on the pleasure and exercise of riding.
❏ The instructor will help the rider to improve balance and strength.
❏ Give assistance when the rider first becomes confused or frustrated.
❏ Show understanding and empathy.
❏ Expect the unexpected since the rider's attention span may be short.

WHAT TO DO WHEN A PERSON HAS APRAXIA

❏ The rider may need to rely on the eyes to compensate for poor coordination and to concentrate on tasks. Give instructions for only one task at a time until it becomes apparent that the rider can handle more.
❏ One may need to help the rider get the "feeling" of the task with physical assistance.
❏ Exercise patience while working with the rider, give ample time for the rider to preform a task. Let the rider do the best he or she can and focus on moving with the horse rather then games.
❏ Do not consider the rider "dense" for having difficulty with a simple task.
❏ Use a smooth gaited horse with predictable behavior.

WHAT TO DO WITH A PERSON WHO HAS AN ARTHRITIS

❏ Riding can be an excellent exercise for a person with arthritis. It provides a good quality exercise, strengthens muscles, increases circulation and strengthens the respiratory system. The ride should be smooth and not longer than the rider can tolerate. Periods of rest may be needed. A horse with smooth gaits and transitions will be more comfortable.
❏ Be gentle when assisting the rider; do not pull on joints that are painful or have contractures. Ask the rider how to help. Most people with arthritis know how to manage their disorder.
❏ The rider should be positioned so pressure does not cause a painful joint. A sheepskin, sponge or gel pad (on the saddle) may protect the rider. A gel saddle pad (under saddle) may make the ride more gentle. Have the therapist give additional advice. A good, balanced posture can help take stress off specific joints.
❏ Exercises to relax the rider are helpful. The gentle rocking of the horse helps to stretch tight muscles and gives overall relaxation. The therapist will provide exercises to assist the rider.
❏ Children may need support. Some may need a therapist to backride with them. The backrider must be careful to provide support without applying pressure or causing the rider to lean to one side.
❏ Special equipment may be used to help a crippled hand or arm become useful. Use a horse with a smooth gait and predictable movements.
❏ A comfortable saddle that fits the rider is important - the "twist" of the saddle must fit the rider.
❏ Do not ride if the rider is having an exacerbation (worsening of disease) or complains of pain.

WHAT TO DO WITH A PERSON WHO HAS A SHORT ATTENTION SPAN

❏ Keep the tasks short but challenging. Repeat them if necessary.
❏ Make sure the rider is attentive before giving instructions. He or she may be looking at the instructor with his or her mind on other things. Speak slowly and clearly. Ask if the rider understands you and have him or her repeat the instructions back to you.
❏ Make the instructional part of the session short and allow for fun and relaxation at the end of the session like a trot.
❏ Be aware of signs of stress such as tenseness, twitching or nervousness, not following through with instructions, chatting, showing no interest, changing the subject, having increased muscle tone, sweating, or difficulty with breathing.

WHAT TO DO WITH A PERSON WHO IS <u>AUTISTIC</u>

❑   Treat the person according to the degree of disability.

❑   Approach the individual slowly and without demands.

❑   Help make this person comfortable with tasks that are easy and that bring the most joy. Add new tasks or skills slowly according to the ability to accept them. Give praise for accomplishments. Do not create stress, the rider may be already stressed due to his or her inability to communicate.

❑   Do not force or expect interaction including eye contact. Be alert to any communication attempts and offer praise for all efforts. Lack of response to your statements does not mean a lack of understanding. Some riders may need to be shown what to do - communication is always a problem.

❑   A person with autism may have low tolerance for stress and may show unusual behavior for no apparent reason. Be ready for actions such as getting off the moving horse or having a tantrum.

❑   Do not allow improper actions. Expect good behavior. Be calm, friendly and firm. Discipline, much the same as with any other child.

WHAT TO DO WITH A PERSON WITH <u>BRACHIAL PLEXUS PALSY-ERB'S PALSY</u>

❑   The therapist will move the involved arm through its full range. Exercise both arms with riding exercises.

❑   Encourage the use of both arms for riding skills, grooming and tacking activities; use two hands on the reins.

❑   The therapist will advise on special exercises or equipment.

WHAT IS INVOLVED WITH A PERSON WHO HAS A <u>BRAIN DISORDERS</u>

Brain disorders have many causes producing varying neurological deficits. Damage to the brain can occur before birth or at any age in life. Damage can be the result of imperfect development of the brain, stress causing injury at birth or during development, infections, drugs, toxins, disease, abuse, coma, drowning, seizures, accidents or injuries to the head.

WHAT TO DO WITH A PERSON WHO HAS A <u>BRAIN DISORDER</u>

❑   Respond to the muscle tone problems as suggested. (See muscle tone and handling techniques).

❑   A rider will need more time to react to stimuli since the messages from the brain to the limbs may be either imperfect, misdirected or slow. Exercise patience.

❑   Be supportive. A great deal of effort may be needed to do a simple task.

❑   Encourage relaxation and a balanced seat. Have fun - laugh and sing. Laughing and singing increases breathing, and in turn, helps relaxation and body control.

❑   Help the rider to maintain the best possible posture. This will help develop muscle balance. Do not give unnecessary help since this does not encourage strength and independence. No not ask for the rider to do too much.

❑   A rider tends to lean into support. Discourage this poor habit. Be careful not to lean on the rider with arms or hands.

❑   Encourage the rider to look up. This improves head control, posture and balance.

❑   Exercises for stretching and balance are important. Exercises should be done while the horse stands. Later, when the rider can maintain balance, they should be done at a walk. The therapist will help with proper exercises.

❑   Ataxia and athetosis make the rider appear as though he or she will fall. The rider can maintain balance better than one may think. Be alert for needed support **but do not be overprotective**. Allow time for independence.

<u>DEVELOPMENTAL DELAY</u>

Developmental delay is an umbrella term used to include most or all functional disabilities that are seen in infants and children. Initially, it was used with infants so that they would not be "labeled" until they were older when their condition could be more accurately assessed. It can include infants with true developmental delays due to premature birth, feeding disorders or due to extensive corrective surgery. With good care and therapy, these children recover and are generally normal. Other developmental delays include all children who are delayed or retarded in major areas of their growth patterns which can include any or all of the following: gross motor behavior, fine motor behavior, adaptive and language behavior and social behavior. Children who are delayed in major growth areas can include those with autism, cerebral palsy, seizure disorders and mental retardation. It is common for this term to be used instead of mental retardation, since it is felt by some to be less offensive. A person with a seizure disorder, cerebral palsy or autism may or may not be retarded in the ability to learn while those who in the past have been termed "retarded" are unable to learn at the normal or near normal rate.

DOWN SYNDROME

Individuals with an intellectual dysfunction can be low normal to severally retarded. Muscles tend to be "soft" and floppy. The joints tend to be loose and almost disjointed. Hips may be formed differently than the normal child. Hands and fingers may be small or stunted. The limbs are out of proportion to the trunk which makes it difficult to find a saddle that fits them well. There may be decreased ability to feel or control movements. Balance may be poor. Other problems can include heart conditions, breathing problems, ear infections, hearing, speech and vision problems. They may also have such disorders as autism and hemiplegia/cerebral palsy. Persons with Down Syndrome tend to act younger than their real age, but they are usually pleasant and affectionate people who love to ride and to please. All persons with Down Syndrome must be diagnosed by X-ray *before* riding since 10% of persons with Down Syndrome have Atlantoaxial instability. This is a condition of weakness and instability of the neck. This condition may cause paralysis if the person receives a jolt to the neck such as in a fall or strong thrust.

WHAT TO DO WITH A PERSON WHO HAS DOWN SYNDROME

❑ Follow suggestions under **Muscle Tone** for weak and floppy muscles. Have your therapist show you how to handle and position this rider.

❑ Support the back if it is weak and balance is poor. Encourage good posture so muscles develop in good form.

❑ This person may have a fear of heights and movement when first starting to ride. Be supportive. Let the rider get used to being on the horse before it moves. The instructor or therapist may backride with him or her one or two times.

❑ The rider's legs should be in a normal riding position--not spread too far apart--so that the hip joints are not stressed. With small children, use a narrow horse.

❑ The instructor should increase riding time slowly to increase strength and endurance.

❑ Provide support as needed.

❑ Riders that have the strength **to steady their heads and bodies** will enjoy trotting.

❑ Encourage coordination activities, mental development and riding skills that challenge the rider. Riders with Down Syndrome may have near normal intellect and can perform all kinds of horsemanship skills successfully.

❑ Do not **over challenge** these riders. They will always try to please. Some can be very manipulative. Set limits for **them** to carry out.

❑ Many riders with Down Syndrome become skilled in all areas of competitive riding and vaulting.

DRUG REACTION FROM MATERNAL DRUG ABUSE

Children who have experienced in utero fetal damage from the drug and alcohol abuse of their mothers can have a wide variety of problems such as mental retardation, cerebral palsy, attention-deficit behavior, impulsive behavior, learning disabilities or other neurological problems. The drugs in their systems may continue to cause behavioral problems for many years. These children may:

❑ Be irritable or get frustrated for unknown reasons.

❑ Have a sudden screaming tantrum due to pain or other sensations.

❑ Get "stuck" in an action or be unable to resolve a problem such as how to move the arm forward.

❑ Daydream, drift, or be unable to attend to the task.

❑ Fidget, be hyperactive, or have tremors.

❑ Appear to have behavioral problems and poor attention.

DWARFISM

People with dwarfism prefer to be called **LITTLE PEOPLE.** Dwarfism is a disproportionately short stature. There are different types of dwarfism. Intelligence, however, is mostly normal. There are characteristics which are of concern to riding programs. Children may have a middle ear infection with balance problems and speech delays. The lungs and breathing patterns may be atypical with less volume because of their small physical structure. There can be hydrocephalus with a shunt or physical problems with hip or elbow contractures, loose joints and poor muscle tone. Immature motor skills may be seen in children due to delay in structural development, decreased strength, deformed and dislocated joints.

WHAT TO DO WITH A PERSON WITH DWARFISM
❑   Check with the therapist for any special directions.
❑   Riding movements should be symmetrical so all limbs are strengthened equally.
❑   Make sure the equipment and tack you use fits the rider; select special equipment necessary for some riders.
❑   Follow procedures used for persons with arthritic conditions when joint problems are present. Check with the therapist for special handling techniques.
❑   Encourage good posture and good joint range.
❑   Follow the therapist's advice for persons with spinal curves.
❑   In growing children, avoid stress on weight bearing joints (such as trotting while standing in the stirrups). Have the therapist approve new activities.
❑   Remember, Little People are generally normal except for their physical structure. Treat them so.

Emotions can be disturbed by any disability due to the impact on the system. In turn, when the brain is damaged, the emotions can be affected because the emotional center of the brain is damaged. A rider can get upset for no apparent reason or over-react to simple things. Frustration and depression can be easily caused by fatigue.

WHAT TO DO WITH A PERSON WHO HAS FRAGILE EMOTIONS
❑   Understand that the rider may not be able to control emotional reactions; what the rider **wants** to do may not be what happens.
❑   Do not react to the inappropriate behavior but react in a matter-of-fact fashion; go on with the lesson.
❑   Give physical and mental support when needed and be patient.
❑   Use a calm, slow moving horse.
❑   Do not allow outrageous behavior. Take a "time out" for children, and adults also. Tell the rider when he or she is doing well and what is not appropriate. End the session if necessary.
❑   Do not get angry with the rider.

EMOTIONAL--BEHAVIORAL DISORDERS
It is important to understand the disorders of a person with emotional problems but do not categorize behavior and label any person with whom you work. A person with behavioral disorders usually does have a pure disorder as listed below but rather a mixture of behavioral characteristics. A rider with emotional problems will take medication to control behavior. A person with severe behavioral problems can function quite normally in a riding situation. Behavioral or psychiatric problems most frequently have a neurological basis and peculiarities may not be under the control of the individual. Do not expect the person to just "stop doing that". They usually cannot.

WHAT TO DO WITH A PERSON WHO HAS EMOTIONAL OR BEHAVIORAL PROBLEMS
❑   Check with the psychiatrist, psychologist, counselor or occupational therapist regarding special handling of any such rider.
❑   Listen carefully to the rider, do not argue or challenge a fantasy. **Direct the rider's attention to the task.**
❑   The therapist or psychologist may set definite goals and limits. Be sure they are carried out as instructed. This helps to prevent manipulation and other undesirable behaviors.
❑   Remember that the instructor is not there to "treat" the rider but to help him or her with horsemanship skills.
❑   If a rider blames **you** for problems that you have no control over, do not take this personally or respond to it. The rider may be projecting his or her feelings for someone else onto you.
❑   Provide the rider with balance and security as needed. Some may need assistance until riding becomes more familiar.

❏ Find in each rider something unique and nice. People with a long term psychiatric problems may be difficult to like but all have some traits to which you can relate on a personal and friendly basis.
❏ Try to develop a relationship between horse and rider. Have the rider spend more time with grooming and touching the horse. Touching brings one in contact with the real world.
❏ Encourage completion of the task and successes.

HEARING IMPAIRMENT

Impaired hearing or loss of hearing can be caused by problems with the ear structure (conductive hearing loss), by nerve damage (**sensorineural hearing loss**), or both. Hearing loss can be of varying levels. A hearing-impaired person uses the other senses for communication: vision, vibrations, feeling and residual hearing. The rider will need to use his or her eyes more to be aware of the surroundings.

(All of the following information refers to the rider with impaired hearing as his or her only disability. It does not address the hearing-impaired rider with multiple disabilities, although the following information may be helpful in such cases.)

WHAT TO DO WITH A PERSON WHO IS HEARING IMPAIRED

❏ Help riders to develop all their senses.
❏ Teach riders to feel the horse's movements and understand what they mean. The horse can provide the riders with much information as they learn to interpret its movements.
❏ Know your riders' skills in communication. Some hearing impaired people lip read and others use sign-language and lipreading together; others use sign-language alone. Be prepared and know how you need to interact with them.
❏ Become as proficient in sign-language as possible or utilize a sign-language interpreter. Also, remember that we all use extensive hand and body language. The hearing-impaired person can understand this in much the same way that a person with normal hearing can.
❏ For riders who lip read be sure you are face to face with them and have their attention when giving directions. Speak clearly and slowly, but use **normal** pronunciation. Use a pause between sentences. Speak slowly with children. Restate sentences which are not understood after two to three repetitions.
❏ Be certain that you are close enough for the riders to see your hands and face clearly in order to read your signs/speech.

EXPECTED BENEFITS

The same benefits which we **all** derive from riding - increased physical, mental and emotional capabilities. In addition - the exposure to **lots** of new vocabulary and language concepts assists in building of American Sign Language (ASL) and/or English skills. The horse has proven to be a very strong "motivator" for communication with children who had previously been non communicative. The relationship with the horse, which is nonjudgmental about the rider's speech and/or signs, promotes the rider's feelings of self-esteem.

PRECAUTIONS

Some hearing impaired riders also have impaired balance; be sure to check on this area with the rider, parent, doctor or therapist. Otherwise, proceed with instruction as with an able-bodied rider with normal hearing.

WHERE TO START THE RIDER IN THE PROGRAM

For a child, it is advisable to start with a leader and possibly a sidewalker (for security and communication purposes). The sidewalker can be taken away when the child's confidence has improved and attention to the instructor or interpreter is **consistent**. The leader can be taken away when sufficient control of the horse has been established. Independent control of the horse must be **excellent** before the leader is taken away; remember that the instructor will not be able to relay **any instructions** when the rider's back is to the instructor! The rider must be able to think and act independently in order to ride safely. Adults may be started with or without a leader at the discretion of the instructor.

SUITABLE RIDING ENVIRONMENT

Any kind of enclosed (safely fenced) riding area is suitable, either indoor or outdoor. It may be necessary to use only part of the enclosed ring or area by blocking off sections with poles on the ground or orange pylons (highway markers/cones). Starting the riders in a smaller area assists with attention to the instructor and improves visibility of signs/speech. When consistent attention has been established and the rider is familiar with the basic vocabulary/concepts and routine, the instructor may choose to enlarge the riding area. For safety purposes, it may be advisable to utilize leaders or riding volunteers to "pony" (the rider's horse is lead by the instructor on horseback) hearing-impaired riders on the trail, at least in the beginning stages.

THERAPIST

The hearing-impaired rider with no other disabilities will probably not require a physical therapist. However, the rider with impaired balance may benefit from the assistance of an occupational therapist with balance/vestibular activities.

TYPE OF HORSE

In the beginning stages, and **especially** for children with impaired balance, a very "unflappable" horse is a necessity! Horses that tend to spook or move very quickly are probably **never** suitable for hearing-impaired riders, since the riders cannot hear the "scary" sounds and will always be caught off-guard if the horses should shy! However, it is not necessary to use very dull, lethargic horses with hearing-impaired riders. If such a horse should "wake-up," the situation could be even more dangerous. An energetic but a calm and sensible horse will be greatly appreciated by hearing-impaired riders (and by **all** riders, for that matter!).

TYPE GAIT/MOVEMENT

Horses with a very **distinct** 2-beat trot and 3-beat canter will be helpful in teaching posting to the trot and canter leads. Learning to post on a horse with a very smooth, "shuffle-y" kind of trot can be very frustrating for a rider who cannot hear the hoof beats!

HORSE TACK

The usual English (or Western) saddle with Peacock-safety stirrups is sufficient for this rider. A handhold attached to the D-rings on the pommel will be helpful for explaining hand placement.

RIDER EQUIPMENT

No special equipment is necessary for the rider other than the usual ASTM-approved helmet. The instructor may find it helpful to have children wear safety belts when they are learning to post to the trot. The belts make convenient "handles" for hoisting children up and down in unison with the two beats of the trot.

LESSON SUGGESTIONS

Treat hearing-impaired riders in the same way as "normal" riders! The following suggestions may be helpful in planning lessons:

❏ Due to the fact that congenitally deaf/hearing-impaired persons have never heard the English language or any other spoken language, some concepts may be unfamiliar to them. Do not hesitate to ask for assistance from an experienced classroom teacher or interpreter when you run into difficulties explaining equestrian concepts to the riders (e.g., diagonals, leads, rein and leg aids, and so forth).

❏ If "a picture is worth a thousand words," a live demonstration is worth a **million** words! Use lots of visual demonstrations by a mounted instructor or other skilled rider, rather than attempting to use lots of lengthy explanations.

❏ Ask the rider(s) to ride into the center of the ring and halt so that the instructor can give explanations or complicated directions. Do not attempt to give any but the simplest directions while the riders are circling the arena!

WHAT TO DO WITH A PERSON WHO HAS HYDROCEPHALUS

A person with hydrocephalus may have a shunt. A shunt is a tube device inserted surgically which allows the drainage of fluid from the brain to a site of absorption usually in the abdomen.

❏ **A child with a SHUNT must have a carefully fitted helmet which protects the head and does not slide. There must not be any pressure on the SHUNT or the area of the head holding the shunt.** If the head is especially large, a light weight helmet may be recommended by the therapist. A special helmet may need to be adapted for this rider.

❏ Have a therapist check the helmet fit, for it must fit exactly right.

HYPER-SENSATION

Hyper-sensation, which can occur in a number of disabilities, is increased awareness to stimuli. Individuals with sensory-integrative dysfunctions or learning disabilities frequently are hypersensitive to touch and may withdraw from contact of surfaces (rough, sharp, furry) that are offensive. Hyper-sensation can occur when nerves are healing or inflamed, as in traumatic injuries or in nerve disorders. When sensation is disrupted, messages may be sent to different brain areas and can cause unpleasant sensations. Hyper-sensation can include feelings of pain, burning, tingling or pinpricks.

WHAT TO DO WITH A PERSON WHO IS HYPERSENSITIVE

1. Touch the rider as little as possible. Firm touch is less offensive than light touch.
2. Do not act as though the rider's behavior is unacceptable if he or she overreacts to touch.
3. Let the rider initiate touch, but do not force this. The deep stimulation from the horse helps to bombard the touch system and desensitization occurs.
4. Long sleeve shirts and long pants help protect against offensive sun, touch and other skin irritations.
5. Do not force the rider to touch things.

HYPO-SENSATION

Hypo-sensation, is decreased awareness of stimuli to the body. It is a loss that can be mild or complete. Sensation may be present but distorted. Pressure may seem like light touch, but the feedback from affected and unaffected limbs will feel quite different. Loss can be in not knowing the position of a limb or not being able to coordinate a limb's movements. Temperature and pain may not be perceived accurately. Loss of sensation can affect how one relates to space or interprets movement in sitting and walking. The rider may not sit up straight because of lack of awareness of how he sits. To say "put your heels down" or "tighten your grasp" may be meaningless. Total loss of sensation is present in complete paralysis, for example, when a nerve has been severed, and to a lesser degree in other injuries. Some losses of sensation may also be present in persons with mental retardation, seizure disorders, cerebral palsy, learning disabilities and sensory-integrative disorders.

WHAT TO DO WITH A PERSON WHO HAS HYPO-SENSATION

❏ Be patient and do not get frustrated as you assist the rider; he or she may not be able to do what is requested of him or her or at least in the **way** which is requested. Imagine how frustrating it would be not to be able to do a simple task such as holding on **tightly** to the reins or having difficulty grasping them at all.

❏ **Show** the rider what is meant or how to do it. Have the rider copy what is expected.

❏ Do not expect the problem to go away quickly. It may take a long time for sensation to improve, or it may never improve.

❏ Use techniques to help overcome the problem, such as adaptive reins or textured reins. Using tape on a finger to increase feeling in the hand, or attaching weights onto the limb may help (check with the therapist before using weights with a person with physical problems).

❏ A rider may not know right from left if the brain cannot distinguish body parts. The instructor may put a red mark on the left hand and a blue mark on the right hand or use one red rein and one blue rein. Say to the rider, "turn red--left" to help the rider learn directions or be able to follow a course.

❏ The therapist will provide exercises to increase sensation, such as putting the hands on the horse's shoulder, to feel the movement. The therapist will have additional ideas. Give the rider feedback on his or her actions.

❑ The horse provides the rider with stimulation in movement, pressure and skin sensation. Let the horse stimulate the rider with a rhythmic walking or trotting pace when this is appropriate. Sometimes it helps to give several taps to the rider's limb or back to increase the sensation.

❑ Remember that poor sensation has nothing to do with intelligence.

❑ For a person with little feeling in the legs and buttocks, be aware that **pressure sores** can develop. A pressure sore happens when there is continuous pressure on skin and muscle tissue without allowing for circulation of blood. Since this person has no feeling, he will not know that damage is occurring. The therapist will instruct you on how to decrease the chances of these sores developing.

❑ The rider, who is sensitive to pressure, should wear pants without seams such as riding britches.

LANGUAGE DISORDERS

APHASIA

Aphasia is the loss or impairment of speech or ability to understand speech caused by damage to the brain. Intelligence is not generally affected. Aphasia can include one or more of the following problems.

❑ **Expressive aphasia** involves the impairment or the loss of ability to produce or recall spoken words.

❑ **Receptive aphasia** is the impairment or loss of the ability to recognize and understand speech. Words can be heard but not understood-as though the words were a foreign language.

❑ **Apraxia of speech** is the loss or impairment of voluntary control of muscles which produce speech sounds. Speech may be slow or slurred.

❑ **Alexia** is word-blindness (failure to recognize written or printed words).

❑ **Agnosia** is the inability to recognize and interpret symbols, shapes, directions, sounds.

WHAT TO DO WITH A PERSON WHO HAS A LANGUAGE DISORDER

EXPRESSIVE DISORDERS:

❑ Keep in mind that intelligence is not the problem (although children with mental retardation can have these problems).

❑ It takes lots of patience to understand these riders. If possible, encourage nonverbal language.

❑ Do not be afraid to say you do not understand what the rider says.

❑ Try to encourage the use of single word responses. Say the word, then have them repeat the word, but do not push them if they cannot respond. Not being able to speak is very frustrating!

❑ It is easier to initiate speech than to respond to someone else, so give the person time to try to express him or herself.

❑ Use directions that do not require an answer. When possible phrase sentences appropriate for a simple verbal or nonverbal yes/no response.

❑ Some people may have only a few words they can say. They may use these words as though they were using full sentences. They may not be aware they cannot be understood. Tell them you do not understand.

❑ Wait a longer time for responses than when talking with people with a language disorder.

RECEPTIVE DISORDERS:

❑ Use as much nonverbal language as possible. Show the rider what you want. Often, visual demonstrations can preclude the use of language.

❑ Speak slowly and look at the rider when you speak. Use single words for children or adults with severe problems. The rider may be able to understand a little. Give him or her time to process what you say. This can take minutes or more.

❑ Do not treat the rider as though he or she is stupid because he or she cannot understand you. Just do the best you can to communicate meanings and smile.

PROBLEMS WITH PERSONS HAVING BOTH A EXPRESSIVE AND RECEPTIVE DISORDER:

❏ Communication is very difficult and frustrating with this rider.
❏ Try different methods of communication and see what works best - ask the caregiver to assist in the best method.
❏ Be patient and relax, for nothing is gained by getting upset.
❏ Use touch, expression and gestures to communicate.

LEARNING DISABILITY

Learning disability is a dysfunction of the brain caused by interference with the normal process of storing, processing and producing information. Learning disabilities can include any or all of the brain's function involving perception, conceptualization, language production and/or reception, control of attention, motor coordination, control of impulses, directional concepts, sensory perception and/or visual perception. Learning disabilities are described by terms such as minimal brain dysfunction, perceptual-motor deficit, dyslexia, attention-deficit disorder or hyper kinetic disorder. A person with learning disabilities has:

❏ Average or above average intelligence
❏ Basically normal abilities in motor, hearing, vision and emotional areas

The disability may be very subtle and unnoticed by others, but the daily performance of tasks may be extremely difficult and take a great deal more energy and effort than others may imagine. The person with this disability can change from day to day or hour to hour since he is affected by fatigue, stress, environmental influences, the complexity of the task or involvement of multi deficit areas. Learning disabilities can be associated with head injuries, sensory integration dysfunction or can be inherited.

Characteristics often seen:

❏ Shows self-centered thinking
❏ Are distractable and/or impulsive and perhaps unable to tune out distracting stimuli
❏ Has poor perception of others' thinking and actions
❏ Has difficulty observing facial and body language which may cause misunderstandings in communication
❏ May not be able to read or see all symbols or letters of a word. May reverse or displace symbols or letters
❏ Auditory perceptual difficulty may cause poor interpretation of comments, not hearing a complete sentence, hearing "slowly" or giving a delayed response
❏ May not be able to judge time and space/space relations, or know right from left
❏ May have difficulty sequencing tasks. May not function well without structure and may need to organize all tasks
❏ May persererate (get stuck in an action)
❏ Maybe able to handle only one task or action at a time, especially if a new task is presented
❏ May have a short attention span and fatigue easily

WHAT TO DO WITH A PERSON WHO HAS A LEARNING DISABILITY

❏ Try to develop some understanding of the rider's problem. The rider may be able to tell you what activities are especially difficult and which are the best ways for him to learn and understand.
❏ Do not use statements such as "Oh, but everyone has some problems like that." "There is nothing wrong with you." "Just pay attention."
❏ Problem areas may require practice and patience. They cannot be corrected easily, and some not at all.
❏ Try to figure out how the rider can learn best through his or her strong areas. Some learn best visually, others through listening. Do not pressure the person. Most people with learning disabilities are already under stress since they must put so much effort into concentration and carrying out tasks. *This lack of being able to perform is frustrating and degrading to them since **their environment** demands more from them. **This** causes a decrease in self esteem.* Try to keep everything light and happy.
❏ Give feedback on what the rider is doing and what the rider should be doing. The rider may also reverse things such as turning left for right. Saying "STOP" may trigger a "GO."
❏ Do not get upset at the rider's slow response. The rider needs time to process information without added pressure.

❏   Remember that the rider is intelligent and generally understands but may not be able to perform exactly as desired.

❏   Make sessions short when necessary, but always challenge the rider. It is depressing for a person with a learning disability to be treated as though retarded or incapable.

❏   End the session with a successful activity and a positive comment.

❏   It is very important that the activities are challenging, not dull. Remember that this rider has normal intelligence. Being slow is not a lack of intelligence!

❏   These riders may need structure. Do not confuse structure with repetition. Repetitions of simple tasks are dull and are not challenging. They do not help the rider to progress and resolve his/her disorder.

LIMB DEFORMITIES OR LOSS OF LIMBS

Limb deformities or amputations can be caused by disease, drugs, toxins or accidents. A person may be fitted with an artificial limb. These are becoming increasingly sophisticated and versatile. The rider with an amputation may choose not to wear the artificial limb since motion can cause rubbing on the skin. A rider who is born without a body part is exceptionally capable and does not seem to miss the limb. The major problem faced by this rider is the lack of balance because one side of the body has less weight and less function than the other. A rider who is missing both legs, for example, has less of a balance problem then a rider who is missing one leg.

WHAT TO DO WITH A PERSON WHO HAS A LIMB DEFORMITY OR LOSS OF A LIMB

❏   Help to develop balance. Give support when necessary.

❏   For a person with a leg missing, it may be necessary to adapt the saddle to help give the rider additional support. The western saddle provides the rider with more securely. A rider with missing lower limbs may need to have a specially constructed saddle.

❏   Give support when a rider lacks balance, security or "feels" off balance.

❏   If an artificial limb is worn, care must be taken not to cause rubbing or sores. Watch for redness. Use sheepskins or sponge to protect the limb or stump if this is appropriate. The therapist will advise you on safe methods for seating and supporting these riders.

❏   Help to develop strength in other areas.

❏   **Never** tie the rider or the residual limb to the saddle.

❏   Add weights to the saddle to give the horse an equal weight on the saddle (if the instructor is unfamiliar with saddle weighing, check with a racing tack shop who are familiar with this technique.)

MENTAL RETARDATION

Mental retardation is a disorder due to brain damage, underdevelopment of the brain or genetic disorders. Difficulties that result can be seen in mobility, vision, hearing, speech, understanding, judgment and behavior. The level of retardation is based on comparison of the level of functioning to the average child or adult of the same age. A **mildly** retarded person is an individual who has an I.Q. below 70 points. This individual can learn basic reading and math, understand social skills and function independently in self-care skills. A moderately retarded individual function at the 50% of the average ability and is considered "trainable." This means that the individual can usually function independently within the home but needs supervision outside of the home due to difficulties with judgement and immaturity in handling social activities. Many people at this level may not understand the concept of money. A severely retarded individual function at 25% or below the average person's abilities. These people can learn, but must do so slowly, and learning is dependent on various problems within the brain. Since it is difficult to test some individuals with mental retardation, it is best in the therapeutic riding area to see what tasks they can do.

WHAT TO DO WITH A PERSON WHO IS MENTALLY RETARDED

❏   Work with the riders on their level of ability and not below it.

❏   Have the rider tell you what he or she likes in general. This will give you some idea of the rider's level of function. **All people can learn** but at different rates.

❑ Keep the activities simple until you know the rider can do more. Most riders will need time to adjust to the feel of the moving horse before they can do any activities.

❑ The rider may need strict guidance to behave in an appropriate way. If this is not necessary, do not provide this structure.

❑ Do not give reins to riders until they have been instructed in rein management and you are sure they will not yank at the horse's mouth. It is easier to set good habits than to correct bad ones. Even if the reins are attached to a halter, pulling on the reins develops poor riding skills. Explain to riders that yanking on reins hurts the horse. If they cannot understand this concept, go on to games that are more at their level. The use of *Peggy the Teaching Horse* allows riders to learn the concept of using the reins without involvement of the horse. The use of reins may be more important to the staff than to the rider.

❑ Encourage situations which produce success.

❑ Give plenty of praise for a job well done.

❑ **Do not praise a poor job** since this does not give the rider proper feedback.

❑ Activities should be challenging and fun.

❑ Make sure the rider understands your directions. Speak slowly and use common words and short sentences.

ALTERED MUSCLES TONE (TONUS)

Muscle TONUS is the degree of tension a muscle needs to maintain the limb or body position in a relaxed state. A relaxed muscle normally shows slight resistance when another person tries to stretch it. If there is too much tension, muscles will be stiff or spastic. If there is not enough tension, muscles will be weak or floppy.

WHAT TO DO WITH A PERSON WITH ALTERED MUSCLE TONE

Spastic, tight and stiff muscles:

❑ Be gentle handling tight limbs. Pulling on tight muscles will make them tighter. The limb will resist quick change.

❑ Give the limb time to relax by itself, if possible.

❑ Have the rider breathe deeply. This helps to relax the rider's muscles.

❑ The rider should be allowed to maintain his postural control over his body as much as possible. Do not do anything to decrease his control since this will increase his stiffness. Help the rider balance, as necessary.

❑ If the altered muscle tone is in the legs, have the rider sit astride a wooden horse or barrel **before** riding for approximately ten minutes to encourage stretch and relaxation.

❑ Initially after the rider has mounted, one may need to let the rider relax while the horse stands so that the rider can adjust to sitting on the horse and the horse relaxes to the rider's weight.

❑ Give the rider extra time to mount or do exercises.

❑ Let the slow rocking movements and warmth of the horse relax the rider's body and limbs.

❑ Use mental image games to help the rider stretch out, such as "pretend to be a rag doll and let everything go or "imagine that there are strings tied to your legs pulling them down."

❑ The therapist may request that the limbs be gently shaken with slow, mild movement to relax the rider. Make sure not to grasp the limb tightly since this pressure will increase muscle tone.

❑ Use a horse with a smooth gait and smooth transitions.

❑ Use a horse with an average barrel to give the pelvis a base of support

HYPOTONIC MUSCLES:

There is a lack of "solidness" to a muscle, a lack of "tone". Muscles controlling the joints are weak. A person with hypotonicity (low tone) generally moves more slowly than the average person, may weigh more or "feel" heavier, because of the low tone muscle mass does not resist against gravity, has difficulty with balance, has trouble keeping his/her back straight and has poor endurance. He/she may have a problem holding his/her arms and legs as instructed since he or she may not "feel" his/her position.

WEAK OR FLOPPY MUSCLES:

❑ When positioning the rider, be careful not to pull so hard as to dislocate a joint. The muscles may be weak and not able to hold the joints firmly together.

❑ Be especially careful with young children whose bones are fragile and developing.

❑ Allow the motion of the horse to add "tonus" to the muscles before doing exercises that demand strength.

❑ Give support where needed until the rider can balance alone. Backriding by your therapist may be necessary to give good support and avoid damage to the joints.

❑ Do not allow the rider's limbs to rest in awkward or abnormal positions.

❑ Make sure the rider's head does not "bob" excessively (this can produce a whiplash effect). Stop trotting or slow down the walk. If the rider's head still bobs, discontinue the ride. A rider with a weak head/neck posture must be carefully watched by the therapist.

❑ If the rider does not have head control off the horse, he or she should not ride unless a therapist is directly treating him or her.

❑ Use a horse that provides a lot of stimulation with gaits energetic enough to increase tone but not so much as to cause an imbalance.

PARALYSIS

Paralysis is caused by the interruption in transmission of nerve impulses so that messages or sensations to a particular part of the body do not get through. There is a complete loss of muscle power and possibly sensation as well.

WHAT TO DO WITH A PERSON WHO HAS PARALYSIS

❑ Do not expect such a limb to move, for it is not possible. The rider needs to learn other ways to function.

❑ The rider will need to work on balance since it will be affected by the paralyzed limb or body parts.

❑ The rider may need special adaptive equipment to carry out activities required.

❑ Use a horse with smooth transitions and gaits.

PARESIS

Paresis is the incomplete loss of muscle power rather than total paralysis. A limb may appear to be immobilized but may have the potential of gaining function. Any movement possible may be weak, clumsy or "floppy" with poor control.

WHAT TO DO WITH A PERSON WHO HAS PARESIS

❑ The rider may not be able to control the muscle actions of the body part affected with paresis. Help the rider to perform the movement.

❑ In some exercises, it may help for the rider to "think" the movements. For example, the rider will visualize squeezing the legs around the horse and say "squeeze" to help do this. The rider is reinforcing the movement of the legs with the mind.

❑ Remember that it will take months or several years for strength and coordination to increase.

❑ The therapist will provide exercises to strengthen weak areas. Give assistance and support as needed to provide good body alignment.

❑ Let the horse's movements help strengthen the rider's movement patterns. The horse's good symmetrical walk challenges the rider with the balance and stimulation exercises needed to increase strength and endurance.

❑ Use special equipment to help balance the rider if needed.

PROTECTIVE REACTIONS

Reactions are automatic movements which occur to help a person to function effectively. When a person trips, his/her hands come forward to keep him/her from hitting his/her head and body against an object. When a person goes down the steps his/her body stays upright to align his/her body against gravity. These reactions, (called righting reactions-against gravity) and equilibrium reactions, to maintain balance, occur without thinking about them, but can be controlled at will with a person who has developed normally.

RANGE OF MOTION
Range of motion is the full swing of a limb up and down, side to side, in or out or around. **Tightness, stiffness, spasticity and weakness** of the muscles can prevent the limb from moving through its full range (limited range of motion). **Weakened or floppy** muscles can allow a limb to move beyond the normal range of the joint and make the joint "loose."

WHAT TO DO WITH A PERSON WHO HAS LIMITED RANGE OF MOTION
- ❑ Move a spastic limb very slowly and gently. **Do not pull on a tight muscle** to increase the range; this can cause the range to become tighter or possibly tear the muscles/tendons.
- ❑ Encourage the rider to move his/her own spastic limbs and also encourage him/her to use his/her voice **with the movement**, e.g., "I lift my arms up - up - up."
- ❑ Give a joint that has excess range support as you help the rider. A loose joint must be handled carefully so that there is no dislocation or tearing of weak muscles/tendons.
- ❑ Have the therapist show you how to handle the rider.
- ❑ Use a horse with smooth movements.

WHAT TO DO WITH PERSONS WITH NEUROMUSCULAR DISORDERS
- ❑ Do not let the rider get too **tired** or stressed. Increase demands in sessions slowly; **stop** for rest periods. **A weak muscle does not become strong when it is tired.**
- ❑ Always encourage good, balanced posture, with a level pelvis, so that spinal curvatures and contractures do not develop. Encourage equal strength and full range of the limbs on both sides of the body to prevent deformities. The therapist will advise you on proper seating and exercises.
- ❑ Provide the rider with support when necessary, making sure the sidewalkers do not lean on the rider or pull him/her off balance.
- ❑ Ask the rider how he/she is doing today, since people with these disorders experience changes from day to day. Get the rider involved in decision making. Remember that this person is generally of average or above average intellect.
- ❑ Be careful of tight hip muscles when putting the rider on the horse. This can cause considerable pain from stretching.
- ❑ A good exercise program is important to increase lung capacity and circulation for overall health.
- ❑ Coordination may be poor due to poor sensation, hyper sensation or weakness.
- ❑ Watch for pressure sores if the rider has poor sensation in the legs and buttocks. The stirrups should be adjusted to provide adequate support for weak legs with poor sensation. A sheepskin saddle cover can protect sensitive skin. Have the therapist assist you in these areas.
- ❑ **Excessive exercise, stress or heat can temporarily increase the symptoms.** This can be prevented or decreased by providing rest periods of ten to twenty minutes. A weakened state can be noticed by unsteadiness, slurred speech, cramping, spasms and/or decreased sensation.
- ❑ Make the lesson stimulating to the rider's intellect. Many riders can develop intermediate to advanced riding skills.
- ❑ In hot weather, have water available for the rider to drink during the lesson and spray the rider's arms and face with a light water mist to cool him/her off. Riders find this light mist cool and refreshing.

PATHOLOGICAL REFLEXES (sometimes called posturing)
- ❑ Pathological movement patterns or reflexes are seen in people with brain injuries. A person with brain damage may have weak or absent protective reactions, which may result in an inability to stay upright in sitting or standing or to rebalance when thrown off balance. Reflexes are seen in specific patterns.
- ❑ The head is lifted and the total body straightens.
- ❑ The arms bend and the total body bends.

❏ The hand is raised to the face while the arm turns inward toward the body.

❏ The legs may cross each other (scissoring).

Examples of reflexes that may be triggered (set off) while a rider is mounting, dismounting or performing exercises and riding skills on the horse include:

❏ A small rider is raised out of his/ her wheelchair by being lifted up under the arms, causing the legs to cross (scissoring).

❏ While riding the rider's head falls forward, which causes the arms to bend and the legs to straighten. This reflex is called a symmetrical tonic neck reflex.

❏ The rider now attempts to raise his/her head and it falls backward, causing the total body to straighten. This is also called a tonic labyrinthine neck reflex.

❏ The rider is turned on his/her stomach across the horse, causing the entire body to flex or bend. This is called a tonic labyrinthine neck reflex.

❏ The rider is asked to point his/her toes, causing the hips and legs to straighten and tending to grip the horse around the barrel (scissoring).

❏ The rider looks to the right and the arm and leg on the face side straightens while the arm and leg on the skull side bend (asymmetrical tonic neck reflex).

❏ The horse blows through his/her nose, and the child startles, with the head extending and arms and legs extending (Moro).

❏ The rider **cannot** control pathological reflexes which are triggered by movement or responses to the environment.

WHAT TO DO WITH A PERSON WHO HAS PATHOLOGICAL REFLEXES

❏ A therapist with neurodevelopmental training will show the team how to avoid triggering pathological reflexes.

❏ Contact your therapist. Therapists have numerous techniques that can be used to normalize reflexes

❏ Do not expect the rider to be able to correct his/her posture easily or at all.

❏ Ask the therapist how you can help the rider obtain better posture and limb movements.

❏ Relaxation will help the rider to control his or her movements with a more normal pattern.

❏ Do not expect the rider to relax upon command. He/she is more likely to become tense to this command. Movement, singing, fun or other tactics are more likely to produce the right response.

❏ See the section on **Helping the Rider Sit Up on the Horse** for assistive techniques.

❏ **Do not expect or encourage** the rider to accomplish skills or tasks that increase abnormal movements.

❏ When the rider is relaxed and having fun, abnormal reflexes may decrease.

❏ Have the rider sit upright on the seat bones and the fleshy part of the butt to create a deep seat. This may encourage a straighter back--but watch out for, and prevent, a posterior tilt and rounded back.

❏ Do not over do the riding. More is not better. Observe when the rider is at his/her peek. Stop the session when the rider has reach his/her peak. This point this may happen at 10, 20, 30 or 45 minutes.

RESPIRATORY DISORDERS
WHAT TO DO WITH PERSONS WHO HAVE RESPIRATORY DISORDERS

❏ Exercise is good for this rider as it improves the lung muscles and stimulates general health.

❏ Exercise should be carefully increased to tolerance.

❏ Dust must be avoided, both the dust from the arena and the dust that comes from the hair of the horse. Wipe the horse with a damp cloth prior to mounting. A surgical or dust mask over the nose of the rider may help decrease dust inhalation.

❏ Cold or dampness may trigger an asthmatic attack.

❏ Have plenty of water on hand for riders with cystic fibrosis since they sweat more than usual and may get dehydrated.

SICKLE-CELL ANEMIA

Sickle-cell anemia is a chronic blood disease, most common in black males. There are periods of crisis where the disease worsens. The disease is characterized by pain in the feet, hands and abdomen. It affects the lungs, the liver, spleen and kidney. A stroke - CVA - can occur because of circulatory problems.

WHAT TO DO WITH A PERSON WHO HAS SICKLE-CELL ANEMIA

❏ The instructor will request extra help in handling such a person for maximum safety since falls must be avoided.

❏ Use protective sheepskin pads or padded supports when necessary. Damage can be caused to the skin rather easily.

❏ Beware of complaints of pain, and inform the instructor immediately.

SPINAL CORD INJURIES

These injuries are due to trauma to the spine, or less often, from tumors. Damage can lead to complete paralysis when the spinal cord has been severely damaged, or it can be partial, with weakness only to areas below the injury. Where there is just weakness, there may be improvement with rehabilitation. Damage in the cervical area of the spine involves the neck, arm muscles and the diaphragm. The thoracic area of the spine involves the chest and abdominal muscles. The lumbar area involves the hips and knee muscles. The sacral segments involve the bowel, bladder and reproductive organs. The degree of dysfunction is related to the specific spinal cord segment and the type of damage.

WHAT TO DO WITH A PERSON WITH A SPINAL DISORDER

❏ The rider's **skin** may be very prone to **pressure problems**. There may be a need for a sheepskin or other seating equipment to cover the saddle to avoid pressure areas. Watch for any reddened areas, and inform the instructor **immediately**.

❏ Remember that this person has had structural damage to his or her body and not to the mind.

❏ This person may wear braces to protect weak areas.

❏ The instructor may select special riding equipment and tack for support and security.

❏ The rider should wear pants without seams to prevent skin irritation from friction.

❏ Be sure that the rider feels balanced after mounting before you move the horse. Provide adequate support.

❏ Include this rider in your team to assist you in understanding his/her specific problems.

❏ A therapist will help to instruct in exercises to develop balance and increase strength.

Spinal curvature which throws the body out of balance is not normal and may be associated with many disorders. A **structural spinal curve** is caused by diseased or abnormal bone structure. A **functional spinal** curve is usually flexible and may be due to persistent poor posture. A functional spinal curve can lose its flexibility, and the person may develop contractures after a period of time.

❏ **Kyphosis** is a "humpback" or rounded upper back.

❏ **Lordosis** is a hollow back of the lower spine or an abnormal forward curve in the neck area.

❏ **Scoliosis** is a side-to-side curve. The vertebrae may deviate to the side but also rotate; scoliosis can cause the hips to tilt and the leg on one side to appear shorter.

WHAT TO DO WITH A PERSON WITH A SPINAL CURVATURE

A rider with a spinal curve must be carefully positioned on the horse with the pelvis level. Improper positioning can cause the spinal curve to worsen. **It is important for a therapist to supervise this rider.** It is important that the person's riding posture keep him balanced and upright.

Muscle balance can be increased by:

❏ A well-balanced horse.

❏ A deep seated, balanced saddle properly centered on the horse.

❏ Circling the horse in large circles in the direction that tends to straighten the spine.

❏ These activities will be initiated and supervised by the instructor.

❑ Supporting the rider from the back by a backrider will not necessarily straighten the spine. The backrider should be a therapist who knows how to best position the rider's spine.

❑ Stirrups should be adjusted to achieve a level pelvis and encourage symmetry.

SEIZURES

Seizures are associated with changes in electrical brain activity. Common symptoms may include headaches, pain, fever, nausea, vomiting, dizziness, fainting, sweating, drowsiness, loss of bladder control and mild to violent motor activity. Most riders with histories of seizures are controlled with medication so they do not have seizures or have seizures that are very slight. Seizures can be influenced by such things as fever, hot weather, boredom, stress or hunger. Some people know when their seizures are about to happen. Seizures can also occur without warning or apparent cause. Riders tend to have seizures before or after riding.

CHARACTERISTICS OF SEIZURES:

❑ Minor or petit mal seizures may involve momentary loss of consciousness, sometimes so short that it can hardly be noticed. Some loss of awareness or increased tone can be noted.

❑ Motor seizures involve rapid and repeated motor movements or jerking. The jerking can involve the whole body or just a limb. These can be with or without loss of consciousness.

❑ There may be a period of restlessness prior to the seizure.

❑ Seizures can cause pain, pleasure, non specific feelings or brain damage. Severe seizures can also cause incontinence.

WHAT TO DO WHEN A SEIZURE OCCURS
MINOR SEIZURES:

❑ A small seizure lasts a second or two. Stop the horse. Support the rider and check to make sure he or she is normal. Follow the instructions of the therapist. If the rider is not all right after a few seconds, stop the ride for the day.

❑ With a seizure that may last "a blink of the eye" without drowsiness or loss of consciousness, the rider may continue to ride if the instructor or therapist makes this decision. If the rider continues to ride, place your arm over his/her legs to steady him/her for a while.

❑ Be aware of loss of balance even after a small seizure.

❑ Do not put demands on the rider after a seizure. There may have been only a pause in awareness with a seizure, but there may be some disorientation. Be sure the rider is completely "oriented" before giving any commands.

MODERATE OR MAJOR SEIZURE:

❑ **Stop the horse.** Calmly lower the rider to the ground and lay him/her on his/her side (in case the rider vomits he or she will be able to clear hi/her throat). All other horses and riders should carefully leave the arena. **Do not try to interfere with the seizure; let it run its course.** Do not give the rider anything to drink. After the seizure, take the rider out of the arena and let him or her rest. The instructor must take charge of the rider as soon as possible. DO NOT ATTEMPT TO INSERT ANYTHING INTO THE RIDER'S MOUTH. CALL THE PARAMEDICS FOR SEVERE SEIZURES.

❑ Instructors or therapists (unless they are RN or LVN) are not qualified to give seizure medicine--or any medicine--and can put themselves "at risk" if they give any medication to riders/program participants.

TRAUMATIC HEAD INJURIES

Traumatic head injuries are caused by an accident or battering to the head. The individual may recover completely with time and therapy or may have permanent neurological damage in mild, moderate or severe form. The period of recovery may vary from within a year to many years.

VESTIBULAR PROBLEMS

The vestibular system affects one's body in relation to space, the direction of one's movement or the lack of movement. This system affects muscle tone, body balance, visual perception, and alertness. When there is damage, or this system does not work well, a rider has difficulty with balance and the muscle tone necessary to maintain balance against gravity. Some riders need increased movement to make their systems work. They may "rock back and forth" frequently and show great joy when the horse trots. Others are hypersensitive to movement, especially subtle movements. These riders may be fearful when they start riding. Sudden movements such as a quick turn or the horse shying might cause these riders to panic. The horse provides vibrations, which are produced by the natural side-to-side, back-and-forth and up-and-down movements: excellent stimulation for both types of riders.

WHAT TO DO WITH A PERSON WHO HAS <u>VESTIBULAR</u> PROBLEMS

❑ For riders who need lots of movement, change directions and speed frequently.
❑ Riders, who are hypersensitive to movement, may need to ride for short periods until they can tolerate movement better. The therapist may have you trot the horse for short periods. Make sure the rider does not slip while trotting.
❑ Do not say things like "It's OK; it's not so bad." Remember that the problem is **disagreeable to the rider**; his/her physical system is over reactive.
❑ Most riders who are hypersensitive to movement have fewer problems with a rough gait or trotting. The therapist may mix slow movements with fast movements, to increase the rider's tolerance to subtle movements. Ask the rider what feels best and repeat that action. Even a nonverbal rider will indicate what is pleasing.
❑ If the rider gets too tense from trotting, trot only for short periods. Help the rider to relax. Have the rider sit on a sheepskin pad and use a vaulting surcingle. The softness of this pad may help to relax the rider and the vaulting surcingle provides good solid handles for security.

<u>VISUAL</u> DISORDERS

Most people with vision disorders have low to partial vision. Normal vision is considered 20/20. A person who is legally blind has 20/200 vision or worse with corrective glasses. This means that a legally blind person can see at twenty feet what a normal eye sees at 200 feet. Moderate impairment is 20/100 to 20/200. A mild visual deficit is 20/70 to 20/100. A legally blind person may see a finger in front of his/her face and general hand movements and may be able to tell where light comes from or to see light but not know its source. A visual impairment that limits seeing to what is seen in front is called **central vision**. Central vision can be limited to tunnel vision where only a small area is seen, as though one were looking through a tube. Or, when one looks ahead and can only see to the sides, the condition is **peripheral vision**. Having good peripheral vision is very important in riding since this is what one uses to see the relationship of the horse to the rest of the arena. Other visual problems include the following:

❑ **Myopia**--near sightedness. Close vision is good, but at a distance objects are blurred.
❑ **Hyperopia**--far sightedness. Objects are clear at a distance but "fuzzy" up close.
❑ **Strabismus**--cross-eyed or squinting. The eyes do not focus together to see an object clearly. The object may "dance," be blurred or move. It may appear as though there are two of everything (double vision). Some people will use one eye for near vision and the other eye for far vision. In such cases it takes more time of focus.
❑ **Nystagmus**--rapid involuntary movements of the eyes. This problem causes difficulty in fixing the eye on an object. The head will often be held at an angle to steady vision.
❑ **Cortical blindness**--there is nothing wrong with the eyes, but the visual parts of the brain do not function. There is no **meaning** to what one sees.
❑ **Ptosis**--the eyelid droops. This does not affect vision.
❑ **Amblyopia**--a lazy eye. One eye may drift. There is difficulty focusing, in depth perception and blurred vision.
❑ **Cataracts** cause blurring of all vision to varying degrees.
❑ **Photophobia**--sensitivity to light, can be painful.

Visual problems can be of varying degrees and in various combinations. Many people are able to compensate well for a deficit. REMEMBER--SOMEONE IS THE RIDER'S EYES AT ALL TIMES. Riders can experience all riding environments with appropriate preparation and leadership.

WHAT TO DO WITH A PERSON WHO IS <u>VISUALLY IMPAIRED</u>

- ❏ Let the rider tell you if vision will cause a problem during riding or other activities.
- ❏ Let the rider help you understand the problem; listen carefully. Observe what the rider can see. Some people may deny their problems.
- ❏ Allow the rider time to interpret what he or she sees and to adjust eye focus or feel. Have the rider feel the saddle and reins. Name aloud the parts of the horse, saddle and bridle. Orient the rider to the surroundings.
- ❏ Give a mental picture if the rider cannot see an object or the environment.
- ❏ Gently touch or speak to the rider. Do not surprise a blind rider with a heavy grasp or a sudden touch. Tell him or her what you plan to do.

GUIDELINES FOR WORKING WITH PERSONS HAVING PSYCHIATRIC AND EMOTIONAL DISABILITIES

Philip Tedeschi, MSSW

Increasing numbers of persons with psychological impairments are being referred to therapeutic riding programs and/or equine-facilitated psychotherapy treatment centers. This section will provide a description of the most commonly seen psychiatric and emotional disorders in clients referred to these programs. Both the risk and potential for these clients will be briefly discussed, and, of necessity, much information will be of a general nature. Specific characteristics and differences among these disorders must be understood if these clients are to benefit from the horse and its environment. Instructors and staff working with these clients need to possess a clear understanding about behavioral and psychological conditions, and should seek help from qualified mental health professionals. Further, the ability of the therapeutic riding program to address such problems must be investigated and validated.

The pervasive impact of emotional disabilities can interfere with every aspect of an individual's life. Unfortunately, the emotionally disordered individual frequently is viewed as "less affected" than someone with more observable impairment. Therefore, despite the absence of physical disability, riding center staff must begin to understand how to provide therapeutic riding and animal facilitation services to address the individual needs of these clients. The primary resource to better understand diagnoses common among persons with "mental" disorders is the Diagnostic and Statistical Manual of Mental Disorders III-R (DSM-III-R), prepared periodically by the American Psychiatric Association. It is considered the primary reference for those in the mental health field since it categorizes the symptomatology and manifestations of each separate diagnosis. The material included in this chapter is drawn from DSM-III-R and is presented in a format useful to those in the therapeutic riding community. This is not meant to substitute for consultation with mental health personnel in regard to individual clients. It is recommended that instructors working with an emotionally disturbed clientele receive additional training specific to their needs and work directly with the mental health team. Therapeutic riding programs working with this population should have a mental health therapy consultant (such as an occupational therapist or social worker with a specialty in psychiatry) on their staff.

Throughout this section, several separate and very different categories of emotional impairment will be described. However, it is important to note that several concepts will apply consistently throughout. For example, any rider who is in treatment for his or her impairment has a therapist or treatment coordinator, called a treatment agent. It is important for the therapeutic riding instructor and staff mental health therapy consultant to confer with the primary treatment agent. If effective therapeutic riding services are to be provided, then a clear sense of each rider's disability and potential, as well as his or her current treatment plan, must be gained. Treatment agents involved with the rider may include psychiatrists, psychologists, social workers, counselors, occupational therapists, special education teachers, recreational therapists and parents. When involved with the rider in the treatment, they will be able to help instructors answer these important questions:

- What are the primary and secondary presenting problems?
- What is it hoped this client will gain from the therapeutic riding experience?
- What are the most debilitating aspects of his or her disorder?
- Are there any special treatment implications or issues that one should be aware of in providing the client therapeutic riding services?
- How will one know if the program is therapeutic for him or her?
- What concerns is this client working on?
- What kinds of medication does this client take? Are there any side effects?
- Can the client's therapist accompany him or her to the therapeutic riding sessions? If not, why?
- How long will this client participate?
- Does he or she have to earn the right to participate?
- Does this client exhibit any inappropriate/dangerous behavior?

- How should one respond if the client acts out?
- Can one attend Individual Education Plan (IEP) and treatment staffings?

In other words, by raising questions, the therapeutic riding instructor creates the expectation that treatment agents respond to therapeutic riding services with the same type of professionalism that would be expected in any other type of service. Information must be shared if clients are to receive maximum help. The treatment agent must also be aware of the services that the center is able to offer. Centers can be developed to provide:

- Generalized riding lessons for a mixed population
- Generalized riding lessons for persons with psychiatric disorders
- An equine-assisted treatment facility for persons with mental disorders
- An equine-assisted treatment facility for a mixed population
- A general riding program with equine-assisted therapy

Regardless of the diagnoses, it is important for a riding instructor to have an accurate history of each client, including any propensity toward becoming easily agitated or disruptive, assaultive or self-destructive. This information is essential to safeguard the horse, the volunteer and the student. The riding instructor should have a basic understanding of the medication that clients receive and the potential side-effects. The staff needs to know if the program area accessible to the client is secure from dangerous items (i.e., no razor blades, first-aid kits, medicines, knives) for those with a tendency for self-destructive behavior. Additional volunteers may be needed when close supervision is required, but the referring agent **must provide staff who are familiar with a client who may be at risk for destructive behavior of any kind or for running away.** The therapeutic riding staff cannot be expected to conduct a session and also be responsible for high risk riders. The exceptions may be centers conducting equine-assisted therapy exclusively with psychiatric clients who have staff especially trained for this work.

Many clients may be referred from group homes or institutional settings where, by law, strict confidentiality rules prevent unnecessary and inappropriate disclosures regarding treatment issues. However, confidentiality protocols can be established within a riding center to fulfill legal requirements, or the riding program can be integrated into a treatment center where the riding modality becomes a part of the client's treatment plan.

Case material must provide pertinent information regarding each individual such as:

- Type of disorder
- Behavior to be expected
- Precautions and contraindications
- Side-effects of medication
- Propensity toward becoming easily agitated
- Disruptive, assaultive or self-destructive behavior toward the horse, staff/volunteers, self
- Need for safe environments--secure from dangerous items (no razor blades, first-aid kits, medicines knives)
- Behavioral objectives
- Expectations from therapeutic riding/equine activities and/or equine-assisted therapy

MAJOR CATEGORIES OF DYSFUNCTION

DEVELOPMENTAL DISORDERS

The term *developmental disorders* refers to several different diagnostic classifications with the primary ones being mental retardation and pervasive developmental disorders. There is also a classification of specific developmental disorders which are generally considered chronic (ongoing) in nature and have pervasive effects that continue throughout the person's life span. Within these broader categories, however, there are specific labels (changed from earlier DSM labels) defining separate types of each of these disorders.

MENTAL RETARDATION

Mental retardation might best be described as a problem of sub-average intellect accompanied by impairments in adaptive and social functioning. Most commonly, a mental retardation onset is prior to the age of eighteen. The condition of Mental Retardation is broken down into five specific diagnostic categories:

- Mild Mental Retardation; previously labeled educationally mental retardation
- Moderate Mental Retardation was previously considered trainable mental retardation
- Severe Mental Retardation
- Profound Mental Retardation
- Unspecified Mental Retardation

Unspecified Mental Retardation is generally used with younger infants and children or individuals who make it difficult to evaluate, and thus to diagnose the degree of retardation present. The **Severe** and **Profound Mentally Retarded** makes up only a small percentage of the entire population. These individuals generally require constant supervision and frequently are found in group homes, residential or institutional settings. It is important to note that despite the unusual and sometimes abnormal behavior attributed to this diagnosis, most mentally retarded individuals referred for therapeutic riding can learn to prevent or reduce, if not eradicate, inappropriate behaviors and live a worthwhile and productive lifestyle. The primary treatment modality for individuals with mental retardation is behavior modification. The more minor forms of mental retardation can benefit from individual and group psychotherapy.

PERVASIVE DEVELOPMENTAL DISORDERS

Pervasive developmental disorders refer to disorders in development seen in early childhood and adolescence, primarily referred to as **Childhood Schizophrenia**, **Autism** and **Child Psychosis**. Of these, the most common condition seen in riding programs is Autism. This is a condition in which a wide variety of intellectual levels are found along with behavioral and motor problems. In order to establish appropriate educational and therapeutic goals, the rider's IQ must be assessed. A therapeutic riding lesson for an autistic rider usually involves breaking down learning tasks into small components, each one separately geared toward success. In addition, behavior modification appears to be the most commonly used and effective means for reducing inappropriate behaviors commonly associated with this particular condition. However, riders with autism frequently are on medication to assist their control of impulsive and inappropriate behaviors, and this may ameliorate many of the most difficult patterns of conduct. (Individuals with autism, who are seen by occupational therapists, may sometimes be treated successfully for both behavioral and motor dysfunctions with the sensory integration approach to treatment).

SPECIFIC DEVELOPMENTAL DISABILITIES

These conditions refer to disorders affecting academic skills, language and speech and motor skills. Generally, individuals with these conditions are referred to neurologists and educational specialists, occupational therapists and speech and language pathologists. These conditions may not be diagnosed until the child has developed other behavioral problems, thus bringing him or her to the attention of school officials or parents. With these students, it is important to gear the lessons toward successful outcome and utilization of the students' strengths, minimizing their weaknesses. IEP (individual educational plan) goals can be integrated into the student's riding lesson plan, thus reinforcing the process of improvement.

DISRUPTIVE BEHAVIOR DISORDERS

As the title suggests, children with these conditions are seen as disruptive, having very low self-esteem, and exhibiting temper tantrums. Parents sometimes report that these children have been difficult from early childhood. Under this category there are three separate disorders:

- **Oppositional Defiant Disorder** describes a child who generally is having difficulty following parental limits or school rules and is getting into frequent conflicts with authority figures, peers, and sometimes the Law. In general, the primary form of treatment used with these children in traditional settings has been behavioral modification systems, reinforcing acceptable behaviors and reducing inappropriate behavior through either ignoring or shaping that behavior. Frequently attention-deficit and hyperactivity are associated with this disorder. It is common to find these children receiving some form of psychotropic medication. In addition, learning disabilities are pervasive as secondary diagnoses with this condition.

- **Conduct Disorders**. The individuals with this diagnosis demonstrate a fairly severe disturbance in behavior. In residents from group homes serving delinquent populations, this is a common diagnosis. These students have had multiple run-ins with the Law, frequently have failed other out-of-home placements, have tendencies toward aggressive or assaultive behaviors, drug use, gang behaviors, suicidal behavior, as well as other delinquent activity. In addition, it is common to find some form of family dysfunction or trauma associated with current or early childhood experiences. These students frequently are on medications. At times, these students are referred with a history of fire-setting, animal abuse or assaultive behavior. It is important for the riding center staff to be aware of the risk of including these clients in their program. The instructor must set clear, firm, and realistic goals within the setting.

Even though, in traditional settings, these individuals may have been difficult to treat, an animal facilitated therapy has proved to be effective. Recognition of the horse as a living creature that requires nurturing, responsibility, and appropriate care-taking are crucial to the student's ability to learn to care for others. The horse becomes a metaphor for how to treat all people.

Inappropriate behaviors cannot be ignored and consequences should be immediate. If the student is being inappropriate or unsafe around the horses, he or she should be removed immediately. Needless to say, there must be good communication between the riding center staff and those mental health professionals who are treating these students, concerning any particularly inappropriate behavior.

- **Attention-Deficit Hyperactive Disorders (ADHD)**.
This diagnosis is frequently associated with learning disabilities and has gone through a multitude of redefinitions. At different times, attention-deficit or hyperactivity were considered entirely separate diagnoses. Usually, onsets of ADHD are during prepubescence or early childhood. It might be most appropriate to view this diagnosis as a multiple handicap. The primary forms of treatment are medication, behavioral modification, sensory-integrative therapy, special education services, family therapy and individual therapy. These various interventions need to be utilized together in order to provide effective treatment. Strategic reinforcement and consequences for behavior are important for the student to learn.

Students, who are unable to sit still and adequately focus in the classroom, can begin to learn in the active therapeutic riding setting. Lesson plans need to be broken down into manageable, understandable steps in order for the ADHD student to successfully complete them. For example, first direct the students to go into the barn, secondly, ask the students to find a grooming bucket; thirdly, ask the students to find the curry comb in the bucket; fourth, ask the student to work with a particular horse; finally, ask the student to pick up the curry comb and use it in a particular manner.

Therapeutic riding program staff, who will be using the behavior modification method, must have training in it before using it with clients. The riding instructor needs to understand the specific behavioral objectives that students are working toward within the equine setting. In order for behavior modification to be effective, timing is everything. Appropriate and inappropriate behaviors need to be addressed immediately and in the same consistent manner as used by the referring agent. Students generally have poor insight into their behaviors and frequently avoid accepting responsibility for their actions. A riding instructor can assist students in looking at their behaviors by demonstrating the way they relate to the impact on the horse and his environment.

PERSONALITY DISORDERS:

Personality disorders are generally considered *Axis II* (see reference) diagnoses. They include three clusters:

- Cluster A
  - paranoid personality disorders
  - schizoid personality disorder
  - schizotypal personality disorders
- Cluster B
  - antisocial personality disorders
  - borderline personality disorders
  - hystrionic personality disorders
  - narcissistic personality disorders
- Cluster C
  - avoidant personality disorder
  - dependent personality disorders
  - obsessive/compulsive personality disorders
  - passive/aggressive personality disorders

It is well beyond the scope of this section to discuss any of these conditions in detail. However, it is common for persons with these diagnoses to be referred to therapeutic riding programs which accept emotionally and psychiatrically impaired riders. The functioning of these people can vary greatly, and may fluctuate, but the conditions are usually chronic. In addition, mood disorders can accompany the primary condition. The chief forms of treatment with persons with personality disorders include pharmacological therapy, cognitive restructuring therapies, and behavioral modification. The therapeutic riding program staff can assist in a variety of ways, working jointly with the treatment team. Again, appropriate supervision must accompany these riders, and high risk clientele must be identified before being received in the riding center's program. The treatment agent should assist the instructor in setting out behavioral objectives and maintaining communication among all team members so that the approach used with each individual is always consistent.

PSYCHOACTIVE SUBSTANCE-ABUSE DISORDERS:

This classification describes persons who engage in pathological use of psychoactive substances. These could include alcohol, opium, amphetamines, heroine, cocaine, inhalants, depressants, hallucinogens and nicotine. Although new in its application, equine-assisted therapy can serve as an additional treatment service for individuals in substance-abuse treatment programs. Those with addictive behaviors, such as drug use, need to break a chain of events and be helped to develop other healthy lifestyle activities. Therapeutic riding can provide replacement behaviors and exciting activity for the chemically dependent client. The riding instructor needs to work closely with treatment staff because treatment of a chemically dependent client can often be very difficult, complicated and dangerous. The staff of the equine-assisted therapy team needs to secure all items such as alcohol, rubbing alcohol, paint thinner, paints, medication for the horses, drugs of any variety and nicotine in order to assist this rider in not relapsing by having access to these items. In addition, the riding center staff must be aware that the withdrawal process can result in extremely inappropriate behaviors. Some programs, without expertise in this field, should decline services to chemically dependent persons until they have received "detox" treatment. Following this stage, therapeutic riding can be an excellent tool for recovery and maintenance of abstinence.

EATING DISORDERS:

The two primary eating disorders, seen among persons most commonly referred to therapeutic riding programs, are anorexia nervosa and bulimia nervosa.

- **Anorexia Nervosa** is a very serious and complicated psychiatric disorder. The anorexic might be defined as an individual who starves him or herself to the point of poor health or even death. The person with anorexia, through a process of severe cognitive distortions, denies the existence of a problem. Significant problems in working with the anorexic client are body strength and body images.

- **Bulimia Nervosa**, another diagnosis considered an eating disorder, is difficult to treat and frequently will require inpatient hospitalization in order to control the overeating and purging characteristic of this condition.

Persons with eating disorders must be under the care of experienced mental health professionals and should not be "treated" by a therapeutic riding team without professional guidance. Suicide is the most common form of death for persons with these conditions, reflecting the emotional devastation of the disorders. While working with the anorexic client, the riding instructor should not conspire with the client in denying the severity of the symptoms or the nature of the problem. The cognitive distortions associated with the image, weight and distorted view of him or herself, which is carried by the client, will be reinforced if volunteers or instructors minimize the seriousness of his or her problem. Discussions related to this problem should be left to the treatment team unless otherwise instructed.

Therapeutic riding can be of significant assistance in the long term treatment and recovery of Anorexia Nervosa and Bulimia Nervosa because it effectively challenges these riders' experience of being out of control of their lives.

The riding instructor must understand the behavioral objectives in order to participate actively with the treatment team. A client's therapist should initially attend the riding session in order to frame the effective metaphor* to confront the pervasive, devastating, distorted thinking of these disorders.

SCHIZOPHRENIA:
It is beyond the scope of this section to fully describe the types of manifestations and effective treatment modalities used in the treatment of schizophrenia. The four different types are categorized as: disorganized, catatonic, paranoid, and undifferentiated schizophrenia. For each the treatment varies somewhat. If working with a rider with schizophrenia or a history of the disease, staff should confer especially closely with the referring party or therapist in order to understand the specific behavioral treatment objectives and interventions. The kind of expectations the therapist has from the riding program and its activities need to be well known in advance. Since schizophrenia can be episodic, even though a chronic condition, it is possible to see fluctuating behavior week by week, as well as extreme and bizarre conduct. However, clients with schizophrenia usually are receiving some form of medication which effectively controls or ameliorates their problems. On the other hand, medications can severely affect their functioning ability and cause ticks, sluggishness, inability to focus, lacks of concentration, involuntary body movement and loss of balance.

Nevertheless, it is important for the riding program instructor, staff and volunteers to treat these clients as much like their normal clientele as possible. Their style of instruction should provide a sense of security and consistency from week to week, as well as provide predictability and caring attitude for their clients. Firm behavioral guidelines and lesson requirements should be carried out so that the clients understand what is expected and the limits set for them.

For example, provide the same rider with the same horse each week, and always start the lesson with familiar material. Allow time before the lesson for the client to orient to the stable environment. This will allow him or her to attach to the activity of coming to the lesson every week, and to perceive the instructor as not threatening or endangering him or her on any way. Further, be sure to give deserved praise.

Inappropriate behavior should be responded to and not avoided. Such behaviors are actually being taught and reinforced by ignoring them. However, unless working directly on the advice of the therapist, it would be unwise to force a schizophrenic client into activity to which he or she is resistant. If a client becomes agitated, it may be appropriate to separate this person from the other riders and guide the client to a quiet area for a "time out." Lastly, many schizophrenic clients are housed in residential and institutional settings and have developed "institutionalized behavior." It is important for volunteers and instructors to be familiar with institutionalized behaviors such as repetitive self stimulation or mutilation.

*An image, figure of speech where one thing is compared to another in such a way that its likeness throws new light on the subject.

MOOD DISORDERS:

Mood disorders include the following general types. All now considered bipolar to characterize the mood swings commonly seen:

- with **manic** features
- with **mild** features
- with **depressed** features

Depression can be categorized as either single episode major depression or recurrent major depression. Some individuals suffer from a manic phase, some with both manic and depressed, and some with simply a depressed phase. The acute features of any of these diagnoses should be treated as very serious emergencies, and clients would not likely be seen at the riding center at that time. Yet, for persons in the subacute or chronic stages of illness, the therapeutic riding center can become an integral part of assisting them to overcome the debilitating effects of this disorder. Many are on medication which provides sustained relief from symptoms and the affected person can function in a relatively normal way. Like eating disorders, mood disorders continue to perpetuate themselves through cognitive distortions of the world and of the images of themselves which these individuals carry around. It is common for these individuals to feel helpless or out-of-control.

Cyclothymia is a form of depression considered to be less serious or to have milder manifestations than a major depression; however, it refers to an episode or recurring episodes of depression. Many individuals with minor forms of depression, such as Cyclothymia, are never formally diagnosed as such. Riders with physical disabilities and other limitations, serious life stressors, or emotional or psychiatric illness, frequently have cyclothymic disorder in addition to their primary diagnosis. These individuals can have their behavior attributed to being lazy, not being interested in anything, and unwilling to participate. Individuals with cyclothymic disorder may have some warning that they will be regressing into their depressive mood and may be able to set up therapeutic riding sessions on an as-needed basis to confront and prevent the mood swing, therefore allowing the client to remain in a stabilized fashion.

Dysthymia, another depressive disorder, is similar to cyclothymia and as far as the therapeutic riding staff are concerned, the clients will be treated with the same procedures. Initially, the staff of therapeutic riding centers can become an integral part of assisting these individuals to overcome the debilitating effects of their disorders, working closely with the clients' treatment or treatment agent to offer strategic interventions. When disorders are well into remission, these clients can safely participate in a regular therapeutic riding program as a volunteer and benefit from the social approbation associated with volunteering. Research in the area of mood disorders shows that exercise in particular can address some of the primary depressive features of bipolar disorders. Metaphoric therapeutic riding challenges the helplessness, distorted thoughts, and out-of-control feelings that these individuals experience.

This condition primarily refers to major depression with a single episode, with recurring or chronic features, and is a very serious and debilitating diagnosis with self-damaging characteristics, and persons affected need to be closely supervised. Persons, who are severely depressed, will have difficulty finding the motivation to participate or volunteer for any activities. If such a student is asked if he would like to take part in an activity, even if the rider has some interest in it, depressive features frequently will prevail and prevent him from participating. The riding instructor needs to approach these persons with a firm, and yet, a sensitive manner. Thus, rather than asking if they should like to participate, they would be given a structured directive to do a specific activity. Volunteers should be made aware, by the treatment agent, of the client's manipulation methods used to avoid activity and participation. In this way, therapeutic riding can be important in assisting, and especially maintaining a client's recovery from depression.

ANXIETY DISORDERS

This label generally refers to a wide range of phobias and panic disorders as well as to post-traumatic stress disorder which can usually be categorized as acute or delayed. There are many different panic disorders and phobias. Anxiety disorders are common in persons with emotional or psychiatric conditions. In these cases, the riding instructor should try to gain understanding of the specific criteria and manifestations of the illness. Some examples of these disorders are obsessive (persistent idea or emotion) compulsive (rituals) behavior, agoraphobia (morbid fear of space) and panic attacks. As with many other psychiatric disorders involving control of impulsive behavior, medication can be used effectively for control. When working with such persons, contact **must** be maintained with the treatment agent in order to understand the overall objectives and strategies of treatment; the instructor and staff **may be asked by the treatment agent** to reinforce specific expressions of feeling and emotion during the sessions.

POST TRAUMATIC STRESS DISORDERS

This disorder is the result of trauma caused by physical injury, emotional stress or sexual abuse. It can be seen as either the acute or the delayed phase of a traumatic occurrence. Delayed onsets usually occur six months or more following the precipitating event. In some populations, it is common for a secondary diagnosis, such as substance abuse disorders, depression, or generalized anxiety to accompany the stress condition. These individuals may also have flashbacks (intrusive memories related to all of their senses).

A program, which provides equine-assisted therapy, offers the treatment agent/team a setting to deal with a variety of problems. Some of the major goals the **treatment team** can accomplish for their clients include improving self-image, confronting the impression of being out of control or powerless, helping to re experience or integrate the trauma into the actual experience, and learning to monitor and manage the intense sensory input of the equine setting. Within the therapeutic riding activities, it is possible to recreate a variety of situations and degrees of stress to assist the treatment team in reaching the deeply buried emotions of the client. In addition, the pervasive need of these individuals to feel in control, and again be responsible for the events that happened to them in their life, can be satisfied.

In working with sexually abused clients, it is important to recognize that the process of spreading the rider's legs and sitting on a warm and moving animal can be a trigger for post traumatic stress symptomology related to their own victimization. With riders who have a history of being sexually abused or have dissociated that experience to the point where nobody is aware that they were sexually abused, one must be sensitive to the possibility of triggering a fastback during the riding lesson. Any event that appears to be a trigger when a rider becomes emotional, frozen, begins to dissociate while in the riding lesson, or starts crying should be addressed by the treatment agent. Through the intentional use of metaphor, post traumatic stress symptomology can be strategically addressed.

CONCLUSION

This concludes the discussion of emotional and psychiatric disorders to be presented. Those chosen for inclusion are considered to be the most commonly referred diagnoses to therapeutic riding centers. This section's purpose has been to encourage the therapeutic riding community to become more familiar with both the disabling features and the interventions useful in working with persons with emotional and psychiatric disorders. In addition, it is hoped that this section will encourage the therapeutic riding instructor and program staff to closely align themselves with the mental health treatment teams. If clients with serious psychiatric or emotional disturbances come to your program without a referring agent or from agents who resist sharing diagnostic and treatment information, the staff of the therapeutic riding center must determine whether it is appropriate and safe to all concerned to work with such persons, despite what they feel could be the benefit of therapeutic riding.

One would never accept the responsibility of a bus load of physically involved disabled riders without medical information and contraindications. The same standard of services should be applied to emotionally, socially at risk, and psychiatrically impaired riders.

Diagnostic and Statistical Manual of Mental Disorders III-R (DSM-III-R) is the primary reference for the mental health field prepared by the American Psychiatric Association.

Axis I -   Includes all mental disorders with the exception of Axis II disorders which are considered to be developmental and personality disorders.

Axis II-   Refers to developmental disorders and personality disorders generally beginning in childhood or adolescence and continuing into adult life. As an example, mental retardation and autism are considered pervasive developmental disorders listed as an Axis II diagnosis.

Axis III-   Though not addressed in the DSM-III-R, this category is used to indicate any physical disability relevant to the understanding of the individual.

Axis IV -   Provides a scale to determine the intensity and severity of psychological or social stressors that have occurred over the past year. This allows better understanding of the individual's presenting problems.

Axis V -   Is a scale assessment of the overall psychological, social and occupational functioning of the individual. This is usually listed as the global assessment of functioning scale which indicates the highest and lowest level of functioning that can be anticipated from that student.

Philip Tedeschi
USA

Reference
DSM III-R
Spitzer, L. R., Et al. (1987). Diagnostic and Statistical Manual of Mental Disorders. (3rd ed, revised).
    Washington, D.C.: American Psychiatric Association.
Spitzer, L. R., Et al. (1989). DSM III-R Casebook: A Learning Companion to the Diagnostic and Statistical Manual Of Mental
    Disorders (Thirded revised). Washington, D.C.: American Psychiatric Association.

SPECIFIC DISABILITIES, DISORDERS OR DISEASES

THE INCLUSION OF DIAGNOSIS LISTED IN THIS ARTICLE <u>DOES NOT</u> SIGNIFY INDICATION OR CONTRAINDICATION FOR THERAPEUTIC RIDING. Please refer to *Therapeutic Riding II Strategies for Rehabilitation,* the *NARHA Guide*, the client's physician or your national guideline for appropriates disabilities to be included in your riding program.

Achondrogenesis

A hereditary disorder characterized by hypoplasia of bone resulting in the shortening of limbs. The head and trunk are of normal size.

Achondroplasia (dwarf)

A hereditary congenital disorder causing inadequate enchondral bone formation resulting in a form of dwarfism. A person who has undergone poor or lack of growth and as a result is of small in stature. The trunk is normal, and the limbs are short, three prong hands, and lardosis.

Acidemia, Methylmalonic

Cause is an inherited autosomal recessive trait due to enzymes deficiency. Mental retardation results due to the deficiency and seizures. The disorder appears in the first months of life with many abnormalities in respiration, digestion, liver disorder seizures, low muscle tone, and developmental delays.

Acne

A noncontagious, inflammatory condition of the sebaceous glands of the skin seen most often in adolescence and young adults.

Acoustic Neuroma or Schwannoma

A tumor on the sheath of the vestibular portion of the eighth nerve. Symptoms include unilateral hearing loss, tinnitus (ringing in the ear) disequilibrium. If the tumor becomes large, it may affect the 5th and 7th nerve causing numbness in the face. Early removal can bring on complete cure.

AIDS (Acquired immune deficiency)

Caused by the HIV lymohotrophic virus. A transmissible retro viral disease The depressed immune system makes infection of the nervous system more prevalent. It is a progressive disorder that causes slow deterioration since the person cannot defend against infections. It can be transmitted through contact with infected blood.

ACTH (Adrenocorticotropic hormone) Deficiency

An endocrine disorder with the decrease or absence of adrenocorticotropic hormone. This hormone is produced by the pituitary gland. Symptoms include severe loss of appetite, weight loss, nausea and vomiting and possibly hypotension and weakness.

Addison's Disease

A chronic, usually progressive disease that affects the outer layer of the adrenal glands which manufacture certain hormones. This imbalance causes increased excretion of water and low blood pressure leading to dehydration. Symptoms include fatigue, loss of appetite, change in skin color, gastrointestinal pain, dizziness, vomiting, diarrhea, apathy and little concern about daily activities. Cause unknown but thought to be related to autoimmune disorders, or due to other disorders which destroy the adrenal glands. It can occur at any age in both sexes.

Agenesis of Corpus Callosum

A congenital abnormality that involves the complete or sectional absence of the fibers which connect the cerebral hemispheres of the brain. Seizures may be present early on. There may be mental retardation, learning problems and a lag in physical development, but also normal intelligent and development may occur.

Albinism

A hereditary disorder that causes absence of pigment from the eyes and/or skin and hair due to a defective metabolism. There maybe associated congenital problems such as visual defects and ocular abnormalities and nystagmus.

Alopecia Areata

Total hair loss in a specific area thought to be an immune disorder. Hair regrows in most cases within a year but a relapse can occur.

Alper's (poliodystrophy) Disease

Onset in infancy to childhood with death within 2 years. Seizures, poor coordination, mental deficits and possible cortical blindness and deafness.

Alstrom Syndrome

An inherited disorder with characteristics of degeneration of the retina leading to visual impairment and childhood obesity. There is involuntary rhythmic movements of the eyes and loss of central vision. In addition, loss of hearing and diabetes mellitus in later childhood.

Alzheimer's Disease

A progressive neurological dementia most often seen in elderly people but can occur as early as 25 years. Cause is unknown but can be diagnosed by brain tissue biopsy. It is a progressive neurogenic disorder lasting from five to twenty years. Both mental and physical capacities are lost over time.

Amelogenesis Imperfecta

A genetic disorder causing defect or the lack of the development of tooth enamel. Loss of teeth, infections, gum disease and bone loss may be secondary. Treatment is by capping teeth. There may be sensitivity to the teeth/gums.

Amyotropic Lateral Sclerosis (Lou Gehrig's Disease)

A disease that destroys the motor neurons of the body, leaving the person unable to move. It effects persons generally between 40 and 60 years but can occur in the 20s. There is no cure. Life span is 3 to 10 years with 3 to 5 the average. Symptoms begin with muscle weakness beginning in the lower limbs and progressing upward, eventually involving respiration, speech and swallowing. Sensation and cognition are not affected.

Anaphylaxis

Extreme hypersensitivity following sensitization to a foreign substance. It is an immediate response to the introduction of specific antigen that is characterized by ulcers, edema, respiratory distress, pulmonary hyperemia and shock. The degree of response can be mild to fatal.

Anemia, Fanconi's

An inherited disorder leading to a deficiency of certain blood cells produced by the bone marrow. Occurs mainly in children, more males than females, resulting in abnormalities of the heart, kidney and skeleton and causes Aplastic anemia. There is easy bruising and nose bleeding. The disorder may cause slowed or no growth, small head, underdeveloped sex organs, pathological reflex reactions and increase patchy pigment. There maybe bones absent, small eyes, crossed eyes. They maybe prone to leukemia.

Anemia, Aplastic

A rare blood disease caused by suppression of bone marrow. The person may experience fatigue, listlessness and weakness. After physical activity, the person may encounter headaches and breathing difficulties. They are more prone to infections to which they react more than normal.

Angelman Syndrome

A neurological disorder with resulting severe mental delays or mental retardation in the severe to profound range with jerky movements and balance impairment, hyperactive and hyper motoric behavior usually observed between ages three to seven. Oral motor incoordination causing feeding problems early on with later absence of speech. Receptive language is higher than expressive non-verbal language. They tend to put hands and toys in mouth with much drooling. They have a happy attitude with frequent laughter and noticeable protruding tongue, difficulty walking with uplifted arms and a stiff gait but hypotonic and ataxic. This may resemble cerebral palsy. Symptoms can include a small head, sleep disorders and seizures with an abnormal EEG. Physical features are normal but may be distorted by their movements. They maybe sensitive to the sun. Scoliosis may appear in adolescence.

Anorexia Nervosa

Avery serious and complicated psychiatric disorder characterized by an individual who starves him or herself to the point of poor health or even death. The person with anorexia, through a process of severe cognitive distortions, denies the existence of a problem. Significant problems in working with the anorexic client are body strength and body image.

Antisocial Personality Disorder

A person whose behavior bring him/her in constant conflict with society and people. This person does not profit from experience, punishment nor maintains loyalties or feels guilt, This person may be irresponsible and immature and rationalized the behavior to be warranted.

Anxiety disorders

Feelings of extreme uncertainty, panic, tension, irritability or crisis. The anxiety may be caused by real or imagined situations. The individual may look fatigued, may sweat, have difficulty breathing or be very apprehensive. Whether the situation is caused by a real or unreal situation, it is <u>real</u> to this person.

Aphasia

A specific language deficit due to cortical brain disease. Aphasia can be divided into two areas, sub fluent aphasia relates to frontal lobe disease with motor problems and fluent aphasia presents strange or incoherent speech that the subject may not be aware of. Fluent aphasia is related to damage to the dominant temporal or temporoparietal damage and does not present motor problems.

Apraxia

The inability to perform a learned motor act due to a lesion of the cerebral hemispheres. Apraxia does not affect mobility or the desire to perform an act. It is thought to relate to the connect of the motor cortical area to the cortical area that makes the decision to perform the motor act.

Arnold-Chiair Syndrome

A disorder caused by the misplacement of the brain stem which becomes elongated and flattened and protrudes into the upper spinal canal. Hydrocephalus is frequent; mental impairment can be present.

Atherosclerosis

A form of arteriosclerosis in which deposits of yellow plaques form within the large and medium arteries.

Arthritis, Degenerative

Or osteoarthritis is caused by trauma or continued stress to joints. Destructive changes to the bones and joints occur which can become painful and cause mild to severe limitations of movement.

Arthritis, Juvenile Rheumatoid

Juvenile rheumatoid arthritis is a chronic disorder which may appear in children between two and four years of age. The disease may involve only a few or many joints. The soft tissue of the joints is inflamed, painful and weak. There may be contractures. The disease has periods of inflammation (active) and periods of remission. In 85% of individuals affected, the disease may disappear at puberty. Others continue on with the adult version of rheumatoid arthritis.

Arthritis, Psoriatic

Arthritis that is associated with psoriatic, a chronic inflammatory skin disease. It can be a type of rheumatoid arthritis or a separate disease. The distal joints of the fingers are most often involved.

Arthrogryposis Multiplex Congenita

A congenital disorder characterized by deformity and ankylosis of joints. Joints are most often in flexion with limited motion and contractures. There is atrophy of muscles.

Arthroplasty

The replacement of a joint. Plastic surgery of a joint such as hip reconstruction.

Asperger's Syndrome

Over development of one facility or skill in an otherwise autistic person.

Asthma

A disorder characterized by an increased response of the trachea and bronchi to various stimuli causing narrowing of the airways, producing wheezing. The problem can be mild to severe. A rider with severe asthma should have instructions in his or her file giving information on what to do in case of severe attacks. An asthmatic person can be allergic to horses, dust, pollens, hay, and perfume. If the rider becomes much worse in the stable environment riding is not appropriate.

Ataxia

Failure or coordination of voluntary muscle actions particularly those involving the limbs. Can be caused by injury, disease or tumors. The exact symptoms will depend on the site of damage. Cerebellar- hypotonia of muscles; frontal lobe-equilibrium disturbance, kinetic or motor-affect motor actions, sensory loss of proprioception between the motor cortex and peripheral nerves, spinal involvement due to diseases of the spine.

Ataxia, Marie's Hereditary

A hereditary ataxia involving the cerebellar.

Ataxia, Telangiectasia (Luis-Bar Syndrome)

An inherited disorder with an onset of progressive cerebral ataxia and nystagmus in infancy or childhood. Liver functions are abnormal, and lung infections are common.

Ataxia, Friedreich's (hereditary ataxia)

(see Friedreich's Ataxia)

Atrioventricular Septal Defects

A congenital heart disorder pertaining to the atrium and the ventricle of the heart.

Attention Deficit Hyperactivity Disorder

Cause unknown, but there seems to be a family tendency. Tendencies include difficulty to attend, hyper motoric activity, short attention span, impulsive behavior, difficulty following directions. Learning disabilities may be present. ADHD may continue into adulthood. Children respond to structured environments with decreased stimulation and areas which allow space to move.

Autism

A non-progressive neurological disorder that clearly appears before 3 years. There is a language and communication dysfunction. The following characteristics are prominent:

1. Self-preoccupation--may not relate to people; avoids eye contact; has delayed or no social smile.
2. Communication dysfunction--lack of speech or unusual speech patterns; may repeat what you say ("parrot-like"); difficulty in expressing wishes.
3. Basically normal physical development with abnormal repetitive movement actions such as moving the fingers continuously; seeking stimulation.
4. Perseveration or sameness--tends to get "stuck" in an action or obsessed with something such as a possession, spinning an object, rocking or perseverance of an idea, and may be fearful of new things.
5. May appear deaf or blind although he or she can hear and see.
6. May be very smart in specific skills. Generally has excellent memory. Autism may be very mild with near normal functioning to very severe with functional retardation.
7. Function can vary from hour to hour or day to day; for instance, a skill can be performed at one time but not at the next try. Autism can exist in combination with other problems created by organic brain disorders.

Bell's Palsy

A not too uncommon nonprogressive disorder resulting from the compression of the 7th nerve or decreased blood supply causing facial nerve paralysis. Cause maybe due to a virus or other causes. Part or all of the face can be effected. Recovery is dependent on the degree of damage- if partial, complete recover, can be within 1-2 months. Eye glasses can protect the open eye from dust.

Binswanger Disease

Refers to multiple white matter infarcts and causes multi-infarct dementia. A chronic, progressive subcortical encephalopathy of later life due to arteriosclerosis of small blood vessels marked by uncertain gait, urinary incontinence, emotional and memory problems, convulsions and hallucinations.

Brain Tumor

Tumors are growths which may be benign or malignant. There are many kinds of tumors which may be located in various parts of the brain. Damage to the brain, if any, will depend on the location of the tumor, pressure on surrounding tissue, or damage to other tissue in its removal.

Buerger's Disease

Cause is unknown. It is often seen with young males who smoke. There are blood clots and restrictions of blood supply to major body parts. Symptoms include coldness, color changes of limbs, ulceration of the skin. The disease lasts 1 to 4 weeks. A rare disease of the small arteries and veins.

Bulimia

An eating disorder that is difficult to treat, and frequently requires in-patient hospitalization in order to control the overeating and purging characteristic of this condition.

Cancer, Skin

Malignant tumors of the skin. Can be in many forms and shapes such as blisters, wart like, mole like, etc.

Carpal Tunnel Syndrome

Caused by the compression of the medial nerve within the carpal (wrist) tunnel producing pain upon flexion of the wrist, edema of the fingers. Pain in the wrist, fingers and can extend to the elbow; can cause dysfunction of the hand .

Cataracts

A irregularity of the lens of the eye that causes a film and loss of clarity. Blindness can occur or poor vision. There are many types of cataracts and many causes. Some respond to treatment; others do not.

Cerebellar Degeneration, Subacute

Causes may include decreased thiamine by alcoholic or nutritional, autoimmune disorder, or pre cancer. It involves the degeneration of nerve cells through out the cerebellum. Symptoms include coordination problems, speech problems, swallowing problems and vision problems. Onset is about 50% more in males than females.

Cerebral Palsy

Caused by damage to the motor (movement) area of the brain. CP is an injury; and not a disease, characterized by a lack of ability to control the body. The injury can occur before birth, during birth or during the early developmental years. Cerebral palsy may be accompanied by other brain disorders such as seizures, mental retardation, vision and hearing problems or learning disabilities. All motor abilities of the body can be affected. The disorder can be very mild or severe, resulting in minimal to extreme movement and coordination difficulties with various body parts moving in unison. When asking the rider to raise his head, his chest and arms may also rise. When bending the arms, the legs may also bend. These actions are not under the rider's control. Types of cerebral palsy include the following:

1. **Spastic:** There is abnormally high "tone" in muscles (hypertonic--stiff arms/legs and trunk) making smooth movement difficult. The feeling is as if the arms are grasping a seventy-pound boulder when picking up the reins. The rider with severe spasticity cannot regulate the amount of movement or tension the arm or leg produces. He or she will also have difficulty with balance and staying upright.

2. **Athetoid:** There is excessive and seemingly purposeless erratic movement. It is as though the limb cannot decide if it will reach or retreat. The muscles alternate between normal and low tone. Posture lacks stability. The body and limbs tend to move at the same time. Speech is also affected.

3. **Ataxia:** There is incoordination of voluntary muscle action. A person with this problem will be clumsy, shaky, may show tremors and walk with a wide based gait. As in the athetoid rider, there is a lack of stability.

4. **Rigid:** There is extreme stiffness. The rider displays constant excessive muscle tightness with little ability to move or bend.

5. **Mixed**: Spasticity and athetosis can be present concurrently in many of those afflicted with cerebral palsy. Some may have spasms in addition to other problems. Spasms are sudden involuntary muscle contractions which cannot be relaxed.

Cerebrovascular accident (CVA, stroke)

Caused by an interruption of the brain blood supply, generally affecting one side of the brain, which causes motor impairment (loss of speech or arm and leg movement) to the opposite side of the body. The incidence of stroke rises with age but can occur in infants as well as the aged. A CVA can cause mild to severe neurological damage or death. The dysfunction may improve over time, from months to years, so that the person heals completely. Other individuals may continue to have mild to severe problems. A child will usually recover more quickly than an adult.

Charcot-Marie-Tooth Disease (peroneal muscular atrophy)

A chronic familial polyneuropathy - an inherited autosomal dominant trait with an onset during childhood or adolescence. Distal muscles atrophy begins in the feet and legs and progress to the hands.

Charge Association

Cause appears to be inherited. A rare disorder involving some or all of the following: a congenital heart disease, retarded growth and development, central nervous system disorders, absence of eye tissue, deformity of oral cavity, ear deformity with loss of hearing and deformity of sexual organs..

Chiair II Malformation

see Arnold-Chiair Syndrome

Chromosome 4

See Huntington's Disease

Chromosome 9

The end part of the short arm of the chromosome number 9 is missing due to a genetic defect during development of the fetus. At birth, one can notice hands and feet defects, eyes are set close together and can be slanted with a flat nose, and the forehead protrudes due to early closure of the frontal bones. Ears maybe malformed and the mouth small. Genitals maybe malformed. Other organs can also be involved, including heart problems, and protrude through the stomach area. The degree of severity depends on the length of the arm of the chromosomal that is missing. Mental retardation with developmental delays are usual.

Chromosome, trisomy 13 (Patau Syndrome)

A congenital disorder due to trisomy of chromosome number13. It is symbolized by failure to thrive, microcephaly, severe mental retardation, seizure disorder, sloping forehead, deformity of eyes, ears, palate, congenital heart condition and other abnormalities.

Chromosome trisomy 18, Ring (Edward's Syndrome)

A congenital disorder that is due to the trisomy of all or most of chromosome 18. Characteristics of this disorder include severe mental retardation, microcephaly, hypertonicity, distortions of the hand, sternum, pelvis, face, and ears. Ventricular septal defects are present. The disorder is seen mostly in females, and they tend not to thrive well.

Chromosome trisomy 21 (Down syndrome)

Individuals with Down Syndrome, (3.6% translocation, 2.4% mosaic) a birth defect, can have any of the following characteristics which may affect their ability to ride. Intellectual function can be low normal to severally retarded. Muscles tend to be "soft" and floppy. The joints tend to be loose and almost disjointed. Hips may be formed differently than the normal child. Hands and fingers may be small or stunted. The limbs are out of proportion to the trunk which makes it difficult to find a saddle that fits them well. There may be decreased ability to "feel" or control movements. Balance may be poor. Other problems can include heart conditions, breathing problems, ear infections, hearing, speech and vision problems. They may also have such disorders as autism and hemiplegia/cerebral palsy. Persons with Down syndrome tend to act younger than their real age, but they are usually pleasant and affectionate people who love to ride and to please. **10% of persons with Down Syndrome have Atlanto-axial instability and must be diagnosed by X-ray *before* riding. This is a condition of weakness and instability of the neck. This condition may cause paralysis if the person receives a jolt to the neck such as in a fall, the horse bolting or strong thrust.**

Chromosome 22, Trisomy Mosaic

An extra chromosome 22 is present in some cells of the individual which affects more females than males. The severity will depend on the percentage of cells involved with the extra chromosome. Features present include unequal development of both sides of the body, shortened limbs and a webbed neck. There may be a hearing loss on one side, missing fingers and toes, drooping eyelids. Intelligence may be mildly impaired. There maybe abnormal kidneys and blood vessels to the heart, and sexual organs can be poorly developed.

Chronic Fatigue Syndrome

Characteristics of this disorder include excessive fatigue or easily fatigued with no relief from bed rest. Activities of daily living reduced due to the fatigue by more than 50% for more than 6 months and may continue for years. Cause is unknown. Effects females more than males.

Cleft Lip and/or Palate (Hare lip)

A congenital deformity caused by the incomplete formation of the closure of the upper jaw bones or the roof of the mouth. May include a complete opening to the nasal cavity, a small opening or a split of the lip. May affect speech and eating.

Clubfoot

Clubfoot includes many deformities of the ankle and foot. The foot can be turned in any direction at birth. It is thought to be caused during the development of the fetus and must be corrected in infancy. Mild cases with treatment will perform as a normal foot. Others may walk with a peg leg effect.

Congenital Dislocation of the Hip

An inherited disorder that is caused by a congenital shallow hip socket.

Cohen Syndrome

A genetic disorder that involves multiple facial abnormalities involving the eyes, ears, and mouth, muscle weakness, mental retardation, delayed growth, and overweight.

Colitis, Ulcerative

Ulceration of the colon

Cor Triatriatum

A disorder where the pulmonary veins enter a separate chamber rather than passing directly into the left atrium.

Cornelia de Lange Syndrome

Congenital malformations characterized by microbrachycephalia, abnormal limbs, abnormal faces, mild to severe retardation and physical retardation. Spasticity can be present.

Creutzfeldt-Jakob Disease

Chronic degenerative disorder of the nervous system with slow progressive dementia. There is a loss of neurons in the cerebral cortex, basal gandlia, brainstem and may also include anterior horn cells of spinal cord. Possibly caused by a slow virus. Myoclonic jerks maybe present along with visual disturbance.

Cri du Chat Syndrome (cat cry)

Called the cat cry syndrome because infants produce a high kitten-like cry. Caused by the partial deletion of the short arm of chromosome 5. The syndrome affects size of body, a small head, low weight, facial features and can involve short bones. Cleft palate may be present. Mental retardation from mild to severe are usually present. Developmental delays of all kinds may be present and respond well to intervention.

Crohn's Disease

A chronic condition that causes cramps, abdominal pain, diarrhea, fever, anorexia and weight loss.

Cushing Syndrome

Causes by adrenocortical hormone. Signs may include rapidly developing fatness, osteoporosis and kyphosis of the spine, hypertension, diabetes, muscular wasting and weakness.

Cystic Fibrosis

An inherited disorder of the exocrine glands. The major complication is chronic pulmonary disease.

Dandy-Walker Syndrome

A congenital disorder causing malformation of the brain. The rear of the head is enlarged with hydrocephalus. There are motor, cognitive and developmental delays. Weakness, seizures and irritability with headaches may be present.

Dementias - see Presenile Dementias, Alzheimer's

An overall decline in cognitive function such as in Alzheimer's Disease.

Depressive disorders

Cause extreme sadness, feelings of rejection, a low self-esteem, feeling constant failure, negative attitudes, feeling let down and feeling guilty. People affected by depression are often quiet and withdrawn. The rider may tell you he did not want to ride or did not enjoy the session even though he actually did.

Diabetes, Insulin dependent

Onset is during adolescence or childhood but can occur at other ages. It is caused due to the lack of the pancreas suppling or producing insulin that cannot convert nutrients into energy needed to maintain activities of daily living. It is believed to be genetic or environmental. Injections are required to control blood sugar. Growth may be hindered in children. The condition can lead to cardiovascular and kidney disorders, damage to nerves and to vision.

Down Syndrome

(see chromosome trisomy 21)

Dupuytren's Contracture

A painless chronic contractor of the hand marked by thickening of the distal processes and of the palmer fascia and the inability to fully extend the fingers.

Dyelexis

Greater then normal difficulty in learning to read, comprehend reading material though has normal to above normal IQ. Can be inherited or congenital.

Dysautonomia, Familial

A dysfunction of the autonomic nervous system.

Dysplasia, Epiphysialis Multiplex

A congential developmental disorder characterized by irregular ossification resulting in dwarfism.

Dystonia

A group of abnormal involuntary movements and the disorders in which the movements are present. The movements are the results of sustained muscle contractions that produce twisting and repetitive movements and abnormal postures.

Dystonia, Torsion

A rare disorder characterized by progressive involuntary movements of the trunk and limbs. It can be an inherited disorder or may be associated with another disorder.

Dystrophy, Myotonia

A rare inherited disease that appears during early adulthood in both sexes. Major symptom is the inability to relax a muscle after a contraction. Loss of muscle strength with atrophy involves all muscles along with dysfunction of speech and motor abilities. Mental deficiency and cataracts may occur.

Encephalitis, Herpetic

An acute viral infection of the central nervous system caused by the complications of herpes simplex virus. Early symptoms can be headaches and seizures. It is contagious and passes through the fluid-filled blisters that are seen on the lips or genitals and can be accompanied by fever. They may be brought on by colds, emotional stress or skin lesions. When the CNS is involved, weakness, fatigue, drowsiness, confusion, stiff neck and paralysis can occur but lesions of the skin are absent. Early antiviral treatment may cure the disease.

Encephalitis, Japanese

An infectious disease that is transmitted by mosquitos. It is most common in Asia. Symptoms are severe and flu like. Neurological impairment can occur including shock and coma.

Encephalitis, Rasmussen's

A disease that affects the central nervous system causing progressive hemiparesis, seizures and mental impairment. It effects children and may follow viral infections.

Encephalomyelitis, Myalgic

An infectious disease - probably a virus affecting the immune system. Mostly seen in adults in both sexes. It affects the central autonomic and peripheral nervous. Symptoms appears as a severe flu but nervous system disorders accompany the flu. It may resolve in a few weeks, can reoccur or last for years.

Epilepsy (seizures)

A disorder associated with changes in electrical brain activity. Common symptoms may include headaches, pain, fever, nausea, vomiting, dizziness, fainting, sweating, drowsiness, loss of bladder control and mild to violent motor activity. Seizures can be influenced by such things as fever, hot weather, boredom, stress or hunger. Some people know when their seizures are about to happen. Seizures can also occur without warning or apparent cause.

Erb's Palsy

Is due to damage to the upper brachial plexus which involves the shoulder and upper extremity. It can be caused by a difficult delivery of a newborn or by a traumatic injury. The damage causes internal rotation of the shoulder and arm. The hand is pronated. Arm maybe flexed. There may be loss of sensation and atrophy of muscles.

Fetal Alcohol Syndrome

Caused by the mother drinking alcohol that in turn causes serious birth defects in the fetus. Both physical and mental developmental lags are present. Physically, the infant is small with a small head and mental retardation. Other symptoms may be failure to thrive. There may be physical signs such as incomplete development of jaw, mouth with cleft palate, a flat face, seizures and heart problems. Problems are non-progressive and vary in intensity.

Fibrodysplasia Ossifications Progressiva

A rare inherited disease involving connective tissue including ligaments, tendons and muscles, which are ossified into bone. It is a progressive disorder which starts in childhood and continues through adulthood leading to skeletal deformity and related problems. Swelling and pain may occur as the ossification process proceeds. Scoliosis and kyphosis are common. As the disorder progresses, limitations of movement occur leading to complete immobilization. Blunt trauma should be avoided since trauma causes abnormal bone development.

Fibromatosis, Congenital Generalized

The occurrence of multiple beign tumor composed principally of fibrous connective tissue.

Fibromyalgia

Cause is unknown. Pain in the muscles and connective tissues. It is recognized as a form of soft-tissue rheumatism. It does not involve the joints. It can occur anywhere in the body. A main symptom is that it moves around. Most people also suffer from sleep disturbance, fatigue, numbness in the extremities, mood changes, difficulty concentrating, gastrointestinal problems and headaches. It can be triggered by other diseases or events that cause extreme fatigue such as multiple sclerosis or lupus. Appropriate exercise is one of the main strategies for easing the pain.

Fragile X Syndrome

An X-linked syndrome associated with mental retardation, enlarged testes, big jaw, high forehead and long ears.

Friedreich's Ataxia

A genetic disorder which begins to appear in late childhood or early adulthood. It is a degenerative (slowly worsening) disease that affects the spinal cord and lower section of the brain. Intelligence is normal, but walking becomes unsteady. All muscles can be affected causing incoordination and balance problems. Spinal curves may develop because of muscle weakness and imbalance. Vision and speech may be affected. Symptoms may vary from day to day.

Graves Disease

It may be due to an imbalance of the endocrine system that causes an increase in the production of thyroid secretion. The eyes protrude, there is sensitivity to light, swelling of the hands and feet, poor tolerance to heat, emotional instability and an irregular heart beat. There maybe a single attack or recurring incidents.

Guillian-Barre Syndrome (GBS)

A rapidly progressive disease that causes inflammation of the nerves leading to weakness and paralysis beginning with the legs and progressing upward to include lips, tongue and voice box. The autonomic nervous system can be involved. Viral disease symptoms maybe present. May be an autoimmune disease. The condition can stabilize within 6 to 24 months and recovery may begins. The sooner recovery begins, the better the prognosis for full recovery.

Hallervorden-Spatz Disease

Characterized by muscle tone disorders, involuntary movements and progressive dementia. Appears early in childhood or adolescence.

Hansen's disease (leprosy)

A slowly progressive infectious disease characterized by lesions on the skin, mucous membrane, nerves, bones and viscera.

Headache, Cluster

A vascular headache with intensity beyond migraines. It attacks in short individual clusters that can last weeks to months followed by remission of months to years. Seen more in middle aged to older men. Attacks last 30 minutes to years with pain around the eyes and radiating to jaw and neck. Usually unilateral in nature.

Headache, Migraine

A genetically disorder that can begin in childhood, adolescence, 20s or later in life. A vascular bilateral attack that is seen more in women. It can affect any part of the body. Symptoms can include anorexia, abdominal pain, nausea, vomiting, diarrhea, gastrointestinal distress, visual blurring, speech slur, and confusion. May respond to stress management.

Hemophilia

An X-linked recessive disorder that occurs in males. The disease can vary in severity from spontaneous bleeding of such areas as the skin, membranes and joints to bleeding due to trauma.

Hepatitis B

A viral infection that is transmitted through blood, needles, transfusions, sexual activity or mother to newborn. The disease appears like a flu and last 4 to 8 weeks.

Hereditary Ataxia

See Frederick's Ataxia.

Herpes, Neonatal

Herpes virus transmitted from mother to fetus.

Heterotopic Ossification

Ossification occurring in a part of the body where it normally does not occur.

Hodgkin's Disease

A form of lymphatic system malignant cancer- especially around or of the lymph nodes. Swollen glands, fever and sweating and loss of weight are common with this disease. Paraneoplastic cerebrellar degeneration is often associated with this disorder.

Hunter Syndrome

An X-linked inherited disorder characterized by excessive sulfate in the tissue and urine. It is a progressive disorder where mental deterioration occurs. There is a large head and a coarse face, skeletal changes and other changes occur. It is a milder form of **Hurler's Syndrome**.

Huntington's Disease

An inherited disease due to genetic abnormality of chromosome 4 with a 10 to 25 year progressive degeneration of the nervous system. Symptoms include involuntary muscle movements and loss of cognitive abilities. Loss of coordination, changes in personality, poor memory and in ability to speak occur as the disease progresses.

Hydrocephalus ("water on the brain")

A condition in which widened cerebral spaces in the brain inhibit normal flow of cerebral spinal fluid between the ventricles of the brain and the spinal canal. This blockage causes an increase in the fluid in the brain which in turn causes pressure on the brain tissue. Fluid accumulates in the skull and can put pressure on the brain tissue. This may causes an enlarged head. Convulsions may be present, vomiting weakness, abnormal reflexes, poor respiratory rate and vision problems. A **shunt** (drain) is placed to release excess fluid and prevent fluid build up. Cause is unknown but maybe associated to other conditions such as birth defects.

Hydromyelia

Dilation of the central canal of the spinal cord with increased fluid accumulation.

Hypertension

Related to high blood pressure levels. A familial progressive disease. It can be related to other abnormalities.

Hypoglycemia

A metabolic derangement. An impairment of the ability to sustain normal serum glucose level. Symptoms can include faintness, paleness, headaches, sweating, feeling hungry and irritability.

Hypothyroidism

Cause can be a congenital inherited disorder, or due to dysfunctions of the pituitary or hypothalamus or dysfunction of the thyroid gland. There maybe enlargement of the heart, the lungs, poor memory, changes in personality, nerve compression in the hands and feet, anemia and low body temperature. In congenital cases, there are slow growth and shortness in height, and mental retardation

Hypotonia, Benign Congenial

Decreased muscle tone originating before birth but not progressive.

Incontinentia Pigmenti

A genetic disorder of the skin during infancy and childhood There is skin discoloration and inflammation and there is warty, rough skin growth. There maybe vision problems and dental problems. There maybe seizures and muscle spasms.

Joseph Disease

A neurological disorder with progressive unsteady gait, spasticity and rigidity of the legs, impaired vision, slow speech and dystonia.

Joubert Syndrome

A neurological disorder involving the abnormal development of the balance and coordination mechanism of the brain. Cause is unknown but may be inherited. Respiration can be affected. Abnormal jerky eye movements may be present. Impaired coordination and gait with tremors and ataxia are present. Mental retardation can occur.

Klinefelter Syndrome

An inherited disorder caused by the extra(s) X-chromosome. It becomes apparent during puberty with deceased growth and sexual development. Testes are small and infertile.

Kohler Disease

Osteochondritis of the tarsal navicular bone. See osteochondritis.

Landau-Kleffner Syndrome

An epileptic syndrome of childhood with partial or generalized seizures, psychomotor abnormalities and aphasia progressing to mutism with the loss of the ability to understand speech. Some may lose the ability to identify environmental sounds. Other symptoms may include those involved in brain dysfunctions, eating problems, behavioral problems (aggressiveness) and sleeping problems.

Learning disability

A dysfunction of the brain caused by interference with the normal process of storing, processing and producing information. It can involve any or all of the following areas of brain function: perception, conceptualization, language production and/or reception, control of attention, motor coordination, control of impulses, directional concepts, sensory perception or visual perception. (Learning disabilities are described by terms such as minimal brain dysfunction, perceptual-motor deficit, dyslexia, attention-deficit disorder or hyperkinetic disorder). A person with learning disabilities has:

1) Average or above average intelligence
2) Basically normal abilities in motor, hearing, vision and emotional areas.

The disability may be very subtle and unnoticed by others, but the daily performance of tasks may be extremely difficult and take a great deal more energy and effort than others may imagine. The person with this disability can change from day to day or hour to hour since he or she is affected by fatigue, stress, environmental influences, the complexity of the task or involvement of multi-deficit areas. Learning disabilities can be associated with head injuries, Sensory-Integration dysfunction or can be inherited. Characteristics often seen:

1. Shows self-centered thinking
2. Is distractable and/or impulsive and perhaps unable to tune out distracting stimuli

3. Has poor perception of others' thinking and actions
4. Has difficulty observing facial and body language which may cause misunderstandings in communication
5. May not be able to read or see all symbols or letters of a word. May reverse or displace symbols or letters
6. Auditory perceptual difficulty may cause poor interpretation of comments, not hearing a complete sentence, hearing "slowly" or giving a delayed response
7. May not be able to judge time and space/space relations, or know right from left
8. May have difficulty sequencing tasks. May not function well without structure and may need to organize all tasks
9. May perseverate (get stuck in an action)
10. May be able to handle only one task or action at a time, especially if a new task is presented
11. May have a short attention span and fatigue easily

Legg-Perthes disease-Osteochondritis

Legg-Perthes disease is a condition of the femur (thigh bone) which causes destruction of the femur due to interruption of circulation to the area where bone and cartilage join.

Lesch-Nyhan Syndrome

A genetic disorder caused by a defective gene. Most cases are males. Symptoms may not appear until age four. Self-mutilation is a telltale sign. They bite their fingers, their lips, poke, gouge their eyes, bang their limbs and have no control of this behavior. Their ability to feel pain appears normal. By age ten, they demonstrate spasticity, choreoathetosis, opisthotonus, and facial dystonia. They may show physical signs as seen in cerebral palsy. They may show aggressive behavior not within their control. Protective devices are used to prevent mutilation of themselves. They have difficulty relaxing for fear they will hurt themselves or others. Reactions to the destructive behavior may increase such behavior.

Leukemia

A progressive malignant disease of the blood forming-organs including blood and bone marrow. Symptoms include anemia, fatigue, weight loss, easy bruising, bone pain, possible persistent bacterial infections.

Leukemia, Chronic Lymphocytic

A form mainly seen in the elderly. Symptoms include fatigue, renal involvement, pulmonary leukemic infiltrates.

Leukodystrophy

An autosomal disorder with degeneration of the white matter beginning at the frontal lobes and extending to the cerebellum of the brain. Associated disorders occur with this disorder involving the frontal lobes and the cerebellum.

Lowe's Syndrome (Lowe-Terrey-MacLachlan)

A condition seen in males (X-linked disorder) leading to abnormalities of the eyes, kidneys and brain (cerebrum). Variables in mental retardation occur. Cataracts and abnormal facial features occur. Hypotonia is significant.

Lupus

An inflammatory disease of the connective tissue. Cause is unknown. Mainly seen in women in the late teens to mid age. The beginning signs include extreme fatigue, fever, loss of appetite with loss of weight, swollen glands, hair loss, edema and headaches. Arthritic symptoms are common with considerable pain but, generally, no destruction of the joints. Pain and inflammation may move from one part of the body to another. The majority of those with Lupus experience skin disorder and sensitivity to light. Other problems associated with Lupus include vascular disorders, respiratory disorders with cough and cardiac problems. In the later part of the disease, the kidneys and urinary systems are involved. Depression and anxiety are behavioral problems. Flare-ups may occur several times a year and can be brought on by infection or stress. Other times may be relatively free of symptoms.

Lyme Disease

A disease that is due to the bite of an infected ticks that causes inflammation and skin lesions. If not treated promptly it can cause neurological disorders with recurring problems, cardiac problems and joint-arthritic type problems. The lesions may be accompanied by flu like symptoms.

Lymphadenopathy

A progressive immune disorder seen in older persons. The disorder appears as flu like symptoms with a skin rash. It can develop into a type of cancer.

Macular Degeneration

A common hereditary eye disorder that causes gradual bilateral decrease of vision. There are several forms: Behr 1- infantile optic atrophy ataxia begins before age 7; Behr 2 adult retinae degeneration occurs between 40 to 50; Stargardt's disease -juvenile macular degeneration occurs between 8-15 years; a senile form and disciform form. It can be static for many years then becomes slowly progressive. Peripheral vision remains intact while central vision becomes impaired or absent. There maybe deformity of shapes. Some forms are not hereditary. There is indication that some forms are due to ultraviolet rays damage occurring over the years. It is the 3rd most dehabilitating disorder to those above 50 yrs.

Manic Depressive- bipolar

See psychiatric disorder (see page 311 under mood disorders)

Marfan Syndrome

An inherited disorder of connective tissue that affects the ligaments, the bones, the eyes, the lungs and the cardiovascular systems. When untreated, failure of the cardiac system can cause death. Persons with this disorder have large hands and feet and are generally tall.

Meningococcemia

Invasion of blood stream by meningococcus.

Microcephalic

Abnormal smallness of the head, usually associated with mental retardation.

Mitral Valve Prolapse Syndrome

A heart disease involving a defective valve of the heart of unknown cause or associated with other diseases. There maybe heart murmurs, irregular beat, chest pains, palpitations, shortness of breath and dizziness. It is most common in middle age women.

Multiple Sclerosis (MS)

A disease which begins in young adults. There are lesions in the myelin sheaths of nerves in the brain and spinal cord which cause "short outs." There may be inflammation, pain, destruction of tissue and weakness; or there may be distorted sensation, contractures, unsteadiness, double vision or loss of vision, dizziness and mixed emotional states. Memory and attention can be affected. Intelligence is usually normal. The rider will be sensitive to extreme hot and cold weather which may increase his symptoms. There may be good and bad periods. Some people with MS are without symptoms for years but may react to heat and cold and fatigue easily.

Muscular Dystrophy, Becker

An inherited disease among men causing a slow and progressive weakness of the pelvic and shoulder girdle. It appears in the 20s and 30s. Contractures develop and mobility is impaired. The lungs eventually may be involved.

Muscular Dystrophy, Emery-Dreifuss

An inherited disorder with resulting wasting-way first in the legs, then the shoulder girdle, neck and spine. Heart conditions are involved. It appears in early childhood.

Muscular Dystrophy, Fukuyama type

An inherited autosomal recessive trait. Symptoms appear before the third trimester. The infant is hypotonic, shows difficulty with initial suck and swallow functions, cries, is mentally retarded, and develops contractures.

Muscular Dystrophy, Labdouzy-Dejerine

An inherited disorder that effects both sexes. Appears during childhood and adolescence. Weakness begins in the face, neck and shoulder girdle. It is progressive and may involve the arms, hands and downward. If present in infants, it is more severe.

Muscular Dystrophy, Limb-Gerdle

An inherited progressive disorder involving the hips and shoulders. Problems appears from childhood to middle age in both sexes affecting walking at first and inability to walk may develop within 20 to 30 years.

Muscular Dystrophy ,Oculo-Gastrointestinal

A progressive inherited disorder seen in females more than males. It involves the external eye muscles and eye lid muscles. It also involves the intestinal walls causing pain and bowel difficulties.

Muscular Dystrophy, Duchenne

A rare, inherited as a X-linked recessive chromosome, neuromuscular diseases manifesting progressive muscular weakness with symptoms beginning between 2 and 5 years in males. Weakening begins in the shoulders and pelvis; then progresses to the upper trunk and the arms. All muscles are eventually involved. Early signs may begin with in-coordination of gait. By 8 or 9 years, the child maybe required to use a wheelchair. Later the muscles begin to shorten and contractures of major joints occur. Also, curvature of the spine increases, and lung capacity decreases leading to respiratory infections.

Mutism, Elective

A mental disorder of childhood characterized by continuous refusal to speak in social situations by a child who is able to and willing to speak to selected persons.

Myasthenia Gravis

A chronic neuromuscular disorder involving the muscles of the oral system, may include vision problems and progresses to the limbs with generalized weakness.

Myelitis

Inflamation of the spinal cord. Causes can include cancer, injury, infections, immune reactions or abessociated with other disorders. Results can include pain, central nervous system dysfunction and paralysis.

Myeloma, Multiple

Multiple bone marrow tumors resulting in bone pain, pathological fractures, hypercalcemis and anemia with increased susceptibility to infection. Renal failure may occur.

Noonan Syndrome

A genetic disorder characterized by heart defects present at birth. A short stature, broad or webbed neck and droopy eyelids are present. Prominent or hollowed breast bones, malformed elbows.

Nystagmus, Benign Paroxysmal Positional

Can occur due to injury to the semicircular canals of the inner ear, infection, surgery or deterioration of the membrane. Oscillation of eye movements occur, set off by a head movement causing severe dizziness, ataxia and vomiting.

Obsessive-Compulsive Disorder

With an obsessive-compulsive disorder the individual may have isolated unwanted thoughts or actions which are constantly repeated or performed and cannot be controlled. This person may have to do things in a specific way only and repeat actions many times. Interference with these acts can cause the individual extreme anxiety or distress. For example the rider may become so concerned with the details of brushing the mane that he/she never gets finished grooming the horse.

Oculocerebrocutaneous Syndrome

Possibly inherited congenital disorder. The brain, central nervous system and skin are involved. Seizures are present. Discolored skin lesions are present.

Olivopontocerebellar Atrophy

A chronic, progressive ataxia beginning in adult or middle age, characterized by progressive cerebellar atrophy with ataxic disorders of the trunk and limbs, equilibrium and gait disorders, tremor and dysphagia.

Opitz Syndrome

A hereditary congenial disorder with characteristics including genital abnormalities, wide-set eyes, strabismus, rotated ears, a widow's hair peak, cleft palate, irregular head shape and mild retardation. Babies may have a variety of feeding problems due to malformations.

Osgood-Schlatter's Disease

A form of osteochrondritis that involves the front, and below the knee joint due to a traction injury to the tibia on the anterior surface.

Osteoarthritis (degenerative arthritis)

Caused by trauma or continued stress on the joints as in a person who is overweight or has an injury. Destructive changes occur to the bones and joints with the loss of cartilage and deformity of bones that becomes painful and can cause mild to severe limitation of movement and activities of daily living.

Osteochondritis

See Leggs-Perthes Disease

Osteogenesis imperfecta

A "brittle bone disease". Children with severe cases should not ride since bones may fracture with little stress. In severe cases, fractures can occur during a routine diaper change. There can be deformities especially in later years. The skin may be thin and bruise easily. Special instructions in handling these children/adults are needed. Intelligence is not involved.

Osteomyelitis

Inflammation of bone that can remain localized or may spread throughout the bone to involved marrow, cortex, cancellous tissue and periosteum.

Osteopetrosis

A disease with increased density of the bone. Deformity and fractures are more common than normal.

Osteoporosis

A disorder that involves the decrease in bone tissue causing weakness of the bone and possibility of fractures. The condition usually is seen in older people.

Paranoid disorders

People with a paranoid disorder may be suspicious, hypersensitive, rigid, jealous, hostile or have feelings of great and superior self-worth. There is a tendency to feel that many acts by the volunteer, a group or even the public are directed specifically at them. The person may feel you came especially to spy on him or her. In other areas, the person functions well. People who have psychopathic personalities have a tendency to blame others for their actions and will cause others to suffer rather than themselves. They may be non-conformist, rebellious, have superficial charm, be untruthful, display poor judgment, and not learn from experience. They truly believe in their actions.

Parkinson's Disease

A slowly progressive neurological condition of unknown cause, demonstrating involuntary tremors, muscular stiffness or rigidity, slowness of movement with a shuffling gate and difficulty carrying out intentional movements. Degenerative changes occur within the brain decreasing dopamine levels in the brain. Symptoms begin usually with mild tremors of the fingers and progressively involve the other parts of the body. Signs become more severe with stress and fatigue. Most cases occur in the elderly but can occur under the age of 40. Intelligence is generally not affected, but dementia is present in some cases. Exercise to maintain muscle tone, prevent speaking and swallowing problems, and emotional well-being can help to reduce the disability.

Peripheral Vascular Disease

Disease of the circulatory systems.

Pervasive Developmental Disorder

Impairment of the quality of social skills, communication skills and interests. Persons may demonstrate stereotype behaviors.

Pica

Compulsive eating of non-nutritive substance such as ice, dirt, gravel. Pica can occur in persons with iron or zinc deficiencies. Children with this disorder are classified as having eating disorders with an onset at 2 years which may stop in childhood but can continue to adolescence.

Poliomyelitis

Caused by three types of viruses which affect the spinal cord or, if life threatening, the lower part of the brain. It can cause paralysis of the lungs and weakness in muscles supplied by spinal or cranial nerves. The result can be mild to severe weakness or paralysis in any part of the body. Sensation is not usually involved.

Polycystic Kidney Disease

An inheritable disorder marked by cysts scattered throughout both kidneys. Can be a congenital disorder or appear during childhood. Characteristics include hypertension. In older persons, there is progressive deterioration of renal function.

Post-Polio syndrome

Most polio victims live fairly normal lives. An unpredictable, progressive weakness may develop after many years of unchanging deficits. Later in life a cluster of new muscle weakness, fatigue and pain can result in a decline of functional abilities. Symptoms can appear 10 to 60 years after the onset of polio. Elimination of stress and strain in their lives are important along with reduced muscle fatigue. It can be caused from nerve compression, surviving motor neuron dysfunction or generalized progressive disuse.

Psychopathic personality

A person affected by continuous and chronic antisocial behavior in which the rights of others are violated. Characteristics includes impulsiveness, egocentricity, irritability, aggressiveness, recklessness, disregard for truth and an inability to maintain consistent, responsible functioning.

Psychosis

A mental disorder characterized by aggregate impairment of reality testing as evidenced by hallucinations, delusions, incoherent speech, disorganized or aggressive behavior. The individual is unaware of his/her inconceivable behavior. The term may also refer to an individual whose mental function is so impaired that they cannot meet their normal daily life requirements.

Prader-Willi Syndrome

A genetic disorder due to a deletion of a chromosome of the father. Found more frequently in males than in females. A multi-system disorder with muscle weakness, poor sucking ability, weak cry, failure to thrive, short stature, impaired intelligence and behavioral abilities. Developmental delays can be seen. Physical features may include a narrow forehead, crossed eyes and oval shaped eyes. There is a tendency to over eat at an early age which is of an impulsive nature and can be life threatening. Sexual development can begin earlier then normal but be abnormal in development. Mental retardation is common in the moderate to mild range. Sun sensitivity is common. Behavior may include temper tantrums becoming severe in the teens.

Presenile Dementias

A presenile dementia can appear from childhood on. It is more frequently seen in the later years - age 50 and up. It can be the symptom of a number of diseases caused by neurological and arteriosclerotic disease marked by intellectual and behavioral changes, uncertain gait, urinary incontinence, convulsions, emotional disorders, hallucinations, memory loss and other brain functions.

Raynaud's Disease and Phenomenon

A disease distinguished by spasms of the blood vessels in the skin, toes and fingers with paleness of the skin which usually occurs bilaterally. It is brought on by emotions, cold or secondary to other diseases such as arterial occlusive disease. It is more common in women.

Reiter's Syndrome

A disorder of unknown cause with inflamation of the urethritis, conjunctivitis (inflammation of the membrane that lines the eye) and arthritis.

Respiratory Distress Syndrome, Infant

This disorder can occur due to a number of diseases involving the respiratory tract and is a symptom of underlying disorders. Apnea is an ominous symptom of respiratory distress syndrome.

Retinoschisis

Splitting of the retina or nerve fiber. The disorder can be benign or slowly progressive. There is an adult form and a juvenile form.

Rett Syndrome

A neurological disorder that is a progressive degeneration of the brain tissue. It appears in early childhood in females only. Symptoms include developmental regression of communication and motor acts, repetitious motor behavior such as "hand washing," and dementia.

Reye Syndrome

An acute illness of childhood usually following a respiratory or intestinal viral infection. Symptoms include fever, vomiting, seizures and deceased consciousness to coma. There can be fatty infiltration of the liver and kidneys and swelling of the brain. Can be fatal.

Rheumatoid Arthritis

Rheumatoid arthritis is a severe crippling condition which involves inflammation and destruction of joints. The joints are progressively destroyed. There are periods of exacerbation and remission. The individual may wear splints to protect the joints. Inflammation of the tendons and muscles accompanies joint inflammation and can be very painful.

Rheumatic Fever

An infectious disease that frequently follows a streptococcal infection. Flu like symptoms occur including swelling of joints. Heart disease can be a result along with arthritis, and treatment can continue for years.

Rubella

An acute, benign, viral, contagious disease that causes a rash, fever, paleness and posterior cervical lymphadenitis.

Rubella, Congenital

Viral infection of the fetus can occur when a woman contracts rubella during the early months of pregnancy. Damage to the fetus can result in deafness, cataracts, glaucoma, retinapathy, congenital heart defects, psychomotor and growth retardation.

Rubinstein-Taybi Syndrome

A congenital condition characterized by mental and motor retardation, short stature, broad thumbs and big toe, high arched pallet and straight peaked nose. Abnormalities of the eyes, lungs and vertebrae occur.

Sanfilippo Syndrome

Characterized by excessive amounts of haparitin sulfate in the urine. Facial features are coarse and similar to Hurler's Syndrome - see Hunter Syndrome.

Scheuermann's Disease

A form of osteochrondritis that involves the lower thoracic and upper lumbar vertebrae in late childhood and early teens. It involves the growth centers of children which begins as a degeneration followed by regeneration or calcification, resulting in structural kyphosis.

Schizophrenia

See psychiatric disorder (see page 310)

Seitelberger Syndrome

A ganglioside storage disorder characterized by petite or grand mal seizures, cyclonic jerks, blindness, incoordination and tremors. Most individuals die between 4 to 8 years.

Sickle Cell Anemia

A chronic blood disease most common in black males. There are periods of crisis where the disease worsens. The disease is characterized by pain in the feet, hands and abdomen. It affects the lungs, the liver, spleen and kidney. A CVA (stroke) can occur because of circulatory problems.

Spina Bifida

A condition in which the spinal cord is not normally closed. The spinal cord may protrude at a point and form a sac. Hydrocephalus maybe associated with more severe cases. Very mild cases may show minimal below the site of cord damage; the degree of dysfunction depends on the level of damage to the spinal cord.

Spinal Cord Injury

The result of a traumatic injury to the spinal cord. The injury may sever the cord with resulting paralysis below the injury. An injury where the spinal cord is injured, but not severed, results in some but not all loss of function below the site of injury.

Sturge-Weber Syndrome

A congenital disorder of unknown cause. There is excessive blood vessel growth, calcium in the brain tissue, and seizures are present. There maybe facial discoloration like wine stains and also on the lips. Associated problems may occur in the majority of those involved include seizures, hemiparesis, eye problems and blindness and mental problems.

Tay-Sacks Disease-also Sandhoff disease is similar but not limited to specific heritage.

Inherited disorder resulting in progressive destruction of the central nervous system. Both parents must carry gene in order for the child to be affected. The body is unable to properly metabolized certain fats due to the absence of an enzyme resulting in the accumulation of fats in the brain. Most prevalent among East European Jewish heritage; 3 to 5 months of age, muscle weakness appears. Abnormal startle response, muscle spasms-myoclonic jerks. Later feeding difficulties, hypotonia, restlessness, abnormal vision with circular red spots appear. 1st year, loss of vision and further loss of coordination and learning skills. Eventually the child is limp, unresponsive and paralyzed.

Tethered Spinal Cord Syndrome

A congenital anomaly resulting from defective closure of the neural tube. Can be associated with spina bifida.

Tetralogy of Fallot

A congenital heart disease involving a defect of the ventricular septal and obstruction to the right ventricular outflow. Children show developmental delays. They are easily fatigued and have difficulty breathing.

Tourette Syndrome

Inherited as a dominant gene. Only 10% with Tourette Syndrome need medication - most improve with age with a normal life span. Onset in childhood or adolescence - more prevalent in males. Bizarre behavior is exhibited from severe to mild tics, jerks, mannerisms, noises and compulsions of many kinds in any part of the body. Behaviors include multiple motor activity, multiple vocal sounds which can occur throughout the day, or every other day, with a sudden onset. Self-mutilating symptoms can be present in severe cases. Those afflicted are not physically disabled to any extent.

Traumatic Head Injuries

An injury to the head, usually by a moving object or the head striking a solid object, resulting in a concussion, external or internal brain damage. Results can involve any or many parts of the brain's ability to function.

Trisomy

When three of a given chromosome occur, instead of two, followed frequently by a deviant chromosome or chromosome group.

Tuberculosis

An infectious disease that can affect any organ but is most commonly involved in the lung. Some strains are curable but others resist intervention.

Tuberous Sclerosis

A congenital disorder identified with benign tumors of the brain, lesions of the skin and other organs. Seizures and mental retardation are common factors.

Tumor

An unusual growth that may be benign, static or malignant which continues to grow. There are many different kinds which can be in any part of the body or its surface. Damage can be caused by its destruction of tissue or organs or by the pressure it places on an organ.

Turner Syndrome

A genetic disorder in females due to the absence or defect of the X chromosome with characteristics of heart defects, loose skin folds, webbing, low hair line, shortness in stature, lack of sexual development and other internal and physical abnormalities. Intellectual abilities may be normal.

Walker-Warburg Syndrome

Syndrome includes hydrocephalus, retinal dysplasia, lack of folds of the brain tissue and difficulty with eyes. Muscle weakness of voluntary nature may increase in time.

Williams Syndrome

A genetic disorder involving the vascular, connective tissue and central nervous system. Cause is due to several missing genes. Early signs include developmental delays such as poor weight gain, poor balance and motor skills, crying, small and missing teeth, poor swallowing, chewing and speech problems, hypotonia, joint contractures and sensory tactile defensiveness. Cognitive and social skills include good visual memory, remembering songs, likes to spin objects, hyperactive with short attention span, poor fine motor skills and difficulty with visual - spatial integration. They are very social and talkative children. They are resistant to change. Repetition and consistency aids in learning.

References:

Advance for Occupational Therapy, 1996 &1997

Dorland'S Illustrated Medical Dictionary, 28th edition, 1994. W.B. Saunders co., Philadelphia.

Kempe, C., Silver, HK, O'Briem, D. 1976. Current Pediatric Diagnosis & TreatmentLange Mediacl Pubiclations.

Blakiston's Gould Medical Dictionary, 4th edition, McGraw-Hill Book Co., New York.

National Organization for Rare Disorders, Inc., Fairfield, CT.